OTHER A TO Z THE SCARECRO

1. *The A to Z of Buddhism* by Charles S. Prebish, 2001.
2. *The A to Z of Catholicism* by William J. Collinge, 2001.
3. *The A to Z of Hinduism* by Bruce M. Sullivan, 2001.
4. *The A to Z of Islam* by Ludwig W. Adamec, 2002.
5. *The A to Z of Slavery and Abolition* by Martin A. Klein, 2002.
6. *Terrorism: Assassins to Zealots* by Sean Kendall Anderson and Stephen Sloan, 2003.
7. *The A to Z of the Korean War* by Paul M. Edwards, 2005.
8. *The A to Z of the Cold War* by Joseph Smith and Simon Davis, 2005.
9. *The A to Z of the Vietnam War* by Edwin E. Moise, 2005.
10. *The A to Z of Science Fiction Literature* by Brian Stableford, 2005.
11. *The A to Z of the Holocaust* by Jack R. Fischel, 2005.
12. *The A to Z of Washington, D.C.* by Robert Benedetto, Jane Donovan, and Kathleen DuVall, 2005.
13. *The A to Z of Taoism* by Julian F. Pas, 2006.
14. *The A to Z of the Renaissance* by Charles G. Nauert, 2006.
15. *The A to Z of Shinto* by Stuart D. B. Picken, 2006.
16. *The A to Z of Byzantium* by John H. Rosser, 2006.
17. *The A to Z of the Civil War* by Terry L. Jones, 2006.
18. *The A to Z of the Friends (Quakers)* by Margery Post Abbott, Mary Ellen Chijioke, Pink Dandelion, and John William Oliver Jr., 2006.
19. *The A to Z of Feminism* by Janet K. Boles and Diane Long Hoeveler, 2006.
20. *The A to Z of New Religious Movements* by George D. Chryssides, 2006.
21. *The A to Z of Multinational Peacekeeping* by Terry M. Mays, 2006.
22. *The A to Z of Lutheranism* by Günther Gassmann with Duane H. Larson and Mark W. Oldenburg, 2007.
23. *The A to Z of the French Revolution* by Paul R. Hanson, 2007.
24. *The A to Z of the Persian Gulf War 1990–1991* by Clayton R. Newell, 2007.
25. *The A to Z of Revolutionary America* by Terry M. Mays, 2007.
26. *The A to Z of the Olympic Movement* by Bill Mallon with Ian Buchanan, 2007.

27. *The A to Z of the Discovery and Exploration of Australia* by Alan Day, 2009.
28. *The A to Z of the United Nations* by Jacques Fomerand, 2009.
29. *The A to Z of the "Dirty Wars"* by David Kohut, Olga Vilella, and Beatrice Julian, 2009.
30. *The A to Z of the Vikings* by Katherine Holman, 2009.
31. *The A to Z from the Great War to the Great Depression* by Neil A. Wynn, 2009.
32. *The A to Z of the Crusades* by Corliss K. Slack, 2009.
33. *The A to Z of New Age Movements* by Michael York, 2009.
34. *The A to Z of Unitarian Universalism* by Mark W. Harris, 2009.
35. *The A to Z of the Kurds* by Michael M. Gunter, 2009.
36. *The A to Z of Utopianism* by James M. Morris and Andrea L. Kross, 2009.
37. *The A to Z of the Civil War and Reconstruction* by William L. Richter, 2009.
38. *The A to Z of Jainism* by Kristi L. Wiley, 2009.
39. *The A to Z of the Inuit* by Pamela R. Stern, 2009.
40. *The A to Z of Early North America* by Cameron B. Wesson, 2009.
41. *The A to Z of the Enlightenment* by Harvey Chisick, 2009.
42. *The A to Z of Methodism* edited by Charles Yrigoyen Jr. and Susan E. Warrick, 2009.
43. *The A to Z of the Seventh-Day Adventists* by Gary Land, 2009.
44. *The A to Z of Sufism* by John Renard, 2009.
45. *The A to Z of Sikhism* by W. H. McLeod, 2009.
46. *The A to Z of Fantasy Literature* by Brian Stableford, 2009.
47. *The A to Z of the Discovery and Exploration of the Pacific Islands* by Max Quanchi and John Robson, 2009.
48. *The A to Z of Australian and New Zealand Cinema* by Albert Moran and Errol Vieth, 2009.
49. *The A to Z of African-American Television* by Kathleen Fearn-Banks, 2009.
50. *The A to Z of American Radio Soap Operas* by Jim Cox, 2009.
51. *The A to Z of the Old South* by William L. Richter, 2009.
52. *The A to Z of the Discovery and Exploration of the Northwest Passage* by Alan Day, 2009.
53. *The A to Z of the Druzes* by Samy S. Swayd, 2009.
54. *The A to Z of the Welfare State* by Bent Greve, 2009.

55. *The A to Z of the War of 1812* by Robert Malcomson, 2009.
56. *The A to Z of Feminist Philosophy* by Catherine Villanueva Gardner, 2009.
57. *The A to Z of the Early American Republic* by Richard Buel Jr., 2009.
58. *The A to Z of the Russo–Japanese War* by Rotem Kowner, 2009.
59. *The A to Z of Anglicanism* by Colin Buchanan, 2009.
60. *The A to Z of Scandinavian Literature and Theater* by Jan Sjåvik, 2009.
61. *The A to Z of the Peoples of the Southeast Asian Massif* by Jean Michaud, 2009.
62. *The A to Z of Judaism* by Norman Solomon, 2009.
63. *The A to Z of the Berbers (Imazighen)* by Hsain Ilahiane, 2009.
64. *The A to Z of British Radio* by Seán Street, 2009.
65. *The A to Z of The Salvation Army* edited by Major John G. Merritt, 2009.
66. *The A to Z of the Arab–Israeli Conflict* by P R Kumaraswamy, 2009.
67. *The A to Z of the Jacksonian Era and Manifest Destiny* by Terry Corps, 2009.
68. *The A to Z of Socialism* by Peter Lamb and James C. Docherty, 2009.
69. *The A to Z of Marxism* by David Walker and Daniel Gray, 2009.
70. *The A to Z of the Bahá'í Faith* by Hugh C. Adamson, 2009.
71. *The A to Z of Postmodernist Literature and Theater* by Fran Mason, 2009.
72. *The A to Z of Australian Radio and Television* by Albert Moran and Chris Keating, 2009.
73. *The A to Z of the Lesbian Liberation Movement: Still the Rage* by JoAnne Myers, 2009.

The A to Z of British Radio

Seán Street

The A to Z Guide Series, No. 64

The Scarecrow Press, Inc.
Lanham • Toronto • Plymouth, UK
2009

Published by Scarecrow Press, Inc.
A wholly owned subsidiary of
The Rowman & Littlefield Publishing Group, Inc.
4501 Forbes Boulevard, Suite 200, Lanham, Maryland 20706
http://www.scarecrowpress.com

Estover Road, Plymouth PL6 7PY, United Kingdom

Copyright © 2006 by Seán Street

All rights reserved. No part of this publication may be reproduced, stored in a retrieval system, or transmitted in any form or by any means, electronic, mechanical, photocopying, recording, or otherwise, without the prior permission of the publisher.

British Library Cataloguing in Publication Information Available

Library of Congress Cataloging-in-Publication Data

The hardback version of this book was cataloged by the Library of Congress as follows:

Street, Seán.
 Historical dictionary of British radio / Seán Street.
  p. cm. — (Historical dictionaries of literature and the arts ; no. 10)
 Includes bibliographical references.
 1. Radio broadcasting — Great Britain — History — Dictionaries. I. Title.
 II. Series.
 PN1991.3.G7S77 2006
 384.540941—dc22   2006045048

ISBN 978-0-8108-6847-2 (pbk. : alk. paper)
ISBN 978-0-8108-7013-0 (ebook)

∞™ The paper used in this publication meets the minimum requirements of American National Standard for Information Sciences—Permanence of Paper for Printed Library Materials, ANSI/NISO Z39.48-1992.

Printed in the United States of America

To Joanne, Jemma, and Zoë

Contents

Acknowledgments	xi
Editor's Foreword (*Jon Woronoff*)	xiii
Acronyms and Abbreviations	xv
Chronology	xvii
Introduction	1
THE DICTIONARY	25
Bibliography	303
About the Author	317

Acknowledgments

Writing this book has been a personally enriching experience, but one that I would not have been able to undertake without the help and support of a number of friends and colleagues within the UK radio industry and among those who study radio as an academic discipline. In the former area of activity, my thanks go to many, including Ralph Barnard of Gcap Media; Tim Blackmore of UBC Media; Helen Boaden, Director of BBC News; John Bradford of the Radio Academy; Paul Brown of the Commercial Radio Companies Association; and Gill Carter of BBC Radio 4. Others who have helped with information, advice, and contacts have included Barbara Bray, Piers Plowright, John Theocharis, John Tydeman, and John Whitney.

I am grateful to the Research Committee of Bournemouth Media School, Bournemouth University, who kindly awarded me a sabbatical that enabled me to work uninterrupted on the text, and to colleagues within the academic community, in particular, Hugh Chignell and Julia McCain, who contributed valuable information drawn from their specific areas of expertise and knowledge, and who read and commented on the text. I am also grateful to my family for their support during the writing of this book and to my editor at Scarecrow Press, Jon Woronoff.

Editor's Foreword

Among all the national radios, British radio has always enjoyed a unique position, probably because of the role of the British Broadcasting Corporation—best known as the BBC. This is partly because of its continuing production of first-class programs of all sorts, whether news, music, or sports. Even more important, in times of crisis or when people abroad cannot trust their own national radio, they tune in to the BBC, which has always proven to be more reliable and still transmits worldwide. But there is more to British radio than the BBC, much more, because it also has a remarkable tradition of commercial radio and public radio, ranging from the early "pirate" stations to more specialized ones of today. This being said, British radio is not without its problems, nor is the BBC, but the industry is adapting to the new technologies, taking on and learning to live with (if not actually defeating) new competitors, and maintaining a distinctive and welcome presence.

The A to Z of British Radio draws a broad picture in several different ways. The chronology traces a long history, from the earliest technical breakthroughs, through the landmark broadcast of Nellie Melba in 1920, and through to the most recent developments. The introduction sums up its role, assessing the many achievements and also the many challenges, from one period to another, with the BBC clearly in charge at first and gradually sharing the field with countless others, and looking toward the future. The dictionary section offers a wealth of detail, with entries on the enabling legislation, the BBC and its many rivals, key persons in the administration and on the creative side, many of the more memorable programs and those who appeared in them, and much of the technical paraphernalia. Last but not least is a bibliography permitting students and radio fans to find further reading.

This sort of book could only have been written by someone with a particularly broad view of British radio, someone who has also approached it from different angles. Seán Street is, among other things, an academic who is currently professor of radio at Bournemouth Media School, Bournemouth University. He has written on radio history, including the recent *Concise History of British Radio,* and is director of the Centre for Broadcasting History Research. But Dr. Street has also written on literary history and several of his plays have been performed, so he knows the creative side. In addition, he is familiar with radio production because that is what he teaches at Bournemouth, where he founded the Bournemouth Internet Radio Station (BIRSt). He is on the boards of two radio stations, and finally, he frequently makes his own features on BBC Radios 3 and 4. This is a rather exceptional foundation for writing a much-needed reference work on British radio.

Jon Woronoff
Series Editor

Acronyms and Abbreviations

AEF	Allied Expeditionary Force
AIRC	Association of Independent Radio Contractors
AM	Amplitude modulation
CBE	Companion of the British Empire
CMA	Community Media Association
COFDM	Coded Orthogonal Frequency Division Multiplex
CRCA	Commercial Radio Companies Association
DAB	Digital Audio Broadcasting
DG	Director-General
DJ	Disc jockey
DMB	Digital multimedia broadcasting
DTI	Department of Trade and Industry
EBU	European Broadcasting Union
EKCO	Brand name of EK Cole, receiver manufacturer
EMAP	East Midlands Associated Press
EMI	Electrical and Musical Industries
ENSA	Entertainments National Service Association
FM	Frequency modulation
GCHQ	Government Communications Headquarters
GFP	General Forces Programme
GLR	Greater London Radio
GTS	Greenwich Time Signal
GWR	Great Western Radio
IBA	Independent Broadcasting Authority
IBC	International Broadcasting Company
ILR	Independent Local Radio
IRDP	Independent Radio Drama Productions
IRN	Independent Radio News
ITA	Independent Television Authority

ITC	Independent Television Commission
ITMA	*It's That Man Again*
ITV	Independent Television
JWT	J. Walter Thompson
kHz	Kilohertz
kW	Kilowatt
LBC	London Broadcasting Company
LW	Longwave
MBE	Member of the British Empire
MHz	Megahertz
MPEG	Moving Picture Experts Group Layer 3
MW	Mediumwave
OBE	Order of the British Empire
OFCOM	Office of Communication
PHILIMIL	Brand name of the Philips-Miller recording system
PMG	Postmaster General
PSB	Public Service Broadcasting
RA	Radio Authority
RAJAR	Radio Joint Audience Survey
RCA	Radio Corporation of America
RDS	Radio Data System
RSL	Restricted Service License
SALLIE	Small Scale Alternative Location Independent
SRH	Scottish Radio Holdings
SW	Shortwave
TRIC	Television and Radio Industries Club
UBC	Unique Broadcasting Company
UPC	Universal Programmes Company
URP	Universal Radio Publicity
VHF	Very high frequency
VOA	Voice of America
WRN	World Radio Network
WS	World Service

Chronology

1864 December: James Clerk-Maxwell delivers his paper, *The Dynamic Theory of the Electromagnetic Field* to the Royal Society.

1877 First transmission of electromagnetic waves without physical means of conduction. **2 April:** First telephone conversation.

1896 2 June: Wireless Telegraphy patent taken out by Guglielmo Marconi.

1901 11 December: First transatlantic wireless signal from Cornwall, England, to Newfoundland.

1906 Triode valve developed, providing the ability to amplify electrical currents in wireless equipment. **24 December:** Early broadcast by Reginald Fessenden in the U.S.

1920 15 June: Dame Nellie Melba broadcasts from the Marconi Company's Chelmsford works.

1922 14 February: Start of broadcasts from 2MT, Writtle. **11 May:** First transmission from 2LO. **18 October:** Form of the British Broadcasting Company agreed upon by the Post Office and radio manufacturers. **14 November:** Daily broadcasting starts from London Station 2LO of the British Broadcasting Company Ltd. **15 November:** Birmingham Station 5IT and Manchester Station 2ZY opens. **23 December:** First regular general news bulletin from London. **24 December:** Newcastle-on-Tyne Station 5NO opens.

1923 8 January: First Outside Broadcast (excerpts from *The Magic Flute* from Covent Garden). **15 February:** Cardiff Station 5WA opens. **6 March:** Glasgow Station 5SC opens. **19 March:** BBC London Station moves from Marconi's Magnet House to 2, Savoy Hill. **26 March:** First broadcast weather forecast. **1 May:** Savoy Hill Studios opens. **28**

September: *The Radio Times* first published. **1 October:** Publication of the Report of the Sykes Committee on Broadcasting. **10 October:** Aberdeen Station 2DB opens. **17 October:** Bournemouth Station 6BM opens.

1924 **5 February:** Greenwich Time Signal inaugurated. **17 February:** Big Ben daily time signal introduced. **4 April:** First broadcast to schools.

1925 **March:** Fashion Talk in English sponsored by Selfridges, organized by Captain Leonard Plugge and broadcast from the Eiffel Tower, Paris. **3 April:** BBC represented at the first General Assembly of the International Broadcasting Union at Geneva. **27 July:** Station 5XX Daventry opens, providing the 2LO service on 1562m longwave.

1926 **5 March:** Publication of the Report of the Crawford Committee on Broadcasting. **4 May:** General Strike begins. **11 November:** Publication of agreement between the postmaster general and the British Broadcasting Company Ltd. providing for the transfer of the Broadcasting Service to the British Broadcasting Corporation on 1 January 1927. **14 November:** Under a plan drawn up by the International Broadcasting Union, the number of wavelengths available to the BBC is reduced. This results in the development of regional, as opposed to local, broadcasting. **31 December:** Expiration of the license of the British Broadcasting Company Ltd.

1927 First shortwave broadcasts to Europe, from Chelmsford station, 5SW. **1 January:** British Broadcasting Corporation constituted by Royal Charter for a term of 10 years. J. C. W. Reith becomes director-general. **22 January:** First Association Football commentary: Arsenal v. Sheffield United from Highbury. **25 March:** First racing commentary (The Grand National from Aintree). **2 April:** First commentary on the Varsity Boat Race. **23 April:** First broadcast from Wembley Stadium (F.A. Cup Final, Cardiff City v. Arsenal). **14 May:** First Cricket commentary (Essex v. New Zealand at Leyton). **13 August:** First broadcast of a BBC Promenade Concert (from Queen's Hall, London). **21 August:** Daventry 5GB Experimental opens.

1928 **12 May:** First broadcast of the BBC Dance Orchestra.

1929 **16 January:** First issue of the *Listener* published.

1930   9 March: The Regional system of broadcasting begins. The Brookman's Park transmitter broadcasts alternative programs for London and the Home Counties. The National Programme replaces 2LO. At the same time, Daventry 5GB starts broadcasting Midland Regional programs. **22 October:** First broadcast of the BBC Symphony Orchestra, conducted by Adrian Boult.

1931   11 October: First International Broadcasting Company (IBC) transmission from Radio Normandy (Radio Fecamp). **29 November:** French station, Poste Parisien, commences English-language commercial broadcasting under the auspices of the IBC with a record program sponsored by HMV, introduced by Rex Palmer, a former BBC staff member.

1932   15 March: Broadcasting House becomes the official London headquarters of the BBC. **15 March:** First broadcast from Broadcasting House, London (Henry Hall, replacing Jack Payne, and the BBC Dance Orchestra). **19 December:** Inauguration of the Empire Service from Daventry.

1933   15 March: Radio Luxembourg begins test transmissions. **21 August:** BBC News read by a woman for the first time (discontinued shortly afterward). **29 October:** Luxembourg begins regular Sunday programs.

1934   15 January: Implementation of the Lucerne Plan, drawn up by the European Broadcasting Convention, on wavelength distribution. **19 January:** First edition of *Radio Pictorial*. Beginning as a general magazine about radio, it gains wider appeal from 31 August 1934, when it becomes the listings journal for Continental commercial stations such as Radio Normandy, Radio Luxembourg, Radio Toulouse, and Radio Lyons.

1935   6 May: King George V's Silver Jubilee celebrations. **16 July:** Broadcast review of the Fleet from Spithead.

1936   20 January: Death of King George V. **28 January:** Broadcast of the king's funeral. **16 March:** Publication of the Report of the Ullswater Committee on Broadcasting. **1 October:** Formation of the Listener Research Unit. **1 November:** Radio Lyons starts broadcasting, with staff announcer Tony Melrose. Programs are produced in London by Vox Productions. This is the last of the major Continental stations to go on air broadcasting English-language commercial radio. **2 November:** Inauguration of BBC Television Service. **10 December:** Publication of Royal Charter for continuance of the BBC and License and Agreement between the postmaster general and the BBC. **10 December:** Broadcast of the announcement of the abdication of King Edward VIII. **11 December:** Broadcast from Windsor by King Edward VIII concerning his abdication of the Monarchy. **12 December:** Broadcast of the Proclamation of Accession of King George VI.

1937 1 January: New Royal Charter and Licence come into force for ten years. **12 May:** Broadcast ceremony of the Coronation of King George VI and Queen Elizabeth. **20 May:** Thomas Woodruffe broadcasts from Coronation Review of the Fleet at Spithead. **31 August:** Broadcast of the Farr/Louis World Heavyweight Championship fight direct from the Yankee Stadium, New York.

1938 15 March: BBC Portuguese and Spanish Service for Latin America begins. **30 June:** Resignation of the first BBC director-general, Sir John Reith. **31 August:** Opening of the Arabic Service, the first BBC broadcast in a foreign tongue.

1938 27 September: Broadcast by the prime minister, Neville Chamberlain, on his return from Munich. BBC German service, Italian Service and French service start. **1 October:** F. W. Ogilvie succeeds Reith as director-general of the BBC.

1939 1 August: First broadcast in English to Europe. **1 September:** The BBC Home Service commences broadcasting at 8:15 p.m., in place of the National and Regional Services. At 9:26 p.m. a supplementary service in foreign languages, for listeners in Europe, begins. BBC Television Services closes down. **3 September:** Broadcast by Neville Chamberlain on the outbreak of war. **5 September:** BBC Hungarian service starts. **7 September:** BBC Polish Service starts. **8 September:** BBC Czech service starts. **15 September:** BBC Rumanian service and Serbo-Croat service to Yugoslavia start. **21 September:** Radio Luxembourg closes down. **30 September:** BBC Greek service starts. **20 November:** BBC Turkish service starts. **31 December:** BBC Slovak service starts.

1940 3 January: Radio International closes down. **7 January:** Opening of Special Programme for the Forces, broadcast from 6:00 p.m.

nightly. **18 February:** Forces Programme extended: now broadcasts from 11:00 a.m. to 11:00 p.m. **13 October:** Princess Elizabeth and Princess Margaret broadcast from Buckingham Palace to the children of the Empire. **15 October:** Bomb explodes in Broadcasting House, London, killing seven people. **8 December:** Landmine causes further severe damage to Broadcasting House.

1941 **17 March:** BBC European Service moves to Bush House.

1942 **26 January:** Resignation of F. W. Ogilvie as BBC director-general. Appointment of Sir Cecil Graves and R. W. Foot as joint directors-general. **26 July:** First broadcast of *Britain to America* series in the BBC North American Service, rebroadcast by NBC in the USA.

1943 **13 June:** Forces Programme becomes the General Overseas Service. **24 June:** Resignation of Sir Cecil Graves as BBC joint director-general. **1 September:** Appointment of R. W. Foot as sole director-general. W. J. Haley appointed as editor-in-chief.

1944 **31 March:** R. W. Foot resigns. W. J. Haley appointed as BBC director-general. **6 June:** D-Day. Allied invasion of Europe. First BBC announcement, 9:32 a.m. **7 June:** Commencement of the Allied Expeditionary Forces Programme. **23 September:** U.S. Twelfth Army commences German-language programming aimed at retreating enemy troops as Radio 1212 from Radio Luxembourg.

1945 **1 March:** Adrian Boult conducts the Orchestre Nationale in the first concert to be broadcast from Paris since the liberation. **8 May:** V-E Day. Broadcasts by King George VI and Winston Churchill. **28 July:** Allied Expeditionary Forces Program discontinued. **29 July:** The Light Programme commences. Regional Broadcasting resumes. **15 August:** V-J Day. Broadcasts by King George VI and Clement Attlee.

1946 **1 January:** W. J. Haley knighted in the New Year Honours List. **1 July:** Radio Luxembourg resumes commercial English-language transmissions, led by Stephen Williams who would be succeeded by Geoffrey Everitt, his assistant and, with Teddy Johnson, an early post-war announcer on the station. **7 June:** BBC Television Service resumed. **19 September:** Third Programme starts.

1947 **1 January:** Third Royal Charter and License (for five years) come into force.

1949 **25 September:** Italia Prize inaugurated.

1950 **12 February:** European Broadcasting Union formed. **15 March:** BBC radio frequencies reorganized.

1952 **6 February:** Broadcast announcement of the death of King George VI. **1 July:** Fourth Royal Charter and Licence (for 10 years). **30 September:** Sir William Haley resigns as director-general of the BBC. **1 December:** Sir Ian Jacob becomes director-general.

1953 **2 June:** Coronation of Queen Elizabeth II.

1954 **1 June:** Combined TV and Radio license cost increased to £3.00. Radio-only license, £1.00.

1955 **2 May:** First VHF transmitter opens at Wrotham supplying BBC radio services to London and the Southeast.

1956 **3 November:** Suez Crisis. Prime Minister Anthony Eden broadcasts to home and overseas audiences.

1957 **1 August:** Combined license £4.00. Radio license remains £1.00. **30 September:** Network Three starts on the Third Programme frequency providing educational programs during the afternoon and early evening.

1958 **14 April:** Radiophonic Workshop starts.

1960 **1 January:** Hugh Carleton-Greene becomes director-general. **31 December:** BBC VHF transmissions now cover 97 percent of the population.

1962 **1 July:** Fourth Royal Charter extended to July 1964. **28 August:** BBC commences experimental stereo radio transmissions.

1964 **1 January:** Hugh Carleton-Greene knighted. **28 March:** Radio Caroline commences broadcasting. **30 August:** Network Three renamed Third Network. Introduction of the Music Programme on the Third Network's frequencies on Sunday, Sports Service on Saturday, and Study Session on weekdays (6:30–7:30 p.m.). The Third Programme continues in the evenings.

1965 **1 May:** General Overseas Service renamed the BBC World Service. **1 August:** Combined license, £5.00. Radio license, £1.5s.

1967 **14 August:** Marine Broadcasting (Offences) Act becomes law. All off-shore "pirate" radio stations except Radio Caroline cease transmission. **30 September:** Radio 1 opens. Other networks renamed Radios 2, 3, and 4. **8 November:** Local Radio experiment begins with the opening of BBC Radio Leicester.

1969 **10 July:** Publication of *Broadcasting in the Seventies*.

1970 **4 April:** Fuller development of BBC generic radio pattern. **19 June:** Conservative Party wins general election.

1971 **1 February:** Radio only license abolished. **16 June:** Death of Lord Reith. **10 November:** Opening of BBC Pebble Mill, Birmingham.

1972 **12 July:** Sound Broadcasting Act comes into force.

1973 **12 July:** Independent Broadcasting Authority comes into existence. **8 October:** First Independent Local Radio (ILR) station, London Broadcasting Company (LBC), begins broadcasting. **16 October:** Second ILR station, Capital Radio, begins broadcasting.

1974 **28 February:** Labour Party wins general election. Halts ILR development, awards more local licences to BBC stations. **10 April:** Government announces the creation of a committee to examine the future of broadcasting (Annan).

1978 **13 November:** Launch of BBC Radio Wales. **23 November:** Major BBC national radio frequency changes. BBC Radio Scotland commences broadcasting.

1979 **27 January:** Radio 2 commences 24-hour broadcasting. 4 May: Conservative Party wins general elections, committed to expand commercial radio.

1982 **4 December:** Complete separation of Radios 1 and 2 in terms of content for the first time.

1988 County Sound, Guildford becomes the first commercial station to "split" frequencies permanently (i.e., to broadcast different services on AM and FM).

1990 **January:** First BBC Digital Audio Broadcasting (DAB) trials from Crystal Palace. **27 August:** BBC Radio 5 begins, the first new UK national radio station since 1967. BBC Radio 2 starts broadcasting on

FM only, the first network to do so. **1 November:** Broadcasting Act published.

1991 **1 January:** Radio Authority established. (Shadow Radio Authority formed, 1990.) **1 May:** Radio 1 commences permanent 24-hour-a-day broadcasting.

1992 RAJAR, the Radio Joint Audience Research organization administered jointly by the BBC and commercial radio is launched, providing industry-approved listening figures for all subscribing UK radio services. **21 January:** Launch of BBC Radio Berkshire, completing the planned BBC Local Radio network as then conceived. **28 February:** Radio 3 ceases AM transmission. **7 September:** Classic FM commences broadcasting on an eight-year license, the first national commercial radio station in Britain. **30 December:** Radio Luxembourg closes down.

1993 **30 April:** Launch of Virgin 1215 (subsequently Virgin Radio). **25 October:** Radio 1 relaunches with new schedule.

1994 **28 March:** BBC Radio 5 Live launches as a replacement for the original Radio 5. **1 July:** Radio 1 ceases AM transmissions.

1995 **14 February:** Talk Radio UK (subsequently TalkSport) begins broadcasting. **27 September:** The BBC begins the world's first Digital Audio Broadcasting (DAB) transmissions from five transmitters around the London area.

1996 **24 July:** Broadcasting Act sets out plans for the development of Digital Broadcasting, including radio.

1997 Radio Authority launches Sallies, small-scale local licenses for smaller communities.

1998 **March:** Radio Authority advertises the first national digital commercial multiplex license. **June:** Applications close for national digital commercial license. Only one applicant: Digital One. **Autumn:** Digital One awarded national digital license. **1 October:** Digital satellite service launches in the UK.

1999 **15 November:** Digital One multiplex commences broadcasting the UK's first commercial DAB radio service with a multiplex containing five stations: Classic FM, Virgin Radio, Talk Radio, Planet Rock, and Core. More follow in 2000.

2000 Spring: Publication of the Communications White Paper on the future of broadcasting and telecommunications.

2001 Radio Authority sets up Access Radio pilot project.

2002 2 February: Launch of BBC 5 Live Sports Extra—the BBC's first digital radio-only service. **11 March:** BBC digital station 6 Music launches at 7:00 a.m. with Phill Jupitus as first presenter on air. Widely billed as "the first new BBC music station for 32 years." **7 May:** Government announces plans for radical changes in media and telecommunications regulation and ownership. **16 August:** 1Xtra, BBC Radio's digital black music station launched. **15 December:** BBC7, BBC Digital speech service focusing on archive comedy and drama launched.

2003 Professor Anthony Everitt, publishes *New Voices*, an evaluation of Radio Authority Access Radio pilot project. **July:** Communications Bill receives Royal Assent. **December:** Ofcom takes over from the Radio Authority as general communications regulator. Communications Act comes into effect.

2004 January: Publication of the Hutton Enquiry into the death of the weapons expert Dr. David Kelly and the BBC's conduct over the matter lead to high-level resignations within the Corporation, including the chairman, Gavyn Davies and the director-general, Greg Dyke. **31 December:** Closure of BBC's Pebble Mill studios.

2005 March: First Community Radio License awarded, to Forest of Dean Radio. **May:** GWR and Capital Radio Groups merge to form GCap Media.

Introduction

The story of British radio is fascinating, beginning long before the birth of the British Broadcasting Company (BBC) in 1922. This book aims to tell this story through its component parts: the makers, the programs, and the policies that together shaped the development of a system of broadcasting, grounded initially in a public service ethic, and subsequently struggling toward an, at times, uneasy balance of public and commercial radio.

The BBC's role in this story is, of course, considerable, and unique, although seldom at any time in its history has the organization been without problems and tensions. The early pioneers, under John Reith, were young men born in Victorian Britain, and their values were instilled in the nature of broadcasting as a sacred cause, a view that created tensions as the medium became established and public needs and expectations changed. Britain, unlike many other countries in the world, did not see the arrival of legal, land-based commercial radio until quite late in its broadcasting history; indeed, commercial television, beginning in 1955, predated radio supported by advertising by almost 20 years. That said, as early as the 1930s, the BBC monopoly was challenged by commercial broadcasters transmitting from the continent of Europe. Indeed, much of the evolution of British radio has come about through external pressures, and conflicts between public service and independent broadcasters. This is a major theme of the book, as is the gradual relaxing of regulation, even if, for some, this process has not happened swiftly or comprehensively enough.

Britain's radio reputation globally has, since the 1930s, been one of great respect and trust, because of the work of the BBC World Service, and the book acknowledges this important aspect of broadcasting in a number of ways through its chronology and within the main body of the dictionary itself. Perhaps the major theme to emerge through the book, however, is British radio's seemingly endless capacity to survive and thrive on change. Once it was predicted that television would bring about the death of the medium; far from this happened. Radio in the United Kingdom has adapted to new audiences and new technologies, including the Internet and downloading of programs. There seems little doubt that it will continue to evolve; the one constant is change, and within the first decade of the 21st century, UK radio is facing new challenges and possibilities in the continuation of that evolution. It will be its capacity to reinvent itself that will ensure its continuing survival as a vital and exciting medium now and in the future.

FOUNDATIONS

Radio in the United Kingdom has seen from its beginnings a tension between its role as a medium of information and a purveyor of popular entertainment, two poles that have frequently manifested themselves in the roles of public service broadcasters and commercial operators. This dichotomy was initially linked to the first uses of radio, as a means of utilitarian one-to-one messaging, and the nature of the signals transmitted, through wireless *telegraphy* rather than *telephony*, sending messages in the form of "electrical impulses and signals" as Marconi's famous first patent of 2 June 1896 had read. The modification of those impulses, the electromagnetic waves that carried the sounds and codes, came about in 1902 at the hand of the Danish scientist, Valdemar Poulsen. The first transmission of the human voice—effectively the first radio program—occurred four years later, the responsibility of R. A. Fessenden, in the United States. It was an event made possible by the invention in 1904 of the thermionic valve, by J. A. Fleming of University College, London.

It was, however, to be some time before the technology was to move into the realms of an entertainment medium. A generation of "wireless amateurs" fell upon the concept of sending and receiving signals prior to World War I, when amateur experiments were banned on both sides of the Atlantic. The war itself—the first in which wireless played a part—helped to develop transmission equipment further, and between the years 1914–1918, a realization was dawning that the medium had a more universal application than utility. In the United States, a former

Marconi company employee, David Sarnoff, the founder of the Radio Corporation of America (RCA), conceived the idea of a "Radio Music Box" in 1916, and two years later, Marconi's head of publicity, Arthur Burrows, wrote an article that was published in the *Yearbook of Wireless Telegraphy and Telephony* in which he predicted the radio as a medium for entertainment, news—and advertising.

The Marconi Company had established itself in the Essex town of Chelmsford in 1903 with a research station conducting transmission tests, and in 1912 had created the world's first purpose-built factory for wireless communications equipment there. After the war, attention was turned to the future development of radio, and in December 1919, an experimental 6-kW telephony transmitter was installed at the works, intended for testing reception of speech signals over long distances. Much of the future application of radio in the UK was determined by the nature of the content emanating from the Marconi station in its new station, MZX; the engineers in charge, W. T. Ditcham and H. J. Round, might have been expected to conduct their rigorous testing through formal scientific parameters and techniques. Instead, they chose to explore the medium's possibilities through the playing of records, linked with speech. Thus, the first ever broadcast in Britain, in the modern sense, given on 15 January 1920, was to set the style of much that was to follow thereafter. Gradually increasing the power of the transmissions, Ditcham and Round created a "schedule" of two 30-minute programs per day through January, February, and March 1920, with content that was not only exciting in the concept of the new but was pleasing and entertaining to listen to. It was as though, instinctively, they had understood one of the precepts that was to inform all electronic media thereafter: that is to say, the first miracle of technology is that it exists at all. Soon, however, it is its role as a platform for content that is interrogated, and in order to prove its continuing relevance, it must satisfy this criterion. In this case, the fact that listeners identified with the content of the broadcasts and therefore understood how it could enhance their day-to-day lives, went a long way to establish radio's relevance as well as its technical possibilities.

The transmissions were received over thousands of miles, and in June 1920, perceiving the immense publicity value of the interest in the experiments, Lord Northcliffe, the proprietor of the *Daily Mail* newspaper, sponsored a recital of "live" music by the famous Australian singer,

Dame Nellie Melba. Broadcasting from the Marconi Chelmsford works on 15 June, Melba delivered a 30-minute program of songs that was heard in Madrid, The Hague, Paris, Sweden, Norway, and Berlin. The event caused a sensation, and the next day the *Daily Mail* carried the story in triumphant terms:

> Art and science joined hands, and the world listening in must have counted every minute of it precious.

On 30 July, the station repeated the idea, with the Danish singer, Lauritz Melchior broadcasting a recital of songs aimed principally at the Scandinavian audience—perhaps the first "targeted" transmission in history. Public interest was extraordinary, and it seemed as though the new medium was about to burgeon. In fact, by demonstrating that wireless/radio had a dual application, the early pioneers had created a tension that would cause a hesitation in its development.

The almost accidental utilization of radio as an entertainment medium, and the enthusiastic public response to the application took both industry and regulatory authorities by surprise. There was concern that the transmissions from MZX would interfere with utility services, in particular wireless communications between aircraft and ground controls. Thus, in November 1920, the postmaster-general, the Right Honorable Albert Illingsworth, banned future Chelmsford broadcasts in an address to the House of Commons, and for a time the use of the medium was returned to message-sending for official purposes only.

There was, however, a growing groundswell of opinion, in the form of wireless amateurs, who now united into large societies around the United Kingdom, proceeding to activate in the cause of radio listening. The Post Office suggested the compromise of a telegraphy station, but the tide had turned in favor of telephony—a medium that could offer speech and music rather than signals and electrical impulses. In March 1921, 63 wireless societies held a conference with the aim of putting pressure on the government to provide a service supplying content of interest to members. The result was a petition, at the end of that year, to which a new postmaster-general, the Right Honorable F. G. Kellaway, responded with an agreement that a service of speech and music should be provided by the Marconi Company once a week. A new station, with the call sign 2MT, was established in a former army hut in the village of Writtle, two miles from Chelmsford, manned by a team of nine, led by Marconi's Captain Peter Eckersley.

Following on from Ditcham and Round's earlier experiments, there was an eccentrically entertaining quality to the 2MT broadcasts, which were transmitted on Tuesday evenings at 7:30 p.m. from 14 February 1922 to 17 January 1923. The content was a mixture of technical information mixed with live and recorded music, banter and doggerel poetry delivered mostly by Eckersley himself. The light-hearted nature of the broadcasts offended some, who felt this new sacred—almost mystical—medium should not be taken lightly, but most listeners enjoyed the informality of Eckersley's presentation, in which he scorned pomposity and employed instead an endearing casualness of style:

> Well, I think we're about ready to begin now, and the first thing I've got to introduce is a record entitled . . . Why are records always entitled, why can't they just be called something?—So here it is, a record entitled . . .

Soon after Writtle began broadcasting, the Post Office issued a second license to the Marconi Company, enabling it to introduce another station, which was established at the Company's London premises, Marconi House on the Strand. The call sign of this second station was 2LO, and its first transmission was on 11 May 1922, under the direction of Arthur Burrows. Broadcasts from 2LO were initially on a twice-weekly basis—Tuesday and Thursday evenings—with half-hour programs. These, however, had a formality not present on the Writtle broadcasts; Burrows and Eckersley were very different personalities, and Burrows's view of the high importance of radio stamped itself on the 2LO output, which was more sober and restrained than that of its Chelmsford counterpart. In a sense, this duality was to prove a metaphor for some of the tensions and debates yet to be encountered, themes that were to characterize and polarize views as to the purpose and nature of radio in the UK, encapsulated in public service versus commercial broadcasting conflicts during the 1930s and beyond.

At the same time as these experiments were taking place in the UK, developments were progressing quickly toward scheduled radio services in the United States. In November 1920, the Pittsburgh station, KDKA, owned by the Westinghouse Corporation, captured the public attention by broadcasting election returns in the race for the U.S. presidency between Warren G. Harding and James M. Cox. The potential for the new medium was immediately clear; within two years, 219 stations were broadcasting, and in August 1922, the first radio advertisement was broadcast, opening a further floodgate of opportunistic entrepreneurship. Chaos threatened as the medium's growth threatened to run out of control, and Herbert Hoover, Secretary of Commerce, was quickly forced to introduce regulation over radio.

In the UK, the government considered its options. It was one thing for radio to proliferate in a country the size of the United States; for a similar expansion to occur in an island the size of Britain was a prospect not to be countenanced, and so, as in 1920, control was deemed necessary. In April 1922, the postmaster-general again addressed the British House of Commons, with a statement that was to inform thinking in Britain relating to broadcasting for almost 40 years:

> It would be impossible to have a large number of firms broadcasting. It would result only in a sort of chaos, only in a much more aggravated form than that which arises in the United States, and which has compelled the United States, or the Department over which Mr. Hoover presides, and which is responsible for broadcasting, to do what we are now doing at the beginning, that is, to lay down very drastic regulations indeed for the control of wireless broadcasting.

COMPANY AND CORPORATION

The dilemma for the British Government was based on the narrow path between allowing an unacceptable and inappropriate proliferation of radio companies on one hand, and the establishment of a monopoly growing out of the Marconi Company's early lead in terms of broadcasting experimentation. In point of fact, a number of other companies, including Metropolitan-Vickers and Western Electric, were already, in 1922, working toward establishing broadcasting based in Manchester and Birmingham respectively. Additionally, pressure was being mounted on the Post Office from receiver manufacturers, who were naturally anxious that there should be a content provider to establish and develop consumer demand for the purchase of sets. From the start, the postmaster-general sought legislation to ensure that Britain should be served by a system that would be "for the benefit of the general public but not for the benefit of individuals."

The solution was to license a number of regional stations run by "bona fide manufacturers of wireless apparatus" under the strict control of the Post Office itself, with only Post Office-approved sets made by the operating companies being offered for sale. In addition, the services should be funded by a listener license fee, levied on all those capable of receiving the new service. Meetings between interested parties were held at the Institute of Electrical Engineers on the Thames Embankment in London in May 1922, and at the second of these, a name was agreed upon for the unified service provided by the various stations. This was to be "The British Broadcasting Company Ltd.," which was accordingly established with £100,000 capital in cumulative ordinary shares. Thus, through a hybrid of government control and commercialism, was British broadcasting established. The studios of 2LO in Marconi House, London, were transferred to the ownership of the new company, and British Broadcasting Company transmissions began on a regular scheduled daily basis on 14 November 1922. This was followed by the opening of regional stations in Birmingham, Manchester, the next day, and subsequently Newcastle, Cardiff, Glasgow, Aberdeen, and Bournemouth over the next 11 months, providing local programming with network potential.

Lord Gainford, a former postmaster-general, was the first chairman of the company, and the first general manager, appointed after interview, was John Charles Walsham Reith, a 33-year-old Scot, who took up his post on 14 December 1922, becoming managing director on 14 November 1923.

From the heady days of experiment and pioneering, there now followed a necessary period of consolidation and rationalization. Issues relating to the manufacture of sets, linked to the issuing of licenses for listeners, caused tension between the Post Office and the BBC. Licenses were only issued to those purchasing receivers carrying a BBC/PMG stamp—in other words, sets manufactured by one of the BBC constituent companies. There were, however, numerous wireless amateurs who constructed their own sets, and therefore fell outside this ruling. In addition, the huge growth in interest in the new medium had resulted in a mass application for licenses, which the Post Office had considerable difficulty dealing with, leading to a backlog in licenses issued, and a further growth in potential listeners constructing their own sets, rather than waiting to purchase a licensed receiver.

The first attempt at the formalization of broadcasting in Britain came with the establishment of the Sykes Committee of 1923, which addressed the matter of licensing, and began the move away from the

BBC's dependence on commercial revenue gained from receiver sales. This was achieved by increasing the proportion of the license fee payable to the BBC from 50% to 75%, and by establishing one form of license, providing the legal right to listen to BBC programs, whether or not the receiver was manufactured by a BBC company. At the same time, the BBC's own license to broadcast was extended until 1926. In May 1923, the new company moved into its own premises, a wing of a building on the Thames Embankment owned by the Institution of Electrical Engineers; the premises were accessed by an entrance at 2 Savoy Hill, a narrow, unprepossessing street flanking London's famous Savoy Hotel. Within a few short months, a catalog of "firsts" was achieved, including the first outside broadcast, the first play written for radio (*Danger*) by Richard Hughes, and the first broadcast symphony concert. At the same time, work was continuing around Britain to enhance technically the BBC's transmitter power through a series of relay stations, improving coverage nationwide.

The BBC's aim was high-minded: to inform, educate, and entertain. It fostered children's programs and encouraged listeners to savor its serendipitous approach to output, with varied content surprising the ear. At the same time there was conflict between the new medium and established institutions; newspaper proprietors feared loss of sales, and agreements were reached limiting the amount of news broadcast, stipulating that it should not be transmitted before the evening, ensuring a continuing public need for newspapers. Theater owners and impresarios also distrusted broadcasting, fearing loss of audiences, while vaudeville entertainers disliked the sterile silence of the studio, and the terrifying capacity of radio to consume material; an act that had lasted touring entertainers for years on stage was now disseminated to a nation in an instant.

The development of radio in the United Kingdom should be seen within the context of the growth of broadcasting within Europe; by 1925, approximately 40 services were operating on the Continent, and listeners were exploring these stations with pioneering zeal. International wavelength regulation became an issue, and was addressed by the formation of the International Broadcasting Union (IBU). In that same year, an experiment in sponsored radio was attempted in the form of a 15-minute fashion talk, supported financially by Selfridges's store in London's Oxford Street. The broadcast, produced by one Captain

Leonard Plugge, was transmitted from the Eiffel Tower in Paris, and, although it had little impact, it was to prove the forerunner of a commercial radio explosion that would have a considerable effect on UK broadcasting through the 1930s.

Set against this, the 1925 Crawford Committee, which was established to explore the future of broadcasting in Britain, came to the conclusion that commercial radio, run by a series of independent companies, was not to be the way forward in the UK, and that the task should be entrusted to a single authority, without ties to industry, run by "persons of judgement and independence, free from commitments." A key to defining this new organization was that the service should be "conducted by a public corporation acting as a Trustee for the national interest." In July 1926, Crawford's recommendations were accepted, and the British Parliament agreed that on 31 December that year, the British Broadcasting Company's responsibilities should be handed to a new authority, with its power derived from a Royal Charter, reviewable and renewable on a regular basis. Thus was born the British Broadcasting Corporation.

Even before this new incarnation came to pass, the BBC was experiencing crisis and expansion in equal measure. The General Strike of 1926 brought the company into conflict with members of the public and the government; the BBC was accused on one hand of progovernment activity, while on the other, criticized for not handing its microphones over totally for government use. Meanwhile Reith, and his chief engineer, Peter Eckersley, were developing new transmitters, affording the possibility of a unified national service, supplemented by regional alternatives.

When the company became a corporation, on 1 January 1927, the number of license holders in the UK numbered 2,178,259. With the coming of its new status, there were those who questioned the BBC's monopoly. This was exacerbated by the perception that the corporation held a paternalistic attitude toward its listeners; the first *BBC Handbook*, published in 1928, states that the BBC's working rule was to "give the public something slightly better than it now thinks it likes." A crucial factor in early BBC policy making was the strict religious upbringing of John Reith, now appointed as the Corporation's director-general. Reith believed firmly in Lord's Day observance, and insisted that Sunday programs did not demonstrate levity or what he perceived as frivolity. Indeed, at one point, BBC stations closed down for one hour at the traditional time for church services, to ensure that there would be no distraction from the business of worship. This policy provided continental-based commercial operators, such as Leonard Plugge, with a golden opportunity to subvert the BBC's monopoly; Plugge, learning from his experiences with the 1925 Selfridge's broadcast, established a business partnership with the owner of the Normandy station, Radio Fecamp. Buying airtime from the station, he then resold it to British advertisers, broadcasting a series of sponsored record programs under the title, "Radio Normandy," specifically targeting the weak BBC Sunday, with its audience starved of popular entertainment.

Radio Normandy went on air in October 1931, and other entrepreneurs followed Plugge's lead, including the U.S. agency, J. Walter Thompson. In 1933, Radio Luxembourg began transmissions from a giant transmitter on the Junglinster Plateau above the city of Luxembourg. Audiences flocked to the populist output of a growing number of stations, many "sub-let," like Radio Normandy, by Leonard Plugge, who formed a quickly growing company called the International Broadcasting Company (IBC). The problem for the BBC was made more serious by the growth of Relay Exchanges under the collective name of Rediffusion, a concept that involved sending wireless signals down telephone cables. Thousands—particularly in poor reception areas—took out subscriptions to these services, which offered good reception of the two BBC services—National and Regional—plus one other. This inevitably meant that one of the commercial stations was included, thus exposing the BBC to direct competition. Ensconced in its gleaming new art deco building, Broadcasting House, at the top of London's Regent Street from May 1932, the BBC stood accused by many of being out of touch with the mood of the time and the needs of its listeners, particularly those of the British working class.

In 1936, with the renewal of the BBC's charter less than a year away, a committee of enquiry into the future of broadcasting chaired by Lord Ullswater examined the development of television; it also explored the issue of commercial competition, which was by this time reaching its prewar height. The Ullswater Report stated that "foreign commercial broadcasting should be discouraged by every available means," but in spite of this and the strenuous efforts of both the BBC and the Post Office, the continental stations enjoyed their most profitable years between

1936–1939. It was partly due to this pressure—and partly from internal opinion—that the BBC somewhat grudgingly created an audience research department under J. R. Silvey; prior to this, such had been the paternalistic attitude within the BBC, that any form of measurement of listening figures was considered an irrelevance and a distraction from the task of its somewhat prescriptive view of public service broadcasting. The late 1930s were turbulent times for the BBC; John Reith resigned in June 1938, under government pressure, and in just over a year, World War II began. Many felt the coming of international conflict saved the BBC from itself. The continental competition was removed at a stroke, while at the same time, the nature of events over the next six years underlined the importance of the BBC as a public service broadcaster, enhancing its reputation immeasurably both within Britain, and internationally.

WAR

The expansion of programs and reorganizing of facilities and resources within the BBC brought about by the coming of war changed the face of British broadcasting forever. International services were developed, and the domestic networks were restructured, creating a Forces Service and a Home Service. In terms of actual content, a raft of programs specifically aimed at maintaining morale was developed, including *It's That Man Again (ITMA)*, *Garrison Theatre*, *Music While You Work* and *Workers' Playtime*. As the war progressed, and the role of war correspondents became defined, portable recording technologies were developed, and the place of on-the-spot journalistic reporting became an accepted part of broadcast news for the first time. BBC monitoring services were complemented by the BBC's own foreign-language transmissions, sometimes involving the development of new techniques. The BBC's German Service utilized short-sentence constructions to subvert Nazi jamming to considerable effect, and the value of the French-language service after the fall of France proved to be immeasurable, enabling ex-patriates to speak to their homeland through the important program *Les Français Parlent aux Français*. By late 1943, in addition to its English-language international service, BBC programs were being transmitted in 45 languages.

In the spring of 1943, William Haley became director-general of the BBC, and from that time onward, the construction of a postwar BBC became a priority. A new generation was running the Corporation now, and there was a determination to learn from the mistakes of the past. The audiences who had been lured by commercial radio in the 1930s, had been further charmed by the influx of American and Canadian broadcasters, with their relaxed, colloquial style contrasting sharply with the traditional formality of prewar BBC presentation. Haley's vision of UK radio included the first moves toward streamed, generic radio. In his words:

> The provision of general contrast, the feeling of competition and choice in the BBC's programmes, should cause what present demand there is for commercially provided competition to subside.

The practical application of BBC philosophy took the form of a tripartite system of radio; the program created for the Forces would remain with modifications, and be renamed the Light Programme; the Home Service, more traditionally "BBC," would continue a mix of speech and light orchestral music, with regional variations; while a third channel, aimed at more "highbrow" tastes, including the arts, classical music, and drama would be created.

These changes were swiftly implemented at the end of hostilities; on 29 July 1945, the Home Service began broadcasting, on the same day as the Light Programme took over from the Forces Programme. The Third Programme did not commence transmissions until September 1946. In the meantime, although the fledgling BBC television service—which had been inaugurated shortly before the war, resumed its transmissions from London's Alexandra Palace in June 1946, the principal investment within the British broadcasting industry remained in radio. In the financial year 1947/1948, £6,556,293 was spent on sound broadcasting, while television saw only £716,666 in terms of financial investment. In 1946, the BBC charter was renewed by the newly elected postwar Labour government under Clement Attlee, but for the first time in BBC history, the term was reduced from 10 years to five. In the meantime, within the last year of the war, the strategically significant Radio Luxembourg had been liberated by U.S. forces, and was used to transmit propaganda at retreating German troops. It was shortly to be returned to civilian operation, heralding a resumption of continental competition, although in a reduced form; Radio Luxembourg was to be the only station from Europe to continue a challenge to BBC programs after the war.

NEW WORLDS

The new structure of British radio after the war began the removal of Reith's beloved concept of serendipity in listening, and may be seen in retrospect to have been the start of a system of generic broadcasting along cultural strands that would eventually lead to the creation of networks, such as BBC Radios 1 to 4 in 1967. On the other hand, a focus was established for producers that enabled some highly significant programs. In 1945, the Features Department was created under Laurence Gilliam; the Third Programme generated some remarkable drama productions, including Samuel Beckett's *All That Fall*; Dylan Thomas's masterpiece, *Under Milk Wood*, with Richard Burton in the role of "First Voice" was first broadcast in January 1954, produced by Douglas Cleverdon, who also fostered the work of other great poets, including David Gascoyne (*Night Thoughts*) and David Jones (*In Parenthesis*); in short, the 10 years following the end of World War II can truly be claimed as a high-water mark for creative radio in the UK.

Light entertainment, too, entered what for some became a "golden era," with the development through the 1940s and 1950s of major—and sometimes long-lasting—comedy series, some of which would later transfer to television, while others, such as the surreal *Goon Show* exploited the concept of "pure radio." From this period come programs that have remained BBC staples to this day, including *Woman's Hour* (October 1946) and *The Archers* (January 1951). The resurgence of listening to commercial radio was not to be stemmed, however, and postwar Radio Luxembourg re-established itself—particularly among the young—as a source of populist entertainment, indeed, modeling much of its programming on its prewar output; *The League of Ovaltineys* returned in 1946 with a virtually identical style and format to that which had captivated a previous generation of children. The station also developed the idea of the record show, and thus this potent form of music radio—relatively unfamiliar to UK audiences despite the work of Christopher Stone and others in the 1930s—manifested itself in Britain for the first time. Initially demonstrating this genre was Radio Luxembourg's *Top Twenty* program, which began in 1948. Starting as a program of the top-twenty sheet music sales of popular songs, illustrated by records, it was an instant success, receiving thousands of letters per week, and paving the way for the growth of music radio generally in Britain, creating an appetite that would in due course challenge the BBC's relationship with its audience—particularly the young—once again.

Postwar Radio Luxembourg was a combination of the familiar and the new; as the 1950s developed, however, its output became increasingly music-dominated, with record shows sponsored by specific companies, such as the Decca Group, Capitol Records, and others. Meanwhile, the BBC's programs for children—including *Children's Hour*—retained and fostered radio audiences among the young in more traditional ways. *Listen with Mother*, aimed at preschool audiences, remained in the affections of generations of youth audiences as they grew, and the science fiction series, *Journey into Space*, broadcast during the mid-1950s, attained a huge following, and was in fact, the last radio drama series to defeat UK television in audience ratings.

Nevertheless, as the mid to late 1950s spawned the rise of rock 'n'roll and the development of a true youth music, BBC radio did little to respond, and Radio Luxembourg, broadcasting to the UK in the evenings, drew increasingly large listening figures.

The BBC faced other crises; just as the General Strike of 1926 had caused tension with the British Parliament, so the Suez Crisis of 1956 pitted the Corporation against Anthony Eden's government. Eden wanted the BBC to put forward internationally a picture of Britain as a united front over the issue of the Suez Canal. The director-general, Sir Ian Jacob, resisted this, maintaining the BBC's right to impartial reporting of internal differences of opinion within the nation on the matter. Had this right been overridden by the government, the nature of the BBC would have been fundamentally changed; as it was, this crucial moment in British broadcasting left the independence of the BBC intact, and maintained its international reputation—and, in particular, the World Service—in an era of increasing global mistrust and Cold War propaganda. As the distinguished broadcaster Desmond Hawkins had remarked of the BBC's wartime role, "if you were traveling in Europe, you only had to mention that you were from the BBC, to be clasped by the hand and welcomed as an honored friend." This sense of trust was at stake—and ultimately preserved—at the time of the Suez Crisis. Throughout the 1950s, the growth of television was inexorable; one of the significant moments for UK audiences was the coronation—in June 1953—of Queen Elizabeth II. The televising of the event had a considerable effect on TV sales in itself, but the growth of the medium as the decade progressed was general and irresistible. In 1955, Britain saw commercial television, the BBC for the first time having its monopoly legally challenged by competition. As it would be later, the death of radio was predicted, while at the same time, the medium continued to develop and innovate. The invention of the portable tape recorder, intended initially as a news tool, was seized on by producers, such as Charles Parker in the BBC's Midland Region, who created a series of classic radio documentaries—*The Radio Ballads*—with Ewan MacColl and Peggy Seeger. These programs, broadcast through the late 1950s and early 1960s, redefined the nature of documentary feature making, dispensing with a narrator, and utilizing actuality and "the voice of the people" in a way that would have a lasting effect on the way speech programs would be made in the future. In creative, news, and current affairs broadcasting, BBC radio remained unchallengeable; it was the youth revolution of the 1960s that instigated the next major change in British broadcasting, with cultural and technological drivers at the forefront of the new order.

REVOLUTION

The 1960s saw two linked issues influencing the development of radio in the UK. First, a growing youth market spawned by popular music, in particular from 1963, when home-grown talent, spearheaded by the Mersey Sound and the rise of the Beatles, created a demand for a media other than television that could be "owned" by this rising audience. Secondly, the development of the transistor enabled a new portability in receiver equipment, typified by the tiny Sony TR620 radio, which first appeared in 1960. That said, what remained lacking, as far as the youth audience was concerned, was appropriate radio content. The BBC Light Programme broadcast a small number of popular music programs, but Radio Luxembourg's evening output was still the only source of a genuine record-based music radio, of the type that had been in existence in the United States for many years. Movements had begun among certain independent radio production companies, which had made programs for Radio Luxembourg, toward the concept of a legal framework for commercial radio within the United Kingdom. These met with a consistently negative response from the Labour government of the time, and the idea of a true competitor for audiences against a BBC that virtually retained its monopoly of radio broadcasting seemed as far away as ever. On 29 March 1964, that breakthrough came in dramatic fashion, with the first broadcast of Radio Caroline, the brainchild of a young Irish entrepreneur, Ronan O'Rahilly. The transmissions came from a ship moored in international waters, five miles off Harwich on the east coast of England. The sound was radically different from anything heard on UK radio before, and it spawned a host of other offshore "pirates" over the next three years. As with the continental stations of the 1930s, the BBC was confronted with a very real attack on its output; a deficiency in its policies had been identified, and it was once again found to be out of step with a crucial part of its audience.

Notwithstanding the growth of the offshore stations, and the demonstrable popularity of their output, Harold Wilson's Labour government would not be swayed. A parliamentary act was devised to silence the stations, making it illegal not only for them to broadcast, but to be supplied from British shores. On 13 June 1967, the Marine Broadcasting (Offences) Act was created; this came into legal effect at midnight on 14/15 August, and all pirates apart from Radio Caroline went off the air. Caroline has continued to broadcast sporadically in various forms ever since, becoming an icon of the free radio spirit of the 1960s and mirroring in many ways the commercial pioneering of the 1930s. The movement created by the activism of the offshore stations made change inevitable; history has shown that BBC policy is often responsive to outside influence, and such was the case in the media climate of the late 1960s. Within two weeks of the ship-based stations coming off the air, many of the stations' presenters were broadcasting once more, this time as part of the BBC's first pop-music station aimed exclusively at a youth market: Radio 1. At the same time, the BBC's director of radio, Frank Gillard, completed the process of generic streaming on BBC radio; the old Light Programme became Radio 2, the cultural channel became Radio 3, while the Home Service was renamed Radio 4.

At the same time, Gillard created BBC local radio. During the early 1960s, there had been a major development in transmitter technology, with the expansion of very high frequency—VHF (FM) to cover 97 percent of the UK population. The high-quality, low-power capability of VHF made it possible for the same or similar frequencies to be used by various broadcasters in different parts of the country. It is important to understand that at this time, the majority of UK radio listening was carried out on either mediumwave (MW) or longwave (LW). VHF also carried with it the capability of stereo broadcasting, and would ultimately be adopted as the standard for UK radio generally. In the meantime, VHF was the ideal carrier for Gillard's experiment in local radio, which began in November 1967 with BBC Radio Leicester. This was followed by stations in Sheffield, Liverpool, Nottingham, Brighton, Stoke-on-Trent, Leeds, and Durham. By 1970, the trial was deemed to have proven a case for local radio, and other stations began to roll out, remaining a part of the UK radio map ever since.

By 1970, the BBC could claim to have regained its radio monopoly, apart from the continuing, although by now culturally diminished, presence of Radio Luxembourg. In that year, however, political events once again conspired to change the UK radio industry. 1970 saw a General Election in Britain, and, somewhat against expectations, the Conservative Party, under Edward Heath, was elected to power. Unlike the Labour Party of the time, the Conservatives stood for free enterprise rather than state-supported industry, and as such, had placed the introduction of commercial or independent radio in its manifesto. A further factor in the chain of events was that the age of voting was reduced to 18, thus admitting a youth vote to the political system for the first time.

The plans for the legal establishment of independent, land-based commercial radio were ratified in the Broadcasting Act of 1972, coincidentally the BBC's 50th anniversary. The new tier of radio broadcasting was to be administered by a new authority, the Independent Broadcasting Authority (IBA), developed out of the Independent Television Authority (ITA), created to administer Independent Television from 1955. Nearly 400 companies prepared for the application process. This was, however, to be a very different concept of commercial radio from the ideals of the offshore stations of the 1960s or the prewar continental pioneers; the early days of Independent Local Radio were to be fraught with financial hardship and political rivalry, combined with overregulation, which together would at times threaten the very future of the new form.

INDEPENDENT RADIO

With the arrival of legally based radio supported by advertising in the UK, the caution exerted by politicians and regulators failed to take into account, at first, the commercial imperatives of the necessary business ethic behind the medium. It is important to understand the distinction between the words "independent" and "commercial" radio within the context of UK radio at this time. Because of a lack of forethought on the part of the politicians who had supported the idea, the new radio service took Independent Television as its model. ITV had been conceived as a public service, and so independent radio, rather than commercial radio was born into a similar ethic, together with a responsibility to answer to listeners rather than to shareholders in the first instance. It was also very heavily regulated, with specific weekly targets for speech content, including prescribed religious programming durations and the requirement to spend a proportion of profits on the development of live music and community events.

Many unexpected and remarkable programs resulted in this overstructuring and regulation, but, within the uncertain and volatile political climate of the 1970s in Britain, the first legitimate radio competition to the BBC found it hard to survive, while at the same time compromising its identity; this was not the concept of commercial radio that the earlier advocates of the form would have envisaged.

The first Independent Local Radio (ILR) station to broadcast was, significantly, an all-speech station, the London Broadcasting Company (LBC), opening at 6:00 a.m. on 8 October 1973. It was as though the intention was to demonstrate that UK radio funded by advertising was a legitimate, worthy form, as far removed as possible from the stereotypical American-style music radio, the style of which had typified the appeal of the offshore stations of the 1960s. The opening of the station was key, conservative (in a nonpolitical sense) and understated. Days later, on 16 October 1973, a second station began broadcasting in London. This was Capital Radio, and was primarily a popular music station. However, such was the nature of IBA regulation at the time, that the station saw fit to employ a drama producer, and to run its own classical orchestra, the Wren Orchestra. As other stations came on air over the coming months and years, the sense was of a diluted "voice," the IBA requirement for a "balanced output" leading often to a certain blandness and a curiously Reithian approach to broadcasting and to the audience. Partly to demonstrate that ILR could produce quality programs to rival its BBC counterparts, a Programme Sharing Scheme was established, allowing participating stations to exchange material that went beyond purely local content, and demonstrate that, whatever the prejudice against the stations, particularly among upper-class professionals and politicians, this was a responsible medium. The funding for this project came from a controversial tax raised by the IBA on ILR profits, which was entitled "Secondary Rental." This fund was raised by taxing a proportion of these profits (if and when they occurred) to create a pool of money that would be made available for communal use among all stations in the network. Another beneficiary of this scheme was a National Broadcasting School. It was, perhaps, little wonder that the early years of the new radio form in Britain were precarious ones financially, set against a time of domestic strife, including a strike by UK miners and a three-day work week.

As more stations were established during the 1980s, there was a growing frustration both within the industry and within the public; on the one hand, excessive regulation continued to threaten the existence and growth of independent radio; in February 1983, two-thirds of ILR stations currently broadcasting were losing money. On the other hand, listeners were being tempted by a new wave of pirate stations, typified by the American-style music radio of Laser 558, broadcasting from a ship off the Essex coast, with a large transmitter reaching considerable audiences with its slogan of "The music is never more than a minute away." The station, with its slick U.S. DJs and uncompromising approach to its output, made considerable inroads into the already fragile output of ILR, while also cutting into the audiences for the BBC's Radio 1. In the meantime, national radio remained the monopoly of the BBC; in 1979, Radio 2 became the first station in Britain to broadcast 24 hours a day.

A further blow to commercial radio development came with th publication of the Annan Report; although primarily concerned w the future of television, the report impacted on commercial radio by clearing the way for morning television for the first time in the UK. In the year 1983/1984, morning radio audiences fell by 10 percent. This was a particularly low point in the industry. In June 1984, the Association of Independent Radio Contractors (AIRC), representing the interests of commercial radio in Britain, held a conference out of which came four crucial resolutions for action on behalf of the industry:

1. To make public the industry's frustration at overregulation
2. To demand an early and substantial reduction in rentals
3. To press the government for new legislation on commercial radio in Britain
4. To commission an independent report on the potential for creating more stations under a lighter regulation

The conference had a major effect; within three months, many of the more petty IBA regulations were dispensed with, within six months rentals were reduced by more than a third, and within a year an independent report, *Radio Broadcasting in the UK*, demonstrated that a new "light-touch" regulation would facilitate genuine expansion in the commercial radio sector. The process that began at the 1984 conference culminated in the 1990 Broadcasting Act, which removed many of the hurdles prohibiting independent radio from being truly commercial, as well as permitting consolidation—the purchasing of radio stations to form groups—and ultimately the creation of the first national commercial radio stations.

DIGITAL

As a result of the 1990 Broadcasting Act, the IBA was abolished, and in 's place were created two separate regulators for independent television ` Independent Television Commission—the ITC) and radio (The ᐯuthority). Beyond this, the Act was pivotal in the development ·ᴄial radio in the UK. Consolidation of company holdings was ᐯme permitted in Britain, seeing the rise of radio groups, ᐯe Capital Radio Group, and Emap, which consumed ᐯng their output to an overall group policy. At the same time, the move toward community radio began, although the reality of "people's radio" was still a full 15 years away. Another outcome of the Act was the creation—for the first time in Britain—of national commercial radio; three licenses were advertised, to be won by Classic FM, which began broadcasting in September, 1992, Virgin 1215, (later renamed Virgin Radio) in April 1993, and TalkRadio UK (later to become TalkSport) in February 1995. The coming of a classical music station as the first national commercial service was significant in the raising of the the sector's profile and image, and played a key part in the following years, which were successful ones for the independent sector. The new "light touch" Authority relaxed regulation on Independent Local Radio, dispensing with the requirement to provide as much "meaningful speech" as previously, and reducing some of the obstacles to profitability which had hitherto existed. The result was a move from an emphasis on programs to programming, a development of the concept of branding within radio groups, and—for some—the deterioration of program standards toward a certain predictability of sound.

Meanwhile, the BBC was changing. New structures led to an opening of its internal systems, with producer choice enabling staff producers to choose facilities beyond the Corporation itself. Also, program making was opened up to independent production companies, which were enabled to bid for program slots across all networks in competition with staff producers and departments. In September 1995, the BBC launched digital radio, and the following year came a parliamentary act, the aim of which was to "make provision for the broadcasting in digital form of television and sound programme services and the broadcasting in that form on television or radio frequencies of other services." The concept of the digital multiplex—a technical conduit clustering a number of separate services transmitted digitally together and offering the potential for a range of new stations in digital quality—came into being. The Radio Authority advertised the first commercial national multiplex in 1997; there was at the time some caution among commercial operators, and in the event, there was only one applicant to operate the service; accordingly, the license was awarded to Digital One, led by the GWR group, and the service was launched in spring 1999.

The technology used to enable DAB in Britain, in common with many other countries in Europe and Asia—although not the Unit States—was known as Eureka 147. Initially, the UK's Digital A

Broadcasting services marketed the system on the basis of improved quality. This, however, proved unsuccessful, and the emphasis was switched to an increase in service choice. Even so, into the first years of the 21st century, a circular problem hindered the public take-up of DAB; sets were expensive, and there was reluctance on the part of consumers to invest in new receiver technology for a service the benefits of which were unclear, and reception—in the early years—intermittent and uncertain geographically. The problem was exacerbated by a proliferation of new radio technologies and platforms, in particular the growth of Internet radio, both as live streaming and audio on demand. Satellite radio, in the form of Worldspace, began in a small way to demonstrate a new concept in global radio, and mobile telephone manufacturers were developing 3G technologies, the first steps toward a new range of portable digital services. Technology also lay at the heart of the program-making process, with digital systems introduced from the mid-1980s for editing and storage of material.

Convergence was in the air—literally. For the first time in the history of the medium, the consumption of radio did not require an eponymous device to enable it; digital television sets carried radio output, and the industry was caught somewhat by surprise as the new century progressed, finding increasing numbers of listeners tuning in via their television receivers. These—and other—technological changes, pointed toward another reshaping of media regulation within the UK, to take the industry forward; in June 2000, the Radio Authority published a paper for submission to the Department of Culture, Media and Sport and the Department of Trade and Industry entitled *Radio Regulation for the 21st Century*, outlining its belief in the requirement for further deregulation. In May 2002, Tony Blair's Labour government announced the draft Communications Bill, which aimed to dismantle existing media regulators in favor of one "super regulator" in the form of the Office of Communications (Ofcom). In May 2003, the Communications Act came into ⁿe, and in December of the same year, the Radio Authority handed sponsibility to Ofcom for an industry that had radically changed years of the former regulator's existence. In 1990, the UK ⁻adio industry consisted of 80 companies; by the end of ⁿk charge of the regulation of 272 local analog services, ⁱ multiplex, and 45 local multiplexes carrying more digital services. The Communications Act also cleared the way for further consolidation, and the potential for international ownership of UK commercial radio services.

In June 2002, the first manufacturer to produce a sub-£100 digital receiver, Pure, launched its Evoke-1, heralding at last the development of cheaper sets, which began an increasing public take-up of the medium. Meanwhile in the BBC sector, a range of new digital services were launched, including BBC 7, a speech service drawing on the Corporation's archive of drama and comedy radio programs. It was said that this one service, making available much-loved material from UK radio's past, was as responsible as anything else for the upsurge in interest in DAB at the time of its launch in the autumn of 2002. Other BBC services available as digital-only stations included 6 Music and 1Xtra, both of which launched during 2002.

In contrast to the developments in new technologies and the potential for new commercial radio giants to inhabit the British media scene, Ofcom progressed the plans of its predecessor, the Radio Authority, to establish community radio within the UK. The concept had been under discussion for some years, and already the germ of "access radio" as it was for a time called, had existed in the presence of short-term licensed stations run by sectors of the community—Restricted Service Licenses (RSLs). These stations, run by student, ethnic, or arts groups, usually operated under license for four weeks or so, often coinciding with a local event or festival. Out of this came the desire to put back into communities a direct local voice that, for many, had been removed by the change in ILR from its early, pre-1990 form, to the branded group-policy-led entity it had increasingly become in the last years of the 20th century and beyond.

In June 2000, the government sanctioned the setting up of 16 stations around Britain as a pilot scheme. The agreed-upon definition of a community service was that of a station run as a small-scale neighborhood project, either as a community of geography or interest. The groups chosen for the pilot covered the whole of the UK, and a commissioned evaluation of the project concluded that this third tier of British radio would ultimately prove itself to be "one of the most important cultural developments in this country for many years." In 2004, the first full-time licenses were advertised by Ofcom, to run for a span of five year and by the summer of 2005, some 20 licenses had been awarded, v a rolling program of further awards being made in the following y

May 2005 saw the first major merger between radio groups, with the GWR and Capital groups joining forces as GCap Media. The event happened at an inauspicious time in commercial radio development, with sales low, and the medium struggling to compete with a content-rich BBC. There were also new trends in the way listeners consumed radio. The phenomenon of the Apple iPod and the ability to download—"podcast" radio programs—gave audiences the potential for creating their own playlists both of programs and of music, and radios with rewind and pause facilities enabled listeners to "spool through" commercial breaks, challenging the traditional means of funding by advertising and prompting the sector to explore new potential revenue streams.

Historically, the tensions within UK radio since its creation, in particular, those created by the continuing evolution and redefining of public service broadcasting and the nature of competition, has created a unique medium, capable of re-inventing itself and adjusting to new times, technology, and challenges. Thus, by the middle of the first decade of the 21st century, British radio continued to be a thriving, vibrant medium. The refining of technology impacted on the medium in many ways; issues of revenue continued to present challenges and promised further changes in structure and funding. At the same time, mobility and questions relating to the inter-relation between content and available platforms pointed to the fact that radio within the United Kingdom was about to embark on a new era of fundamental change.

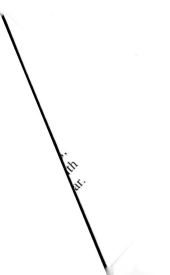

THE DICTIONARY

– A –

ABRAMSKY, JENNY (1946–). After reading English at the University of East Anglia, Abramsky joined the **British Broadcasting Corporation (BBC)** in 1969 as a programs operations assistant, moving to the **Radio 4** lunchtime news program, *The World at One*, in 1973. After editorships on *PM* and *Today*, she became editor, News and Current Affairs, Radio, in 1987, in charge of all news and current affairs programs on the five BBC radio networks and was founding controller of **Radio Five Live** when it launched in March 1994.

In 1995, Abramsky won the Sony Radio Academy Award for an outstanding contribution to radio, and in 1998 she was made a fellow of the Radio Academy. In January 1999, she was appointed director of BBC Radio, a role that was subsequently extended under the title of director of BBC Radio and Music. Her responsibilities in this capacity included the five main networks and the BBC's digital stations, **Radio 1Xtra**, **6 Music**, **BBC 7**, **Five Live Sports Extra**, and the **Asian Network**. Additionally, she was responsible for the three **BBC Orchestras** in England, **The Proms** Television Classical Music and Radio Resources. She was awarded the honor of CBE in 2001.

ACK-ACK BEER-BEER. This popular show formed a twice-weekly variety series on the **Forces Programme** broadcast from July 1940 to February 1944, with no less than 324 episodes. The title derives from the Morse Code words for the initials of the Anti-Aircraft and Balloon Barrage commands during World War II, for whom the program was intended. Among many artists who regularly appeared were **Sandy MacPherson**, **Elsie and Doris Waters**, **Vera Lynn**, **Kenneth Horne**, and **Doris Arnold**.

ACKERLEY, JOE (1896–1967). Writer and poet Joe Ackerley was for 24 years the literary editor of the *Listener*, a post to which he was appointed in 1935. Prior to this, from 1928, he had been an assistant producer in the Talks department of the newly constituted **British Broadcasting Corporation (BBC)**. One of his most enduring friendships was with E. M. Forster, whom he had met in 1922, and it was through Forster that Ackerley acquired a wide circle of acquaintances from the world of literature, and he was able to call on many of these acquaintances when recruiting speakers for talks.

As editor of the *Listener*, he was radical, energetic, and fearless, commissioning poems and features and frequently coming into conflict with the hierarchy of the BBC, which he saw as being characterized by philistines and prudes. Overtly homosexual, his charm, integrity, and insistence on the highest standards earned him the reputation of being the finest literary editor of his generation; he sustained his role in the job for nearly a quarter of a century.

ADAMS, DOUGLAS (1952–2002). Adams was the creator of one of the great classics of radio comedy, the highly innovative *The Hitchhiker's Guide to the Galaxy*. It was the producer Simon Brett who, receiving a synopsis from Adams for a science fiction comedy series, saw its potential and achieved a **Radio 4** commission. The first program was transmitted in March 1978. Its transfer to television was not generally considered an unqualified success; however, books based on the series have continued to achieve remarkable sales, and in 2005 a feature film was issued, based on the stories. Up to his death, Adams remained fascinated by the possibilities of technology, and his last radio series, *The Hitchhiker's Guide to the Future*, featured him as both writer and presenter, exploring various forms of digital communication.

ADIE, KATE (1945–). Kate Adie, familiar to both radio and television audiences in the UK as a **British Broadcasting Corporation (BBC)** war correspondent, began her career as a studio technician in **local radio**. At Radio Bristol, she worked on farming programs, joining BBC TV news in 1979. She became the BBC's chief news correspondent in 1989 and in radio terms became well known as the presenter of the **Radio 4** program, *From Our Own Correspondent*. Among the many honors she has received is the Broadcasting Press Guild's Award for an Outstanding Contribution to Broadcasting.

AEOLIAN HALL. This famous concert hall, built in Bond Street, London, in 1904, was taken over by the **British Broadcasting Corporation (BBC)** in March 1943 after the destruction by German bombs of the Variety Department's former home, **St. George's Hall**. From that time on, Aeolian Hall was the home of **Variety** programs and remained so for 30 years. At its peak in the 1960s, 20 shows a week were being recorded or broadcast live from two studios, Aeolian 1 and 2.

ALAN, A. J. (1883–1941). The name was a pseudonym for Captain Leslie Harrison Lambert, a London civil servant. For years before World War II, Alan enthralled listeners to the **National Programme** with his mysterious radio stories. In January 1924, his first story, *My Adventure in Jermyn Street*, was broadcast from **Savoy Hill**, and his last was transmitted in March 1940, just a year before his death. His cult status was added to by the mystery of his identity. His broadcasts were limited—only about five a year—which heightened his impact and mystique. It was only at the time of his death that his identity was revealed. In his obituary, the *Times* stated: "Broadcasting has lost one of its most popular storytellers, and one—possibly the only one—who maintained his anonymity to the end." His catchphrase was "Good Evening Everyone," which gave its title to a book of his stories that was published in 1928.

He also broadcast a series of 15-minute talks from **Radio Luxembourg**, from July 1939, entitled "Story Telling." Outside of broadcasting, he worked in the cryptographic analysis section of the Admiralty, which subsequently became known as GCHQ and was responsible for breaking the "Enigma" code. He was strongly aware of the magic of the radio form, and in order to allow nothing to come between him and his listeners, he pasted each page of his script onto cards to prevent paper rustle. His is a classic image of the early British broadcaster: **Stuart Hibberd** described him as "a neat figure in perfectly cut evening dress, with eye glass and a slim black brief case."

ALDISS, BARRY (1932–1982). Aldiss was a **disc jockey (DJ)** particularly associated with postwar **Radio Luxembourg**. He came to London in 1955 after working on a number of radio stations in his native Australia. Aldiss could have had a successful career as a musician and composer; he wrote more than 100 songs and was a talented pianist, working for a time as such in a Knightsbridge club after his arrival in Britain. While so occupied, he met a member of the German presentation team for the BBC program, *Two Way Family Favourites*, who helped him to make the contacts that led to his joining the staff of Radio Luxembourg a year later.

For eight years, he presented the *Top Twenty* program with an audience, which at its peak was said to be close to 10 million. In 1966, he moved to London and worked as a freelancer on such programs as *Housewives' Choice* before joining the original team of presenters on **Radio 1**, in 1967, presenting, among other programs, *Late Night Extra*. He returned to Radio Luxembourg in 1975, this time as general manager and presenter, positions that he held until his death at the early age of 52.

ALLIED EXPEDITIONARY FORCES (AEF) PROGRAM. The radio service for the Allied Expeditionary Force opened on 7 June 1944, the day after D-Day. Programs were divided jointly between Britain, Canada, and the United States. The service gave many British civilians a taste of the more relaxed style of broadcasting on the other side of the Atlantic and influenced postwar **British Broadcasting Corporation (BBC)** policy, which previously had come under fire from prewar commercial interests attacking its controversial **Sunday Policy**. Many famous American radio shows were heard on AEF, including *Amos 'n' Andy*, *The Bob Hope Show*, and regular concerts by Glenn Miller and the American Band of the AEF. The British Band of the AEF was led by George Melachrino, and among the stars who appeared on the service were Bing Crosby, Jessie Matthews, Webster Booth, and Marlene Dietrich. The service ended on 28 July 1945.

ALLISON, GEORGE (1884–1957). George Allison was a legendary football commentator from the early days of sports **outside broadcasts**. His first broadcast was only the second ever match transmitted, the cup-tie between Corinthians and Newcastle United on 29 January 1927. Born at Hurworth-on-Tees in County Durham, he began his career in Plymouth as a journalist, and in 1912, having secured an exclusive interview with Lord Kitchener, he joined the U.S. Hearst newspaper group, working as European correspondent for *The American Weekly*, a post he held for more than 30 years.

His 1927 debut as a **British Broadcasting Corporation (BBC)** soccer commentator opened up a new career; his rich voice and colorful descriptive powers, together with his skill at capturing the atmosphere of major sporting occasions quickly made him a favorite with listeners; in 1928 he was the natural choice as commentator for the FA Cup Final—the first to be broadcast. He went on to become a director of Arsenal Football Club and later resigned his directorship to become manager, leading the club through great years of achievement during the mid-1930s. He retired in 1947.

ALL THAT FALL. In 1957, Samuel Beckett wrote this, the first of his works for radio, and his first published play written in English rather than French, for broadcast on the **BBC Third Programme**. It was produced by Donald McWhinnie and featured in the cast a number of actors who have become strongly associated with his work: J. G. Devlin, Mary O'Farrell, Jack MacGowran, and Patrick Magee. The script's subtle sonic requirements led to new developments in audio production and ultimately to the formation of the **BBC Radiophonic Workshop**.

AMPLITUDE MODULATION (AM). First utilized in 1906 by Reginald Fessenden, the signal is transmitted by varying the radio wave to match the sound wave variations being transmitted, and converted back into sound waves at the receiver. **Mediumwave** and **longwave** transmissions still use amplitude modulation, although with the advent of **Digital Audio Broadcasting (DAB)** it became increasingly arcane.

ANALOG. Until the latter years of the 20th century, traditional radio systems were exclusively **amplitude modulation (AM), frequency modulation (FM), longwave (LW),** and **shortwave (SW)**. These services used analog technology. The analog system consists of transmitting the actual audio signal modulated onto the Radio Frequency carrier. Drawbacks related to analog broadcasting include its susceptibility to unwanted interference, noise, and hiss, which undermine the audio signal. For listeners of FM, this can usually be remedied to various extents by adjusting or improving the receiver aerial, or resiting the receiver itself. With the development of digital radio services in the 1990s, pressure began to grow for the British government to set a date for an analogue "switch-off," thus moving the UK industry into a totally digital climate. The slow initial take-up of digital radio receivers has made the decision relating to such a move somewhat problematic, and at this time no such date has been set.

ANALYSIS. This **Radio 4** program was created by **Ian McIntyre** and **George Fischer** in 1970. It is characterized by the serious and committed tone of its engagement with current affairs—frequently political—and the informed nature of its narrative. It has benefited from a number of distinguished presenters, notably, for more than 10 years, **Mary Goldring**.

ANDERSON, MARJORIE (1913–1999). Initially employed by the **British Broadcasting Corporation (BBC)** as an actress, Anderson, who had trained for the stage at London's Central School of Speech and Drama, she was among a number of women trained to become the BBC's first female presenters of record programs. For many years she was the main presenter of *Woman's Hour* from its beginning in 1946. In 1955, she hosted a spin-off program, *Home for the Day*, remaining with the program until its demise in 1968. She continued on *Woman's Hour* until she retired from broadcasting in 1972. Her style influenced many women presenters.

ANDREWS, EAMONN (1922–1987). Born in Dublin, Andrews's first job was as an insurance clerk, a post he lost when it was learned he was broadcasting boxing commentaries on Radio Eireann. Gradually, his work increased on Irish radio, and in 1948 he was MC of a stage show called *Double or Nothing* at a Dublin theater, where he was spotted by the British band leader, Joe Loss, who signed him—and the program—for a tour.

In 1949, when **Stewart MacPherson** left the **British Broadcasting Corporation (BBC)**, Andrews successfully applied for his job as

MC of *Ignorance is Bliss*. The rich Irish brogue immediately proved popular with UK audiences, and Andrews was asked to present the live weekly program, *Sports Report*. He continued to host this for many years, alongside work as a boxing commentator for BBC radio. By 1951, television was emerging in the UK, and Andrews was offered the role of host for the panel game, *What's My Line*. Other TV successes included the UK version of U.S. television's *This Is Your Life*, which he hosted both for BBC and ITV.

In 1964, he became a papal knight of St. Gregory, and in 1970 he was appointed an honorary CBE. After his death in November 1987, more than 3,000 people attended his memorial service.

ANNAN COMMITTEE/REPORT. From 1974–1977, a government committee led by Noel Gilroy Annan (Baron Annan, 1916–2000), considered the future of broadcasting in the UK, and produced a 500-page report that laid down the terms of operation for both radio and television over the next decade. The report, written by Annan himself, recommended the further development of local radio, and suggested that broadcasters be more responsive to the public. It advocated high standards in broadcasting, and insisted on the need to resist what it saw as extreme commercial pressures. There were implications in this for the new and developing medium of **commercial radio**, which was to struggle to establish itself financially for some years to come.

ANNOUNCERS. The earliest announcers on British radio were at **2LO**, including **Arthur Burrows** and **Cecil Lewis**, who combined the task with their other roles. **Stuart Hibberd** was made chief announcer in 1928; others were **John Snagge**, **Derek McCulloch**, and **Alvar Liddell**. For a time, announcers were anonymous voices, but during World War II, the practice was introduced of announcers identifying themselves when reading the news to ensure that the audience would be aware of the authenticity of what they were hearing. In **commercial radio**, the first staff announcer was Max Staniforth on **Radio Normandy** in 1931. Also on this station was **Bob Danvers-Walker**, while on **Radio Luxembourg**, **Stephen Williams** was chief announcer, and Tony Melrose became "The Voice of **Radio Lyons**." It is true to say that, as the "voice" of their respective stations, radio announcers became the first recognizable personalities in the new medium, leading to the famous song, "Little Miss Bouncer Loves an Announcer," recorded by the comedy duo, **Flotsam and Jetsam**.

ANY ANSWERS. Initially the program, which started in October 1954, was the opportunity for listeners to respond to the previous week's edition of *Any Questions*. From 1989, it became a 'phone-in and follows the second transmission of *Any Questions*.

ANY QUESTIONS. This long-running discussion program began as a six-week series in the **British Broadcasting Corporation**'s **(BBC)** West Region in October 1948, and continues to this day. It was conceived by **Frank Gillard** and from the start it dealt with controversial issues of the day, with a panel of guests debating with a live audience who supplied the questions. Among early panelists were **A. G. Street** and **John Arlott**. The program has evolved into a harder-edged debate, usually politically oriented. From 1954 it had an appendix in *Any Answers*. *See also* THE BRAINS TRUST.

ARABIC SERVICE. Apart from its domestic transmissions in Welsh and Gaelic, the BBC only broadcast in English until 1938, when it began its Arabic Service. As a crucial and frequently controversial arm of the **World Service**, its output was increased during the Gulf War crisis of 1991, and continues to actively debate issues in the Middle East, now supported by a developed online presence.

THE ARCHERS. This daily radio serial, originally billed as "the everyday story of country folk" began its long career on Whit Monday, 1950, broadcast in the **British Broadcasting Corporation**'s **(BBC)** Midland Region only. The writers in the first instance were Geoffrey Webb and Edward J. Mason, who were responsible also for *Dick Barton, Special Agent*. The program idea had been conceived in Birmingham in the late 1940s, as a support for government policy to encourage the nation's farmers to grow more food. The concept was that current issues would be debated within the form of popular drama, and to this end the program always carried a farming advisor. Over the many years of its existence it has become a national institution, and in addition to its Monday to Friday 15-minute episodes, there is a week-end omnibus edition. Its theme tune, "Barwick Green," is also nationally famous.

The fictional home of the farming family, The Archers, is Ambridge, somewhere in Central England, and although this is fiction, the concerns dealt with in the **serial** remain very real, and reflect the current affairs world of British farming accurately. For instance during the Foot and Mouth Disease epidemic in the early years of the 21st century, storylines were recorded as near to transmission as possible in order to reflect the rapidly changing situation.

The Archers has always held a reputation for headline-gathering, notably in 1955, on the night of the first transmission from Independent Television, when the story editors "killed" one of the program's star characters, the young Grace Archer, in a stable fire. The effect was to send the nation into "mourning" and to defuse—whether intentionally or otherwise—the launch of Great Britain's first commercial television service.

Another aspect of the program's continuing cult status is its ability to attract star names for cameo appearances, including members of the British Royal Family (Princess Margaret appeared in 1984, playing herself). The program has its own, highly organized fan club, appropriately known as *Archers Addicts*.

"ARCHIE ANDREWS." Following the success on U.S. radio of Edgar Bergen, ventriloquist Peter Brough, in association with **Ted Kavanagh** (who chose the name) created "Archie Andrews" in 1944 for a series entitled *Archie Takes The Helm*. In June 1950 came the start of *Educating Archie*, which was to become the most popular comedy **series** on British radio. The concept of ventriloquism on radio is an odd one, but was in this case successfully supported by off-air visual campaigns, including comic strips, and the naughty small boy persona of Archie, by all accounts an upper-class prep school attendee dapper in a striped blazer and scarf, became readily identifiable to its 1950s audience.

ARLOTT, JOHN (1914–1991). One of the best known of all cricket commentators, John Arlott was also a published poet, and it was this quality that informed his work with the spoken word to memorable effect. His early work—as an attendant in a psychiatric hospital, and later as a policeman—was a long way from his ultimate career, although his time in the Hampshire Police Force demonstrated a keen interest in—and talent for—playing the game of cricket.

His first job in the **British Broadcasting Corporation (BBC)**—mentored by John Betjeman—was in 1945, when he became a producer of poetry programs for the **World Service**'s Eastern Service. In 1946, he covered the England tour of India, and produced a delighted response among listeners. It was the start of a career that would last for 34 years. He retired in 1980, appropriately after commentating on the Lords Centenary Test Match.

ARNOLD, DORIS (?–1969). Although her main fame rests on her being the first female **disc jockey** in UK radio, through her work on *These You Have Loved*, Arnold's association with broadcasting goes beyond this long-lasting request program. Originally a shorthand typist, she joined the **British Broadcasting Company (BBC)** at its start as a secretary. As an accomplished pianist, her career changed forever when in 1930 she stood in at short notice as an accompanist for *Children's Hour*. Thereafter she formed a partnership with the pianist Harry S. Pepper and as a duo they made many successful and popular broadcasts together. Arnold was also a respected musical arranger. She became hostess of *These You Have Loved* in 1938, and remained associated with the program for many years.

ASHBRIDGE, NOEL (1889–1975). One of the original **Marconi Company** team at **Writtle**, Ashbridge had served as an officer with the Royal Engineers in World War I, and was one of the first wireless operators at the front line in France. He joined the Marconi Company in 1919 and worked at **Writtle** constructing the 2MT transmitter, and he worked with **Peter Eckersley** on the first broadcasts. In 1926, Ashbridge joined the **British Broadcasting Company (BBC)**, and became assistant chief engineer under Eckersley. Three years later he succeeded him as chief engineer.

In 1935, he received a knighthood; the previous year he was made a knight of the Danish Royal Order of Dannebrog in recognition of his work within Europe, establishing radio services. After spending time with the BBC team developing high definition television in the 1930s, and the subsequent wartime closure of the service, Ashbridge was appointed deputy director-general of the BBC in 1943, with special responsibility as technical advisor. In 1948, he relinquished the post to become director of technical services, and from this position played a major role in the postwar expansion of both radio and television in the UK.

In 1950, Ashbridge was the BBC's engineering representative at the Torquay conference, which established the European Broadcasting Union. He retired from the BBC in 1952, thereafter spending a further seven years as a board member of the Marconi Company.

ASKEY, ARTHUR (1900–1982). The diminutive Askey was a much-loved comedian who was associated from 1938 with the hit radio show *Band Waggon*. Together with **Richard Murdoch**, Askey developed a style new to British radio, of fast cross-talking nonsensical dialogue with ad-libbing, using the microphone in a focused way, which owed more to an understanding of the potential of this new medium rather than the world of the music hall, from which many of their contemporaries had come. Askey remained popular up to the end of his life, latterly becoming a regular member of the panel of the comedy ad-lib program, *Does the Team Think*. He coined numerous catchphrases, among them, "Hello Playmates" and "Before your very eyes."

ASSOCIATION OF INDEPENDENT RADIO CONTRACTORS (AIRC). This trade organization for **commercial radio** in Britain was created by the first Independent stations in 1973. The Association's purpose was to negotiate on the companies' behalf on all issues relating to working practice, regulation and marketing. It continues its work today under the name of the **Commercial Radio Companies' Association (CRCA)**.

AT HOME AND ABROAD. The program was an important development in **Current Affairs** radio in Britain, first transmitted in January 1954 and continuing until 1960. Broadcast twice weekly, and featuring speakers from all over Britain and overseas, who discussed issues of topical interest, it was heralded in *Radio Times* prior to its first edition as aiming to be "the essence of Current Affairs broadcasting . . . [bringing] to the microphone the *right* contribution on the *right* subject at the *right* time."

AUDIENCE RESEARCH. The **British Broadcasting Company/Corporation (BBC)** came relatively late to the concept of audience research, largely due to early paternalistic attitudes toward public service broadcasting. The way was led in the 1930s by U.S. advertising agencies, creating **commercial radio** programs for transmission from the Continent to the UK; these organizations needed to demonstrate to prospective clients that radio held potential as an advertising medium, and set about creating their own research units. In 1936, the BBC set up its Listener Research Unit under **Robert Silvey**, who devised a number of means of exploring audience tastes and listening habits (*See also* STEPHEN TALLENTS). In latter years, radio listening has become increasingly dominated by ratings, which are measured and monitored quarterly by the **Radio Joint Audience Research (RAJAR)** unit, co-owned by the BBC and the **Commercial Radio Companies Association**.

– B –

BALDWIN, PETER (? –). Peter Baldwin was deputy director of radio at the **Independent Broadcasting Authority (IBA)** under **John Thompson** until 1987, when he succeeded Thompson as director of radio. He held the post until the IBA was dissolved, and was thereafter the first chief executive of the **Radio Authority**, until 1995, when he was succeeded by **Tony Stoller**.

BALLAD OF JOHN AXON. In 1957, the **BBC** commissioned **Charles Parker** and **Ewan MacColl** to make a documentary feature on the life and death of a north country railway engine driver called John Axon. Together with Peggy Seeger, the two men created a new form of program, utilizing the newly acquired technology of the portable tape recorder, and replacing scripted narrative with actuality and musical commentary. This was to be the first of what came to be known as the **Radio Ballads**, of which there were eight, broadcast between 1957 and 1964 on BBC radio.

BAND WAGGON. This highly influential program, running from January 1938 to December 1939, effectively created the genre of the radio "sitcom." Starring **Richard Murdock** and **Arthur Askey**, the premise was that of the two comedians occupying a fictitious apartment on the top floor of **Broadcasting House**. Peopled with fast-moving banter and many catchphrases that entered public consciousness and usage at the time, the show became extremely popular, and spawned a touring stage version, a series of commercial records, and a film.

BANDWIDTH. The development of radio in the UK has frequently revolved around the availability of bandwidth, or spectrum. This is allocated to the industry regulator by the government. When the first Independent Local Radio (ILR) stations launched in 1973, all contracts issued included two frequency allocations—**amplitude modulation** (**AM**-mono) and **frequency modulation** (**FM**-stereo). Initially, stations broadcast the same service on each of their frequencies. Subsequently, companies used the two frequencies to broadcast alternative services.

As **commercial radio** developed, the initial bandwidth allocation was filled. By 1989, FM allocation of local frequencies was divided equally between independent radio and the BBC. The development of national commercial radio in the early 1990s was driven by government-approved allocation of one national FM frequency and two national AM frequencies. Commercial radio's coverage was further enhanced in 1996 by the allocation of the bandwidth between 105 and 108 MHz. The increasing pressure to launch new services with a finite amount of bandwidth was one of the factors taken into account with the development of **digital radio**.

BANNISTER, MATTHEW (1957–). Matthew Bannister has had an unusual career in radio, moving between management and presentation. He began at Radio Nottingham in 1978, before joining the news department of **Capital Radio**. Between 1988 and 1991, he ran GLR, the London station operated by the **British Broadcasting Corporation (BBC)**. As controller of **Radio 1** between 1993–1998, he was responsible for taking the station through a difficult period in which the network redefined its place in the youth music-radio market, and within the BBC. In doing so, he removed many of the older presenters, some of whom had worked for the station since its inception, and introduced a "new music first" policy in the network's playlist. Other management posts included chief executive of production, director of radio, and director of marketing and communication. Bannister subsequently left management and joined the presentation team at **Radio 5 Live**.

BARKER, ERIC (1912–1990). Barker was a writer, actor, and comedian most associated with his 1950s series, *Just Fancy*. He first worked in radio in 1933, and during the war he appeared in *Merry-Go-Round*, writing a contribution to the program featuring life in the Royal Navy (in which he served) aboard "HMS Waterlogged." His catch phrase was "Steady Barker," and the words became widely used by the public and formed the title of his autobiography. A spinoff after the war helped to launch the career of **Jon Pertwee**. In addition to *Just Fancy*, in which he starred with his wife, Pearl Hackney, who had also appeared in *Merry-Go-Round*; other radio series included *Passing Parade*, *Barker's Folly*, and *Law and Disorder*.

BATCHELOR, HORACE (1899–1977). Batchelor became a household name during the 1950s through his **Radio Luxembourg** program in which he advertised his "Infra-Draw" method for winning football pools. An ex-insurance collector, he won his first dividend in 1948. For a number of years his system became famous, although the actual success of it was debatable. Based in Keynsham near Bristol, the program is today remembered mostly for the announcer's careful spelling of the name—"K-E-Y-N-S-H-A-M."

BBC. *See* BRITISH BROACASTING COMPANY; BRITISH BROADCASTING CORPORATION.

BECKETT, SAMUEL (1906–1989). Radio was in many ways an ideal medium for the Irish playwright, and he created many works for the **Third Programme** and **Radio 3**. Some fine examples of his poetry, prose, and plays were written specifically for the medium, including the 1957 work, *All That Fall*. *See also* DRAMA.

BEERLING, JOHNNY (1937–). During a long, varied, and distinguished career in British broadcasting, Johnny Beerling was often at the forefront of the industry's music development. Beginning as a technical operator with **British Broadcasting Corporation (BBC)**

radio in 1957, he became a studio manager and then producer for the **Light Programme**. When **Radio 1** was created, Beerling devised the first jingle package, recruited many of the presentation team, and produced the first program—with **Tony Blackburn**. In 1971, he devised the first **documentaries** on the network, establishing a long tradition, and in 1973 he conceived and launched the program for which he became most remembered, *The Radio 1 Roadshow*. He became controller of Radio 1 in 1985.

In 1993, Beerling left the BBC to work as a broadcasting consultant for both radio and television, and has continued to be active as a freelance producer. In 1997 and 1998, he worked with Mark Tully on **Unique Broadcasting**'s *Something Understood* and produced an audio cassette, *Kenny Everett at the Beeb* for BBC Worldwide. In 2001, on behalf of Unique Broadcasting, he acted as consultant on the company's acquisition of the **Classic Gold** digital stations.

Beerling has been chairman of the **Radio Data System (RDS)** Forum, an international body that coordinates the interests of the world's broadcasters and radio manufacturers involved in data broadcasting. In May 1993, he received a **Sony Radio Award** for "Outstanding Services to the Radio Industry." His autobiography, *In Search of 1's Navel*, was published in 2007 to coincide with the 40th anniversary of the start of Radio 1.

BENN, TONY (1925–). This Labour Party politician has had a long and varied association with radio, beginning as a producer in the **British Broadcasting Corporation**'s **(BBC)** North American Service from 1949–1950, prior to fighting—and winning—the Bristol Southeast parliamentary seat for Labour.

In 1967, as postmaster general in the Harold Wilson government, Benn was instrumental in the creation of the Marine Broadcasting Offences Act that outlawed the offshore **pirate radio** stations, of which he was an active and extremely vocal opponent. An accomplished broadcaster himself, he recorded his own audio diaries over many years.

BENTINE, MICHAEL (1922–1996). After Royal Air Force service in World War II, comedian Michael Bentine developed his surreal sense of humor into a stage act, which won him considerable success, including seasons at the London Palladium. In 1951, he was one of the founder members of the radio show, *Crazy People*, later to become *The Goon Show*. Bentine withdrew from the program after the second series, claiming the original concept behind it had changed. Thereafter, he resumed his solo career, initially making *The Bumblies*, a comic program that appealed equally to children and adults. He moved into television, creating a range of anarchic programs, including many for children, which won him a wide following. He also wrote three volumes of an autobiography, five novels, four books relating to psychic phenomena, and five children's books. He was awarded the CBE in 1995.

BENZIE, ISA (1902–1988). Glasgow-born Isa Benzie joined the **British Broadcasting Corporation (BBC)** as a secretary in 1927. In 1933, as director of the Foreign Department, she took responsibility for a huge range of negotiations and cultural exchanges with overseas stations, listening to output and liaising over program matters with broadcasters from all over the world. When she married John Royston Morley, one of the BBC's first television producers in 1937, she had to temporarily leave the Corporation due to the Reithian rule stipulating that married couples could not both work for the BBC. She returned when the ban was lifted in World War II.

Thereafter, Benzie worked from 1943–1964 producing talks for the **Home Service** principally. One of her preoccupations of this time was to find a means of expression for women seeking to combine motherhood with a career. In 1957, she was central to the creation of the *Today* program, which she conceived and named. With her friend and exact contemporary, **Janet Quigley**, she developed the early style of the program. Benzie was the program's first editor, although her official title was "senior producer." She retired in 1964.

BERNARD, RALPH (1953–). Prior to the merger of the **GWR** Group and **Capital Radio** to form **GCap Media** in May 2005, Ralph Bernard was executive chairman of GWR. He trained as a journalist, and after agency and newspaper work in his early career, he became one of the original newsroom staff at Radio Hallam in Sheffield in 1975. His pioneering radio **documentaries**—among the first in Independent Local Radio—included the award-winning *Dying for a Drink*, a five-part dramatized documentary on alcoholism. He joined

Hereward Radio as head of news, moving to Wiltshire Sound as program controller in 1982; three months after the station went on air, he became managing director and later, chief executive. It was from here that the GWR Group began.

In 1991, Bernard formulated the proposal that eventually led to **Classic FM** winning the independent national radio license in which GWR took an initial 17% interest, later to buy out the remaining 83% of shares. As well as being chief executive of GWR, he became chief executive of Classic FM in 1996 in addition to his GWR group responsibilities. With the creation of the new radio group—the UK's largest commercial radio organization—in May 2005, Ralph Bernard became executive chairman, GCap Media. He holds the title of CBE for services to the UK radio industry.

BEVERIDGE REPORT (CMND 8116 REPORT OF THE BROADCASTING COMMITTEE, 1949, CHAIRMAN, LORD BEVERIDGE). This important report relating to the preservation of the **British Broadcasting Corporation (BBC)** monopoly in British broadcasting and the potential for commercial enterprise was presented to Parliament in January 1951. In many respects, it was to predict many of the changes in the British media over the next 50 years. Beveridge reviewed the debate relating to the preservation of the broadcasting monopoly and the possibility of the introduction of commercial television. At the time, the report recommended the continuing existence of a broadcasting monopoly and came down against advertising and sponsorship of programs.

A minority report by the Conservative Party MP Selwyn Lloyd disagreed with the findings. This report proposed creation of a Commission for British Broadcasting to oversee the BBC as a radio broadcaster, a British Television Corporation, a number of other national commercial broadcasters for radio and television, and the provision for a potentially large number of local radio stations.

BEYOND OUR KEN. This comedy **series** began in July 1958 and ran through a number of series until 1964. It was scripted by Eric Merriman and Barry Took, and produced by Jacques Brown. The program starred **Kenneth Horne**, **Kenneth Williams**, Hugh Paddick, and Betty Marsden. In the first series, the cast also included Ron Moody and Stanley Unwin, who left before series two, to be replaced by Bill Pertwee. The format was later revamped with the same ensemble as ***Round the Horne***.

"BIG BEN." This is the name given to the main bell in the clock tower of the Palace of Westminster, home of British Parliament. It has long been a part of **British Broadcasting Corporation (BBC)** radio output, first broadcast in 1923, and the chimes continue to be heard, "live" prior to certain broadcasts, including the 6:00 p.m. news on **Radio 4**. For a time during the 1930s, it was also relayed from a loudspeaker behind the clock on **Broadcasting House**. It is also heard on the BBC **World Service**, and in 1932 was voted the most popular broadcast by BBC overseas listeners.

BILLY COTTON BAND SHOW. This highly popular entertainment program was broadcast on the **Light Programme** initially in February 1949. It featured a blend of comedy songs sung by Alan Breeze, and more romantic fare, originally by Doreen Stephens (later replaced by Kathy Kay) linked by Cotton himself. The show ran until October 1968, and became a staple part of the nation's Sunday lunchtime listening, with its familiar theme, "Somebody Stole My Gal." It also transferred successfully to television.

BINAURAL RECORDING. This is a highly specific method of stereo recording that seeks to replicate the conditions of actual human hearing. Usually using a model of the human head, microphones are placed where the ears would be. It is a complex procedure and is most often used in programs requiring specialist effects. From the listener's point of view, binaural stereo is best experienced using headphones rather than loudspeakers. *See also* BLUMLEIN, ALAN.

BIRT, JOHN (1944–). Subsequently Sir John Birt and Lord Birt of Liverpool, he came to the **British Broadcasting Corporation (BBC)** from London Weekend Television in 1987 as deputy **director-general** with special responsibility for **News** and **Current Affairs**. With **Michael Checkland**, he devised the concept of **Producer Choice**, an internal market system that offered producers the choice between using internal facilities or external suppliers.

Shortly after he replaced Checkland as director-general, Birt was criticized when it became known that he had joined the BBC as a freelancer contracted to the Corporation through a personal company. As a result, he became a staff member, and, as director-general from 1992, he oversaw the development of digital and online services and pursued further areas of restructuring, including the separation of broadcasting and commissioning.

Although his style of management was unpopular with many of the staff, Birt was undoubtedly responsible for giving the BBC a secure place in the emerging digital world of broadcasting, and gained a favorable license fee settlement. He resigned to become the first director-general since **John Reith** to sit in the House of Lords.

BLACKBURN, TONY (1943–). After early aspirations to become a singer, Blackburn joined the pirate station, **Radio Caroline** South in July 1964. He transferred to rival pirate, **Radio London** in 1966, and, after a short spell on the **Light Programme**'s *Midday Spin*, he was, as breakfast show presenter, the first broadcaster on air when **Radio 1** launched in September 1967. In 1980, he took over the Saturday morning children's request program, *Junior Choice*, prior to joining BBC Radio London to present *Morning Soul* in 1984. Subsequently, he has returned to **commercial radio**, working for such stations as **Capital** Gold, **Jazz FM**, and the **Classic Gold Network**.

BLACKMORE, TIM (1944–). Beginning his radio career as a studio manager and announcer, Tim Blackmore was one of the team who helped to launch **Radio 1** in 1967. Among many programs for the network, he wrote and produced the 26-part **series**, *The Story of Pop*, before leaving to join **Capital Radio** in 1977. Over the next six years, he served as head of music and then head of programs.

In 1984, Blackmore was appointed as the first director of the **Radio Academy**, leaving in 1989 when with Simon Cole he launched the **Unique Broadcasting Company**, providing independent productions for the UK's **commercial radio** sector, moving in 1999 into independent production for BBC radio. In the same year, Blackmore saw the company floated on the Stock Market as **UBC Media Group** plc.

In 2004, he resigned from the staff of UBC Media and was appointed the Group's consultant editorial director. In addition to his radio work, he wrote and produced the Brit Awards show for four years, and the Ivor Novello Awards show for 21 years. Since 1983, he has managed the career of **Alan Freeman**. He has been the chair of the radio industry's Sony Radio Awards Committee. In 1994, he was awarded a fellowship of the Radio Academy, and in 1999, received the MBE for services to independent radio production.

BLAND, CHRISTOPHER (1938–). Sir Francis Christopher Buchan Bland, knighted in 1993, had served on the boards of both the Independent Broadcasting Authority (IBA) and London Weekend Television prior to becoming chairman of the **British Broadcasting Corporation (BBC)** in 1996. He had disagreements with the Conservative Party over the appointment of a Labour donor **(Greg Dyke)** to the position of **director-general**. He resigned in 2001 to become chairman of British Telecom.

BLATTNERPHONE. During the 1920s, the German Louis Blattner developed a concept pioneered by Kurt Stille for the magnetic recording of sound on metal. Blattner was for a time the manager of the Gaiety Cinema in Manchester and used early versions of his machine as an attraction for members of the public, who could pay to hear a recording of their own voice.

In the late 1920s, The British Blattnerphone (Stille System) Company Ltd. was formed and studios set up in Elstree. In 1929, **British Broadcasting Corporation (BBC)** engineers witnessed a demonstration of his recording method and were sufficiently impressed that they arranged for a research trial. Subsequently, the machine entered service at Savoy Hill, and the BBC Year Book for 1932 (covering the year November 1930 to October 1931), claimed the device to be "in some ways the most important event of the year." In 1934, **Val Gielgud** and Holt Marvell used the Blattnerphone as the key plot element in their novel, *Death at Broadcasting House*. *See also* MARCONI-STILLE SYSTEM.

BLUMLEIN, ALAN (1903–1942). Blumlein, an electronics engineer, was born in London and received a BSc in electrical technology from Imperial College, London, in 1923. He worked first conducting research into telephone technology and, in 1929, joined the Columbia

Graphophone Company, which was to become part of Electrical and Musical Industries (EMI) in 1931. At EMI, Blumlein worked to develop new recording techniques, his most notable invention being "binaural sound," which was to become known as stereo. Blumlein's thinking was based on the concept that the positioning of the human ears means that sound is received with slightly differing perspectives. He incorporated this principle into an electronic system using two output speakers to reproduce the effect.

In the late 1930s, Bluemlein applied some of the ideas developed from his binaural sound system into research relating to radar. On 7 June 1942, he was killed in a plane crash while experimenting with this technology. Although he was only 39 at the time of his death, he had amassed no less than 128 patents in his short career. *See also* BINAURAL RECORDING.

BOADEN, HELEN (1956–). Helen Boaden was controller of **Radio 4** from 2000 to 2004. She was also the first controller of **BBC 7** when the network launched in 2002. She began her radio career in the UK at Radio Tees and Radio Aire before joining the **British Broadcasting Corporation (BBC)** in 1983 as a news producer at Radio Leeds. She later became a reporter and subsequently editor of the Radio 4 current affairs program, *File on Four*. She presented *Woman's Hour* from Manchester as well as a wide range of features and **documentaries**, winning a number of awards, before becoming head of Business Programs in 1997, and a year later, head of **Current Affairs**, the first woman to hold the post. In September 2004, she left Radio 4 to assume the role of director of BBC News.

BOOK AT BEDTIME. This late-night series began on the **Light Programme** in August 1949, growing out of an experiment in January that year entitled *Late Night Serial*, when Arthur Bush read *The Three Hostages* by John Buchan. The concept is that of dividing up a book into a number of 15-minute readings, broadcast at the same time on successive evenings. By so doing, the program predicted the development of "talking books" and similar latter-day attempts at broadcast readings on stations such as **Oneword** and **BBC 7**. The first book to be read in August 1949 was Sir Arthur Conan Doyle's Sherlock Holmes story, "The Speckled Band," read by Laidman Browne.

The program continues today, in the late evening on **Radio 4**. Although the premise behind the program—that of a straight reading—has never changed, the time of transmission has, relating to the broadcasters' perceptions of British nocturnal listening habits. Originally transmitted at 11:00 p.m., it has been broadcast at 10:15 p.m., and since 1989 has been broadcast at 10:45 p.m.

BOYLE, JAMES (1946–). James Boyle was a controversial controller of **Radio 4**, succeeding **Michael Green** in 1996. Born in Scotland and coming from an academic background, he joined the **British Broadcasting Corporation (BBC)** in 1975 as further education officer, Scotland and Northern Ireland. In 1983, after a period as further education officer, Southwest England, he became manager of educational radio, BBC Scotland in 1983, and in 1985 was appointed head of educational broadcasting for Scotland. In 1992, he became Head of Radio Scotland, and under his leadership, Radio Scotland became UK Radio Station of the Year in the 1994 **Sony Radio Academy Awards**.

During his time as controller, Radio 4, he radically reshaped the schedule and also introduced a wide-ranging study of listener habits that informed production decisions and scheduling in a way not previously seen on the network. He left Radio 4 in 2000 on his retirement from the BBC and was succeeded in the post by **Helen Boaden**.

BRADEN, BERNARD (1916–1993). Braden was born in Vancouver, Canada, and was a successful actor, singer, announcer, and writer on Canadian radio before becoming a household name in the UK. He moved to Great Britain permanently with his wife, Barbara Kelly, in 1949, Braden himself having first come to the UK on behalf of Canadian radio in 1947. From that time on, the couple became highly popular in British radio and later in television.

Among many programs, the most important was *Breakfast with Braden*, a fast-moving comedy show written by **Frank Muir** and **Denis Norden** dating from 1950. Later in the year, it was moved in the **Light Programme** schedule to an evening slot, becoming *Bedtime with Braden*, and it was in this version of the program that Barbara Kelly joined the cast. Braden also appeared as an actor in many West End theater productions. He received many awards, including the BAFTA Features Personality Award and the British Variety Club Light Entertainment Personality. In 1955, he was made honorary chancellor of the London School of Economics.

BRAIN OF BRITAIN. The series, which evolved out of another program, *What Do You Know?* began in January 1968, chaired by **Franklin Engelmann**. Later, the quiz show was hosted by Robert Robinson for many years. A straightforward general knowledge quiz, each series seeks to eliminate contestants until a "Brain of Britain" is found. There is no prize, simply a title. Spin-offs have included winners from successive series competing for the title, "Brain of Brains."

THE BRAIN'S TRUST. This program began in January 1941 on the **Home Service** under the title, *Any Questions*. It should not, however, be confused with another program of the same name. It changed its name to *The Brain's Trust* in January 1942 and continued until May 1949. It also transferred to television. In its original form—that of a wide-ranging debate on issues and topics of current interest—it had a regular panel consisting of Professor Julian Huxley, Dr. C. E. M. Joad and Commander A. B. Campbell. Over the years, panel members changed, and there were guests, among them Kenneth Clark and Hannen Swaffer. The format, however, remained constant. *See also ANY QUESTIONS.*

BRAY, BARBARA (1924–). Barbara Bray was born in London and graduated with a first class honors degree in English from Cambridge. After university, and some lecturing in Egypt, she joined the **British Broadcasting Corporation (BBC)** as script editor, Drama, in 1953 and then worked as a writer and director within the same department. Her role made her responsible for finding, commissioning, and bringing to realization all dramatic scripts for BBC radio.

Bray, a seminal figure, was instrumental in developing and directing works by Marguerite Duras, Harold Pinter, and **Samuel Beckett**, all of whom she continued to collaborate with after first encounters. She also was active in the development and encouragement of new writers both in Britain and throughout Europe, Africa, India, and the West Indies. In 1960, she left the BBC, and the following year she moved to Paris, where she has continued to work as a writer, translator, critic, and broadcaster. She was succeeded in her BBC post by her deputy, **Martin Esslin**.

Bray continued to write and/or direct a number of film and theater plays, and many pieces for radio, as well as making many dramatic adaptations and translations. She collaborated with Harold Pinter and Joseph Losey on a film adaptation of Marcel Proust's *A La Recherche du Temps Perdu*. She has won many international prizes for translation, including the George Scott-Moncrief Prize for translation from French, which she has received four times. In 1991, she cofounded the Anglo-French Theater Company, Dear Conjunction.

BRIDGEMAN, WILLIAM (1864–1935). Lord Bridgeman of Leigh, 1st Viscount, William Clive Bridgeman, was a Conservative politician who joined the Board of Governors of the **British Broadcasting Corporation (BBC)** in 1933. Becoming chairman in 1935 on the death of **J. H. Whitley**, he himself died in the year of his appointment.

BRIDSON, DOUGLAS GEOFFREY (1910–1980). D. G. Bridson began his career in 1933 as a freelance radio writer, joining the **British Broadcasting Corporation (BBC)** as a feature programs assistant in the North Region in 1935, at a time of considerable cultural development in social action feature-making within the department. In 1941, he moved to London to become Overseas Features Editor, and after the war, assistant head of Features. From 1964–1967, he was program editor for arts, sciences, and **documentaries** (sound). He retired from the BBC in 1967 after more than 35 years; 800 programs had carried his name. His autobiography, *Prospero and Ariel—The Rise and Fall of Radio: a Personal Recollection*, was published in 1971.

BRITISH BROADCASTING COMPANY (BBC [1]). Initially, the full name of the BBC included the word "Company," not "Corporation." This grew out of the initial commercial origins of the organization. In 1922, a number of firms were involved in the development of radio; the technology to manufacture receivers had been developed with the advent of World War I, and a number of wireless amateurs were seeking a broadcasting service. Clearly, there was a commercial imperative for manufacturers; in order to sell receivers, there needed to be a purpose for those receivers, that is to say, a regular schedule of programs.

At the same time, the British government considered the "chaos of the ether" resulting in the U.S. nonregulation of radio practitioners to be unacceptable in the UK, while at the same time ruling out the idea of one commercial company having a monopoly. On 4 May 1922, the British Post Office announced to the House of Commons that "bona fide manufacturers of wireless apparatus" would be given permission to establish a number of broadcasting stations around Great Britain under the eye of the Post Office.

On 23 May 1922, a meeting was held at the Institute of Electrical Engineers in London under the chairmanship of Frank Gill, the chief engineer of the Western Electric Company. Among those attending were representatives of the six companies concerned with establishing a broadcasting base in Great Britain: **Marconi**, Metropolitan-Vickers, the General Electric Company, the Radio Communication Company, the Western Electric Company, and the British Thomson-Houston Company. This group was to guide the course of British broadcasting toward one service, and two days later, another meeting was held, at which the name, "The British Broadcasting Company Ltd." was agreed upon.

The new company was established with £100,000 capital in cumulative ordinary shares. Additional continuing finance was to be provided by the introduction of a 10-shilling **license** payable by all those receiving the service. The steering committee also agreed that the Post Office should be requested to approve for sale only sets made by companies constituting the British Broadcasting Company.

The company's first offices were in Magnet House, Kingsway, London, owned by GEC. At the same time, **2LO**, the Marconi station in Marconi House on the Strand, was placed under the control of the company, which commenced regular transmissions in November 1922.

Thus, the birth of regular, organized broadcasting in Britain was a curious hybrid of commercial interests and government intervention and control. The BBC achieved its initial coverage of the UK through the establishment of a series of local or regional stations, run by its commercial company members. These, in chronological order of first BBC broadcasts, were as follows:

> **2LO.** This was the callsign and title of the first London station, initially run by the **Marconi Company** from Thursday 11 May 1922, out of studios in Marconi House on the Strand. Its

original name was Marconi's London Wireless Telegraphy Station. Formal programming began on 20 July 1922, and from 14 November of that year 2LO became the London Station of the British Broadcasting Company, broadcasting a daily schedule. On 1 May 1923, the station moved to new premises and studios at nearby **Savoy Hill** in a building on the banks of the River Thames, owned by the **Institution of Electrical Engineers**. 2LO continued broadcasting until 9 March 1930, when it was superseded by the **National** and **Regional Services** of the **British Broadcasting Corporation**.

2ZY. Metrovick began experimental broadcasts from this Manchester-based station on 16 May 1922. It became part of the British Broadcasting Company, and, on 15 November, the day after the first daily programs from 2LO, began transmitting BBC programs. It was the first UK station to broadcast a program for children, *Kiddies Corner*.

5IT. This was the station operated by the British Broadcasting Company in Birmingham, going on the air on the same day—15 November 1922—as 2ZY began its BBC transmissions.

5NO. Opened on 24 December 1922, the BBC's Newcastle station developed an early interest in **radio drama**, and one of its associates, Gordon Lea, wrote what has been claimed to be the first book on the genre, *Radio Drama and How to Write It*, in 1926. As early as September 1923, its first drama production was a 15-minute excerpt from Shakespeare's *Romeo and Juliet* (Act III, Scene 5).

5WA. The BBC's Welsh service, 5WA, began broadcasting from Cardiff on 17 February 1923.

5SC. The Glasgow station of the BBC opened on 6 March 1923.

2BD. Opened on 10 October 1923, 2BD was the call sign of the new BBC station serving Aberdeen. It was the second Scottish station, after **5SC** (Glasgow).

6BM. Opened on 17 October 1923, the BBC's Bournemouth service established an early relationship with the Bournemouth Municipal Orchestra (later the Bournemouth Symphony Orchestra) under its founder, Dan Godfrey, and weekly concerts—eventually networked—became a feature of its output.

2BE. The BBC established its Belfast station, 2BE, on 15 September 1924, although its official opening was on 24 October that year. It was the last of the regional stations responsible for originating program content to be established by the company.

BRITISH BROADCASTING CORPORATION (BBC [2]). On 1 January 1927, the British Broadcasting Company became the British Broadcasting Corporation, licensed under Royal Charter. *See* BBC CHARTER.

BBC CHAIRMEN. Since its creation as the **British Broadcasting Company (BBC)** in 1922, the organization has had 19 chairmen presiding over its board of governors. In chronological order, these have been:

Lord Gainford	1922–1926
George Clarendon	1927–1930
Rt. Hon. J. H. Whitley	1930–1935
Viscount Bridgman	1935
R. C. Norman	1935–1939
Sir Allan Powell	1939–1946
Lord Inman	1946
Lord Simon of Wythenshawe	1947–1952
Sir Alexander Cadogan	1952–1957
Sir Arthur fforde	1957–1964
Lord Normanbrook	1964–1967
Lord Hill	1967–1973
Sir Michael Swann	1973–1980
George Howard	1980–1983
Stuart Young	1983–1986
Marmaduke Hussey	1986–1996
Christopher Bland	1996–2001
Gavyn Davies	2001–2004
Michael Grade	2004–

BBC CONCERT ORCHESTRA. The Orchestra was founded in 1952, and for nearly 20 years, from 1970–1989, its principal conductor was Ashley Lawrence. Light orchestral and classical music are its main staples, and it is the mainstay of the weekly program, *Friday Night Is Music Night*, now broadcast on **Radio 2**. In 1989, it performed the entire Gilbert and Sullivan Savoy Operas for the network. The Concert Orchestra is also heard on occasion on **Radio 3**.

BBC DANCE ORCHESTRA. The history of this institution may be divided into three distinct eras. The first orchestra, led by Jack Payne, made its debut in March 1928, and in the four years of its existence made more than 4,000 broadcasts. In March 1932, the new orchestra made its debut under the baton of Henry Hall, celebrating the opening of the **British Broadcasting Corporation**'s **(BBC)** new headquarters, **Broadcasting House**. One of its most enduring recordings was "The Teddy Bear's Picnic." In September 1937, the Orchestra performed under the BBC name for the last time; thereafter it carried Hall's own name, and toured widely.

The third BBC Dance Orchestra was formed in 1939, shortly after the start of World War II, under the directorship of Billy Ternent. He remained until 1944, when he resigned for health reasons and was replaced by Stanley Black who led the orchestra for the next nine years.

BBC DIRECTORS-GENERAL. The role of director-general of the **British Broadcasting Corporation (BBC)** dates from the year 1927 onward and is probably the most important, prestigious, and frequently controversial appointment in British broadcasting. The first director-general of the BBC was **John Reith**, who held the post from the creation of the BBC as a corporation in 1927, until 1938, prior to which he was general manager of the **British Broadcasting Company (BBC)**. From 1942–1943, Cecil Graves and **R. W. Foot** jointly served as directors-general, succeeding F. W. Ogilvie, before Foot continued individually in the role for a further year, after Graves became ill. This was the only time such an event occurred. Incumbents in the position of director-general have been, in chronological order:

F. W. Ogilvie	1938–1942
Cecil Graves	1942–1943
R. W. Foot	1942–1944
William Haley	1944–1952
Sir Ian Jacob	1952–1960

Hugh Carleton Greene	1960–1969
Charles Curran	1969–1977
Ian Trethowan	1977–1982
Alastair Milne	1982–1987
Michael Checkland	1987–1992
John Birt	1992–2000
Greg Dyke	2000–2004
Mark Thompson	2004–

BBC DRAMA REPERTORY COMPANY. As early as 1924, the playwright George Bernard Shaw advocated the creation of a specific company, run by the **British Broadcasting Company (BBC)**, to support the specialist requirements of radio drama. In fact, it was not until the start of World War II, in September 1939, that such a company was founded, run initially from Evesham, and subsequently for the duration of World War II from Manchester. Many distinguished British actors—including Marius Goring, Valentine Dyall, and Carleton Hobbs—have been members. Indeed, the BBC Carleton Hobbs competition continues to foster and motivate radio acting talent from Britain's drama schools. In the 1980s, the company was renamed "The BBC Radio Drama Company."

BBC HANDBOOK. The public annual report of the **British Broadcasting Corporation (BBC)** was published from 1928–1987 in book form, and is an indispensable source for historians of UK broadcasting. Sometimes entitled *BBC Yearbook* or *BBC Annual*, the work is not to be confused with the *Annual Report and Accounts* that have been presented to parliament every year since incorporation in 1927. The handbooks contain a wide variety of articles, statistics, and photographs depicting the life of the BBC. Most follow the same template: a review of the BBC's year, information on notable programs, and other factual information, including the names of senior staff and governors, engineering developments, audience trends, the accounts, and a copy of the BBC's **charter**.

BBC MONITORING SERVICE. The Monitoring Service, based at Caversham Park Reading since 1943, operates a 24-hour watch on more than 3,000 radio, TV, press, Internet, and news agency sources, translating from as many as 100 languages. It was created on the eve of World War II as an aid to tracking foreign propaganda. Its first mission was in 1938, when at the request of the Foreign Office, it began monitoring Italian broadcasts to the Middle East, which were seeking to undermine the British presence in the region.

Initially based at Evesham, the Monitoring Service produced its first full Summary of World Broadcasts in August 1939, but by the middle of the war, the importance of its work and the employment of 500 monitoring staff necessitated a move to premises at Caversham Park, an English country mansion that had formerly been a school. The Monitoring Service collaborates with its U.S. equivalent, the Foreign Broadcast Information Service in Washington, DC. Its continuing relevance has been highlighted through numerous global conflicts and upheavals, among them the Cold War, the collapse of communism, and crises in the Gulf and the Balkans.

BBC NORTHERN DANCE ORCHESTRA. In 1951, the **British Broadcasting Corporation (BBC)** formed the Northern Variety Orchestra, and four years later, with the disbanding of the string section of the orchestra, the Northern Dance Orchestra was created. Under its first musical director, Alyn Ainsworth, the band became well known and respected, and its appearances on such programs as *Make Way for Music* gained it an almost cult status.

In the 1960s, with the changing face of popular music, a new image was sought, and this was provided by Ainsworth's successor, Bernard Herrman, rebranding the orchestra as the "NDO." In 1969, with a view to cost cutting, the BBC put forward a plan to disband the NDO. This was met with great animosity from all sides, and questions were even tabled in the House of Commons on the matter. For a time, the corporation maintained the band, but in 1974 it was reorganized as the Northern Radio Orchestra and was finally disbanded in 1981.

BBC PHILHARMONIC. The orchestra, which is based in Manchester, has had a long and complex history, always linked to broadcasting. In 1922, with the creation of the Manchester station 2ZY, a small orchestra of 12 players, known as the 2ZY Orchestra, was founded. Many significant works—including Edward Elgar's *Enigma Varia-*

tions and Gustav Holst's *The Planets*—received their first broadcast performances from this ensemble. In 1926, it was renamed the Northern Wireless Orchestra (NWO).

In 1930, as a result of a **British Broadcasting Corporation (BBC)** decision to establish a national symphony orchestra in the form of the **BBC Symphony Orchestra** and to reduce commitment to regional orchestras, the NWO was disbanded and was replaced by a small studio ensemble known as the Northern Studio Orchestra. The decision was reversed in 1933, with the creation of the BBC Northern Orchestra, which played at public concerts throughout the region during World War II. During the 1960s the reputation of the orchestra—now as the Northern Symphony Orchestra—grew, and between 1982 and 1984, its playing strength was augmented to 90 and it was renamed the BBC Philharmonic.

BBC RADIO ORCHESTRA. The Radio Orchestra was formed in 1964 by the combining of the BBC Revue Orchestra and the BBC Variety Orchestra. This made it a considerable musical force of 56 players, and under its joint musical directors, Malcolm Lockyer and Paul Fenoulhet, it created a familiar sound and was a major contributor to the **Radio 2** output up to the 1980s, finally led by Iain Sutherland. It had also been conducted by Robert Farnon, at its first public concert in 1971 among other occasions. In 1988, it played at a gala banquet in the presence of Prince Edward but was disbanded two years later as a cost-cutting measure.

BBC RADIOPHONIC WORKSHOP. Formed in March 1958 as a response to growing requirements for sonic innovation within radio drama, the Radiophonic Workshop fostered some remarkable talents, including Delia Derbyshire, David Cain, and John Baker, among others. It also created distinctive sounds for both radio and television up to its demise in 1996.

All That Fall by **Samuel Beckett**, written in 1956 for the **Third Programme** and broadcast in 1957, epitomized the sound climate into which the Workshop was born. Out of this production came others, notably *The Disagreeable Oyster* by **Giles Cooper**, which required sound to be treated as a caricatured style of an audio cartoon. The lessons learned here moved to the logical creation of the Workshop in 1958.

In 1978, Workshop member Paddy Kingsland was involved in possibly the most notable of its accomplishments—the creation of the sound universe for *The Hitchhiker's Guide to the Galaxy* by **Douglas Adams**. In April 1979, the Workshop produced its own history for **Radio 3**, *We Have Also Soundhouses*, a title borrowed from Francis Bacon's treatise, *The New Atlantis*.

BBC REVUE ORCHESTRA. An orchestra of 28 players, it played for many variety programs in the 1940s and 1950s. It joined with the **BBC Variety Orchestra** in 1964 to form the **BBC Radio Orchestra**.

BBC SCOTTISH SYMPHONY ORCHESTRA. The orchestra was founded by composer and conductor Ian Whyte in 1935 as the first full-time musical ensemble in Scotland. Growing out of a background as a small studio orchestra, one of many employed in its early years by the BBC around Britain, Whyte's vision—of a Scottish symphony orchestra that would play music by contemporary Scottish composers—bore fruit with the growth of the Orchestra into the formidable force it had become by the time of his death in 1960. An award for young composers was established in his honor, and today its ability to play contemporary music with a unique commitment has made it renowned among composers and audiences alike.

BBC SINGERS. This choir dates back to 1924, when Stanford Robinson was engaged as the BBC's first chorus master, at **Savoy Hill**. One of his first acts was to establish the Wireless Chorus, which made its debut with a broadcast performance of Rutland Boughton's *The Immortal Hour*. In 1927, an offshoot of eight performers became the Wireless Singers. When the ***Daily Service*** began in 1928, this ensemble was to be a regular part of it. In 1934, Leslie Woodgate became chorus master, and held the post for more than 25 years.

During World War II, the Singers were evacuated, first to Bristol and then to Bangor and Bedford. In 1943, they performed at the famous National Gallery concerts in London, and in 1945, took part in the first performance of Francis Poulenc's *Figure Humaine*. By 1950, now named the BBC Singers, they had built an international reputation through foreign tours, and when Leslie Woodgate died in 1961, to be succeeded by Peter Gellhorn, they were renamed the BBC

Chorus. During the 1960s, they began a long and fruitful relationship with the French composer and conductor, Pierre Boulez. John Poole was appointed chorus master in 1971, reforming and renaming the BBC Chorus with the name it has borne since—the BBC Singers.

BBC SOUND ARCHIVE. This huge resource includes many thousands of recordings, many of which date from long before the birth of radio. Most, however, are of **British Broadcasting Corporation (BBC)** broadcasts and include many of the most historic moments of contemporary history. There are also recordings of drama and music, and a number of these have been made commercially available through the BBC's own marketing arms. There is a continuing argument for more public sharing of this collection, and the BBC has been exploring ways in which this might be made more accessible. Copyright has been an inhibiting factor; on the other hand, there have been a number of occasions when the BBC itself successfully sought help from the listening public in locating "lost" recordings from its own past.

BBC SYMPHONY ORCHESTRA. Founded in 1930, its first principal conductor was Sir Adrian Boult, who directed the Orchestra until 1950. During World War II, it was evacuated to Bedford. It has always retained a commitment to contemporary music, and since its foundation it has given premieres of over 1,000 works, by composers such as Bela Bartók, Benjamin Britten, Paul Hindemith, Gustav Holst, Igor Stravinsky, Dimitri Shostakovitch, and Ralph Vaughan Williams. It is the resident orchestra for the BBC Henry Wood Promenade Concerts each year, making at least a dozen appearances, including the first and last nights.

BBC THEATER ORGAN. In the interwar years, coinciding with the growth of interest in theater organs in the great cinemas of the time, the **British Broadcasting Corporation (BBC)** introduced its own instrument. The first broadcast was from St. George's Hall in October 1936. The first resident organist was **Reginald Foort**, who was replaced in 1938 by **Sandy Macpherson**. The original organ was destroyed in the Blitz of 1941. Thereafter, the BBC purchased Foort's own instrument and it began its career in Jubilee Hall, London, in 1946. There continues to be a following and enthusiasm for popular organ music from the BBC, as is witnessed by the longevity of the weekly **Radio 2** show, *The Organist Entertains*, which began in 1969.

BBC VARIETY ORCHESTRA. An ensemble of 28 players, serving the same purpose—that is of providing mostly incidental music for **British Broadcasting Corporation (BBC)** variety shows and series—as the **BBC Revue Orchestra**, with which it combined in 1964 to form the **BBC Radio Orchestra**.

BBC WRITTEN ARCHIVE CENTRE. Housed at Caversham, Reading, the Centre holds thousands of files, scripts, memos, and working papers dating back to the formation of the **British Broadcasting Company (BBC)**, together with information relating to programs and broadcasting history. Academics and accredited researchers can visit the Centre to study these resources.

BRITISH FORCES BROADCASTING SERVICE (BFBS). In early 1944, a British Forces Experimental Service was established in Algiers, and by the end of the year, five stations were broadcasting. This was to be the foundation of the service that has become known as the British Forces Broadcasting Service, although this title was not used until the start of the 1960s.

Two days after the German surrender, on 10 May 1944, the disparate broadcasting services were unified under the name, "British Forces Network" (BFN), using studios in Hamburg (and subsequently in Cologne). At about the same time, parallel services began operating in India, the Pacific, and the Middle East. This network grew over the next decade to include Kenya, Malta, Cyprus, Libya, and Gibraltar. The service became familiar to domestic audiences largely through the regular weekly Sunday link-ups for the Light Programme's *Family Favourites*, which, beginning in October 1945, enabled service men and women and their families, to exchange messages and musical requests.

In February 1956, BFN moved to fully FM transmission, the first English-speaking network to do so. When UK military conscription ended, staffing of the now renamed BFBS was extended outside the armed forces, and a number of young UK broadcasters gained their early experiences of radio broadcasting from employment this way.

A London headquarters was established, and programs reached various parts of the globe either by satellite—as the technology developed—or in some cases by prerecorded tape.

In 1982, BFBS—previously a part of the Ministry of Defence—became a branch of the Services Sound and Vision Corporation and thereafter derived income from the UK government and a range of commercial activities. With the cessation of the Cold War, BFBS operations in Germany were reduced considerably. The service continues globally, however, and has responded to the need of the UK armed forces wherever they are, including new programming initiatives in the Gulf during the first years of the 21st century. By 2005, personnel in 23 countries were receiving BFBS programs in some form.

BRITISH FORCES NETWORK (BFN). *See* **BRITISH FORCES BROADCASTING SERVICE (BFBS).**

BRITISH LIBRARY SOUND ARCHIVE. This resource, formerly known as the National Sound Archive, is housed in London and holds over a million discs, nearly 200,000 tapes, and many other sound and video recordings. The collections come from all over the world and cover the entire range of recorded sound, including music, drama, literature, oral history, and wildlife. Copies of commercial recordings issued in the UK are kept, together with selected commercial recordings from overseas, radio broadcasts, and many privately made recordings.

The catalog includes over two and a half million entries and is updated daily. It also provides public access to a wide range of specialist books, magazines, and journals covering every aspect of recorded sound, including radio. Seven main subject areas are within the archive, each headed by its own curator. These are

Classical music
Drama and literature
Jazz
Oral history
Popular music
Wildlife sound
World and traditional music

BROADCASTING FROM THE BARRICADES. On 16 January 1926, a talk by Father Ronald Knox included simulated reports of rioting in London by the mass unemployed. Although fictional, the aim of the exercise was to draw attention to social issues that were to culminate in the general strike of May that year. Twelve years before Orson Welles's famous *War of the Worlds* broadcast on CBS radio in the United States, the event actually convinced a number of listeners that Britain was in the throes of revolution.

BROADCASTING HOUSE. "B. H." as it is affectionately known to staff, was established as the headquarters of the **British Broadcasting Corporation (BBC)** on 15 May 1932, when the Corporation moved from **Savoy Hill**. Standing in Portland Place, facing down London's Regent Street, the building was designed by Lieutenant-Colonel G. Val Myer and decorated with sculptures of Prospero and Ariel by **Eric Gill**. By 1928, it had become clear that the BBC had outgrown the space available at Savoy Hill, and the search had begun for a suitable site upon which to establish new, purpose-built premises. A number of London locations were considered, the most favored being one on Park Lane. However, while this was under consideration, it became known that another site, on the corner of Portland Place and Langham Street, was about to become available at much lower cost. The building was completed in 1931, with the BBC initially renting it, the freehold being transferred to the Corporation on 16 July 1936. Its structure took into account the requirements of sound broadcasting in a way that had not been possible in Savoy Hill; the studios were centrally located in a tower, separated from street noise by offices and corridors. It is a building in the Art Deco style and the Latin inscription, mounted in bronze Roman lettering in its entrance hall, is indicative of the sacred cause in which early British broadcasters considered themselves to be engaged:

> To Almighty God
> The first Governors of this institution dedicated this Temple of the Arts and Muses under the first directorship of John Reith, Knight, praying for Divine help that a good sowing may have a good harvest and that everything impure and hostile to Peace may be banished from this building, and that whatsoever things are sincere and beauti-

ful and of good report and loveable, the people, inclining its ear to these things with a contentment of mind, may follow in the path of virtue and wisdom.

The building was badly damaged in World War II, although broadcasting continued uninterrupted. In the first years of the 21st century, there was a large-scale redevelopment on the eastern side of the building. Since its creation, the term "Broadcasting House" has been adopted as generic for all main UK regional BBC premises.

BROADCASTING IN THE SEVENTIES. This **British Broadcasting Corporation (BBC)** paper of 1969 created considerable controversy. In terms of radio, the practical result was to strengthen the identities of the main networks established in 1967, developing further the generic form of "branded" broadcasting, which was to increasingly dominate UK radio in the latter part of the 20th century and into the 21st.

BROADCASTING POLICY (CMND 6852. GOVERNMENT WHITE PAPER, JULY 1946). This was the first postwar government white paper dealing with broadcasting. As well as announcing that the BBC **charter** would be renewed without extensive review and that a new structure of consumer licensing would be introduced, combining radio and television for a £2 per annum cost, the newly installed Labour government's policy review proposed a new cultural radio station, to be known as the **Third Programme**. Another innovation as a result of this paper was the instigation of a daily radio review of proceedings in the British Parliament.

BROOK, NORMAN (1902–1967). Norman Craven Brook, Lord Normanbrook of Chelsea, was given a peerage in 1963 and became **BBC chairman** the following year. He took the role very seriously, and his relationship with incumbent director-general, **Hugh Greene**, was amicable. He died in office, and his place was briefly taken on a temporary basis by Robert—later Sir Robert—Lusty.

BROOKMANS PARK TRANSMITTING STATION. Situated in Greater London, between Potters Bar and Hatfield in Hertfordshire, the Brookmans Park Transmitting Station, completed in October 1929, played a key part in the development of British broadcasting. It was the first purpose-built twin transmitter station in the world capable of broadcasting two radio programs simultaneously; it also played an important role in the initial development of television. The commissioning of the station was one of the first acts of the newly formed **British Broadcasting Corporation (BBC)**, and signaled the development of the BBC's regional broadcasting scheme, conceived in 1924 by its chief engineer, **P. P. Eckersley**. Brookmans Park was the first transmitter in this scheme, serving London and the Home Counties.

BROUGH, PETER (1916–1999). *See* "ARCHIE ANDREWS" and *EDUCATING ARCHIE.*

BROWN, PAUL (1945–). Paul Brown is the chief executive of the **Commercial Radio Companies Association (CRCA)**. From 1970–1984, he worked in Forces radio and in UK commercial radio. In 1984, he joined the Independent Broadcasting Authority as head of radio programming. He was deputy chief executive of the Radio Authority from 1990–1995, chairman of the UK Digital Radio Forum from 1999–2001, and president of the Association of European Radios from 1998–2000. He is a fellow and ex-chairman of the UK Radio Academy and a board member of **Radio Joint Audience Research (RAJAR)**. He was made a CBE for services to the radio industry in 2003.

BUCKERIDGE, ANTHONY (1912–2004). Creator of one of the most affectionately remembered children's series of the late 1940s and 1950s, Anthony Buckeridge was a prep school master who wrote stories in his spare time. Among his stories, he created a schoolboy character called Jennings, and in 1948, he submitted a script based on the story to the ***Children's Hour*** producer, ***David Davis***. The result was a series of radio productions under the title ***Jennings at School***. The series was so successful that in 1950, Buckeridge gave up teaching to concentrate on writing books based on the radio characters. By 1977, 23 books had been published and, despite the period nature and the extreme "Englishness" of the scenario, translated into 12 languages, proving particularly popular in Norway, where the characters of the fictional Linbury Court School were dramatized afresh.

Buckeridge wrote more than 100 radio plays for adults as well as children, but it is for *Jennings* that he will be remembered. In the 1980s, after a period when the stories went out of fashion, they were revived in book form, and Buckeridge wrote two new *Jennings* stories in 1994. By that time, however, there was very little in the way of children's radio that could provide an audio platform for dramatizations of the stories. The stories were, however, issued as audio cassettes.

THE BUGGINS FAMILY. Created by **Mabel Constanduros**, this series of radio sketches, later growing into larger playlets, created the first radio "family" and continued through intermittent appearances from 1925 until 1948 in various guises and on numerous programs, of both the **British Broadcasting Company/Corporation (BBC)** and **Radio Normandy**. Mabel Constanduros herself played the main character of Grandma Buggins, who became an extremely popular feature of the program, particularly during the war years.

BURROWS, ARTHUR (1882–1947). Burrows was the first program director of the **British Broadcasting Company (BBC)** and a major figure in radio's pioneering days. He had begun his career as a journalist and specialized in wireless telegraphy. In 1920, he was working for the **Marconi Company** in Chelmsford and organized the highly important broadcast by **Dame Nellie Melba** from the factory. He was program organizer for 2LO during 1922, as well as chief announcer, and continued these duties when the BBC took over the station in November of that year. He was also the first newsreader in British radio, was coeditor of *The Radio Times,* and authored an early book on radio, *The Story of Broadcasting* (1924). In 1925, he left the BBC to assume the post of the first secretary-general of the Union Internationale de Radiophonie based in Geneva.

BUSH HOUSE. Contrary to some ideas, the name "Bush" is not named for the well-known radio and television manufacturers, but for Irving T. Bush, an American businessman, head of an Anglo-American trading organization, who financed the creation of the original building.

Designed by Harvey Corbett, Bush House was built in 1923, with extensions added between 1928 and 1935.

During the 1930s, the imposing building in London's Aldwych, looking up Kingsway, was occupied by the Radio Division of the **J. Walter Thompson Organization**. Near the end of the decade, the division built state-of-the-art studios designed to record programs for transmission on **Radio Luxembourg** and other Continent-based commercial stations. Technology included variable studio wall textures to change acoustics and the high-quality **Philips-Miller recording** machines.

In 1941, the Foreign Language Broadcasting Service of the **British Broadcasting Corporation (BBC)** relocated to Bush House from **Broadcasting House** after the latter was damaged by bombs, thus inheriting the J. Walter Thompson facilities. Through the years, the BBC's External Services occupied the building, and for many it will always be associated with the BBC **World Service**. The corporation has never owned Bush House, which has been the property, sequentially, of the Church of Wales, the Post Office, and a Japanese business organization. The BBC, however, continues to broadcast from there in more than 30 languages around the world until its lease expires in 2008.

– C –

CADOGAN, ALEXANDER (1884–1968). The Right Honorable Sir Alexander George Montagu Cadogan was **chairman** of the **British Broadcasting Corporation (BBC)** from 1952–1957, appointed the same year as **Director-General Ian Jacob**. The relationship between the two men was a good one, due partly to Cadogan's tactful interpretation of his regulatory powers. As both a director of the Suez Canal Company and a friend of the Tory prime minister, Anthony Eden, Cadogan was in a potentially difficult position at the time of the Suez Canal Crisis when he successfully defended the BBC's impartial reporting of the crisis in the face of government pressure.

CAMPBELL, ARCHIBALD (1881–1966). A. B. Campbell came to broadcasting in August 1935 when he gave a talk entitled *The Last*

Voyage of the Otranto, an eyewitness account of the loss of the warship upon which he had been serving in World War I. The success of the talk led to others, including **Men Talking**, and later **The World Goes By**. He proved himself to be a natural, fluent, off-the-cuff speaker, someone for whom radio broadcasting was instinctive—a born storyteller.

Campbell became nationally famous as a member of the original team—with **Julian Huxley** and C. E. M. Joad—of *The Brains Trust*, in 1940. Campbell had a key role—that of forming a bridge between his intellectual fellow panelists and the listeners. His blend of style and commonsense gave him an air of being the listeners' friend, and he became extremely popular. On *The Brains Trust*, Campbell made more than 200 appearances between 1941–1946, as well as working as an advisor to troops preparing for the Normandy landings.

After the war, Campbell continued to give radio talks, based on his maritime experiences, including *The Old Sea Chest*, a series for **Children's Hour**, and *Commander Campbell Talking* for **Woman's Hour**. He made a series for the newly formed Independent Television (ITV) in 1956, and made his final radio appearance—on the *Today* program—in February 1959. He wrote a number of books, including memoirs, one of which, *When I was in Patagonia* (1953), took its title from a phrase with which he had become associated during his time on *The Brains Trust*.

CAPITAL RADIO. Britain's oldest commercial music station began operations on 16 October 1973 (eight days after the first commercial station, **London Broadcasting Company [LBC]** commenced broadcasting). Originally housed in Euston Tower, London, it is now established in the city center's Leicester Square. Over the years, the station has been involved with many metropolitan initiatives, including The Capital Radio Music Festival. When the 1990 Broadcasting Act eased the regulations governing consolidation of ownership, Capital was at the heart of an expanding empire of radio stations nationwide. Between 1993 and 2005, the Capital Radio group expanded its operation from 2 to 52 analog and digital stations, with a total of nearly 8 million listeners. In May 2005, the Group merged with the other major UK radio group, **GWR**, to form **GCap Media plc**.

CARPENTER, HUMPHREY (1946–2005). Carpenter was a prolific writer of biographies, including those of J. R. R. Tolkien, W. H. Auden, Ezra Pound, and Benjamin Britten. In addition, he wrote the definitive history of the **Third Programme** and **Radio 3**, *The Envy of the World* (1996). It was an appropriate subject for him; he became a notable presenter on the network, presenting among other programs, the nightly arts and cultural magazine, *Night Waves*, and a wide range of other musical programs, to which he brought an infectious enthusiasm and thorough research. Carpenter began his radio career as a trainee in 1968 and joined Radio Oxford when it was established in 1970. In his last years, he contracted Parkinson's disease, but continued to work with his accustomed energy. He died suddenly on 4 January 2005, shortly after returning from a New Year's trip to France with his wife, Mari.

"CAT'S WHISKER." This was the popular term for a piece of early, rather crude radio technology that consisted of a length—usually of about two inches—of thin wire positioned on a piece of suitable material, such as a crystal of gallenium arsenide, which rectified and thus "detected" amplitude modulation (AM) broadcasts. The device was patented by the German scientist, Ferdinand Braun in 1899, and because of its cheapness and convenience, was used in preference to **John Ambrose Fleming**'s **Valve** in the initial years of wireless receiver development. *See also* CRYSTAL SET.

CELLO AND THE NIGHTINGALE. In 1924, a series of extraordinary outside broadcasts began which, at an early stage of radio history, demonstrated more than anything else the power of the sound medium for a mass audience. The celebrated cellist, Beatrice Harrison (1892–1965), had discovered that while playing her instrument in the garden of her house, Foyle Riding, in Surrey, a nightingale in the woods nearby would sing to her playing. She contacted **John Reith**, suggesting that the BBC broadcast the event, and on 19 May 1924, more than a million listeners tuned in at midnight to hear her play a duet with the bird. For 12 years, every May, the nightingale concerts continued, and thousands of people came to Foyle Riding every May to witness the phenomenon. Harrison used the image of the bird on her publicity material and on her concert dresses.

A commercial recording was issued and the "duet" became world famous. Some time after the event, while Harrison was engaged in recording Edward Elgar's *Cello Concerto* at HMV's Abbey Road, London studios, she met King George V who was on a tour of the building. On being introduced to her, he said "Nightingales, nightingales! You have done what I have not yet been able to do. You have encircled the Empire."

CELLULOSE-NITRATE DISC. *See* DISC RECORDING.

CHARTER. The **British Broadcasting Corporation (BBC)** is constitutionally established by a Royal Charter, usually reviewed for renewal every 10 years, although the period is variable. Attached to this is an accompanying agreement whereby the corporation's editorial independence is recognized and its public obligations are stated. The creation of a British Broadcasting Corporation in 1927 under charter, to replace the previously commercially founded **British Broadcasting Company (BBC)**, has been at the center of British broadcasting for many years. The first charter, which ran for 10 years, from 1 January 1927, was very much the product of **John Reith**'s wish to place the organization above political machinations and commercial interest; it was he who pressed for a charter to be granted to the BBC under Royal Seal. A key element of the charter renewal process, and in latter years, an increasingly contentious issue in its own right, has been that of the funding of the BBC through a public requirement to purchase a receiving **license**. The frequently permissive nature of successive charters has also frequently proved controversial, particularly among commercial broadcasters and some politicians. The current BBC charter was granted in 2006 and runs for 10 years. Details of charters are as follows:

1927: The first charter came into force on 1 January 1927 and led to the creation of the **British Broadcasting Corporation**. It was granted after Parliamentary consideration of the **Crawford Committee** report (1925), which recognized the need for an independent responsible body to further develop radio in the national interest along the lines already established by the British Broadcasting Company. This established the long-term policy of a Board of Governors responsible for the day-to-day control of the BBC, although Parliament would have the "ultimate control." The charter was awarded for a span of 10 years.

1937: The second charter was granted after Parliament considered the findings of the **Ullswater Committee** of 1925. It was granted for a further 10 years and permitted the BBC to further develop overseas broadcasting, which had begun to be transmitted to various parts of to the Empire in 1932, "for the benefits of Our dominions beyond the seas and territories under Our protection." The charter also followed up the findings of the Selsdon Television Committee of 1934, which had been endorsed by Ullswater, permitting the BBC to develop a television service, which accordingly began on 2 November 1936, from Alexandra Palace.

1947: Initially this, the third BBC charter, was granted only until 1951, although it was ultimately extended until June 1952. Following World War II and the BBC's extension of its **Empire Service** to encompass an overseas service of many languages and destinations, the document authorized the BBC to provide broadcasting services that could be received "in other countries and places" outside the British Commonwealth.

1952: The fourth charter took into account the report of the **Beveridge Committee** of 1949 as well as various government white papers, notably that of May 1952, issued by the Winston Churchill administration, in which the government stated that it had "come to the conclusion that the expanding field of television provision should be made to permit some element of competition." Therefore, the license received by the BBC from the postmaster general was for the first time a nonexclusive one. The charter provided for the establishment of National Broadcasting Councils for Scotland and Wales, with powers for radio, and was extended to July 1964.

1961: This charter was, for the first time, granted on the basis of a duration of 12 years. It had been preceded by the report of the Pilkington Committee of 1960. It authorized the BBC to borrow up to £10m. for temporary banking accommodation and up to £20m. for capital expenditure subject to the approval of the postmaster general. Secondly, the Broadcasting Councils for Scotland and Wales were granted powers over decisions relating to local/regional content similar to those already in place regarding radio. In 1969, a Supplemental Royal Charter was granted in order to take account of the transfer of powers, formerly exercised by the postmaster general in relation to broadcasting, to the minister of posts and telecommunications. In 1973, the government announced its intention of extending the duration of the charter to July 1981.

1981: The charter of 1981 took into account the findings of the **Annan Committee**, in the context of a developing climate of commercial competition, both in radio and television. The charter was granted for 15 years, expiring on 31 December 1996.

1996: This charter coincided with the start of one of the most significant times in UK—and global—media development. Running for 10 years, ending at the end of 2006, its life included the development of digital media, and the publication of the 2003 Communications Act, highlighting greater convergence, and enabling the creation of **Ofcom**. In 2003, the process of charter review commenced, to be concluded at the end of 2006, at which time the next BBC charter, expected to be granted for a further 10 years, commenced.

CHECKLAND, MICHAEL (1936–). Sir Michael Checkland joined the Finance Department of the **British Broadcasting Corporation (BBC)** in 1964 from a background as a chartered accountant. He subsequently held the posts of director of Television Resources and chairman of BBC Enterprises prior to his appointment as **director-general** in 1987, following the resignation of **Alastair Milne**. He described his objectives as introducing efficiency measures, diverting money toward programs, and accommodating new independent production quotas. He was committed to a more economical BBC, and he was robust in his defense of its independence. Like his predecessor in the post, Checkland was publicly critical of Chairman **Marmaduke Hussey**. He resigned and was replaced in 1992 by his deputy, **John Birt**, 21 months before the end of his contract.

CHELMSFORD. This Essex town, 30 miles northeast of London, is credited in UK broadcasting history as being the "birthplace of radio." In 1896, **Guglielmo Marconi** came to the town, found premises in 1898, and the following year opened the world's first wireless factory there, in a former silk mill in Hall Street, employing about 50 workers. The building is now occupied by Essex and Suffolk Water. A plaque proclaims: "In this building was established in 1899 the first radio factory in the world, by the Wireless Telegraph and Signal Co Ltd, later known as Marconi's Wireless Telegraph Co Ltd."

Business expanded rapidly, and in 1912, the company moved into a purpose-built factory in New Street. This was the first purpose-built factory for radio communications, built in 17 weeks. In 1920, from the New Street works, came the first officially publicized sound entertainment broadcasts in the UK, one of them featuring the prima donna, Dame Nellie Melba (*see* the "MELBA" BROADCAST). Two years later, the first regular wireless programs, also operated by the Marconi Company, were transmitted from the nearby village of **Writtle**. The original New Street building was extended in the 1930s.

Evidence of the presence of the Marconi Company is to be found throughout Chelmsford; from 1968–1994, the company produced radar components at their Writtle Road factory. The old building remains, and has been converted into apartments as part of a wider housing development on the former factory site, while in Waterhouse Lane, Marconi Applied Technologies continues to design and manufacture optical components for space, medical, industry, and radar markets.

CHESTER, CHARLIE (1914–1996). Chester was well known as a comedian in Britain from the 1930s, having made his radio debut in 1937 and come to further prominence through appearances in programs such as *Stand Easy* and *Workers' Playtime*. In 1969, he was given a daily radio show on **Radio 2**, which later moved to Sunday early evenings, becoming his *Sunday Soapbox*. The program's premise was a mix of records and social help; Chester and the program offered help and assistance to the poor and disadvantaged, helping to recycle items for the benefit of those in need, both nationally and internationally. He continued on the program virtually until his death in June 1996.

CHILDREN'S CHOICE. This Saturday morning **Light Programme** record request show started on 25 December 1952 and was created as a youth version of the long-running weekday program *Housewives' Choice*. Presenters included Donald Pears and "Uncle Mac" **(Derek McCulloch)** who was to see it into its second incarnation as *Children's Favourites*.

CHILDREN'S FAVOURITES. This was the new name for ***Children's Choice*** from January 1954. It ran in its original form—starting at 9:05 a.m. on Saturday mornings, and presented initially by **Derek McCulloch**, and played a mixture of novelty records and some light classics. As the children who had first listened grew into teenagers, so the 1960s boom influenced the music choice, and "old school" presenters like "Uncle Mac" gave way to DJs, while the music became more pop orientated. In 1965, a second edition was introduced on Sunday mornings, but by this time it was already something of an anomaly. When the **Light Programme** was succeeded by **Radio 1** in 1967, the program died and was replaced by ***Junior Choice***, which, by dropping the word "Children" from the title, allowed for the growing teen market fostered by the new network.

CHILDREN'S HOUR. This iconic program began in December 1922 and ended on Good Friday, 27 March 1967. In the first **BBC Handbook** is a suggestion of the origin of its title; in an article devoted to the program, the writer quotes from the poet, Henry Wadsworth Longfellow:

> Between the dark and the daylight,
> When the night is beginning to lower,
> Comes a pause in the day's occupations,
> that is known as the Children's Hour.

Over the years, a number of distinguished and devoted staff broadcasters were associated with it, including **Derek McCulloch** ("Uncle Mac") and **David Davis**, who was in charge of the program at the end of its life. It was a blend of stories, quizzes, music, natural history features, **serials**, and plays. Among the most famous and popular were ***Toytown*** and ***Jennings at School*** and the boy-detectives ***Norman and Henry Bones***. The controversial decision to take the program off the air was made by **Frank Gillard** when he was director of sound broadcasting, provoking a heartbroken David Davis to end the final edition with a reading of Oscar Wilde's *The Selfish Giant*, a tale of a bully who prevents children from playing in his garden. Despite its title, it was for most of its existence, aside from the years 1937–1939, less than an hour in duration.

CHILTON, CHARLES (1918–). Chilton is best known as the writer of *Journey into Space*, the cult science fiction series that captivated British radio audiences in the 1950s. He joined the **British Broadcasting Corporation (BBC)** as a messenger boy at the age of 14 in 1932, and worked his way up to the position of producer, being involved in, among other things, the first American broadcasts of **Alastair Cooke**. He also created *Riders of the Range* and *Blood on the Prairie*, as well as the original stage show of *Oh What a Lovely War* for Joan Littlewood. He remained on the staff of the BBC until his retirement in 1979, but continued to write and in 1981, created a 90-minute sequel to *Journey into Space* and another series, *Space Force*, in 1984. He was awarded the MBE.

CHRYSALIS. The Chrysalis group was founded in 1967 by Chris Wright and Terry Ellis, who together set up an agency for music management, the Ellis Wright Agency. From this grew a record label, Chrysalis (a combination of Wright's first name and Ellis's last). In 1993, the radio division was established with the first station, 100.7 Heart FM launched in Birmingham in September 1994, followed by the London station, Heart 106.2 a year later. Then came the creation of the Galaxy brand of stations in Bristol (since sold), Manchester, Yorkshire, and Birmingham. In September 2002, the group acquired the London talk station, **London Broadcasting Company**, making Chrysalis one of the largest players in the UK commercial radio industry.

CLAPHAM AND DWYER. Charlie Clapham and Billy Dwyer are notable in British radio history as the first major comedy double act to have had their reputations created by radio. In 1926, just one year after their formation as an amateur duo, they made their first radio appearance, and after two years they were featuring on variety stages around Britain, beginning in 1928 with an appearance at Shepherd's Bush Empire. Some of their routines were controversial in the somewhat censorious climate of the 1930s **British Broadcasting Corporation (BBC)**; for one routine, deemed to be in bad taste, they were banned from the BBC for several months, and the Corporation even broadcast a public apology in its evening news bulletin. Clapham and Dwyer's career as a double act ended in 1943,with the sudden death of Billy Dwyer.

CLARENDON, GEORGE (1877–1955). George Herbert Hyde Villiers, the Sixth Earl of Clarendon, was the first **chairman** of the **British Broadcasting Corporation (BBC)** as opposed to the **British Broadcasting Company**, taking over the role vacated by **Lord Gainford** in 1927. There was tension between Clarendon and **John Reith** over their respective spheres of authority relative to one another. Clarendon left the BBC in 1930 to become governor-general of South Africa.

CLASSIC FM. In September 1992, Classic FM became Britain's first national commercial radio station. The 1990 Broadcasting Act had provided opportunities for three national channels, but initially the successful bid for the license ultimately won by Classic FM went to another consortium, Showtime, with a format of music from West End shows. In the event, the company behind Showtime was unable to raise the required capital, and the license went to the second in line, Classic FM.

Initial reaction to an all-classical commercial station was mixed, but after nearly five months on air, the station was boasting 4.3 million listeners a week, almost double its expectations at launch, making it the fourth largest in the country.

CLEVERDON, DOUGLAS (1903–1987). Cleverdon was one of the most imaginative and creative radio producers of his era. Joining the **British Broadcasting Corporation (BBC)** in 1939, for a short period held the post of war correspondent. It was, however, in the period from the 1940s to the 1960s that his most lasting work was done. He was skilled in particular at developing radio work with poets, producing, among others, David Jones's *In Parenthesis* (1946) and **David Gascoyne**'s great radio poem, *Night Thoughts* (1955). He is, however, best known for his collaboration with **Dylan Thomas** on *Under Milk Wood* (1954). It was Cleverdon who commissioned the work and who guided and cajoled the unreliable Thomas for seven years and beyond, after the poet's death, when he saw the work through to transmission with Richard Burton as "First Voice."

THE CLITHEROE KID. This popular situation comedy starred a diminutive Lancashire comedian called Jimmy Clitheroe (1922–1973) who played a mischievous school boy in a **series** that ran from 1958 to 1972—16 series, a total of 280 episodes—and was regularly listened to by more than 10 million people.

COATES, ERIC (1903–1957). This composer of light orchestral music created melodies that continue to be heard on **British Broadcasting Corporation (BBC)** programs today. His *By a Sleepy Lagoon* is the theme tune for the long-running celebrity record show, *Desert Island Discs*. Previously the *Knightsbridge March* from his *London Suite* achieved huge popularity when it was selected as the theme for the weekly series, *In Town Tonight*, and the introductory music to *Music while You Work* was Coates's *Calling All Workers*.

COCK, GERALD (1887–1973). Although Cock was most associated with the birth of high-definition television in the UK, he began his broadcasting career in radio. Joining the **British Broadcasting Company (BBC)** in 1925, he was responsible for widening and enhancing the range and quality of programs and events covered by BBC microphones. Among significant broadcasts organized by Cock were the broadcasts of King George V. In February 1935, Cock was appointed the first director of television for the **British Broadcasting Corporation (BBC)**, a post he held until transmissions ceased at the outbreak of war, when he became the BBC's North American representative. He retired for reasons of health in 1945.

COLE, ERIC KIRKHAM (1901–1966). E. K. Cole was a radio engineer who, in 1922, set up his own business manufacturing radio sets, taking advantage of the demand following the establishment of the **British Broadcasting Company (BBC)** that year. In partnership with fellow businessmen in his native Essex, in October 1926, he established a private company, using his own name to form what was to become a famous acronym in UK radio manufacture, Ekco.

In 1930, Ekco began manufacturing radios in the new material of Bakelite, and this enabled a more adventurous design of cabinets than the more conventional wood had allowed. Some of the Ekco designs from the early 1930s became classics, and by 1934 Eric Cole's company had increased its turnover to more than one million pounds a year.

Cole set high standards, and as a result, Ekco sets gained a reputation for reliability. During World War II, the company worked on a number of projects for the government, including radio sets for bombers. After the war, Ekco took over Dynatron (1955) and Ferranti (1957), and moved into television manufacture. In 1960, the company merged with **Pye** to form British Electronic Industries, with Cole as vice-chairman. Following a management disagreement, he retired in 1961.

COLLINS, NORMAN (1907–1982). Collins was the creator and first controller of the **Light Programme** and the instigator of numerous programs in the extraordinary period of innovation between the birth of the network in 1945 and his transfer to television, where he became controller in 1947. Always a pioneer, Collins later moved to the newly formed commercial television sector, where he was vice-chairman of Associated Television (ATV) from 1955–1977.

COMMERCIAL RADIO. Although commercial—"independent"— radio officially began in Great Britain on 8 October 1973, its history considerably predates that year. Sponsored broadcasts from stations on the Continent were part of the early radio scene even before the birth of the BBC. On 15 June 1920, the opera singer Dame Nellie Melba broadcast from the Marconi works at **Chelmsford**, a recital sponsored by the *Daily Mail*, owned by Lord Northcliffe, a fervent supporter of commercial radio. There were many other experiments, notable among which was a 1925 fashion talk sponsored by Selfridges and transmitted from the Eiffel Tower. The broadcast lasted 15 minutes and received little attention at the time. It was, however, a precursor of much more extensive activity, and its producer, **Captain Leonard Plugge**, went on to found the **International Broadcasting Company (IBC)**, establishing **Radio Normandy** on 11 October 1931, broadcasting populist material from the French port of Fécamp.

The IBC's programming interests grew throughout the 1930s, and by the middle of the decade English-language sponsored broadcasts were extensively attacking the BBC monopoly and reaching large UK audiences who felt dissatisfied and disenfranchised by the BBC's strict Sabbatarian **Sunday broadcasting policy** introduced by **John Reith**. Among European stations involved in the broadcasts were

Radio Toulouse, Poste Parisien, Radio Côte D'Azur, Radio San Sebastian, Radio Ljubljana, Radio Lyons, Radio Valencia, Radio Madrid, Radio Athlone, and Radio Aranjuez. In addition, and significantly, on 3 December 1933, transmissions began from **Radio Luxembourg**, using a giant transmitter on a pirated wavelength in contravention of international broadcasting law.

Through the latter years of the 1930s, a highly successful commercial industry broadcast increasingly sophisticated popular programs, including soap operas and quiz shows, recorded in well-equipped studios in London by major advertising agencies, the largest of which was the American **J. Walter Thompson Organization**, occupying premises in London's **Bush House**. World War II ended these operations, and after the war, only Radio Luxembourg returned and resumed highly successful evening broadcasts that provided alternative listening through the 1940s, 1950s, and early 1960s.

Further commercial attacks on public service broadcasting began in March 1964, with a station broadcasting from a ship in the North Sea. **Radio Caroline**, owned by the Irish entrepreneur Ronan O'Rahilly, was the first of many marine-based stations that flourished for three years as once again the **BBC** found itself out of tune with popular youth culture. "Free Radio" became a political issue, as it had been in the 1930s, with Harold Wilson's Labour government establishing a determined campaign to outlaw the stations. Labour Postmaster Generals Edward Short and subsequently **Tony Benn** were instrumental in removing most of the stations from the airwaves under the new Marine. Broadcasting (Offences) Act, which became law in August 1967. Commercial pirates continued spasmodically even after this; Radio Caroline has continued in a number of forms, gaining iconic status. In the 1980s, the U.S.-run **Laser 558** proved popular until it was removed under the same legislation.

Meanwhile, pressure had been mounting for the establishment of legally constituted land-based commercial radio, and in 1972, the Conservative government under Edward Heath passed the law that permitted the **London Broadcasting Company (LBC)** to be the first station in Britain to be legally supported by advertising. The station went on air on 8 October 1973, and was followed shortly afterward by **Capital Radio**. The early days of Independent Local Radio (ILR), as it was known, were difficult ones. Overregulated by the **Independent **Broadcasting Authority (IBA)**, stations found it difficult to succeed financially initially, although through the 1980s growth in advertising revenue created a somewhat healthier climate. The 1981 Broadcasting Act developed the system laid down in 1972, without changing the original public service ethic upon which ILR had been based. Control remained tight; the 1981 Act limited the concept of program sponsorship, although the IBA sanctioned the first sponsored program in *The Network Chart Show*. Notwithstanding, station owners lobbied for more relaxed regulation.

The Broadcasting Act, published on 1 November 1990, abolished the IBA and established the **Radio Authority (RA)** as the body for specific regulation of commercial radio. The RA also permitted stations to concentrate more on developing successful business plans, rather than being forced to adhere to the unrealistic public service model of programming under which they had been forced to operate previously. As a further consequence, the RA permitted consolidation —the ability of companies to buy other stations and form groups, thus establishing the pattern of ownership that was to lead UK commercial radio into the 21st century.

Through the late 1990s, commercial sound broadcasting continued to develop; on 7 September 1992, the first national station opened in the form of **Classic FM**. In March 1998, the Radio Authority advertised the first national digital commercial multiplex license, and in the spring of 2000, **Digital One** began transmissions. In December 2003, the newly implemented Communications Act disbanded the Radio Authority, putting in its place the **Office of Communication (Ofcom)**, a regulatory body the role of which was seen as encompassing the increasingly diverse platforms available to broadcasters. The possibility of overseas ownership of UK interests became a real issue, with most British commercial radio stations already in the hands of a relatively small group of companies. *See also* PIRATE RADIO.

COMMERCIAL RADIO COMPANIES ASSOCIATION (CRCA).
The Commercial Radio Companies Association is the trade group for **commercial radio** companies in the United Kingdom. It is voluntary and nonprofit, and was formed, as the Association of Independent Radio Contractors (AIRC), by the first radio companies when independent radio began in 1973.

It has always enjoyed the overwhelming support of the radio industry—all but a handful of stations are in membership—and has been an influential force in British broadcasting throughout its existence. As well as promoting the importance of commercial radio, CRCA plays an active role in campaigning for conditions that will enable the industry to thrive in the future. It is funded by the subscriptions of its member radio companies, which share the cost in proportion to their shares of the industry's broadcasting revenue.

CRCA represents the interests of UK commercial radio to government, Parliament, the **Office of Communication (Ofcom)**, the European Commission, the European Parliament, and other organizations concerned with radio and broadcasting. Since 1984, CRCA has been especially active in this area, having provided significant input to the 1987 green paper, "Radio: Choices and Opportunities," to the 1990 Broadcasting Act, which substantially deregulated independent radio, to the 1996 Broadcasting Act, to the Communications Act of 2003, and to the 1996 and 2006 BBC **charter** reviews. CRCA lobbied hard to ensure that commercial radio's views were taken into account throughout the passage of the 2003 Communications Act through Parliament; key concessions were agreed upon in content-regulation and ownership rules, which led to consolidation in the UK commercial radio industry.

Together with the **British Broadcasting Corporation (BBC)**, CRCA owns **Radio Joint Audience Research (RAJAR)**, the company that oversees radio audience measurement in Great Britain. It administers the Radio Advertising Clearance Centre (RACC)—the UK commercial radio industry's advertising clearance body—and jointly owns the Joint Industry Commercial Radio IT Futures Group (JICRIT) with the Institute of Practitioners in Advertising (IPA).

COMMITTEES OF ENQUIRY. Significant committees of enquiry in the development of UK broadcasting have been:

Sykes Committee
Broadcasting Committee: Report
Appointed: 24 April 1923
Reported: 25 August 1923
Discussed: **British Broadcasting Company (BBC)** funding by license, and its monopoly on broadcasting.

Recommended:
- license fee funding
- no advertising
- broadcasting transfer from private to public

Outcome: The Company continued its monopoly and funding by license, eventually becoming a public corporation (see below).

Crawford Committee
Report of the Broadcasting Committee, 1925
Appointed: 20 July 1925
Reported: 2 March 1926
Discussed: broadcasting organization and its effect on audiences.
Recommended:
broadcasting to be run by a public service corporation
no direct parliamentary control
license fee funding for 10 years
educational programs
Outcome: The establishment of the **British Broadcasting Corporation (BBC)** by Royal **Charter**.

Selsdon Television Committee
Report of the Television Committee
Appointed: 14 May 1934
Reported: 14 January 1935
Discussed: television broadcasting in the UK, and whether the Baird or **Marconi** systems should be adopted.
Recommended:
- television broadcasting should be established within the public sector
- a London station should be set up using both systems until one proved better

Outcomes: The BBC commenced broadcasting from Alexandra Palace. Eventually the Marconi system was adopted.

Ullswater Committee
Report of the Broadcasting Committee, 1935
Appointed: 17 April 1935
Reported: 31 December 1935
Discussed: broadcasting, including overseas, funding and the nature of programming.

Recommended:
- regional broadcasting decentralization and expansion
- government control during national emergencies
- freedom to report anti-government views
- no funding by advertising
- increase in license fee
- impartiality of news programs
- increase in Schools broadcasting
- increase in numbers of BBC governors by two

Outcome: Further expansion of the BBC and programs.

Hankey Television Committee
Television
Appointed: September 1943
Reported: 29 December 1944
Discussed: postwar television services
Recommended:
- BBC monopoly of television services
- television in the regions
- high-definition television on 405 lines
- television receiver standards
- more coordinated research and development
- financial independence for television

Outcomes: The postwar BBC television service, which remained monopoly until 1956; expansion of BBC research and development.

Beveridge Committee
Report of the Broadcasting Committee, 1949
Appointed: 21 June 1949
Reported: 15 December 1950
Discussed: BBC monopoly and funding
Recommended:
- BBC to continue as sole broadcaster
- Charter renewal and license fee funding, but under review
- regional devolution
- broadcasting of minority views
- more political broadcasting
- trade union recognition

Minority Report: Selwyn Lloyd recommended the end of the broadcasting monopoly

Outcome: When the Conservative Party won the 1950 General Election, Selwyn Lloyd's recommendations were consolidated into a White Paper, leading ultimately to the establishment of Independent Television (ITV).

Pilkington Committee
Report of the Committee on Broadcasting
Appointed: 13 July 1960
Reported: 1 June 1962

Discussed: organization of the broadcasting industry and programs
Recommended:
- renewal of BBC charter and license fee funding
- extended radio hours
- adult education broadcasting
- second BBC television channel
- color television on 625 lines
- local broadcasting
- better commercial television regulation

Outcomes included: creation of the Open University, BBC **local radio**, BBC 2 and the color television license.

Annan Committee
Report of the Committee on the future of broadcasting
Appointed: 10 April 1974
Reported: 24 February 1977

Discussed: the whole broadcasting industry, including the development of new technologies and their funding, the role and funding of the BBC and **Independent Broadcasting Authority (IBA)** and program standards

Recommended:
- BBC funding by license fee
- fourth television channel, to be independent
- long-term restructure and diversification of broadcasting
- establishment of the Broadcasting Complaints Commission
- privatization of BBC local radio
- BBC independence from direct political control

- increase in independent production

Outcomes: increased license fee, Channel 4 created (1980).

Hunt Committee
Report of the Enquiry into Cable Expansion and Broadcasting Policy
Appointed: 6 April 1982
Reported: 28 September 1982
Discussed: the organization and future of cable broadcasting
Recommended:
- a cable regulatory authority
- cable providers able to make programs
- BBC and ITV programs to be carried free

Outcome: expansion of cable broadcasting, eventually overtaken by satellite broadcasting.

Peacock Committee
Report of the Committee on Financing the BBC
Appointed: 27 March 1985
Reported: 29 May 1986
Discussed: BBC funding (taxation, sponsorship, advertising or license fee), efficiency, cable and satellite broadcasting
Recommended:
- license fee to continue
- **Radio 1** and **Radio 2** to be privatized
- more broadcasting hours
- independent production quotas
- ITV companies franchise auctions
- removal of cable and satellite broadcasting restrictions

Outcomes included: Charter renewal and license fee, BBC staff cuts and efficiency drives, night-time broadcasting, independent production sector growth, deregulation of ITV, satellite broadcasting.

Davies Committee (Independent Review Panel)
The Future Funding of the BBC
Appointed: 14 October 1998
Reported: 28 July 1999

Discussed: funding of the BBC until Charter Review in 2005/6
Recommended:
- license fee frozen after 2001
- license fee to be the sole income for domestic services
- new money from efficiency savings
- digital services funded by a license fee supplement
- sale of part of BBC Worldwide and Resources

Outcome: Digital license fee plans were dropped because of Government opposition. Instead, funding was incorporated into the main license fee.

COMMUNITY RADIO. The UK community radio movement grew out of a number of initiatives during the early 1980s, which culminated in the establishment of the Community Radio Association (CRA) in 1983. This organization evolved as a broad coalition of campaigners, academics, unlicensed stations, workshops, and community activists. From the beginning the aim was to establish a third sector of UK radio alongside the **British Broadcasting Company (BBC)** and commercial interests.

The CRA gained early recognition in 1985 when the UK government, acknowledging the demand for community radio, agreed to a limited experiment. In the event, the experiment was cancelled due to the fact that the government concluded that no satisfactory regulatory structure existed whereby community radio could operate. In 1987, a green paper, *Radio: Choices and Opportunities*, was published. It proposed a rapid expansion in local and community radio services. Legislation reached the statute books with the Broadcasting Act 1990. The newly formed **Radio Authority (RA)** then recognized the CRA as the representative body for community radio in Great Britain, and confirmed that the new legislation would provide scope for the development of community radio.

Following a resolution passed at the 1997 Community Media Conference, it was decided that the name of the Association should be changed to reflect the growth of diversity of community expression through various media, including television and the Internet. Accordingly, the movement is now known as the Community Media Association (CMA).

As the UK moved toward a third tier of radio provision in the form of community radio, a number of experiments took place, involving Incremental Stations (1989–1990) set up by the IBA, specializing in specific forms of output relating frequently to ethnic groups, and "SALLIE"s (small-scale, alternative location independents). For a time, the regulator toyed with the title of "Access" radio for the new services, before the word "Community" was reinstated.

In the fall of 2002, the Radio Authority was replaced by a new "super regulator" in the form of the **Office of Communication (Ofcom)**. One of the first acts of the new regulator was to sanction the development of community radio, and accordingly a number of experimental stations was established around Britain. The success of this prompted the regulator to invite license applications for five-year franchises for community stations, advertised in the winter of 2004–2005. In response to the advertisement, 292 applications were received. Of these, the first to be successful was **Forest of Dean Radio** in Gloucestershire, one of the initial experimental stations, which was awarded its license in March 2005.

CONSTANDUROS, MABEL (1880–1957). Coming quite late to the world of entertainment, Mabel Constanduros trained as an actress at the Central School in London, where she discovered an ability for writing and creating cockney character sketches. She joined the **British Broadcasting Company (BBC)** Repertory Company in February 1925 and made her first broadcast in March the same year.

Constanduros is best remembered for her creation of the *Buggins Family*. Initially, she played all the characters, but ultimately became known for her portrayal of "Grandma Buggins." She was also instrumental in the creation of *The Robinson Family* with her nephew, Denis Constanduros. Her work was significant in establishing and developing a "voice" for British radio comedy. Outside radio, she wrote more than 100 plays for the stage, her most successful being *Acacia Avenue* (1943). *See also* WOMEN.

CONVERSATIONS ON A TRAIN. This important **series** was created in 1931 by **Hilda Matheson**. The concept behind the program was a number of simulated chance encounters on train journeys, made up of content that would be entertaining and/or topical. Initially, the programs used the work of literary figures, such as E. M. Forster, Dorothy L. Sayers, and Aldous Huxley, supported by relevant train sound effects. The formula was not a success, and actors were used instead, in cooperation with the **Drama** and **Features** Department of the **British Broadcasting Corporation (BBC)**. This transformed the series, which became extremely popular, running from 1932–1938 and drawing considerable audiences.

COOKE, ALASTAIR (1908–2004). Alastair Cooke's most famous contribution to radio broadcasting was his long-running *Letter from America*, a weekly 15-minute talk broadcast on the **Home Service** and later **Radio 4** from 1946 to within weeks of his death in 2004. Cooke was born in Manchester, England, but became a U.S. citizen in 1941. He had worked in radio in the United States, serving as NBC's London correspondent from 1935–1937. He continued working for the network until 1938, and then from 1939–1940 took over the role of film and theater critic for the New York station WQXR.

In 1938, Cooke made his first full series of radio programs for the **British Broadcasting Corporation (BBC)** entitled *I Hear America Singing*, a set of talks illustrated with a range of actuality material gathered on location across the United States. The material was destroyed by German bombs during World War II.

One of Cooke's greatest influences was the U.S. critic H. L. Mencken (1880–1956); in his weekly *Letters* on BBC radio, he delighted listeners with his cool appraisal of American events and political developments, always delivered in elegantly crafted scripts. Beyond these weekly programs, he continued to make various major contributions to BBC Radio, including a return to his interests in American music in a series made with the producer Alan Owen between 1974–1987 and broadcast on Radio 4 and **Radio 2**.

COOPER, GILES (1918–1966). Cooper was a major influence on the development of radio drama, particularly in his use of sound effects as part of the aural narrative. Plays such as *Under the Loofah Tree* and *The Disagreeable Oyster* were instrumental in the development of the **BBC Radiophonic Workshop** in the late 1950s. Of more than 60 dramas, produced on the **Light Programme**, **Home Service,** and **Third Programme** in the 1950s and 1960s, his first to be broadcast was *Thieves Rush In*, which was produced for the Home Service in 1950. His disturbing *Unman, Wittering and Zigo*, produced on the Third Programme in 1958, was later produced as a film starring David Hemmings. Cooper was also a masterly adapter, and his creations in this area included radio dramatizations of *Lord of the Flies* and *The Day of the Triffids* as well as the works of Charles Dickens and Rudyard Kipling. In 1966, he died after falling from a train on his way to his home in Midhurst, Sussex. In 1978, his work was commemorated by the foundation of the annual **Giles Cooper Awards** for radio drama.

COSTA, SAM (1910–1981). Sam Costa began his radio career as a dance band singer with the **Jack Jackson** Band in 1935. In 1939, he changed the emphasis from music to comedy when he joined the cast of ***It's That Man Again (ITMA)***. After the war, a third career in radio opened up when he became the presenter of the **Light Programme** show, *Record Rendezvous*. With the advent of **Radio 2**, Costa hosted a number of programs, including *Sam on Sunday*, *Melodies for You*, and *Glamorous Nights*. His adopted signature tune was "Sam's Song."

COTTON, BILLY (1899–1969). Billy Cotton was a cockney bandleader who hosted the *Billy Cotton Band Show* on the **Light Programme** and (for the program's last year) on **Radio 2** from 1949 to 1968. An ex-racing driver, Cotton was famous for his trademark opening of the program, "Wakey-Wakey!" followed by his theme tune, "Somebody Stole My Gal." Vocalists on the program included Al Bowlly, Alan Breeze, **Sam Costa**, Kathy Kaye, and Doreen Stephens.

COUNTY SOUND. This Independent Local Radio (ILR) station, serving Surrey, is noteworthy in that it was the first in the UK to divide its **amplitude modulation (AM)** and **frequency modulation (FM)** transmissions to provide separate services on a full-time basis. Prior to this, Hull-based **Viking Radio** had divided its FM and AM services on Saturdays only, to provide an alternative for Rugby fans in its area, from 1986. In June 1988, County Sound launched a completely separate gold service on AM, alongside, and independent of its FM service, which it renamed Premier. In 1990, it also launched a localized FM service, Delta Radio, for Haslemere. County Sound, in developing these services, was also one of the pioneers in the use of computerized radio programming in Britain. *See also* VIKING RADIO.

CRAWFORD COMMITTEE (Cmnd. 2599). This important government committee was set up by the postmaster general in 1925 under the chairmanship of the Earl of Crawford and Bacarres to explore the future of the **British Broadcasting Company (BBC)** beyond its initial form. Through its deliberations, it moved the company from the status approved by the 1923 **Sykes Committee** toward the established **British Broadcasting Corporation (BBC)** it became in 1927, thus formalizing the model of public service broadcasting that the BBC was to represent thereafter. Crawford was also interested in the social effects of broadcasting, based on the early evidence; there were concerns from some quarters that wireless listening would encourage a cultural passivity, while at the same time undermining the financial security of public entertainments such as concerts and theater. Crawford's conclusions led to the creation of the British Broadcasting Corporation (the committee's recommendation, that it should be the British Broadcasting *Commission* was one of the few to be rejected) under **charter**, and to the replacement of the nine main regional broadcasting stations around Britain by two main services— **Regional** and **National**. It also recommended no direct parliamentary control, license fee funding for 10 years, and the development of educational programs. The license fee—set at 10 shillings, and under the authority of the postmaster general—was to continue and be collected by the Post Office.

CRAZY PEOPLE. See GOON SHOW.

CROOK, TIM (1959–). Tim Crook is an author, teacher, and producer. He worked as a presenter and reporter for the **London Broadcasting Company (LBC)** and in the field of **radio drama** formed **Independent Radio Drama Productions (IRDP)** in 1987. As a writer and producer, he has created work for UK independent radio, National Public Radio (NPR) in the U.S., and for **British Broadcasting**

Corporation (BBC) radio. He has written numerous books on aspects of radio, including drama and journalism. He is a senior lecturer in communications at Goldsmiths College, University of London, where his research interests include media law and ethics, the practice and history of radio drama, and propaganda in radio.

CRYSTAL SET. This was the term given to the earliest and simplest radio receivers. The key part of the technology was a diode detector made up from the junction of a fine wire (*see* CAT'S WHISKER) touching a mineral crystal, hence the name. No "plug-in" electrical source was required, and thus the device became popular after the introduction of the **valve** or tube among young hobbyists. *See also* FLEMING, JOHN AMBROSE.

CURRAN, CHARLES (1921–1980). Sir Charles John Curran was the first person from a nonpublic school background to be appointed as **director-general** of the **British Broadcasting Corporation (BBC)**. Having served in the Indian Army, he first worked for the BBC in the **Talks Department** but resigned after a dispute. He rejoined the Corporation in 1951 in the **Monitoring Department**, subsequently holding the posts of secretary, and director of **External Broadcasting**. As director-general, he was more popular with the Board of Governors than with staff, who criticized his decision-making abilities. During his time, he was president of the European Broadcasting Union for three terms. He died of a heart attack in 1980.

CURRENT AFFAIRS. The origins of current affairs radio in the UK lie in the "Topical Talks" of the late 1920s and 1930s. Most talks were educational, but some dealt with political, economic, and social issues of the kind that we might today term "current affairs." One of the main topical issues concerned unemployment; however, this type of talk was less concerned with explaining the causes or examining the effects of unemployment than in trying to create social cohesion.

It was the perceived ignorance of modern affairs demonstrated generally by the British soldier before World War II, which led to one of the earliest known uses of the term. An attempted remedy for this ignorance was provided in the form of provision of a series of "current affairs" classes in European geopolitics.

Within the BBC itself, the term appears in the staff lists for 1958, where "Current Affairs Talks Department" is mentioned. There are many examples of current affairs radio programs, almost all of them on the BBC. They can be broadly divided into "magazine" and single-subject documentary strands. Of the former, the most important is the *Today* program, while of the latter, *Analysis* is the most significant. In the early days of **Independent Radio News (ILR)** the weekly program, *Decision Makers* offered the **commercial radio** network a form of current affairs in a half-hour format.

CUTFORTH, RENE (1909–1984). As with some others of his generation of news correspondents, Cutforth was a reporter whose love of words and the observance of detail marked him out as a highly distinctive voice in radio. He broadcast reports from the Korean War, and subsequently worked as a freelancer, specializing in travel programs, capitalizing on his clear eye and ear.

– D –

DAILY MAIL. This national newspaper can claim to have had a longer association with the development of radio than any other in Britain. In 1920, it was the *Daily Mail* that sponsored the **Marconi Company**'s famous broadcast of Nellie Melba from **Chelmsford**, later declaring the event a success in these terms:

> Art and Science joined hands, and the world listening in must have counted every minute of it precious.

DAILY SERVICE. This 15-minute act of worship, broadcast now at 9:45 a.m. on **Radio 4 longwave (LW)**, began in 1928. It is one of the world's longest running radio programs, with a formula that has remained virtually unchanged since it began, as the direct result of one listener, a Mrs. Kathleen Cordeux, who maintained a determined campaign of pressure on **John Reith**, and wrote in a 1926 edition of *The Radio Times*, putting forward the idea of a daily service containing "a little sacred musc, hymns, a brief reading or address to comfort the sick and suffering and the lonely."

DAMAZER, MARK (1955–). Mark Damazer was appointed controller, **Radio 4** in October 2004, having been deputy director of news at the **British Broadcasting Corporation (BBC)** since April 2001. He was previously assistant chief executive of the News Division from December 1999, with responsibility for the quality and standards in news programs across all BBC networks.

Educated at Cambridge, where he attained a double-starred first in history, he joined the BBC **World Service** in 1981 as a **current affairs** producer. He then spent two years with ITV as a producer with TV-a.m., returning to BBC TV in 1984, helping to launch the *Six O'Clock News*. He became output editor on *Newsnight* in January 1986 and deputy editor on the *Nine O'Clock News* in 1988, becoming editor of the program in 1990.

In 1996, Damazer became head of weekly programs, news, and current affairs; the department was restructured and renamed current affairs in 1997, and his responsibilities then ranged across radio and television, overseeing radio policy affecting such programs as *File on Four*, *From Our Own Correspondent*, and *Law in Action*.

DAN DARE. In July 1951, **Radio Luxembourg** broadcast the first episode in what was to become a remarkably popular **series** of science fiction programs featuring *The Adventures of Dan Dare, Pilot of the Future*. Dan Dare was a character originating from the children's comic, *The Eagle*, and the radio version, which was sponsored by Horlicks and announced by Bob Danvers-Walker, starred **Noel Johnson** as Dan. The identity of Johnson was kept secret, due to the fact that he also starred as **Dick Barton, Special Agent** in the eponymous **British Broadcasting Corporation (BBC)** series, which had received its final episode (prior to a 1970s revival) in March 1951, just over three months before the Dan Dare programs started. Radio Luxembourg broadcast the last in the series on 25 May 1956. However, in April 1990, to mark the 40th anniversary of the first publication of *The Eagle*, **Radio 4** created a new stereo version of the first of the Dan Dare serials in four episodes.

DANGER. Also called *A Comedy of Danger*, it has been claimed to be the first play specifically written for radio as a medium, although a children's play by Phyllis M. Twigg entitled *The Truth about Father Christmas* (broadcast, 24 December 1922) has also been suggested as the first. The author, Richard Hughes, was invited by the **British Broadcasting Company (BBC)** to write it in January 1924, and the work was created over one weekend. Made in an era when film was still silent, Hughes's introductory remarks to the published edition of the play become significant, describing as they do how the brief was "to write a play for effect by sound only, in the same way that film plays are written for effect by sight only." This was thus the first "Listening-Play." Nigel Playfair was the producer, and the play was broadcast from **Savoy Hill** on 15 January 1924. The action was set in a coal mine, and the first two lines were:

Mary: Hello! What's happened?

Jack:The lights have gone out!

It was suggested to the audience that they listen in darkness; thus, Hughes and Playfair had identified very early in its development, the unique imaginative interaction between broadcaster and audience, something that would continue to inform radio ever after.

DAVENTRY. The name "Daventry" is one of the most significant in British broadcasting history. Within two years of the **British Broadcasting Company (BBC)** commencing broadcasting, a network of nine main **mediumwave (MW)** transmitters, augmented by 11 relay stations, each with its own studio, had been established around the United Kingdom. Due to the qualities of mediumwave transmissions, however, it was not possible to adequately serve all stations with a common program from London. The BBC therefore set up plans to create a giant **longwave (LW)** transmitter that would be capable of such coverage. The requirement was for a site in central England, and after investigation, Borough Hill, on the outskirts of Daventry in Northamptonshire, was chosen.

The station, using the callsign 5XX on a frequency of 187.5 kHz, was opened with considerable pomp by the postmaster general on 27 July 1925. A poem was even commissioned from the poet Alfred Noyes and read during the opening ceremony. An extract demonstrates the almost mystical aspirations of early broadcasting:

... My mirth and music, jest and song,
Shall through the very thunders throng.

You shall hear their lightest tone
Stealing through your walls of stone;

Till your loneliest valleys hear
The far cathedral's whispered prayer,

And thoughts that speed the world's desire
Strike to your heart beside your fire;

And the mind of half the world
Is in each little house unfurled . . .

With an output power of 25 kW, Daventry was the most powerful transmitter in the world, and the first to use longwaves. Reception reports of the time soon confirmed that the range of the station was 300 km for valve receivers, and that 85% of the United Kingdom population could receive transmissions from the station.

In March 1992, after 67 years, the Daventry transmitter was closed down because of a reduction in the BBC's total transmission requirements. The site is now a broadcasting maintenance depot.

DAVIES, GAVYN (1950–). Davies, who became **chairman** of the **British Broadcasting Corporation** in 2001, came from a background as an economist, and chaired a 1999 enquiry into BBC funding. He joined the Board of Governors as vice-chairman in 2001 and took over the chairmanship in the same year, on the departure of **Christopher Bland**. He resigned after the 2004 **Hutton Report**.

DAVIS, DAVID (1908-1996). This producer and presenter of **British Broadcasting Corporation (BBC)** children's programs was born in Bishops Stortford and joined the staff of *Children's Hour* as a pianist in 1935, remaining with the program until its demise in 1964. From Queen's College, Oxford, his career prior to the BBC included four years as a schoolmaster from 1931. During the war he served in the Royal Naval Volunteer Reserve (1942–46) after which he returned to the BBC. He became head of *Children's Hour* in 1953, and from 1961–1964 rose to head of children's programs. When *Children's Hour* ended, as part of the program policy of **Frank Gillard**, it is said that it left Davis a broken man. It was his decision to end the final edition with a symbolic reading of Oscar Wilde's *The Selfish Giant*. Davies then moved to the BBC Radio Drama Department as a producer until his retirement in 1970. He fostered many talents and program ideas, among the most successful being *Jennings at School* by **Anthony Buckeridge**.

DEARMAN, GLYN (1937–1998). Dearman was originally a child actor and appeared in two film adaptations of Charles Dickens's *Nicholas Nickleby* and *A Christmas Carol*. He also played the part of Jennings for a time in Anthony Buckeridge's school series for radio, *Jennings at School*. Later, he became a respected radio producer and made drama and features of the highest quality. He produced Andrew Sachs's wordless play, *The Revenge* (1973), and the *Earthsearch* series by James Follett among much other distinguished work. At the lighter end of production, he worked on the popular **serials**, *Mrs. Dale's Diary* and *Waggoner's Walk*. He died in an accident in 1998.

DEATH AT BROADCASTING HOUSE. This thriller novel, published in 1934, under the authorship of **Val Gielgud** (head of productions at the **British Broadcasting Corporation [BBC]** since 1929, and brother of the famous actor, John Gielgud) and "Holt Marvell," the pseudonym of **Eric Maschwitz**, at the time editor of *The Radio Times*, was unique in showing the action driven by radio production, within **Broadcasting House** itself.

Filmed in November 1934, on location within Broadcasting House, the story revolves around the murder of an actor perpetrated during the recording of a play and "captured" on a new piece of recording technology—the **Blattnerphone**.

DECISION MAKERS. This weekly half hour **documentary** program was produced by the Parliamentary Unit of **Independent Radio News (IRN)** and funded by the **Independent Broadcasting Authority (IBA)**. Dealing with major **current affairs** issues of the day, it started in 1976, and was distributed by IRN to the commercial radio network for 10 years. *Decision Makers* was taken off the air in 1986, when IBA funding was withdrawn, at a time when commercial radio stations were becoming increasingly reluctant to broadcast 30-minute speech programs.

DEE, SIMON (1935–). Dee's was the first voice on **Radio Caroline**, the **pirate station** run by **Ronan O'Rahilly** from a ship in the North

Sea from Easter Sunday, 1964. Absorbed by the **British Broadcasting Corporation (BBC)** in 1966, even before the creation of **Radio 1**, he presented such programs as *Housewives' Choice*. He also worked for **Radio Luxembourg**, and, in a chequered subsequent broadcasting career, became for a time a considerable television personality, hosting his own chat show, *Dee Time,* on Saturday evenings.

DELL, ALAN (1924–1995). Dell was a sophisticated and knowledgeable presenter of music programs, with a long-running association with the **Light Programme** and **Radio 2** from the 1950s until shortly before his death. Born in Cape Town, South Africa, he joined the record library staff of the South Africa Broadcasting Corporation in 1943, and was one of the first presenters on Springbok Radio when it started in 1950. He then went to the United States and the United Kingdom to study radio production and acoustics, and settled in England in 1953.

In addition to his work for the **British Broadcasting Corporation (BBC)**, Dell made programs for **Radio Luxembourg**. His style was relaxed and intimate, and the music played on his programs was usually that of big bands, swing, and middle-of-the-road artists, such as Frank Sinatra. On Radio 2, he presented *Sounds Easy* for a number of years, up to his death from cancer in 1995.

DE MANIO, JACK (1914–1988). De Manio was an idiosyncratic and eccentric broadcaster who presented the **Radio 4** program, *Today*, from 1958–1971. He had joined the **British Broadcasting Corporation (BBC)** in 1946 as an announcer, but it was on *Today* that he gained his reputation, largely, ironically due to his notorious inability to give listeners the correct time. Up until 1970, he was the only presenter of the program; thereafter it became a two-person presentation show, and he was joined by John Timpson. De Manio left the year after, and began a new Radio 4 afternoon series, *Jack De Manio Precisely*. This lasted until 1978, after which his radio career effectively ended.

DEPARTMENT OF TRADE AND INDUSTRY (DTI). The British government's Department of Trade and Industry has historically been a major influence on the development of radio in the United Kingdom. It has been responsible for the allocation of frequencies, notably for amateur, marine, and mobile services, and has policed **pirate radio** over many years.

The DTI has actively supported the development of radio technology in the UK, and through its Global Watch industry missions it has funded comparative research trips exploring the possible future of radio to countries such as the United States, Korea, and Singapore.

DERBYSHIRE, DELIA (1937–2001). This gifted and innovative composer joined the **British Broadcasting Corporation (BBC)** as a trainee studio manager in 1962, but was soon seconded to the Corporation's **Radiophonic Workshop** based at studios in Maida Vale, London, to create sound effects and theme music for BBC drama. Working in both radio and television, her best known work was her realization of Ron Grainer's music, which became the theme tune of the popular TV series *Dr. Who*. She created many other themes and sounds for BBC media, and worked outside of the Corporation with many leading contemporary composers, including Karlheinz Stockhausen and Peter Maxwell Davies. Derbyshire left the BBC in 1973, disillusioned by what she saw as an increasing artistic conservatism. She continued to innovate for the rest of her life, and shortly after her death, she was celebrated in a **Radio 4** play, *Blue Veils and Golden Sands*, written by Martin Wade and titled after one of her own compositions.

DESERT ISLAND DISCS. This program is probably the best known of all UK radio record shows. Devised by **Roy Plomley** in 1942, the format continues to be the same as it has ever been. Each week, a guest celebrity is invited to choose eight records he or she would wish to take, were they to be marooned on a desert island. Together with these, they are permitted one luxury and one book, other than the Bible and Shakespeare. In the process of explaining their choices, the guest is interviewed about his or her life.

Over the years, individuals from every walk of life have appeared on the program. Plomley himself summed up the essence of the show's continuing appeal in his 1975 book, *Desert Island Discs*: "I believe *Desert Island Discs* adds a dimension to a listener's mental picture of a well-known person, giving the same insight he would receive from visiting the celebrity's home and seeing the books, pictures, and furniture with which he surrounds himself."

Since Plomley's death in 1985, the program has been presented by Sue Lawley and then Kirsty Young.

DICK BARTON, SPECIAL AGENT. Dick Barton was a dashing ex-commando hero of postwar British radio, the eponymous central character played initially by Noel Johnson. First broadcast on the **Light Programme** in October 1946, this was the first daily radio **serial** on the **British Broadcasting Corporation (BBC)**. Famous for its theme tune, "The Devil's Gallop," the program quickly gained an enormous audience; initially aimed at adults, it also appealed to the young, and the BBC adjusted the content accordingly, making Barton (the hero) a teetotaler. At its peak, it was required listening for approximately 15 million listeners every evening. It ran for 711 episodes, with a final episode broadcast in March 1951. It was revived for a short series in 1972, for the BBC's jubilee, with Johnson reprising his original part.

DIGITAL AUDIO BROADCASTING (DAB). The **British Broadcasting Corporation (BBC)** initially pioneered Digital Audio Broadcasting in the UK, and was the first broadcaster in the country to build a transmission network, commencing in 1995. In 1998, the first commercial digital radio license was awarded to **Digital One**. By 2003, Digital One was covering 85% of the United Kingdom.

Subsequently, DAB has been enthusiastically developed by both commercial and public service sectors, using the Eureka 147 system, utilizing both MPEG and COFDM (Coded Orthogonal Frequency Division Multiplex) technology, which converts the content from an analog signal into a digital (binary) code. The result of this conversion is a greatly reduced possibility of transmission interference. With DAB, there is virtually no possibility of hiss and fade as with previous methods of transmission.

The other principal quality of DAB is its ability to transmit radio signals in clusters, known in the UK as multiplexes. The technology permits broadcasters to transmit more radio stations within the same comparable amount of radio spectrum, compared to **frequency mod-**

ulation (FM). This has provided listeners with a wide range of digital-only stations: for example, the **GCap Media** group have created stations such as Core and Planet Rock, which are aimed at specialist or niche audiences, while BBC radio launched five digital-only stations in 2002, including **1Xtra** and **BBC7**.

DAB receivers have the capability of accessing data, and small screen displays scrolling text with program or auxiliary information. The initial public takeup of digital radio in the UK was slow; receivers were priced too high to attract potential listeners, and initially there was a blurred focus as to the benefits of the new service. Since the turn of the century, however, manufacturers have marketed increasingly cheaper, stylish receivers, and growth has been more rapid.

DIGITAL ONE. A pioneer of the role of **digital** broadcasting in UK **commercial radio**, Digital One was the sole applicant for the 1998 UK National Multiplex license and was thus awarded the license by the **Radio Authority**. It started broadcasting in November 1999 on a renewable 12-year term. Founder stations on the multiplex were **Classic FM**, **Virgin Radio**, **Talksport**, Core, Life, **Oneword**, Planet Rock, and Primetime Radio.

DILLON, FRANCIS (1899–1982). Known to all his colleagues as "Jack," Dillon saw active service in World War I, after which he spent time with a number of fighting units, including, it was said, the White Army in Russia and the Black and Tans in Ireland. In contrast, his next work was as a tax inspector in Manchester; he retained the job until 1936, when he began writing for the burgeoning **British Broadcasting Corporation (BBC)** North Region radio Features Department under **E. A. Harding**.

In 1938, Dillon moved to Bristol to take up the post of West Regional Features Producer before moving to London in 1941 to work in the Features and Drama Department. Here, he met **Louis MacNeice**, and the two men became close friends and working colleagues. In MacNeice's autobiographical poem, *Autumn Sequel*, Dillon is represented by the character, "Devlin." In 1942, Dillon started the radio series, *Country Magazine*, on which he worked with **Desmond Hawkins**. The program was a response to a request from the government's Ministry of Agriculture, which felt that such a concept would raise morale at a time when travel restrictions brought about by war meant that public access to the countryside was limited. In fact, the program ran for 12 years.

In 1949, Dillon won a Prix Italia award in the first year of this competition's existence for one of a series of fairy tale adaptations he undertook at the time, *The Old and True Story of Rumpelstiltskin*. He retired from the BBC in 1959 but continued to work as a freelance writer and producer from his Sussex home. He died of pneumonia on 9 December 1982—his 83rd birthday.

DIMBLEBY, RICHARD (1913–1965). Latterly Dimbleby became well known to television audiences, notably for his presentation of the **British Broadcasting Corporation (BBC)** news and current affairs program *Panorama*. He was, however, first and foremost a radio correspondent of the highest order, and in 1936, he virtually created the role of radio reporter, insisting that the BBC needed the voice of an on-location observer to bring many news events alive. As the BBC's first war correspondent, he had a unique ability to portray a scene in words so graphic that listeners felt they had been present with him at some of the most extreme locations of the conflict. Famous among these were his recorded commentaries of an Allied bombing raid on Germany, in which the audience could hear the very gunfire of German antiaircraft batteries exploding around him, and his memorable account of the liberation of Belsen. The first reporter to enter the camp, he completed his recorded report, and then, so he later confessed, was physically sick.

After the war, Dimbleby moved more into radio light entertainment, presenting ***Down Your Way*** for five years, and being a panel member of the ***Twenty Questions*** program for 18 years. In 1990, he received the unique posthumous honor for a broadcaster of having a memorial dedicated to him in Westminster Abbey, where, in 1953, he had commentated on the coronation of Queen Elizabeth II.

DISC JOCKEY (DJ). The term is an American one, which crept into usage in the United Kingdom as a result of United States broadcasts to Europe during the war. Prior to this the **British Broadcasting Corporation (BBC)** and **commercial radio** had employed personalities as "presenters of Gramophone Record Recitals." There can be some variance of opinion as to the first UK representative of the role. **Peter Eckersley** introduced occasional records from **Writtle** in the earliest **Marconi Company** experiments in 1920.

The first regular scheduled weekly program from the BBC began in March 1924, presented by **Compton Mackenzie**, editor of the *Gramophone Magazine*. Mackenzie's son-in-law, **Christopher Stone**, however, holds the claim to being the first UK "professional" DJ, broadcasting from 1927 on both the BBC and subsequently on **commercial radio** from the Continent. Other key presenters from this time included **Radio Luxembourg**'s **Stephen Williams**. The first woman DJ was **Doris Arnold** who presented *These You Have Loved* on the BBC **National Programme** from November 1938, and continued presenting the program into the mid-1960s.

After World War II, the concept of the personality DJ developed, notably on BBC programs such as *Housewives' Choice*. Specialist music DJs emerged, as well as wholly original talents such as **Jack Jackson**, who, from 1948, redefined the role in his interaction between music and speech in programs such as *Record Roundabout*. Postwar Radio Luxembourg continued to develop new household names, familiar particularly to the popular music-seeking young, including **Teddy Johnson**, **Pete Murray**, and **Barry Alldiss**.

The North Sea **pirates**, such as **Radio Caroline** and **Radio London**, took up the mantle in the 1960s, and presenters such as **Simon Dee** and **Tony Blackburn** brought a new informality and U.S.-style pace and dynamism to music broadcasting, which was to be the foundation of the late flowering of music radio in Britain.

Toward the end of the 20th century, the role of the DJ on local stations was frequently diminished by automation and format-based programming in which personality broadcasting gave way to formulaic and functional-link-based presentation. There remained however a key role for major figures to play, and presenters such as **Jonathan Ross**, **Chris Tarrant**, Johnny Vaughan, and **Terry Wogan** remained important definers of the modern role of the disc jockey in the early 21st century.

DISC RECORDING. Discs were for many years the favored means of reproduction for radio, and in 1930, **Cecil Watts** created a system of economic, efficient recording, using an aluminum-based cellulose-nitrate laquer-coated disc that enabled playback directly after recording. The advantage of the Watts system was that while the coating was soft enough to enable the recording stylus to cut, it was durable enough to withstand repeated play-backs of up to 20 times. The system was widely used through the 1930s and beyond.

DOCUMENTARY. The development of documentary program making in Britain is almost as old as the medium itself. For many years, however, the form of radio documentary was dictated by the limitations of technology. Scripted **talks** and **discussions** were frequent examples of factual programs on the **British Broadcasting Company/Corporation (BBC)**, and this persisted into the 1930s. The introduction of recording, and in particular, mobile recording, created more creative possibilities, and the development of features units, such as those in Manchester run under **E. A. Harding** before the war, and in London under **Laurence Gilliam** postwar, gave producers the opportunity to interrogate the factual genre in varied ways.

As radio freed itself from restrictions imposed by early agreements formed between the BBC and the newspaper associations, programs became more journalistic and investigative. Postwar, the radio documentary has been an increasingly significant form, with important and sometimes difficult topics explored by experienced journalists and producers in the field of **news** and **current affairs**. From 1973, with the coming of UK-based **commercial radio**, a new generation of documentary-makers were given the opportunity of adding documentary voices, and some powerful work resulted from outside the BBC. The documentary form has been flexible, and the use of drama-documentary to explore the implication of facts beyond the explicit statement has been used to considerable effect on occasion.

Many distinguished program makers from the field of news have been associated with the documentary genre, among them **Rene Cutforth**, **Richard Dimbleby**, and **Feargal Keane**. Programs as diverse as *File on Four* for BBC radio, and, in the 1970s and 1980s, *Decision Makers* from **Independent Radio News (IRN)**, *Face the Facts* contrasted with the more impressionistic work of producers such as **Charles Parker**, who sought to explore the realm of documentary through location and direct contact with his subjects in **series**, such as *The Radio Ballads*.

DOES THE TEAM THINK? This was one of British radio's longest running comedy quiz shows, a parody of the **British Broadcasting Corporation**'s **(BBC)** *The Brains Trust* and *Any Questions* with four comedians, including **Jimmy Edwards**, who devised the program, ad-libbing answers to listeners' questions. It ran from 1958–1976.

DONOVAN, PAUL (1949–). Paul Donovan has been radio columnist for the *Sunday Times* since 1988, in addition to much other distinguished writing on radio matters, including *All Our Todays* (Cape, 1997), marking 40 years of **Radio 4**'s *Today* program. He has been a judge on several occasions for the **Sony Radio Academy Awards**, and until 2005 had been convener of the Broadcasting Press Guild radio awards.

DOUBLE YOUR MONEY. A popular quiz show, which ultimately became a major attraction on the newly formed Independent Television (ITV) in 1955, running until 1968. *Double Your Money* was originally a radio program for **Radio Luxembourg**. Broadcast on the station from October 1954, it was sponsored by Lucozade and devised by Hughie Green, who also acted as the show's MC.

DOUGLAS, LESLEY (1963–). Lesley Douglas was appointed controller, **Radio 2** and **6 Music** in October 2003, and took up the post in January 2004, succeeding **James Moir**. She began her career as a production assistant and, in 1986, joined Promotions. In 1988, she became a producer in the Music Department, returning to Promotions in 1990 as a producer, before being promoted to editor, Radio 2 Presentation and Planning in 1993.

In May 1997, Douglas became managing editor, Radio 2, and in 2000, was appointed head of programs. In 2004, she was awarded the top prize in the UK music industry's Woman of the Year Awards. She is a fellow of the Radio Academy.

DOWN YOUR WAY. A program that was part travelogue, part record request show, *Down Your Way* ran in its original form from 1946 to 1987. Successive presenters were **Stewart MacPherson**, **Richard Dimbleby**, **Franklin Engelmann**, and **Brian Johnson**. Always broadcast at the same time on the **Home Service/Radio 4**—late afternoon, Sundays—the format never varied, consisting of a radio visit to a village or town, interviews with local characters and personalities, and the invitation to these participants to choose a piece of music of their choice.

DRAMA. Radio drama has been a feature of British radio from the earliest days. The first broadcast drama in the UK is said to have been scenes from three Shakespeare plays, broadcast in February 1923, and the first play specifically written for the sound medium has been claimed to be *Danger* by **Richard Hughes**, broadcast by 2LO on 15 January 1924. The first novel dramatization was of Charles Kingsley's *Westward Ho!* in April 1925. As early as 1926, the first book on the subject, *Radio Drama and How to Write It*, had been written by Gordon Lea, who worked in Newcastle, and who had made some drama productions for the local station, 5NO.

It soon became clear to producers that radio had the potential to create drama in a completely new image; experiments were conducted in which casts for radio plays were anonymous, with details of the actors being neither broadcast nor published. This was resisted and opposed by the actors' union, but the principle—of retaining realism and maintaining illusion in a "blind" audience by maintaining an "anti-personality" policy—was an interesting and radical one. By the early 1930s, the work of producers such as **Val Gielgud**, **Lance Sieveking**, and Tyrone Guthrie had made the art of the radio drama a specific genre, and the era saw a rise in use of poetic drama, including works by T. S. Eliot, such as *Murder in the Cathedral* and *The Waste Land*, which was produced by **D. G. Bridson** in 1938.

The 1930s also saw the concept of multistudio productions, sometimes live plays being produced by various regions in a complex, layered sound-picture. Drama-documentary and drama-features sometimes utilized this technique, which was costly and tied up resources to a considerable degree. Many playwrights have been drawn to the medium, and some, such as **Giles Cooper** and **Samuel Beckett**, have understood and exploited the uniqueness of storytelling in pure sound, taking the concept to an extraordinarily sophisticated level.

In the early days of **commercial radio**, a number of companies, including **Capital Radio** (Anthony Cornish), **Radio Clyde** (Hamish

Wilson), the **London Broadcasting Company** (**LBC**—Tim Crook) and 2CR (Seán Street), Swansea Sound, and Downtown Radio in Northern Ireland were active in drama production. After the 1990 Broadcasting Act, with its relaxation of regulations relating to speech content, such work became rarer, and by 2006, drama was virtually nonexistent in the commercial sector.

At the same time there was a growth in drama productions made by independent production companies for **British Broadcasting Corporation (BBC)** radio. **Radio 4** remains the biggest commissioner of new drama in Britain, with a daily afternoon play, Monday–Friday, and at least one play in its schedule on every day of the week. **Radio 3** broadcasts substantial dramas, including classics, cutting edge new drama, and experimental work.

Drama **serials** have ranged from the first, *Dick Barton, Special Agent*, first heard in 1946, and *The Archers*, to Radio 4's *Classic Serial*, broadcast on Sunday afternoons. At the outbreak of World War II, 1930s commercial radio had already begun to develop "soap opera" popular drama based on the U.S. radio model and produced by agencies, with such productions as *Young Widow Jones*, *Stella Dallas*, and *Dr. Fu Manchu*. Postwar, **Radio Luxembourg** serialized *Dan Dare, Pilot of the Future*, during the 1950s, while roughly parallel in chronological terms, BBC radio captured the imagination of a generation with the science fiction serial, *Journey into Space*. *See also* INDEPENDENT RADIO DRAMA PRODUCTIONS.

DR. FU MANCHU. The series began on **Radio Luxembourg** on 6 December 1936, adapted from the novel by Sax Rohmer, and sponsored by Milk of Magnesia. The program ran for 62 episodes, ending with "The House of Hashish" on 6 February 1938.

DROITWICH. The **British Broadcasting Corporation (BBC)** transmitter at the Worcestershire town of Droitwich was opened on 6 September 1934 and took over the transmission of the **National Service** from **Daventry** on 7 October at a power of 150 kW, broadcasting on the 15000 meters, **longwave (LW)** frequency. The mast height was 700 feet, and the transmitter equipment was installed by the **Marconi Company**.

During World War II, the site was used by the BBC for overseas broadcasts and subsequently as a blocking device to disorientate enemy aircraft. At this time, it also expanded to house the transmitter for the **Forces Programme** and a high power **mediumwave (MW)** transmitter. In a major overhaul in 1960, the 1934 transmitters were replaced with more powerful units, increasing longwave capability to 500 kW. By 2006, the site was still active, transmitting **Radio 4** on longwave and **Radio 5 Live**, **TalkSport**, and **Virgin Radio** on mediumwave.

DUNHILL, DAVID (1917–2005). Dunhill was a well-known **British Broadcasting Corporation (BBC)** "voice," who joined the Corporation at the end of World War II as a staff announcer and newsreader for the **Light Programme**. His voice was also associated with the comedy series, *Take It from Here*, during the 1950s. When BBC local radio was created, he worked as a voice and presentation coach, remembered with affection by a new generation of radio broadcasters.

DUNN, JOHN (1934–2004). This much-loved presenter began his radio career as a studio manager with the **British Broadcasting Corporation (BBC) External Service** in 1956. In 1958, he became an announcer and news reader in the **General Overseas Service**, before moving into domestic radio in 1959. Among **Light Programme** shows, he was most associated with *Friday Night Is Music Night*, *Housewives' Choice*, and *Roundabout*. At the launch of **Radio 2** in September 1967, he hosted the breakfast show, a role in which he continued until 1973 when he moved to the early evening slot, remaining as a highly popular host until 1998, when he retired. In 1983, Dunn was voted the Variety Club's Radio Personality of the Year and gained a Sony Award in 1998 for the best drive time music show. In 2003, he was inducted into the **Sony Radio Academy**'s Hall of Fame, almost exactly a year prior to his death from cancer.

DYKE, GREG (1947–). Dyke was **director-general** of the **British Broadcasting Corporation (BBC)** from 2000 to 2004, when he was forced to resign after the **Hutton Report**, which investigated the death of the government weapons expert, Dr. David Kelly. The report severely criticized the editorial decision of the **British Broadcasting Corporation (BBC)** to broadcast a report in the **Radio 4 *Today*** program about the government's decision to go to war in Iraq. The event overshadowed a period in the BBC in which Dyke, coming from a commercial TV background, had emphasized directing money into programs and making savings in non-program-making departments. In so doing, he came closer to program makers and was largely popular with BBC staff.

– E –

EAQ MADRID. Working under the subtitle of "Radio Aranjuez," this shortwave station carried half an hour of English language programming per night produced by the **International Broadcasting Company (IBC)** from 1932 until July 1936, when the Spanish Civil War made UK transmissions untenable. Although it was never fully developed by the company, this policy—known as "keeping a station warm"—was one adopted by the IBC elsewhere in Europe.

The idea here, as far as **Leonard Plugge** and his company were concerned, seems to have been to undermine the BBC's newly formed **Empire Service** (December 1932). The IBC added the name "IBC Empire Service" to its EAQ transmissions, continuing to do so in spite of BBC insistence that it should not use the title. Although it ended in 1936, the IBC retained intentions of reopening EAQ as a transmission site, although in the event this did not occur.

ECKERSLEY, PETER PENDLETON (1892–1963). This dynamic, controversial, and charismatic visionary was truly a pioneer of radio: an engineer who also understood the entertainment potential of the medium from the start. Eckersley directed and took part in experimental transmissions from the **Marconi Company**'s site in the village of **Writtle** in Essex. These began on 14 February 1922, and he subsequently was appointed by John Reith as the first chief engineer for the **British Broadcasting Company (BBC)** in 1923. He was dismissed in 1929 after being cited in divorce proceedings, and subsequently became involved in the development of **commercial radio**, and in particular the **radio relay** system.

Eckersley's controversial career was complicated by his association with Sir Oswald Mosley, founder of the British Union of Fascists, and by the involvement of his wife and stepson in a 1945 trial, charged with "conspiring to assist the enemy" through the medium of propaganda. In his 1942 book, *The Power behind the Microphone*, Eckersley set out his thinking relating to the future of radio broadcasting, predicting both the coming of digital sound and cable transmission.

EDMONDS, NOEL (1948–). Edmonds worked in radio first for **Radio Luxembourg** in 1968 before joining **Radio 1** in 1969, taking over the Saturday morning show from **Kenny Everett**, in the process becoming the network's youngest presenter. From 1970 to 1974, he switched to Sunday mornings, introducing the formula of prank telephone calls, which was to characterize much of his subsequent career both in radio and latterly after his move into television. In 1974, he inherited the breakfast slot from **Tony Blackburn**, and remained its host until 1978, by which time his career in TV was burgeoning. In 1989, he became a founding director (with **Tim Blackmore** and Simon Cole) of the independent production company, **Unique**. Edmonds cashed in his stake in the company in August 2005, for £1.35m.

EDUCATING ARCHIE. The idea of a ventriloquist act on radio— although apparently anomalous—has a number of precedents, not least the Edgar Bergen Show on the U.S. network NBC, which began in the 1930s, and the UK ventriloquist Saveen. In Britain, without doubt the partnership of **Peter Brough** and his dummy, **Archie Andrews** (a name invented by **Ted Kavanagh**, one of the brains behind the show), was one of the most famous in radio. First broadcast in June 1950 and running for 10 series on the **Light Programme** throughout the decade, the show was significant in its fostering of new talent, including Julie Andrews, **Max Bygraves**, **Tony Hancock**, **Hattie Jacques**, and **Beryl Reid**. The storylines revolved around the adventures of a naughty schoolboy, Archie, and his girlfriend, Monica (Beryl Reid). The first seven series were written by **Eric Sykes**, whose inventive scripts contributed much to the success of the program.

EDWARDS, JIMMY (1920–1988). Edwards came into broadcasting shortly after the war. In 1948, he joined Dick Bentley and Joy Nichols in the successful comedy series, *Take It from Here*. He was also a regular member of the spoof panel game, *Does the Team Think*. Famous for his large handlebar mustache, he carried the nickname "Professor." He also had a successful career in television, and was a musician, frequently using his playing of the trombone as a part of his comedy act.

EKCO. This famous receiver manufacturer was founded in 1922 by **Eric Kirkham Cole** (1901–1966) and during the 1930s and 1940s created a series of sets that became highly collectable due largely to their unique circular design, made possible partly by the use of Bakelite in their manufacture.

ELECTROPHONE. This important early precursor of "wireless" was invented by a Frenchman, Clement Ader in 1881, and introduced first in France that year as the "Theatrephone." The principle was that of relaying audio entertainments down telephone lines; thus Ader demonstrated live performances from the Paris Opera to audiences at the Paris Electrical Exhibition of that year. The system became popular in Europe and the United States, and was introduced to Great Britain in the early 1890s by the National Telephone Company, licensed by the Post Office under the title of "Electrophone" with its central exchange in Gerrard Street, London. Queen Victoria became an early adopter of the system, having it installed at Windsor Castle.

A subscription service, it offered customers a choice of theater performance and other events, including church services, via headphones. "Receivers" were installed in domestic homes and public places, where it offered a "pay-per-listen" service. There were two levels of subscription: a £5 charge enabled listeners to connect to a preselected service, whilst for £10, subscribers could choose from a selection themselves. During World War I, the Electrophone was installed in some hospitals for the entertainment of convalescent troops. On Sundays, church services were relayed.

The system survived for some years after the introduction of wireless radio services, offering as it did choice and "live" quality relays at a time when the fledgling wireless service was overcoming early transmission and reception issues. Reputedly the last Electrophone relay service ended as late as 1938—in Bournemouth—when the final subscriber died.

EMAP. Formed as a newspaper and magazine company in 1947, Emap has expanded into all areas of media, including radio. In 1990, the company acquired the London dance station, **Kiss FM**, and the following year, bought Radio City in Liverpool. Other acquisitions followed, with a strong north-country bias to purchases. In 1998, Emap bought the London station, Melody FM, renaming it Magic 105.4. This began the development of the Magic brand—nine stations aimed at the 35–44 year-old audience age group, and complementing the group's Big City brand (8 stations) targeting the 15–34 year-old audience. Emap also moved into digital radio, operating 13 multiplexes across the UK. In April 2005, the group's burgeoning radio aspirations were demonstrated by the creation of a new division, "Emap Radio," and Emap acquired **Scottish Radio Holdings** in June 2005.

"EMPEROR ROSKO." Born Michael Pasternak, the son of the film producer, Joe Pasternak, this iconic **disc jockey** joined **Radio Caroline** in 1966, where his brash American style gained him great popularity. Educated in Paris, Switzerland, and California, "Rosko" was equally at home broadcasting in French, and after leaving Caroline, he worked on the French services of Radio Monte-Carlo and **Radio Luxembourg**, where he worked under the pseudonym, "Le Président Rosko."

His style was strongly influenced by the U.S. DJs, Emperor Hudson and Wolfman Jack. In 1967, he was one of the original team at **Radio 1**, although initially, due to his continental commitments, his programs were prerecorded. From 1968, now a resident of the UK, his shows went "live," and he stayed with Radio 1, broadcasting on various shows, until September 1976, when he returned to the United States to be near his ailing father. He returned to the network in 1982 for a further four years, being part of its 25th anniversary celebrations in 1992. He then worked for **Virgin Radio**, before returning to the U.S. to work in California, continuing to be heard by UK audiences on the **Classic Gold** Network.

EMPIRE SERVICE. Launched by the **British Broadcasting Corporation (BBC)** in December 1932, this was the beginning of the Corporation's international aspirations as a broadcaster. Studios were initially at **Broadcasting House**, later moving to **Bush House** and transmitted from **Daventry**. From the start, the service broadcast across five time zones, targeting Canada, West Africa, South Africa, India, and Australasia. It later became known as the General Overseas Service, BBC External Services, and ultimately as the **World Service**.

ENGELMANN, FRANKLIN (1908–1972). Engelmann was a popular broadcaster on British radio for more than 30 years, and his warm tones were associated with many programs, including *What Do You Know* and the program that replaced it, *Brain of Britain*. He was the original host of *Pick of the Pops* but is mostly remembered for his role as presenter of two long-running programs, *Down Your Way*, which he hosted from 1955–1972, and *Gardeners' Question Time*. Having chaired the latter program from 1961–1972, he died in the week of the 1,000th edition. His nickname was "Jingle."

ENNALS, MAURICE (1919–2002). Maurice Ennals was the first manager of a **British Broadcasting Corporation (BBC)** local radio station, **Radio Leicester**. This opened in 1967, prior to which, he had worked on the introduction of local radio, and was jointly responsible for deciding where many of the stations were to be sited. In 1970, he was responsible for the launch of BBC Radio Solent, part of the second tier of stations to roll out after the success of the initial experiment. He remained as manager of Radio Solent until his retirement in 1976, after which he lived in Dorset, acting as a talent scout for local football teams.

THE EPILOGUE. The program was a part of **John Reith**'s Sabbatarian policy of broadcasting, and was heard at the close of transmissions on Sunday evenings from 1926. In its original format, it was a Bible reading, although this was later added to by hymns and psalms, broadcast on the **Home Service**. The final broadcast was in 1980.

ESSLIN, MARTIN (1918–2002). Of Hungarian origin, born and educated in Vienna, Esslin was a theater scholar and radio producer, who came to London because of the Anschluss, and joined the **British Broadcasting Corporation (BBC)**, becoming a producer and scriptwriter. He worked for the European Service from 1941–1955, eventually becoming head of the European production department. He translated many pieces of European theater into English, and this in turn led to a number of significant **drama** productions. In 1961, Esslin became assistant head of radio drama, becoming the department head in 1963, a post he retained until 1977 when he began spending more time each year in the United States. He received an OBE in 1972. A scholar of theater, his book *The Theatre of the Absurd* (1962) defined a movement and created a term that remains extant.

EUREKA 147. The system, developed by a consortium of 12 partners, has been widely adopted since 1994 as an international standard for the transmission of **Digital Audio Broadcasting (DAB)**. Today, a large proportion of the world's broadcasters have implemented the system. Exceptions have been the United States, which has embraced both satellite digital radio and high definition (HD) radio—In Band, On Channel (IBOC)—and Japan, where cable is the chosen method of new radio format delivery. Other countries, including South Korea, have used Eureka 147 as the delivery system for the development of Terrestrial Digital Multimedia Broadcasting (T-DMB) in mobile devices.

EVANS, CHRIS (1966–). Born in Lancashire, Evans's first job in radio was for Manchester's Piccadilly Radio. He soon moved to the **British Broadcasting Corporation (BBC)** London station, GLR. In 1992, he gained national prominence as the host of the TV show *The Big Breakfast* and built on his new-found celebrity by establishing his own production company, Ginger Productions, responsible for his Channel 4 quiz program, *Don't Forget Your Toothbrush*. The program format was sold worldwide, and much of Evans's media empire was built on the money from the show.

In 1994, Evans left *The Big Breakfast*, and the following year he signed with **Radio 1** to present the breakfast show at a time when the network was moving—under the controllership of **Matthew Bannister**—toward a new image and definition of itself after a period of decline and stagnation. Between his arrival at the station and October 1996, he had increased the breakfast show audience from one million to seven million listeners. His time at Radio 1 was, however, not without controversy, and he was frequently censured for his remarks and inappropriate jokes. In January 1997, he was sacked after his demands to work a four-day week were refused by Bannister.

Evans moved to **Virgin Radio**, where he worked as a presenter, but in 1997, his Ginger Media Group bought the station for £85m. Less than three years later, the station was sold again, this time for £225m. Evans continued to broadcast for the station, but in 2001 he was sacked after failing to appear for his program for five consecutive days. After some unsuccessful TV ventures, during 2005 he made a number of guest appearances on BBC programs, including a charity broadcast in aid of the Asian Tsunami appeal, and an outside broadcast from the London *Live 8* concert held in Hyde Park. Also in the summer of 2005, he signed a contract to present programs on **Radio 2**.

EVERETT, KENNY (1944–1995). Everett was a **disc jockey/** presenter of genius who developed a style of radio which used the medium's technical resources in a creative and innovative way, unlike much of the pop music programming of the 1960s and 1970s. He first came to the attention of the British public on the **pirate radio** station **Radio London** and joined the **Radio 1** team when the station was created in 1967. He was sacked by the **British Broadcasting Corporation (BBC)** in 1970 after a joke in which he suggested on his program that the transport minister's wife had passed her driving test because of a bribe. He came back to the BBC in 1981, but two years later he was again the subject of controversy after a remark about Margaret Thatcher. He also worked for **Capital Radio**. He died of AIDS in 1995.

– F –

FAMILY FAVOURITES. This highly popular record request program began in 1945 on the **Light Programme** and ran until 1984. The format was that of a two-way link-up between the **British Broadcasting**

Corporation (BBC) and the **British Forces Network** in Germany. Created by **Maurice Gorham**, the program had two famous presenters, **Jean Metcalfe** in London and **Cliff Michelmore** in Hamburg, who subsequently married. From January 1960 the program became known as *Two Way Family Favourites*. On certain occasions, the brief was widened to include other British Forces around Europe, including Cyprus and Malta. Broadcast on a Sunday lunchtime, it was a focus for many in the immediate postwar years, linking as it did, servicemen and women abroad with their families at home. Its theme tune was "With a Song in My Heart."

FARMING PROGRAMS. British radio has maintained specialist programs for farmers since 1929, although in many cases research has shown that the programs are listened to by an audience beyond the farming community itself. In 1937, a new program, *Farming Today*, was launched, presented by Anthony Hurd of the *Times*, father of future Conservative Party home secretary, Douglas Hurd. Initially, the program was broadcast weekly, but since 1960, it has become a daily part of the output, first of the **Home Service** and subsequently of **Radio 4**. It is broadcast Monday to Saturday, in the early morning, while on Sunday agricultural interests are catered to by *On Your Farm*. Most **British Broadcasting Corporation (BBC)** farming programs have historically originated from Birmingham, and it was here, in 1948, that the well-known and perennially popular serial *The Archers* began, and from where it continues to be produced.

FEATURE. The concept of the radio feature has had a particularly rich history in UK broadcasting. Developed early as a hybrid between **documentary** and **drama**, its growth in the 1930s was particularly enhanced by the development of mobile recording technologies. The sense that the radio feature could explore facts from a dramatized or stylized stance gave program makers the freedom to create material that had considerable emotional impact, and could also at times express the implicit opinion of the producers themselves. The work of **E. A. Harding**, **D. G. Bridson**, **Olive Shapley**, and others in Manchester at this time was particularly powerful in examining issues of poverty, unemployment, and inner-city and industrial strife.

The use of poetry as a strand in features continues to be a strong narrative device, as does the use of music and adapted or created material utilizing actors, blended with journalistic techniques such as interviews. The postwar radio Features Department of the **British Broadcasting Corporation (BBC)** under **Laurence Gilliam** was extremely fruitful and creative in the development of the genre, and from this time comes the work of major producers such as **Douglas Cleverdon** and **Louis MacNeice**. Dylan Thomas's great verse drama, *Under Milk Wood*, originated from this department. From the BBC regions, as before the war, work of great importance originated, including the programs of **Charles Parker** in Birmingham.

The works of Simon Elmes, Peter Everett, Alan Hall, **Piers Plowright**, **John Theocharis**, and Matt Thompson have continued the tradition, and a younger generation of program makers, many working for **independent production** companies, is using digital technology to reach new, younger audiences on such networks as **Radio 1** and **1Xtra**. The duration of the radio feature has proved to be infinitely flexible, from large-scale 90-minute programs to short form. The heart of the feature has always been the desire and ability to tell stories in imaginative ways.

FESTIVAL OF NINE LESSONS AND CAROLS. This annual radio Christmas institution was first broadcast from King's College, Cambridge on Christmas Eve 1928 and has continued ever since. It is also now broadcast on television.

FFORDE, ARTHUR (1900–1985). Sir Arthur Frederic Brownlow fforde held the post of **chairman** of the **British Broadcasting Corporation (BBC)** from 1957–1964. An unobtrusive incumbent, he suffered intermittently with periods of ill-health, during which his vice-chairman, Sir James Duff (1898–1970), deputized for him.

FILE ON FOUR. This weekly **current affairs** program was created by **Michael Green** in Manchester for **Radio 4** in 1977, and has included among its reporting team a future controller of the network, **Helen Boaden**. It is an investigative series that specializes in first-hand reporting on topical issues, either of international or domestic concern.

FISCHER, GEORGE. Fischer was a key figure in the development of the **Radio 4 current affairs** program, *Analysis*. He joined the **BBC** in 1963 as a program assistant in **External Services**, and moved to network radio in 1967, where he met **Ian McIntyre**, with whom he worked as a producer. He was the first producer of *Analysis*, and produced 45 editions of the program from 1970–1974, most of them with McIntyre as presenter. From 1972–1987, he was editor, Documentaries and Talks, Radio/head of Talks and Documentaries, Radio. He remained a close ally of McIntyre, and together they continued to espouse Reithian broadcasting values into the 1980s.

FIVE TO TEN. This short religious program was broadcast on weekday mornings from 1950–1970 on the **Home Service/Radio 4**. Its subtitle was "A story, a hymn and a prayer."

"**FLEET'S LIT UP.**" In 1937, Lieutenant Commander Thomas Woodruffe was scheduled to broadcast a commentary on the Coronation Review of the Fleet at Spithead. Unfortunately, Woodruffe was aboard his old ship, HMS *Nelson*, and had enjoyed considerable boardroom hospitality prior to the broadcast, and was demonstrably drunk by the time of the broadcast. After some minutes, he was faded off the air, but the incident was far-reaching, leading to the introduction of continuity announcers whose role was not only to link programs but to monitor output. Such a sensation did Woodruffe's commentary cause—"The Fleet's lit up . . . It's lit up by fairy lights . . . It's like fairyland . . . the ships are lit up . . . even the destroyers are lit up"—that the incident even produced a West End stage musical called *The Fleet's Lit Up*.

FLEMING, JOHN AMBROSE (1849–1945). Fleming was an English engineer, born in Lancaster but brought up in north London. He made numerous contributions to electronics and wireless telegraphy and in 1899 started working with the **Marconi Company**. He was responsible for designing the transmitter that facilitated the first transatlantic message, but is best known as the inventor of the thermionic or Fleming **Valve**, which was patented in 1905 and which was highly significant in the development of radio technology. Fleming became a consultant to the Edison Electric Light Company, and was a fine and popular tutor at University College, London. He was knighted in 1929 for his valuable and wide-ranging contributions to electrical and electronic engineering.

FLETCHER, CYRIL (1913–2005). Fletcher was a well-known comedian and raconteur, famous for his rich voice and comic verse, which he coined as "Odd Odes." This aspect of his work became popular in 1938 when he recited "Dreamin' of Thee," a Cockney caricature of "The Lovesick Tommy's Dream of Home" by Edgar Wallace. Others followed, and his success with comedy voices made him a natural favorite on radio. He made his first series in 1940, *Thanking Yew*. He frequently worked with his wife, the actress and singer, Betty Astell, notably in the 1952 comedy series, *Fletcher's Fare*. He also worked in television, and was one of the first comedians to work in the medium in the UK, from the BBC studios in Alexandra Palace in 1936.

FLOTSAM AND JETSAM. This comedy duo comprised B. C. Hilliam (Flotsam) (1890–1968) and Malcolm McEachern (Jetsam) (1883–1945). They made their broadcasting debut in 1926, and their contrasting high and low voices made them immensely popular for nearly 20 years, with a series of successful radio programs: *Round the World with Flotsam and Jetsam*, *Our Hour*, and *Signs of the Times*. Many of their songs took radio as their theme; for example, "Weather Reports," "Big Ben Calling," and most famously, "Little Betty Bouncer loves an announcer down at the BBC."

FOOT, R. W. (1889–1973). Robert William Foot, OBE, was joint **director-general** of the **British Broadcasting Corporation (BBC)** with **Cecil Graves** from 1942–1943 and sole director-general until 1944 after Graves retired in 1943. He had been a solicitor and became general manager of the Gas, Light, and Coke Company. He had been originally commissioned to investigate inefficiencies and overspending within the BBC under the director-generalship of **F. W. Ogilvie**, and was appointed joint director-general on Ogilvie's departure. Essentially an administrator, after Graves retired, he worked with **William Haley** who managed programming as editor-in-chief until succeeding him as director-general in 1944. Foot's contribution during his time with the BBC was to decentralize management and improve relations with the British government.

FOORT, REGINALD (?–?). Reginald Foort was the first resident organist to be appointed by the **British Broadcasting Company/Corporation (BBC)**, holding the post until 1938, when he went freelance as a performer. Such was the public feeling at the time of his resignation that the BBC received some 10,000 letters from listeners, all of which Foort replied to personally. In 1926, at the height of his radio success, his recording of Albert Ketelby's *In a Monastery Garden* sold 3,250,000 copies.

He continued to broadcast, and amassed over 2,000 programs up to 1951, when he immigrated to the United States, making his home in Florida. He returned to the UK for a tour, at the age of 78, when his familiar style of mixing "popular classics and light melodies" renewed memories for the many listeners who recalled nostalgically his time at the BBC.

FORCES PROGRAMME. It was launched on 7 January 1940, at 6:00 p.m., as a specific channel of entertainment for British service personnel, and quickly drew civilian audiences away from the **Home Service** by virtue of its more relaxed mix of dance band music and comedy. From 27 February 1944, it was retitled as the **General Forces Programme** and after the end of the war, metamorphosed into the **Light Programme**.

FOREST OF DEAN RADIO. Following the experiment into the viability and desirability of a UK **Community Radio** sector, the government media regulator, **Ofcom**, granted the first five-year license to Forest of Dean Radio in Gloucestershire in March 2005.

FRANCIS, RICHARD (1934–). Sir Richard Francis was director of **British Broadcasting Corporation (BBC)** Radio from 1982–1986. It was he who conceived the idea of the **Radio Academy** to provide a radio equivalent of film and television's British Academy of Film and Television Arts (BAFTA).

FRANKAU, RONALD (1894–1951). This highly popular comedian and reciter of monologues was a personal favorite of **John Reith**.

This is surprising, given the nature of much of Frankau's material, which was frequently risqué. He first broadcast in 1925 in a relay of his concert party, *Cabaret Kittens*. He appeared in films, wrote books, and in 1932 alone sold more than 100,000 records of his comic routines and songs. His regular accompanist was Monte Crick, who went on to become one of four actors to play the character Dan Archer in the serial *The Archers*. He became a close friend of **Tommy Handley**, and they worked together many times, notably as the comedy duo, "Mr. Murgatroyd and Mr. Winterbottom."

FREEMAN, ALAN (1927–). Beginning his radio career as an announcer for the Melbourne station, 7LA in 1952, he spent two years at **Radio Luxembourg** before joining the **Light Programme** in 1960. Here, he was one of the presenters for *Housewives' Choice* and, in 1962, took over the program with which he was mostly to be associated, *Pick of the Pops*. In 1972, he became a regular presenter on **Radio 1** and the following year presented the first *Radio 1 Roadshow*. For 10 years, from 1979–1989, he worked for **Capital Radio** before rejoining the BBC to present *Pick of the Pops* in a new format, once more, until his retirement. He is widely known by his nickname, "Fluff."

FREQUENCY MODULATION (FM). Previously known as **very high frequency (VHF)**, it relates to wavelengths within the 87.5 to 108 MHz range. British radio moved progressively away from the use of **mediumwave** transmission in the 1970s, 1980s, and early 1990s toward the exclusive use of FM for its domestic services, a status quo that was to remain until the introduction of **Digital Audio Broadcasting (DAB)** at the end of the century. Even given that, because of the slow roll-out of digital services and receivers, it is likely to remain the main source of radio listening for some years.

FRIDAY NIGHT IS MUSIC NIGHT. One of British radio's longest-running music programs, having started on the **Light Programme** in 1953 as a showcase for the then newly formed **BBC Concert Orchestra**, it continues on **Radio 2**. A key figure in its policy was the conductor, arranger, and composer Sidney Torch who created a format of light music reflecting everything from popular classics to show tunes. There is usually a guest singer or singers, and the program is recorded in front of a large audience. Originally, it was broadcast from the Camden Theatre, and subsequently from the Golders Green Hippodrome, although it has also toured the country extensively.

FROM OUR OWN CORRESPONDENT. The program consists of short talks from news correspondents around the world, and is broadcast on **Radio 4** and the **World Service**. Now introduced by the distinguished broadcast journalist **Kate Adie**, usually the theme is topical and either relates to the main news or—frequently—is based on other issues within the correspondent's geographical sphere of work. As such, it has produced some of the finest reflective **current affairs** writing to be heard on British radio. **John Tusa** likened the program to "postcards from the world," adding, "like real postcards, they come at unexpected times from unlikely places, telling improbable adventures." The program first began in October 1946 as a 15-minute series on **Radio 3** and remained on the network throughout the 1940s. It was first heard on Radio 4 in its now familiar half-hour version from September 1955.

– G –

GALTON AND SIMPSON. Ray Galton (1930–) and Alan Simpson (1929–) are considered to be among the finest of all UK comedy writing partnerships, and the innovation of their situation comedy writing—both for radio and television—has helped to define the genre. Galton and Simpson met as teenagers in 1948, while convalescing from tuberculosis in a sanatorium. They started writing material for hospital radio, and submitted material to the **British Broadcasting Corporation (BBC)**, attracting the attention of the comedian **Derek Roy**, who commissioned them as writers for his radio program, *Happy-Go-Lucky*. Mentored by the show's producer, **Dennis Main Wilson**, they progressed to work on *Calling All Forces*, where they first wrote for **Tony Hancock**, in 1952, and *Star Bill*, again with Hancock, in 1953–1954.

It was at this time that they approached Dennis Main Wilson with the concept of a half-hour program, featuring Hancock, but using only one storyline per episode, rather than sketches. The result was

Hancock's Half Hour, which ran from 1954–1959 on radio, and successfully transferred to television. They also wrote extensively for **Bernard Braden**, and, moving increasingly into television, created *Steptoe and Son* in 1962. Ray Galton and Alan Simpson were awarded lifetime achievement awards by the Writers' Guild in 1997, and received OBEs in 2000.

GARDENERS' QUESTION TIME. The program, one in a long tradition of broadcast information and advice services for UK horticulturalists, began under the title of *How Does Your Garden Grow?* in 1947, capitalizing on a newly developed enthusiasm for gardening, arising from the government's wartime "Dig for Victory" campaign. The name change came in 1951.

The format was that of an audience, often comprising members of a local horticultural society, putting questions and problems to a resident team of experts. When the program began this team comprised Fred Loads and Bill Sowerbutts, who were joined in 1950 by Alan Gemmell. So close was the team that when Loads died in 1981, Gemmell retired the following year and Sowerbutts a year later.

Since then, there have been various teams and chairmen, and the location-based format in front of a live audience continues, with the series produced in Manchester, where it originated. One change has been the introduction of every third program being studio-based, answering listeners' queries submitted by post.

GARRISON THEATRE. This Saturday evening wartime comedy series began in August 1940 and attained high popularity ratings, making a star of its central figure, **Jack Warner**. It was devised by **Charles Shadwell** and produced by **Harry S. Pepper**. The program recreated the atmosphere and mood of troop shows from the previous war, and was broadcast—usually before a boisterous invited audience and typically from Clifton Parish Hall in Bristol. A stage version of the show was also broadcast, and toured until 1942 although the program in its original form ended in 1941.

GCAP MEDIA. Through the merging of the **GWR** and **Capital Radio** groups in May 2005, the newly formed GCap Media Group became the UK's largest **commercial radio** company, with one national and

54 local **analog** stations and 100 **digital radio** stations. In addition, the company could boast an interest in 28 digital radio multiplexes, and a controlling shareholding in the UK's only national commercial digital radio multiplex, **Digital One**.

The geographical spread of ownership was also enhanced by the merger, giving the group ownership or interest in local and regional analog stations in the Southeast and Southwest of England, the Midlands, East Anglia, Northern England, Wales, and Scotland. **Ralph Bernard** of GWR became the group's first executive chairman, with Capital Radio's **David Mansfield** as chief executive. Mansfield resigned within six months of the merger.

GENERAL STRIKE. Beginning on 4 May 1926, the General Strike was a major event in British broadcasting, and the first time that the **British Broadcasting Company (BBC)** faced a crisis in its relationship with the government. As the country came to a standstill and newspapers ceased publication, radio became the only source of information available. **John Reith**, who later referred to the time as "those exciting but very difficult days of the General Strike," had the task of trying to keep the BBC free from the influence of right-wing politicians, and was criticized by left-wing activists for progovernment policy in its broadcasts. Winston Churchill demanded that the BBC be commandeered to become the voice of government; this did not happen, although at times some critics felt it had come close to this.

Reith's own assessment, recorded for the 1961 program *Scrapbook for 1926*, summed up both the problem and the opportunity of the strike for the BBC, in its last year prior to becoming a corporation:

> It was a tremendous opportunity to show what broadcasting could do. Hitherto the BBC had not been permitted to give news before seven o'clock in the evening; now arrangements were made for bulletins at 10.00 a.m., 1, 4, 7 and 9.30 p.m. The major issue was whether or not the BBC was to become part of government, broadcasting only what was passed by some government representative, or whether BBC independence was to be preserved, the BBC being trusted to broadcast or not to broadcast as it thought in the best interests of the country.

GERALDO (1904–1974). Born Gerald Bright, this popular dance band leader broadcast on radio through the 1930s, and during World War

II. His music was always that of the "easy listening" variety, and many of his broadcasts came from major hotels, such as the Savoy in London. His radio shows had a number of lead singers over the years, notably in the late 1930s the crooner Al Bowlly. After the war, he organized bands for P & O transatlantic liners.

GIBBONS, CARROLL (1903–1954). Born in the United States, Gibbons came to the United Kingdom in 1924, playing at the Savoy hotel as a pianist. The resident band at the time was the Savoy Orpheans, which he took over as leader in 1927. Capitalizing on the close proximity of the hotel to **British Broadcasting Company (BBC)** headquarters in Savoy Hill, literally next door, the band made frequent appearances in the early days of radio.

The band disbanded in 1928, and Gibbons joined HMV as director of light music. He returned briefly to the U.S. to work in films, and was back in Britain by 1931, when he reformed the Orpheans, running the band until the end of his life. From December 1933, he took the band to new popularity through its numerous appearances on commercial radio, in particular on **Radio Luxembourg**, where it attracted keen sponsorship from major advertisers while maintaining a BBC presence. He also appeared solo in such series as *Carroll Calls the Tune*. His signature tune was "On the Air."

GIELGUD, VAL (1900–1981). The elder brother of Sir John Gielgud, Val was the founding father of British radio drama, a department he led within the **British Broadcasting Corporation (BBC)** from 1929 until 1963. Among his famous productions, one of the most significant was *The Man Born to be King*. He also pioneered international work in *World Theatre* and was a prolific writer in his own right. He collaborated with Holt Marvell (the pen name of **Eric Maschvitz**) on a crime novel, *Death at Broadcasting House*, which was also filmed in Broadcasting House itself, and in which he himself played a central role. He famously rejected **Samuel Beckett**'s *Waiting for Godot* for broadcast in 1953.

GILES COOPER AWARDS. Founded in 1978 in honor of the radio playwright **Giles Cooper** who died in 1966, this annual award for plays broadcast on **British Broadcasting Corporation (BBC)**

networks other than the **World Service** has over the years marked the work of many famous writers, some of whom, at the time of their award, were new names. In the first year of the awards, recipients included Richard Harris, Don Haworth, and Fay Weldon. Among winners in subsequent years have been Harold Pinter, Peter Barnes, John Arden, Wally K. Daly, Peter Tinniswood, and Anthony Minghella.

GILL, ERIC (1882–1940). The carvings of Prospero and Ariel on the façade of **Broadcasting House** in London are among the best-known work of this artist, stone carver, and writer. The adoption of Shakespeare's Ariel, the invisible spirit of the air, from *The Tempest* was an appropriate metaphor for the new science of broadcasting. As well as the two figures of Ariel and his master over the main entrance, others develop further metaphors for sound broadcasting, showing "Ariel between wisdom and gaiety," "Ariel listening to music," and "Ariel piping to children." Inside the main reception, Gill created a carving entitled "Sower," a man broadcasting seed. Below it is the inscription, "Deus incrementum dat" ("God giveth the increase," from Corinthians, Chapter 3, verse 7). Gill's work on Broadcasting House was not universally liked; the carving Prospero and Ariel in particular caused controversy, claimed by one critic to be "objectionable to public morals and decency."

Gill was born in Brighton, the son of a nonconformist minister. While he was apprenticed in London to a firm of architects as a young man, he became fascinated by the art of calligraphy. Absorbed by the Arts and Crafts movement and its philosophies, Giles during his life he set up three self-sufficient religious communities where worked with others as a sculptor, wood-engraver, and type designer. (His most famous typeface is Gill Sans, which was used by a number of corporate institutions—including the BBC for its logo).

GILLARD, FRANK (1908–1998). Born in Exford, Somerset, Gillard was a distinguished broadcaster and war correspondent who proved himself to be as forceful and effective a manager of broadcasting as he was a presenter. For nine years, he practiced as a school teacher before working as a freelance broadcaster from 1936. He joined the staff of the **British Broadcasting Corporation (BBC)** in 1941, and, using the then new portable recording technology equipment made available for war correspondents, he broadcast reports of the Normandy landings and broke the news of the link-up between the American and Soviet forces at the River Elbe in 1945.

After the war, as head of programs for the BBC West Region in Bristol, Gillard conceived the highly successful program *Any Questions*. Later, as director of sound broadcasting in 1964, he was more controversial in his decision to take the much-loved *Children's Hour* off the air permanently. Moving to the post of managing director of BBC Radio, he oversaw the creation of **Radios 1**, **2**, **3**, and **4** in 1967, and was the driving force behind the creation of BBC Local Radio in the same year. He was awarded the OBE in 1946, and the CBE in 1961.

GILLIAM, LAURENCE (1907–1964). Gilliam worked first in the UK recording industry, for the Gramophone Company, before freelancing as a journalist, actor, and producer until 1932, when he joined the staff of *The Radio Times*. The following year, he moved to the Drama Department, where his particular interest was in creating programs characterized by their sound pictures. Typical of this was *'Opping 'Oliday*, a sound picture of hop picking in Kent, which he produced in 1934 using the newly created mobile recording van, then being developed by the **British Broadcasting Corporation (BBC)** for location work.

In 1933, Gilliam began his lifelong association with the production of worldwide Christmas Day programs, which traditionally aired prior to the annual message from the monarch on Christmas afternoon. These programs were complex technically, and helped develop radio's potential in the UK. In 1936, drama and features divided, with Gilliam having responsibility for the latter, and during the war, his work in this field reached new heights, culminating in his editorship of **War Report**.

Postwar, his work encouraged writers and poets to enrich the radio **feature**, and inspired great loyalty amongst his colleagues, generating some of the most memorable radio of all time, including the work of **Francis Dillon**, **Nesta Pain**, **Wynford Vaughan-Thomas**, and **Douglas Cleverdon**. It is true to say that the development of the radio feature owed more to Laurence Gilliam than to any other single person. In his last years, he saw the BBC begin to dismantle his department, which was disbanded in 1965, a few months after his death.

GILLIGAN, ANDREW (1968–). As defense and diplomatic correspondent for the **Radio 4** *Today* program, Andrew Gilligan was the journalist at the center of the issue relating to the 2003 controversy over reporting of Iraqi weapons capability, a major factor in the UK government's prosecution of the Iraq War. The case led to the Hutton Enquiry, which resulted in a number of high-level resignations within the BBC, and ultimately Gilligan's own, in January 2004.

GLENDENNING, RAYMOND (1907–1974). This sports commentator was known for the extreme speed of his live description of events. He had begun his working life as a chartered accountant, but joined the **British Broadcasting Corporation (BBC)** in 1932 as an organizer on *Children's Hour* based in Cardiff. He left the staff in 1945 and from then on worked as a freelance full-time sports commentator, equally at ease describing the action in football, boxing, racing, tennis, show jumping, greyhound racing, and other athletics. For many years until his retirement in 1963 he was the voice of sports on BBC radio.

GOLDRING, MARY (? –). A journalist with an ability to pinpoint issues and detail, Goldring was the business editor of *The Economist* and a key member of the presentation team for the **Radio 4** program *Analysis*. She won many awards for her work, including the Broadcasting Press Guild Award for "an outstanding personal contribution to radio." She received an OBE in 1994.

GOON SHOW. Growing out of a 1951 program, *Crazy People*, this ground-breaking comedy show first aired on 22 January 1952 and featured **Spike Milligan**, **Peter Sellers**, **Harry Secombe**, and **Michael Bentine**, although Bentine left after the first series. Also integral were the musicians Max Geldray and the Ray Ellington Quartet. The style—a blend of army and surreal—was anarchic and hugely influential in the development of postwar broadcast comedy.

Mostly written by Spike Milligan, for whom the strain of writing material over 10 series and eight years produced several breakdowns, the program was broadcast on the **Home Service** from 1952–1960, with a revival edition, *The Last Goon Show of All* in 1972, produced as part of the 50th anniversary celebrations of the **British Broadcasting Corporation (BBC)**. Among the program's greatest admirers was HRH, the Prince of Wales.

GORDON-WALKER, PATRICK (1907–1980). A leading academic before World War II, Gordon-Walker became increasingly interested in politics, eventually becoming a Labour Party MP, and finally, as Lord Gordon-Walker, a member of the European Parliament in 1975–1976. During the war itself, he became closely involved with the European Service of the **British Broadcasting Corporation (BBC)**, and after a number of freelance talks, he joined the staff at **Bush House**. When U.S. forces reached Luxembourg in 1944 and took over control of **Radio Luxembourg** from the retreating German army, Gordon-Walker was among BBC staff seconded to the station; from there, he traveled with Allied troops into Germany, reporting as he went, including powerful broadcasts from the Belsen concentration camp. After the war, he became an MP for Smethwick and thereafter devoted himself to politics.

GOSLING, RAY (1940–). Having begun his broadcasting career as a researcher for **Charles Parker**, Ray Gosling went on to become one of the most unique program makers in British radio, with a personal style both reflective and perceptive. He has made many series exploring the specifics of living, commentaries often characterized by the style and stance of an outsider, written with a poet's eye and objectivity, and delivered in his own idiosyncratic style of speech.

GRADE, MICHAEL (1943–). Michael Ian Grade, CBE, became **chairman** of the **British Broadcasting Corporation (BBC)** on the resignation of **Gavyn Davies** as a result of the **Hutton Report**. Having begun in print journalism, he worked in his family's theatrical business, and subsequently moved into television. Among numerous management roles, he was controller of BBC 1 and chief executive of Channel 4 Television.

GRAND HOTEL. A long-running program of light orchestral music that had its first transmission from the Palm Court of the Grand

Hotel, Eastbourne, on 28 July 1925, under the leadership of the well-known violinist Albert Sandler. It was hugely popular up to the outbreak of World War II. In 1943, it was revived from the Concert Hall of **Broadcasting House**, still with Sandler and the Palm Court Theatre Orchestra, and with potted palms specially imported for the transmissions to create an appropriate ambience. The first program in its revived form featured the popular tenor Frank Titterton. (There was always a guest singer who performed with the small musical forces, usually comprising a piano trio, augmented occasionally by extra musicians and instruments, including a Mustel Organ and Celeste). It continued for many years after the war, and its theme tune of "Roses from the South" by Johann Strauss II became a familiar part of Sunday evening listening.

GRAVES, CECIL (1892–1957). After the departure of **F. W. Ogilvie** as **director-general** of the **British Broadcasting Corporation (BBC)** in 1942 Graves took on the role jointly with **R. W. Foot** for just one year, being responsible for programming while Foot took administrative control. Graves had joined the BBC in 1926 from a military background. He was the first director of the **Empire Service** and deputized for both **John Reith** and Ogilvie. Indeed, Graves was Reith's preferred choice to succeed him. However, he had been plagued with ill health and retired from the BBC in 1943.

GREENE, HUGH CARLETON (1910–1987). Sir Hugh Carleton Greene OBE, KCMG, who was the brother of the novelist, Graham Greene, was **British Broadcasting Corporation (BBC) director-general** from 1960 to 1969, succeeding Sir **Ian Jacob**. Originally joining the Corporation to lead the **German Service** in 1940, he took on, successively, the roles of director of news and **current affairs** and director of administration. He was heavily involved in modernizing the BBC and encouraged new program ideas and program making, including, for radio, *I'm Sorry I'll Read That Again*, and a range of satirical material. He was admired for his leadership and his evidence to the **Pilkington Committee** helped in the renewal of the BBC's **charter**. He resigned due to marital problems but subsequently served for two years on the **BBC Board of Governors** where he robustly defended the corporation's editorial independence. After his retirement, he took over the running of the family business of the Greene King Brewery.

GREEN, HUGHIE (1920–1997). Green was born in London, but moved to Canada, becoming a Canadian citizen. Returning to Britain at the age of 13, he gained a reputation as a gifted impersonator, and came to public notice after an appearance on *In Town Tonight* in 1933. By the time he was 15, he was the highest-paid child star in Britain. Green worked extensively on commercial radio, including **Radio Luxembourg**, appearing on programs such as *Horlicks Picture House* before World War II. After the war, he devised and presented *Opportunity Knocks* for Radio Luxembourg. Later, the show transferred to television. He was involved in an unsuccessful legal battle with the **British Broadcasting Corporation (BBC)** for alleged blacklisting.

GREEN, MICHAEL (1941–). Green became controller of **Radio 4** in 1986 and was largely popular with staff for his work, although his decision to move *Woman's Hour* from its afternoon slot to a morning place in the network schedule provoked considerable controversy. Among his many achievements was the establishment of *File on Four*. He began his broadcasting career with Swiss Radio International, before joining BBC **Local Radio** when it began in 1967. He went on to a distinguished career in radio journalism, including work as a producer on the *Analysis* program. He retired in 1996, and was succeeded as controller of Radio 4 by **James Boyle**.

GREENWICH TIME SIGNAL. On 5 February 1924, at 5:30 p.m., the **British Broadcasting Company (BBC)** first broadcast the Greenwich Time Signal. The event was preceded by an introductory talk by the astronomer royal, Frank Dyson. The idea for the time signal—affectionately referred to ever after as "the pips" came from **John Reith** after a radio talk by horologist Frank Hope-Jones at the introduction of British Summer Time in 1923. It was Hope-Jones who devised the system, based on two clocks built by E. Dent and Company in 1874, with Dyson.

Electrical contacts attached to the pendulum of the clocks at the Greenwich Observatory sent pulses to the BBC's headquarters at **Broadcasting House**, where an oscillatory valve circuit converted the signal to the tones. The clocks operated until 1949, when more up-to-date technology was implemented. The system was the first of its kind in the world, and was the model for time signals on all other broadcasting services.

Today, the BBC keeps its own time, using two atomic clocks in Broadcasting House, kept in step by signals received from the Global Positioning Satellite system and by information received from the Rugby radio transmitter facility operated by BT Aeronautical and Maritime, under contract to the National Physical Laboratory. Since 1972, all time signals have been based on atomic time, due to the fact that Greenwich Mean Time drifts as the speed of the Earth's rotation changes, thus causing discrepancies.

Differences between atomic time and Greenwich Mean Time are compensated for by occasional extra seconds that need to be added to the signal. This is the reason for the last "pip" being slightly longer; if—as very occasionally happens—a seventh tone has to be added in order to compensate, an elongated last tone is required to demonstrate the true end of the signal.

GREGG, HUBERT (1916–2004). Although Hubert Gregg was for a short time an announcer on the **BBC Empire Service** in 1936, it was his radio programs that linked to his long and illustrious theater career—and the memories engendered by it—that made his **Radio 2** series *Thanks for the Memory* such a long-running success. Beginning in 1972, it was still a staple part of the network's output and remained so at his death in March 2004, with its blend of popular songs from the past and personal anecdotes. Gregg was an actor, singer, director, writer, and composer, in addition to his role as a broadcaster; he was the author of probably the most famous song ever written about London, "Maybe It's Because I'm a Londoner."

GRENFELL, JOYCE (1910–1979). Joyce Grenfell was a much-loved, multitalented broadcaster with a special skill at monologues that characterized and often gently satirized the English middle class and certain colonial attitudes. She was the first radio critic of the *Observer* newspaper, and after the war, she created, with **Stephen Potter** the *How To. . .* series for the fledgling **Third Progamme**. The series ran from 1943–1962.

GRISEWOOD, FREDDY (1888–1972). Grisewood was noted as the chairman of *Any Questions* from 1948, when the program began, until his retirement through ill health in 1968. He had joined the **British Broadcasting Corporation (BBC)** in 1929 as an announcer and was assistant chief announcer under **Stuart Hibberd**. His voice became a well known part of the program schedule from that time onward. Grisewood appeared in many radio shows, including *Children's Hour*, *In Town Tonight*, and the long-running *Scrapbook* series from 1933. He was the cousin of **Harman Grisewood**.

GRISEWOOD, HARMAN (1906–1997). Grisewood began his career as an actor and a radio announcer during the 1930s. In 1941, he moved from presentation to organization, and became assistant controller to the European Service of the **British Broadcasting Corporation (BBC)**, based at **Bush House**, London. After the war, he worked briefly in talks but resigned in 1947, although he was almost immediately offered a post in the planning department of the newly formed **Third Programme**, of which he became controller from 1948–1952. While there, he launched the long-running *Record Review* program, which later became *CD Review*.

From 1952–1955, he was director of the spoken word, and finally chief assistant to the **director-general** of the BBC from 1955–1964. During the Suez Crisis, Grisewood did much to maintain the BBC's political independence, under considerable government pressure. He was awarded a CBE in 1960 and retired from the BBC in 1964, briefly joining the *Times* under **William Haley**, with whom he had worked in the Corporation. He was the cousin of **Freddy Grisewood**.

GWR. In 1985, the Independent Local Radio station, Wiltshire Radio, merged with Radio West in Bristol, which was relaunched as Great Western Radio (GWR), although the acronym was from the start more identifiable than the full name and has remained so. GWR acquired Plymouth Sound in 1987, Radio 2-Ten in Reading, and Two Counties Radio (2CR, Bournemouth) in 1989. This was the foundation of the GWR Group, which was to become, prior to the merger with **Capital Radio** in May 2005 to form **GCap Media**, the largest pure radio group in the UK.

In 1991, under the leadership of **Ralph Bernard**, the GWR Group took an initial 17% share of the first national commercial radio station in Britain, **Classic FM**, later, in 1996, buying the remaining 83% of the shares for £71.5 million.

The local radio operations of the GWR Group continued to grow, with the Chiltern Radio Group, the Mid-Anglian Radio group, East Anglian Radio, the Orchard Media Group, and the Marcher group of stations all joining GWR, giving the group control of 32 local licenses in addition to Classic FM. In May 2005, the group merged with the **Capital Radio** Group to form **GCapMedia**.

– H –

HALEY, WILLIAM (1901–1987). Sir William John Haley KCMG, a native of Jersey, was a journalist and one-time editor of the *Manchester Evening News* who joined the **British Broadcasting Corporation (BBC)** in 1943 and became its **director-general** in 1944. A widely respected figure, he was admired by **John Reith** and was largely instrumental in the establishment of the BBC's role after World War II, with the establishment of the tripartite structure of the **Home Service**, **Light Programme**, and **Third Programme**. After leaving the BBC in 1952, he became editor of the *Times* and finally, prior to his retirement, the *Encyclopaedia Britannica*.

HANCOCK, TONY (1924–1968). Tony Hancock was a troubled genius whose comic persona of "Anthony Aloysius St. John Hancock" was the basis for *Hancock's Half Hour*, which has been hailed as one of the greatest radio comedy series of all time. He made his radio debut in 1941 in a light entertainment program called *A La Carte* but gained more recognition from his time in *Educating Archie* from 1951–1953. His partnership with writers **Ray Galton** and **Alan Simpson** and producer **Dennis Main Wilson** was first formed in the radio comedy show *Happy Go Lucky* and was to prove the potent root of his success. By all accounts, Hancock was a difficult man to work with, and his career dwindled toward the end of his life. He died by his own hand.

HANCOCK'S HALF HOUR. The show ran from November 1954 to December 1959, transferring to television in 1956. The central character was **Tony Hancock** himself, or rather a version of himself, and through various series he was joined by a number of others, played by Sid James, Bill Kerr, Hattie Jacques, and Kenneth Williams. The programs were a blend of well-drawn and played characters and skillful plot lines that revolved around Hancock's fictional home of "23, Railway Cuttings, East Cheam." At its best, the writing of **Ray Galton** and **Alan Simpson** elevated the situation comedy genre to a series of unique short television plays akin in some ways to the work of **Samuel Beckett**.

HALL, HENRY (1898–1989). Hall was probably the most famous dance band leader in all British radio. He first broadcast in August 1924 with the Gleneagles Hotel Band from Glasgow. He came to the attention of **John Reith** and, in 1932, succeeded **Jack Payne** as leader of the **BBC Dance Orchestra**. Five years later, he went freelance, but his programs remained a staple part of BBC Radio's schedule. His presentation style was somewhat hesitant and diffident, but this only endeared him to audiences all the more. His regular greeting was, "Hello everyone, this *is* Henry Hall speaking," and it may be said that his program, *Henry Hall's Guest Night*, was the first British radio "chat show." Over his career, Hall was in charge of no less than 32 dance bands. His most famous commercial recording was that of "The Teddy Bears Picnic."

HANDLEY, TOMMY (1896–1949). Handley was a greatly loved comedian, who, for his generation, became an institution. Coming from a music hall background, his career was boosted by his first radio appearance in 1924. It was, however, for his work on *It's That Man Again (ITMA)* that he was best remembered, and his fast-moving delivery, together with producer **Ted Kavanagh**'s concept of a show full of running gags and oddball characters, was perfectly suited to the war years and changed radio comedy forever. When Handley died in 1949 of a brain hemorrhage, there was unprecedented national mourning; the **director-general** of the **British Broadcasting Corporation (BBC)**, **William Haley**, broadcast a tribute, and a memorial service was held in St. Paul's Cathedral. Handly's funeral was attended by 10,000 mourners.

HAPPIDROME, THE. A comedy series set in an imaginary variety theater, and broadcast in fact from the Grand Theatre, Llandudno, *The Happidrome* ran through a number of series from 1941–1947, with a "special" final show on 14 November 1947 marking the Silver Jubilee of the **British Broadcasting Corporation (BBC)**. A live transmission on Sunday evenings, it was performed before an audience of war workers and was fronted by a regular trio of characters played by residents Harry Korris, Cecil Frederick, and Robbie Vincent. Around these three, an impressive range of guests from the world of variety would appear. The program's popularity was enormous; the first series, initially intended to run for six episodes, was extended several times and finally lasted for 53 editions. Stage and film spin-offs came out of the format, and a number of records relating to the show were made.

HARDCASTLE, WILLIAM (1918–1975). Hardcastle was a distinguished print journalist for many years prior to the start of his radio career, working both in Great Britain and the United States, rising to the role of editor of the *Daily Mail*. He lost this job in 1963, only to find a new life in radio from 1965 when the new **Home Service** lunchtime news program, *The World at One*, was launched. He quickly adapted to the medium and became the recognizable voice of the program, reveling in the speed and immediacy of radio. Hardcastle brought a new edge to British radio journalism, born of his experience in the United States, and his uncompromising interviewing style—particularly of politicians—was to be of lasting influence. His excessive self-imposed workload led to his premature death, after a stroke, in November 1975. He had presented *The World at One* until within a few days of this event.

HARDING, EDWARD ARCHIBALD (1903–1953). E. A. ("Archie") Harding joined the **British Broadcasting Corporation (BBC)** London station in 1927 as an announcer, and quickly became a member of a group of producers working within the Drama Department, experimenting with new formats. Out of this period of innovation came the concept of narratives conveying aura pictures, utilizing sound words, and music. This was the birth of the radio **feature**, a form that was to preoccupy Harding for the rest of his life.

In 1931, he produced *Crisis in Spain*, the first British example of radio reportage, and the following year, he made the first Christmas Day program linking speakers from various Commonwealth countries. It ended with a message from King George V. As a result, Harding was asked to make a similar program linking European countries. *New Year over Europe*, broadcast on New Year's Eve 1932, created a storm of controversy due to Harding's political approach, when a statement in the program about Polish armaments led to an official protest from the Polish ambassador and a debate in the British Parliament. As a result, Harding was removed to the BBC's headquarters in Manchester.

Harding embraced this three-year period of "exile," and within that time, he established a thriving left-wing Features Department, surrounding himself with new, talented writers committed to making radio a medium for the voice of ordinary people. He recruited **D. G. Bridson**, encouraged **Francis Dillon**, and nurtured the talent of **Wilfred Pickles**, among many others.

In 1936, Harding returned to London to work in the BBC's Staff Training Department, initially as chief instructor, and subsequently as director. After the War, in 1948, he became deputy director in the Drama Department under **Val Gielgud**. He recruited **Louis MacNeice** to the BBC and is represented as "Harrap" in MacNeice's *Autumn Sequel*.

HARDING, GILBERT (1907–1960). Harding was a major figure in 1950s radio, and was the first chairman of *Twenty Questions*. He also hosted *Round Britain Quiz* and, for a time, *The Brains Trust*. His first work for the **British Broadcasting Corporation (BBC)** had been shortly before the war, when, as a skilled linguist, he worked for the **BBC Monitoring Service**. Gilbert Harding had an extremely complex personality, and his persona was irascible and often downright rude. He was fired from *Twenty Questions* after an infamous incident when he presented the program while drunk.

HATCH, DAVID (1939–). Hatch moved from being a member of the anarchic radio comedy show, *I'm Sorry I'll Read That Again*, which ran for nine years from 1964, to become controller of two radio networks. As a member of the Cambridge Footlights, he worked with future stars, such as John Cleese. Hatch joined the **British Broadcasting Corporation (BBC)** in 1964 as a producer. In 1980, he became controller of **Radio 2** and the following year became controller of **Radio 4**. In 1987, he was appointed managing director of BBC Network Radio.

HAVE A GO. This traveling quiz program was one of the most popular UK radio shows of all time, running for 21 years with the same format. At the center was **Wilfred Pickles** and his wife Mabel; they traveled the length and breadth of Britain with their production team, interviewing and questioning members of communities in front of audiences made up from those communities. In so doing, the program was a celebration of everyday people. The main strength was the telling of stories. Beginning in the Northern Region in March 1946, it ran until January 1967, always from a different location, and at its peak it attracted listening audiences of up to 20 million.

HAWKINS, DESMOND (1908–1999). Desmond Hawkins worked for the **British Broadcasting Corporation (BBC)** initially as a freelance writer and producer. He worked with Francis Dillon on *Country Magazine* and was on the staff from 1945 to 1970, primarily in **features**. It was in this capacity that he worked at the receiving end of many of the great contributions from BBC correspondents in the last year of the war, on the nightly program *War Report*. He went on to become head of West Region programs and finally regional controller for the South and West of England, based at Bristol. During this part of his career, he developed wildlife programs and founded the Natural History Unit.

Hawkins was a passionate advocate of the English countryside, literature, and ecology; he was also an expert on the work of the novelist and poet, Thomas Hardy, and became well known for his radio dramatizations of some of Hardy's finest novels. After his retirement, he continued to work as a freelance writer and broadcaster until his death at the age of 90.

HAYES, BRIAN (1937–). Born in Perth, Hayes worked in radio in Western Australia for a number of years before coming to Britain to work for **Capital Radio** in 1973. Between 1976–1990, he was the controversial host of the **London Broadcasting Company's (LBC)** morning **phone-in** program, inspiring many imitations around the UK. He has worked for **Radio 2** and has won many awards for his work, including a number of **Sony Radio Academy Awards**.

HEMSLEY, HARRY (1877–1951). Hemsley was a child impersonator who became most famous for his imaginary "family" of children, Elsie, Winnie, Johnny, and baby Horace—collectively known as the Fortune Family—in the 1930s **Radio Luxembourg** program, **The Ovaltiney's Concert Party**. He was the son of a scenic artist, W. T. Hemsley, and was born in Swindon, Wiltshire. His father's intention was to develop his son in his footsteps, as an artist, but Hemsley took to the stage at a young age and appeared in a number of productions as a child and young adult, including the ill-fated production of Sir Arthur Sullivan's opera *Ivanhoe*. Work as a bass-baritone in a number of concert parties followed, and in 1901, he joined *The Follies*.

It was while working with this troupe that Hemsley developed his child mimicry, and, by 1905, had perfected his act to the degree that he became nationally known with juvenile audiences, appearing regularly at St. George's Hall, London, and on national tours.

Hemsley also developed his inherited artistic talent as a cartoonist, and utilized the skill in a series of spin-off books based on his characters. He first broadcast in 1927 and was a part of the hugely successful *Ovaltineys* radio project from its inception in December 1934. After the war, his radio series included *Old Hearty* (1947) and *Hemsley's Hotel* (1949). He also appeared on television toward the end of his career.

HENRY HALL'S GUEST NIGHT. The program evolved almost accidentally. **Henry Hall** had been in charge of his own program for two years when, in 1934, on the evening of the Oxford/Cambridge boat race, a number of guests joined him in the studio; these included Lupino Lane, **Elsie and Doris Waters**, and Anona Winn. The resulting informality of unscripted conversation relating to social and show business gossip struck a chord with both listeners and staff alike, and when Hall invited his guests to return the following week, effectively the "chat show" was born. The program ran right through the war and finally ended in the late 1950s, by which time it had been broadcast

972 times, and had included some of the greatest variety performers in the world, including Noel Coward, Laurel and Hardy, and Bob Hope. Hall had two theme tunes: to start his program the band played "It's Just the Time for Dancing," while his closing signature was "Here's to the Next Time."

HENRY, STUART (1942–1995). Having trained first as an actor, Stuart Henry came to radio in 1965, at the height of the **pirate radio** boom, working as a **disc jockey** for **Radio Scotland** and broadcasting from a converted lightship off the Scottish coast. Because of his severe seasickness, he was permitted to record his programs on land, enabling him to develop personal appearances at Scottish dance halls. He was among the first intake of **Radio 1** presenters in 1967 and became best known for his Saturday show; his unique style, quiet, with a gentle Scottish brogue, was in direct contrast to the louder mid-Atlantic style of some of his contemporaries. In 1974, he moved to **Radio Luxembourg**, settling in the country with his wife, Ollie. Shortly, however, he began showing the first symptoms of multiple sclerosis, including a slurring of his speech, which ultimately made it impossible for him to continue broadcasting. He spent his last years campaigning for MS research, and cowrote a book, *Pirate Radio, Then and Now*. He died at his Luxembourg home in November 1995.

HIBBERD, STUART (1893–1983). After a military career, this well-known **announcer** joined the **British Broadcasting Company (BBC)** on its second anniversary, 13 November 1924, becoming chief announcer four years later. He was at the microphone for many historic events, including the **General Strike**, when he broadcast bulletins that sometimes lasted for an hour. He announced the news of the death of Adolf Hitler, and nine years earlier, had created his most memorable phrase when reporting the impending death of King George V in 1936: "The King's life is drawing peacefully to its close." He was also remembered for his close-down announcement: "Goodnight everybody . . . Goodnight." He explained when asked that the pause was to permit the listener to respond. Another of his well-known phrases, "This—is London," became the title of his autobiography. He retired from the BBC in 1951 but continued to broadcast on certain programs for a time.

HILL, CHARLES (1904–1989). Charles Hill, Lord Hill of Luton was a medical doctor and was well known to listeners from 1942 to 1950 as "The Radio Doctor." He became an MP for Luton and held a number of posts in both the House of Commons and the House of Lords, including that of postmaster general at the time of the Suez Crisis, when he was in conflict with the **British Broadcasting Corporation (BBC)**. Later, as chairman of the Independent Television Authority (ITA), he was at times openly hostile to the BBC. Thus, his appointment as BBC **chairman** in 1967 came as a shock to many, and a number of the Board of Governors resigned in protest. As chairman, he was encouraged by the then prime minister, Harold Wilson, to take an active role in editorial decisions. This frequently brought him into conflict with Hugh Greene as **director-general**. He retired in 1972.

HILL, TREVOR (1925–). Born in Southampton, Trevor Hill joined the **British Broadcasting Corporation (BBC)** in 1942 as a sound effects assistant on *It's That Man Again (ITMA)*. From then on, Hill worked as a writer, producer, and director and with his wife, the author Margaret Potter, was strongly involved with the production of *Children's Hour*. In his career, he was involved with drama and **features**, as well as producing such programs as *Round Britain Quiz* and *Transatlantic Quiz*. His final staff post in the BBC was that of assistant head of BBC Network Radio, from which he retired in 1983. However, he remained an active freelance broadcaster, and in 1998 and 2001, he made two feature series, broadcast by the **British Forces Broadcasting Service (BFBS)**, in which listeners in England and Germany were taken back to the days of wartime broadcasting in both countries. In 2005, he published a memoir, *Over the Airwaves*.

HITCHHIKER'S GUIDE TO THE GALAXY. This unique comedy drama **series** created from the writing of **Douglas Adams** gained a cult following on **Radio 4** from the time of the first series in 1978. It later transferred to television, formed the basis for a series of novels, and became a feature film. Radio, however, remained its true home, and in its early years the program fused skillful writing with technical sound innovation (created by Paddy Kingsland of the **BBC Radiophonic Workshop**) in a way that pushed back the boundaries of radio comedy. The parodying of everyday "little English" values and petty bureaucracy, set within a cosmic context, was central to the show's continuing success. It was revived in 2004 and 2005 in its original radio form. A feature film based on the program was also made.

HOFFNUNG, GERARD (1925–1959). This German-born eccentric, raconteur, artist, writer, and musician came to the attention of producer **Ian Messiter** in 1951, who enlisted him as a member of the team for his new series, *One Minute Please* (which later became *Just a Minute*). Hoffnung, although only 34 when he died of a brain hemorrhage, looked and sounded much older, and this quality, together with his original wit, made him a unique radio personality. His most famous creation was *The Bricklayer's Story*, supposedly built on a genuine letter to a builder's trade press journal, which the BBC recorded in 1958 during a presentation by Hoffnung to the Oxford Union. It was later commercially issued on records and cassettes.

HOME SERVICE. Prior to the outbreak of World War II, **British Broadcasting Corporation (BBC)** radio services consisted of two networks, the **National Programme** and the **Regional Programme**. On Friday, 1 September 1939, two days prior to the declaration of war, these were merged into one and called the Home Service. From 7 January 1940, with the creation of the **Forces Programme**, the name acquired a new significance for listeners. Also at this time, many of the lighter programs were transferred to the Forces Programme; this was to pave the way for the postwar establishment of the **Light Programme**. With the reorganization of radio services under **Frank Gillard** in September 1967, the Home Service was renamed **Radio 4**.

HORLICKS PICTURE HOUSE. This major weekly variety **series** began on **Radio Luxembourg** in April 1937 and ran for over 200 editions. A one-hour program, it attracted the greatest stars of its time and was prerecorded at the Scala Theatre in London. The film star Jessie Matthews featured in its first transmission, Maurice Chevalier in the second, and Richard Tauber in the third. The producer was Stanley Maxted.

HORNE, KENNETH (1907–1969). A Cambridge University graduate, Horne began in the retail trade, selling safety glass, but gained his first major radio opportunity in the service **series**, *Ack-Ack Beer-Beer*. He then linked with **Richard Murdoch** for the long-running comedy series *Much-Binding-in-the-Marsh*. He returned to his work in senior business management after the war and continued there until he suffered a severe stroke. From his recovery onward, he devoted himself to radio comedy. After the dismissal of **Gilbert Harding** from *Twenty Questions*, he assumed the role of chairman. His respectable, avuncular style was exploited to its greatest effect in the two comedy programs for which he is most remembered, *Beyond Our Ken* and *Round the Horne*.

HOUSEWIVES' CHOICE. This record request program began in 1946 on the **Light Programme** and ran until shortly before the launch of **Radios 1** and **2** in 1967. It was created by the Light Programme's first controller, **Norman Collins**. In its heyday, the 1950s, it was immensely popular in its morning transmission slot of 9:10 a.m., and within two months of its first broadcast was receiving 4,000 requests a week. It caught the mood of postwar Britain, with its theme tune, "In Party Mood," and its range of presenters, each of whom took charge of the program for two weeks at a time. These included Godfrey Winn, **Gilbert Harding**, **Sam Costa**, and **Eamonn Andrews**.

HOWARD, GEORGE (1920–1984). Lord Howard of Henderskelfe was a long-serving governor of the **British Broadcasting Corporation (BBC)** who was appointed **chairman** in 1980. Nicknamed "Gorgeous George" because of his habit of dressing in caftans, he owned Castle Howard and also chaired the County Landowners' Association. He was a strong defender of the BBC's public service status and its impartiality, particularly during the Falklands War. His relationship with his **director-general**, **Ian Trethowan**, was supportive, and his wide knowledge from the arts to engineering was valuable at a time when content and technology were becoming key issues in the modern media. He retired in 1983 due to ill health.

HOWE, PAMELA (1929–2004). Pamela Howe joined the **British Broadcasting Corporation (BBC)** as a secretary at the age of 18, working in the **Features Department** with writers and producers such as **Laurence Gilliam**, **Francis Dillon**, **Rene Cutforth**, and **Louis Macneice**. This background, together with her own love of literature, colored all her later work, and after her arrival in the BBC West Region, at Bristol in the late 1960s, she concentrated on producing a range of programs reflecting this, including *A Good Read* and her recordings of Martin Jarvis's readings of Richmal Crompton's *Just William* stories.

While working as a producer of a regional edition of ***Woman's Hour***, Howe was sent the manuscript of Winifred Foley's memoir of the Forest of Dean, which she recorded with June Barrie as the reader, provoking huge interest in the story, which was to be published as *A Child in the Forest*, in turn, leading to a best-selling trilogy.

HOWERD, FRANKIE (1917–1992). After an undistinguished prewar career, this much-loved comedian found his niche during World War II as a concert party entertainer, and shortly after the war, due partly to the foresight of **Jack Payne**, Howerd made his first radio appearance in *Variety Bandbox* in December 1946. He became an immediate success with radio audiences, although because of manipulation of contracts by Payne and his agency, for many years, Howerd did not receive appropriate financial gain from his work.

From radio he moved into films, and became a major television star, and after a period of professional failure in the late 1950s and early 1960s, his career revived, and by the end of his life he had become something of an institution for UK audiences, young and old.

HUGHES, DAVID (1831–1900). David Edward Hughes was a British-born inventor who grew up and was educated in the United States. He is best known as the inventor of the carbon microphone, which he invented in 1878. Hughes discovered that a loose contact within a circuit containing a battery and a telephone receiver created the potential for sounds in the receiver, which could match the vibrations on the diaphragm of a telephone or transmitter. His device was crucial to the development of the telephone but also played a part in microphone development for broadcasting during the 1920s.

Hughes also researched the theory of magnetism and in 1857 received a U.S. patent for a telegraph printer. He brought this printer to the UK when he returned to live and work there in 1857, after some years teaching and studying the science of sound at St. Joseph's College, Bardstown, Kentucky. Using his research, he created what was in essence the world's first transmitter at his home in Langham Street, London, just a few yards from where **Broadcasting House** now stands.

HUGHES, RICHARD (1900–1976). Hughes's association with UK radio was brief but important. While at Oriel College, Oxford, immediately after World War I, he began to write—and publish—poetry and plays. In 1924, commissioned by the **British Broadcasting Company (BBC)**, he wrote *Danger*, in response to a request for a piece of drama that could only succeed in a purely sound medium. Produced by Nigel Playfair, it was broadcast from the London station on 15 January of that year.

Thereafter, Hughes abandoned drama, and in a varied career wrote novels, screenplays, histories and worked in academia. His 1929 novel, *A High Wind in Jamaica*, brought him international celebrity.

HUMPHRYS, JOHN (1943–). John Humphrys joined the *Today* program on **Radio 4** in January 1987, and remained as a presenter thereafter, becoming known for his powerful and stringent interrogation of interviewees, particularly politicians, and he has become one of the most respected journalists of the **British Broadcasting Corporation (BBC)**. He had joined the BBC as a reporter based in Liverpool in 1966 and a year later became the BBC's northern industrial correspondent. He moved to London in 1970, and at the age of 28 he became the BBC's youngest ever television correspondent and the BBC's first full-time television correspondent to the United States.

Other television posts followed, including that of news presentation to camera. From 1987, however, he has become mostly associated with the Radio 4 output; in addition to *Today* he has presented *On the Ropes* for the network, in which well-known personalities recalled difficult times in their lives and careers.

HUSSEY, MARMADUKE (1923–). Lord Hussey of North Bradley, Marmaduke Hussey was the only **chairman** of the **British Broadcasting Company/Corporation (BBC)** to sit for two full terms.

Coming from a background in print journalism, he admitted on his appointment in 1986 that he knew nothing about broadcasting. Notwithstanding this, he presided over the dismissal of **Director-General Alastair Milne** and the resignation of **Michael Checkland**. He later came into conflict with **John Birt**, when he disapproved of the latter's style of management. Lord Hussey left the post in 1996.

HUXLEY, JULIAN (1887–1975). The older brother of the novelist, Aldous Huxley, Julian was a zoologist and philosopher who became nationally famous through his radio talks and, in particular, his membership in the successful wartime radio discussion program, *The Brains Trust*. A major figure of his time in the philosophy of science, one of his great skills was as the popularizer of his subject to a mass audience. He was particularly significant as the mentor of the German sound recordist, **Ludwig Koch**, whom he championed on his arrival in Britain in 1936.

– I –

IMPERIAL WIRELESS COMMITTEE (1920). During World War I, it became clear that wireless was an important form of strategic communication. Even prior to this the use of the telegraph had been recognized for business and government (*See also* TELEGRAPH ACTS). After the war, it became increasingly clear that there was an immediate priority to extend this new medium for the uses of business, governmental concerns, and journalism as widely as possible. It was also becoming clear that there was a potential for home entertainment inherent within the medium, which was highly significant, but which relied on the spread of receiver-ownership. In May 1920, Sir Henry Norman was appointed chairman of a committee to examine the possibilities for the creation of an imperial wireless network. Among its findings, the committee stated: "that an Imperial wireless scheme . . . would afford reliable, expeditious and economical communication for commercial, social and press purposes throughout the Empire . . . ." Thus, it might be seen that the concept of an **Empire Service**, later to become the BBC's **World Service**, was present in legislative thinking even prior to the establishment of a domestic broadcasting service.

I'M SORRY I'LL READ THAT AGAIN. This comedy show broadcast on **Radio 2** from 1964–1968 epitomized a sea-change in British humor following the boom in satire in the early part of the decade, in particular, *Beyond the Fringe*. Previously, much radio comedy had grown out of the music-hall tradition and wartime conventions. Coming largely from an Oxbridge review background, notably the Cambridge Footlights, the main cast members of *I'm Sorry I'll Read That Again* purveyed a themeless, anarchic silliness in their quick-fire presentation that caught the mood of the time and even turned its satire onto the **British Broadcasting Corporation (BBC)** itself. The program helped to launch many successful media careers, among them those of John Cleese, Tim Brooke-Taylor, Jo Kendall, Graham Garden, Bill Oddie, and a future **Radio 2** and **Radio 4** controller, **David Hatch**.

I'M SORRY I HAVEN'T A CLUE. Subtitled, "The antidote to panel games," *I'm Sorry I Haven't a Clue,* devised by Graeme Garden, grew out of the comedy show, *I'm Sorry I'll Read That Again*, with all the original panel members—Garden, Bill Oddie, Jo Kendall, and Tim Brooke-Taylor—coming from the latter program. Later, Kendall and Oddie were replaced by Barry Cryer and Willie Rushton. After Rushton's death, the program continued with a variety of guests joining the regulars. Hosted by **Humphrey Lyttelton**, it was first broadcast on 11 April 1972 and has been heard on both **Radio 2** and **Radio 4**. Its appeal is based largely on word play and punning, and the popularity of the program has increased over its existence of more than 30 years. One of its most enduring components is a parody of a board game, "Mornington Crescent," the humor of which is in its impenetrably complex rules. Originally recorded in front of an invited audience in a number of London venues, such as the Playhouse and Westminster Theatres, and the Paris Studios in Lower Regent Street, more recently the program has been taken on the road and tours to regional venues.

INDEPENDENT BROADCASTING AUTHORITY (IBA). When legalized **commercial radio** began in Britain in 1973, regulatory responsibility was placed in the hands of the Independent Broadcasting Authority, a body developed from the Independent Television Authority (ITA). In 1990, it was dissolved, and a radio-specific regulator, the

144 • INDEPENDENT LOCAL RADIO

Radio Authority, was established in its place. The IBA had two directors of radio: **John Thompson** from 1973–1987 and **Peter Baldwin** from 1987–1990, when he became the chief executive of the new authority. The IBA was criticized by many commercial operators for what was seen as the overstringency of its regulatory powers, which at first threatened to stifle development of the new sector. At the same time, this same regulatory rigor produced much imaginative programming on Independent Local Radio (ILR) in its first 17 years.

INDEPENDENT LOCAL RADIO (ILR). *See* COMMERCIAL RADIO.

INDEPENDENT PRODUCTION. In 1994, BBC Radio initiated a commitment to commission a minimum level of 10% of nonnews programs from the independent production sector. Certain networks, such as **Radio 4**, controlled this by setting up an approved supplier list, in order to ensure that only companies with appropriate skills and a known track record of production could offer program ideas at commissioning rounds. The policy of having in-house and independent program makers providing content for **British Broadcasting Corporation (BBC)** networks is one that had previously been introduced in television. Since its inception, the amount of independently produced content on BBC Radio has grown across all networks.

INDEPENDENT RADIO DRAMA PRODUCTIONS (IRDP). Independent Radio Drama Productions, a non-profit-making company formed with the intention of promoting radio drama to expand opportunities for writers coming to the medium for the first time, started in 1987. Run by Tim Crook, Richard Shannon, and Marja Giejgo, the company ran festivals and competitions resulting in the production and broadcast of writers who otherwise would not have had the chance to hear their work on air. IRDP's work was frequently heard in the United States via the National Public Radio (NPR) network, and NPR commissioned a number of original productions, including *The Sherlock Holmes Stories.*

IRDP had a theater subsidiary, On Air Theatre Company, that mounted a number of stage productions in and around London during the 1990s, as well as a U.S. sister organization, the Anglo-

American Radio Drama Company, run by Charles Potter, with Crook and Shannon as vice-presidents. Like IRDP, this company has achieved a number of prestigious commissions from NPR, and continues to develop. Independent Radio Drama Productions supplied a season of drama to **Oneword Radio** in 2003 but subsequently ceased trading in the UK. It has developed the Internet as a means of disseminating its work globally.

INDEPENDENT RADIO NEWS (IRN). Independent Radio News began broadcasting on 8 October 1973, the day that **commercial radio** was officially launched in the United Kingdom. The first bulletins came from basement studios in Gough Square, just off Fleet Street in London, at that time the center of the British national newspaper industry, and IRN's first client was the **London Broadcasting Company (LBC)**. IRN's role, then as now, was to provide a 24-hour service of national and international news to the UK commercial radio network. Initially, it was funded by cash payments from the stations receiving the service, and material was distributed by landline and teleprinter.

The method of funding changed in 1987, when *Newslink* was introduced. This was a system whereby advertising airtime replaced cash payments from stations, thus making the service free to companies receiving it. By the early 1990s, the *Newslink* scheme was so successful that IRN was able to pay its client stations an annual loyalty bonus.

Other innovative developments that have contributed to IRN becoming one of the world's most successful radio news providers have been the introduction of computer technology (in 1985, the switching of distribution from landline to satellite (in 1989), and the introduction of Internet distribution (in 2001).

By 2005, the number of stations taking the IRN service in the UK had risen to almost 300, with a total audience of 26 million listeners.

INMAN, PHILIP (1892–1979). Philip Albert Inman, Lord Inman of Knaresborough, held the post of **chairman** of the **British Broadcastin Corporation (BBC)** for just four months in 1947. Involved with both the medical profession and the church, he was also a member of the Labour Party and resigned shortly after his appointment to take up the post of Lord Privy Seal in the Labour government of Clement Attlee.

INTERNATIONAL BROADCASTING COMPANY (IBC). The purpose of the IBC, established by **Leonard Plugge** in March 1930, was to sell and broadcast sponsored programming to Great Britain from transmission sites on the Continent, thus breaking the BBC's monopoly. This began with **Radio Normandy** in 1931, and the company applied its principles of buying airtime to resell to clients on other stations, including Radio Paris, Radio Rome, Radio Toulouse, Radio Ljubljana, and Radio Côte d'Azur. Initially, headquarters were at 11 Hallam Street, London, adjacent to Broadcasting House, but as the Company gained in financial strength it moved to larger premises in Portland Place. Program information was carried by only one national newspaper, the *Sunday Referee*, due to a boycott of commercial radio stations by the British newspaper industry. This was countered by the establishment of the *IBC Program Sheet* in 1933, and subsequently by the establishment of the more sophisticated **Radio Pictorial** from August 1934 until the outbreak of World War II.

During its existence, the IBC instigated a series of initiatives to develop listenership and create a sense of itself as a truly international organization. Among these was the *IBC Club*, advertised in June 1933 in the newspaper the *Sunday Referee* and—according to its own publicity—attracting a nationwide membership. Other uses of the IBC brand included the "IBC Empire Transmission" from Spain, shortwave transmissions sponsored by Philco All-Wave Radios (*see* EAQ MADRID), and the I. B. C. Yankee Network, a series of transcription programs from WNAC, Boston, and WEAN, Providence. These ran from December 1934–September 1935.

After World War II, despite strenuous but unsuccessful efforts to reestablish its flagship station, Radio Normandy, the IBC was unable to operate as it had previously, but it remained in existence as a production house in one form or another into the 1970s.

IN TOUCH. This weekly **Radio 4** program for the visually impaired began in 1961, and was believed to be the world's only national radio series for the blind. The show's presenters have always been blind themselves, from its first, David Scott Blackhall, to **Peter White**, who also became disability affairs correspondent for the **British Broadcasting Corporation (BBC)**.

The aim of the program is to bring **news**, issues, and **current affairs** topics relating to the blind to as wide an audience as possible. One of the program's great strengths has long been the fact that there is a strong interactive spirit between the production team and the audience, from whom many of the issues that make up the content arise.

IN TOWN TODAY. This program, broadcast on Saturday lunchtimes on the **BBC Light Programme**, was an attempt at preserving the formula that had sustained *In Town Tonight* since 1933 in the face of changing listener habits brought about by the coming of television. The first edition, on 24 September 1960, came exactly one week after its predecessor's final broadcast. A blend of interviews with current personalities and celebrities presented by Nan Winton, Michael Smee, and Tony Bilbow, it ran for more than five years, finally ending in December 1965.

IN TOWN TONIGHT. The program was a significant development in popular UK radio entertainment and broke new ground in its reflection of the "working-class" voice juxtaposed with "star" names of the day. The first edition was broadcast on 18 November 1933 and featured, among many others, Bette Davis. The last program was broadcast on 17 September 1960. One of the key features was its use of outside broadcasting as an integral part of its content. It became a key part of UK Saturday evening radio entertainment for 30 years, with its iconic opening announcement—"Once again we stop the mighty roar of London's traffic"—and its signature tune, "The Knightsbridge March" by Eric Coates.

IPOD. The computer company Apple launched the iPod **MP3** player in 2002. The device quickly became a style icon for the young, at the same time becoming a key part of the download revolution that began to change the music industry significantly. The capability to download songs cheaply, create playlists (effectively the listener's own schedules), and gain control of music consumption forced new thinking among music stations globally. In an extremely short time, executives perceived that programming had the potential to move from a "push" culture (output determined by radio stations and sent to a largely passive audience) to a "pull" culture, whereby listeners selected what they wanted to listen to, and with the aid of such devices as the iPod, could choose to listen when and where they wanted to. *See also* PODCASTING.

IT'S THAT MAN AGAIN (ITMA). *It's That Man Again* was the most popular and well-known radio comedy program of the World War II years and, some would argue, of all time. Created by **Ted Kavanagh** and starring **Tommy Handley**, it took its title from a *Daily Express* headline on Adolf Hitler. It ran for 310 episodes, through many series from July 1939 to January 1949, and captured the heart of the nation with its blend of quick-fire humor and zany characters who became familiar through their regular appearances.

– J –

JACKSON, JACK (1907–1978). Jackson was originally a band leader in the 1930s, with a series on **Radio Luxembourg** sponsored by Oxydol which started in January 1939 and introduced a new style of dance music combined with zany humor. After the war, Jackson turned more to radio record shows, including his highly successful *Record Roundabout*. Produced in his own studio, it was this program that developed his new style of intercutting comedy recordings to make a dialogue between the records; it was highly innovative and predicted the later developments of presenters such as Adrian Juste and **Kenny Everett**. On Radio Luxembourg, after the war, he presented a series of Decca-sponsored music shows. In the late 1960s, he was heard in a highly popular Saturday lunchtime slot on **Radio 1**. It might be said that Jackson was, for some years, the only exponent in Britain of a U.S.-style music presentation.

JACOB, IAN (1899–1993). Sir Ian Jacob, who was **director-general** of the **British Broadcasting Corporation (BBC)** from 1952 to 1959, succeeding **William Haley**, came from an army background, having served as military assistant secretary to the British War Cabinet. In 1946, he was invited by the BBC to run its **European Service**, from which his responsibility extended to the management of all **Overseas Services**. After a period out of the corporation, working at the Ministry of Defence in 1951, he returned as director-general in 1952, with an emphasis on corporate planning rather than direct involvement with programs. He was a popular figure within the BBC.

JACOBS, DAVID (1926–). Jacobs's varied career has included work as a **disc jockey**, actor, and quiz show host. After serving in the Royal Navy from 1944–1947 (during which time he made his first broadcast, in *Navy Mixture*), he joined Radio Seac in Ceylon in 1945 as chief announcer, becoming assistant station director prior to his departure for the **British Broadcasting Corporation (BBC)** Overseas Service in 1947, where he worked as a newsreader before going freelance. He narrated *Journey into Space* as well as contributing a number of small parts to the series. It was, however, as a music presenter that he made his most enduring mark; he hosted numerous programs, including *Housewives' Choice* and *Pick of the Pops*. More recently, he has presented *The David Jacobs Collection* on **Radio 2**. He has been voted "Top DJ" six times, and other radio awards include BBC Radio Personality of the Year (1975) and the Special Sony Award for an Outstanding Contribution to Radio (1984). He has also established himself as a major television personality. Jacobs was awarded the CBE in 1996, and was inducted into the **Radio Academy Hall of Fame** in 2004.

JENNINGS AT SCHOOL. This series of plays came from the pen of a former prep school teacher, **Anthony Buckeridge**, at the suggestion of the *Children's Hour* producer, **David Davis**. Jennings was a young boy in the fictitious "Linbury Court" school, and he and his friend, Darbishire, and their teachers, Mr. Wilkins and Mr. Carter, became household names to British children in the late 1940s and the 1950s. The first program in the first series was broadcast in October 1948. So popular did the series prove that from September 1954 the plays were broadcast in adult schedules as well as in *Children's Hour*. Today, the few extant recordings and their situations might seem anachronistic, given the stories' clearly "upper-class" origins, but in their time they were hugely successful and remain the object of some affectionate memories among the older generation. Among the actors to play the part of Jennings was **Glyn Dearman**, later to become a distinguished **British Broadcasting Corporation (BBC)** radio producer.

JOAD, CYRIL (1891–1953). The philosopher C. E. M. Joad, a scholar of Plato and Aristotle, and one-time head of philosophy at Birkbeck College, University of London, came to popular public attention as a member of the team of thinkers on *The Brains Trust* in 1941. Together with **Julian Huxley** and **Commander A. B. Campbell**, he became a household name, with a distinctive high-pitched voice, and a habitual proviso, presaging everything he said, "It all depends what you mean by . . . ," which became a national catchphrase.

Such was his fame from the program that he became a celebrity, opening bazaars, giving after-dinner speeches, and even advertising tea. His fame lasted until April 1948, when he was convicted of boarding a train from Waterloo without a ticket. He was fined £2.00, but the event reached the press, and he was withdrawn by the BBC from *The Brains Trust.*

JOHNSTON, BRIAN (1912–1994). Johnston joined the **British Broadcasting Corporation (BBC)** in 1946 as a member of the radio **Outside Broadcast** team. From 1948–1952, he had his own outside broadcast feature, *Let's Go Somewhere*, within the magazine program, *In Town Tonight*. He became the BBC's first cricket correspondent in 1963, working initially in television. In 1970, he switched to radio as part of the *Test Match Special* presentation team, and became notable for his gaffes, his rather school-boy interplay with the other presenters, as well as his propensity to "break up" on air. From 1972–1987, in addition, he presented *Down Your Way* on **Radio 4** and was a familiar voice over the years on many outside broadcast commentaries, including the coronation of Queen Elizabeth II and the wedding of Prince Charles and Lady Diana Spencer in 1981. He retired in 1993 and died the following year.

JONES, PETER (1920–2000). Best known to radio audiences for his roles in the *Hitchhiker's Guide to the Galaxy* and *Just a Minute*, Peter Jones joined the theater on leaving school at the age of 16. Over the early years of his career, he established himself as a comedian and writer, costarring with Richard Attenborough in 1952 in his own play, *Sweet Madness*. In the same year, he created a successful radio partnership with **Peter Ustinov** in the series *In All Directions*, a groundbreaking program in its time, using an improvised format at a time when many programs were still strictly scripted. In the 1960s, he became famous to millions of TV viewers in his role as the put-upon factory manager in the sit-com *The Rag Trade*; subsequently, he developed further the somewhat confused persona of this character and built it into his own style, carrying it into his most enduring work, that of an avuncular but permanently bewildered member of the team of *Just a Minute*. As the "Voice of the Book" in the cult series the *Hitchhiker's Guide to the Galaxy*, he reached new audiences and generations. He worked almost to the very end of his life and died after a short illness in April 2000.

JOURNALS. The first broadcasting journals were aimed at the enthusiastic market of amateurs who wished to construct their own crystal sets, through which they could "listen-in" to radio experiments on headphones. As curiosity grew, the number of technical journals proliferated, and the first part of the 1920s saw a large number of weekly papers in circulation with the words "wireless" or "radio" in the title. This phenomenon reached a peak by the autumn of 1924, when the *Wireless Constructor* alone had a circulation of a quarter of a million. Some of those involved in the experiments, such as **Arthur Burrows**, who was then working for the **Marconi Company**, cooperated closely with technical radio magazines such as *Amateur Wireless*, the *Popular Wireless Weekly,* and the *Broadcaster*.

As wireless sets became more complicated something of the tinkering quality that had made radios so attractive to some individuals was lost. The market could not sustain the large number of broadcasting titles, many of which had faded away by 1927. Home-construction no longer required extensive technological knowledge, but could be achieved by buying and assembling a pre-prepared kit; in some cases a screwdriver was even supplied along with the component parts. According to the advertisement, the 1928 *Melody Maker* could be assembled by those with "something less than the average amount of dexterity." Moreover, greater attention was becoming focused on the nature of the material being transmitted. Initially the

British Broadcasting Company (BBC) depended upon the national and local press to advertise its programs, but following a brief boycott, the idea was conceived for the BBC to publish its own journal, and the first number of *The Radio Times*, published by George Newnes Ltd., rolled off the press on 28 September 1923.

In keeping with its heritage from the technical magazines, its pages featured articles explaining wireless technology, and educational items, in addition to program information. It also carried regular columns, including a weekly letter from the company's general manager, **John Reith**, and articles, with photographs, of the broadcasters and artists behind the microphones. Meanwhile, another aspect of radio interest was spreading through the population, that of "distant listening." With careful tuning and patient listening for the stations' identifying call signals, the programs being broadcast by foreign radio stations could be picked up. It became quite a competitive activity, with enthusiasts vying as to whom could pick up the most distant signal. In 1925, the BBC launched its *Radio Supplement*, afterward renamed ***World-Radio***, which listed the program details of foreign radio stations; it, too, included articles for the more technically minded reader.

A third BBC publication, the ***Listener***, was launched in January 1929. The original idea had been to add gravitas to the spoken word by printing some of the more erudite broadcast talks. In fact, the journal soon established its reputation for the high quality of its articles and reviews. In contrast to this "highbrow" publication, ***Radio Pictorial*** began circulation in 2 January 1934. This journal, published by the **International Broadcasting Company (IBC)**, was specifically pitched as a populist magazine. The IBC had set up the journal in response to a government ban on newspapers printing the listings of continental commercial radio stations under pressure from the BBC, which was trying to protect its monopoly from the competition of entrepreneurs buying airtime from European radio stations, and selling it to advertisers. In the event, this competition was defeated by the advent of World War II, which eventually forced the closure of the European stations and put the BBC back at the center of the broadcasting map.

After the end of the war, and with the rise of television, radio-specific journals ceased publication, with *Radio Times* remaining the sole journal to carry radio programs listings alongside an increasingly dominant television section.

JOURNEY INTO SPACE. Written by **Charles Chilton**, the first **series** of the Light Programme's highly successful science fiction **serial** opened on 21 September 1953, with Captain Jet Morgan, played by Andrew Faulds, leading his crew into an adventure that originally was intended to last for no more than eight episodes. In fact, so great was the program's grip on the public imagination that it went through a number of series, finally ending in 1958, by which time it had been translated into 17 languages and broadcast globally. Other characters were "Doc" Matthews (Guy Kingsley-Poynter), "Mitch" Mitchell (Don Sharpe, later David Williams), and Lemmy Barnett (David Kossoff, later Alfie Bass). Other parts were played by **David Jacobs**. It is notable in the history of radio in that it was the last program of its era to attract an audience to the medium larger than that watching television at the same time.

JOYCE, WILLIAM "LORD HAW-HAW" (1906–1946). It is a strange fact of British broadcasting that one of the most remembered and listened-to personalities of the mid-20th century was also one of the most hated and feared of all enemy propagandists of World War II. Born in New York, of Irish descent, but with a forged British passport (his undoing, since because of this he was convicted and executed after the war as a traitor), he joined Oswald Moseley's Blackshirts in the 1930s and formed his own National Socialist League before moving to Germany in 1938. His thin, nasal tones, the sneering quality of his voice, and his trademark call of "Germany Calling, Germany Calling" transfixed British audiences, who tuned in to the broadcasts in vast numbers (at one point 27% of the whole population), as if hypnotized, to hear his uncanny predictions and inside knowledge of what was happening in the country—and where the next strike would fall. It was said that six million listeners tuned in nightly to hear him.

His nickname, "Lord Haw-Haw," was coined by a journalist working on the *Daily Express*, Jonah Barrington, although Barrington's original target for the name was not actually Joyce but another broadcaster altogether. By mid-1940, even German radio was introducing him, using the name. Broadcasting from Hamburg, his transmissions were relayed via **Radio Luxembourg** while the station was held in German hands. Joyce's last broadcast, on 30 April 1945, was slurred by drink. He was hanged for high treason at Wandsworth Prison, London.

JUNIOR CHOICE. When **Radio 1** went on the air on Saturday, 30 September 1967, one of the first programs was *Junior Choice*, the successor to the **Light Programme**'s *Children's Favourites*. Broadcasting on Saturday and Sunday mornings, the first presenter was Leslie Crowther, who was succeeded by **Ed Stewart** in 1968. The program, a record request show, took into account the changing youth music trends that had created Radio 1, and differed from its predecessor in that music was chosen by the program producer for its overall mix, rather than program policy being governed—as previously—by demand and volume of request for specific items. By the time Stewart was succeeded by **Tony Blackburn** in 1979, the show had attained a remarkable audience of—at its height—16 million listeners. In the early 1980s, with audience trends changing and the growth of **Independent Local Radio (ILR)** the program was taken off air.

JUST A MINUTE. Devised by **Ian Messiter** as a successor to *One Minute, Please*, the program revolves around the idea of being able to talk without hesitation or deviation for one minute on a set subject. The four panelists are permitted to challenge one another and, if successful, take up the remaining time on the clock. Panelists have included Clement Freud, Derek Nimmo, **Peter Jones**, Paul Merton, Wendy Richard, and **Kenneth Williams**. When the program began in 1967, producer **David Hatch** originally invited **Jimmy Edwards** to take the role of chair. Edwards was unavailable, and the chairmanship was offered to Nicholas Parsons, who has fulfilled the task ever since.

JUST FANCY. This gentle comedy series was written by **Eric Barker** and performed by him, with Deryck Guyler, Kenneth Connor, and Pearl Hackney. A sketch show that was largely based on

Barker's gift for human observation, it ran from 1951–1962; thus it was almost exactly contemporaneous with the more famous ***The Goon Show***. In its own way, it was equally popular in its time, with similar listening figures, and was quietly revolutionary in its development of radio comedy, notably by the absence of a studio audience.

JUST WILLIAM. A phenomenon of British children's radio postwar, Richmal Crompton's own adaptations from her original stories were first heard in October 1945 and captured the hearts of a generation. "William Brown" was the central character, a naughty but loveable small boy, whose antics and misdemeanors attracted large audiences of children and their parents. The stories had come from a magazine called *Happy Mag*, the earliest dating from 1919. The radio dramatizations continued until 1952, and included actors such as Charles Hawtrey, Anthea Askey (daughter of **Arthur Askey**), Andrew Ray (son of **Ted Ray**), and Patricia Hayes.

From 1986, a new generation was to discover "William" through a series of highly popular readings on **Radio 4** by the actor, Martin Jarvis, which continued until 1990, when the last **series** was simultaneously released as an audio book by the **BBC**, with unprecedented success in terms of commercial sales of the spoken word.

The author, Richmal Crompton (1890–1969) was a classics mistress at a girls' school in Kent, but when she was struck by polio, she devoted herself to writing full time, producing more than 400 *Just William* stories.

J. WALTER THOMPSON ORGANIZATION. This major United States advertising agency was a crucial part of the development of prewar commercial radio in Great Britain. Having learned from its American experience, it set up the first purpose-built radio studio for commercial radio in Britain. The Ariel Studio, in **Bush House**, was highly sophisticated, and used the **Philips-Miller** system of recording on film. At its peak, in 1938, the unit was run by a staff of 40, producing 44 programs a week to be shipped to continental stations, including **Radio Luxembourg** and **Radio Normandy**, for transmission back to the United Kingdom.

– K –

KALEIDOSCOPE. This daily arts magazine program began in 1973. Conceived by **Radio 4** controller, **Tony Whitby**, the original premise was to provide a spectrum for both arts and sciences, but this proved a failure and science devolved to a new strand entitled *Science Now*. Until the program was removed in 1997 by the then controller, **James Boyle**, it remained an arts-only strand, moving through a series of formats and incarnations. The last of these utilized a series of presenters, identified with a particular day and specialty, with a "live" afternoon transmission and an evening edited repeat. There was also the addition of a weekly *Kaleidoscope Feature*, a half-hour **feature** program on a specific topic.

KALEIDOSCOPE 1. This gigantic radio experiment was broadcast by the **British Broadcasting Corporation (BBC)** in 1929. Produced "live" in eight studios by **Lance Sieveking** and utilizing more than 100 performers, it was described by *The Radio Times* as "a play too purely radio to be printed for reading." It represented the life of man from the cradle to the grave.

KAVANAGH, TED (1892–1958). New Zealand-born Kavanagh was a significant figure in the development of radio comedy, understanding as few had done before him the nature of the medium in relation to comic writing. He began working with **Tommy Handley** in the 1920s, but it was their collaboration on the series *It's That Man Again (ITMA)*, considered by many to have been the most popular radio comedy show ever broadcast, that both men are principally remembered. The combination of Kavanagh's writing and Handley's comic timing made the show one of the great radio memories for a generation of listeners.

KEILLOR, GARRISON (1942–). Keillor began his broadcasting career on Minnesota Public Radio in 1968 as a presenter on a morning classical music program. It was from 1974 that he developed his most famous show, the live *Prairie Home Companion*, and out of his warm, quiet melancholic humor came a series of books, such as *Lake Wobegon Days* and *Leaving Home*, which introduced him to British audiences through readings on **Radio 4** from 1986. It was thus radio that launched his work as an author in Britain and his Radio 4 readings were all subsequently issued commercially by the **British Broadcasting Corporation (BBC)**. When the Corporation launched its digital speech station, **BBC 7**, in the fall of 2002, British audiences were also able to listen for the first time to *The Prairie Home Companion*.

KEITH, ALAN (1908–2003). Born Alec Kossoff in 1908, he changed his name to Alan Keith in the 1920s while studying at the Royal Academy of Dramatic Art. He was the brother of the actor David Kossoff and the uncle of the rock guitarist, Paul Kossoff. His radio career began in 1935 as a variety show MC and an interviewer on *In Town Tonight*. He was always most associated with the program of his own devising, *Your Hundred Best Tunes*, which he presented from 1959 until his death. He had announced that the program broadcast on 30 March 2003 would be his last. Between recording it and transmission, he died, at the age of 94. By way of a tribute, **Radio 2** broadcast the program as planned.

KISS FM. This purveyor of dance music started its life as a **pirate** unlicensed station, and from its beginnings in 1985 to 1988 it became something of a cult. Founded by London club **disc jockey** Gordon McNamee and entrepreneur George Eracleous, it finally closed down as a pirate in 1988, only to apply successfully for one of the new **incremental licenses** then being offered by the **Independent Broadcasting Authority (IBA)**. Supported by **Virgin** and **Emap**, it continued its policy of broadcasting club-based music, but this time legally. Now part of the Emap group's raft of stations, it is available far beyond its original London base over wide parts of Britain via **digital multiplexes**.

KERSHAW, ANDY (1959–). Kershaw is known for his love and fostering of world music. A broadcaster of **Radio 1** and subsequently **Radio 3**, his music shows champion work that would find it hard to gain a hearing elsewhere. Kershaw is notable, however, for his active interest in the cultures from which the music springs, and he has made documentary features that examine, for example, issues and problems in West Africa. Significant among these was a three-part series he made in 1989 in Mali for **Radio 4**.

KOCH, LUDWIG (1881–1974). Born in Frankfurt am Main, Germany, Ludwig Koch was to become one of the most significant figures in the sound recording of the natural world. Before World War I, he was a developing musical talent and was a successful concert singer. With the outbreak of war in 1914, he worked in German military intelligence and remained with the German government until 1925, when he resumed his musical career; from 1928, he worked for the German subsidiary of Electrical and Musical Industries (EMI).

As a child, Koch had been given an Edison phonograph recorder and some cylinders, which he had used to record the sounds of family pets. In his new post he returned to this enthusiasm, using state-of-the-art equipment to make wildlife recordings. He developed the idea of "sound books," the inclusion of sound recordings within conventional illustrated books on animals. With the coming of the Nazi regime, Koch, a Jew, came to Britain, where, in 1936, ornithologists encouraged him to participate in a sound book on British birds. By the end of 1936, *Songs of Wild Birds* was published, followed by two other sound books.

One of Koch's mentors in the UK was **Julian Huxley**, who suggested, early in World War II, that Koch should offer his services to the **British Broadcasting Corporation (BBC)**. By the end of the war, his voice was a familiar part of radio programming, and from 1946 he became an integral part of the growth of natural history programs from the BBC's west regional center in Bristol.

In 1948, the BBC purchased his private collection of animal recordings, at which time, he joined the staff and continued to record on location and to broadcast in his distinctive manner, retaining a strong German accent that became instantly recognizable to British listeners during the 1940s and 1950s. His collection is now housed at the British Library Sound Archive. He is rightly credited for bringing the true sounds of the countryside to radio, which had, hitherto, been limited by studio-bound discussions on the subject. He was awarded the MBE in 1960.

– L –

LASER 558. This popular **pirate** station operated for a few years off the Essex coast from the motor vessel (MV) *Communicator*. The station was American owned and staffed by U.S. **disc jockeys**. The station came off air after severe storms and **Department of Trade and Industry (DTI)**-based blockades in November 1985. In its short life, it highlighted the fact that the bland **Independent Broadcasting Authority (IBA)** version of Independent Local Radio had failed to replace the excitement in music-radio provided by the 1960s pirates. Ultimately, another station that began operations at about the time Laser came off air, **Kiss FM**, was to provide a groundswell of pressure from popular listener support to actually gain legal status.

LAUGH AND GROW FIT. Hailed as the first daily on-air keep-fit program on radio, *Laugh and Grow Fit* was broadcast on **Radio Normandy** during 1937 and 1938. Devised and presented by the Northern comedian Joe Murgatroyd, accompanied at the piano by his wife, "Poppet," the 15-minute programs went out—usually live—at 7:45 a.m. on weekday mornings and consisted of a series of jokes and exercises to music.

LEAGUE OF OVALTINEYS. This was the radio club linked to the *Ovaltineys Concert Party*, which began on **Radio Luxembourg** in February 1935. Children joining the club received a badge, rulebook, and details of the Ovaltineys' code, which enabled them to interprete "secret" messages on the program each week.

LETTER FROM AMERICA. This weekly 15-minute talk was broadcast to **British Broadcasting Corporation (BBC)** listeners from 1946 until the death in 2003 of the broadcaster with whom it was inextricably associated, **Alastair Cooke**. Originally called *American Letter*, the program was a reflection of **current affairs** in the United States, interpreted from a personal standpoint by Cooke. The elegance of his prose style and the intimate presentation gave the program a quality that ensured its longevity for approximately 3,000 editions, heard in 52 countries, worldwide. Many of the broadcasts have, by their very nature, become historical documents, responding as they do to some of the most significant moments in U.S. and world history but with the eye of an interested observer and chronicler. Cooke's *Letters* gave many outside America a view of great issues and events beyond the journalistic angle of the news reporter, including John F. Kennedy's assassination, Watergate, the Clinton impeachment hearings, and the attack on the World Trade Center. Since Cooke's death, a selection has appeared in book form.

LEVIS, CARROLL (1910–1968). Associated with prewar **British Broadcasting Corporation (BBC)** and **Radio Luxembourg** amateur talent shows, Carroll Levis had achieved a successful radio career in his native Canada, prior to his arrival in Great Britain in 1935. He toured the country, auditioning hopeful entertainers, choosing the best of them to appear on his program, *Carroll Levis Discoveries*. After the war, he continued with the broadcasts, but a mental breakdown resulted in his temporary return to Canada in 1947.

In 1950, Levis had resumed his touring talent shows, but with an unsuccessful lawsuit brought by **Hughie Green** against Levis and the BBC over an alleged conspiracy to keep Green's own talent show, *Opportunity Knocks*, off the air, Levis's career began to decline. He had moved into television by this time, but after November 1959, he did not broadcast. Despite numerous attempts at relaunching his career, he died, financially impoverished in obscurity in London.

LEWIS, CECIL (1898–1997). In a long and remarkable life, Cecil Lewis made his mark in many areas of entertainment, including work in Hollywood as a script writer, where he won an Oscar for his screenplay of *Pygmalion*. It is, however, as one of the founding fathers of the **British Broadcasting Company (BBC)** that he is widely remembered in Great Britain. After winning the Military Cross for his work as a pilot in World War I, he joined the staff of the engineering firm, Metropolitan Vickers. In the early 1920s, this company became one of a consortium seeking to launch broadcasting in Britain, and thus Lewis became the partner of **John Reith** in the foundation of the British Broadcasting Company, as program manager.

Lewis mounted the first plays to be heard on radio, and also produced the early broadcasts of *Children's Hour*, in which he appeared as "Uncle Caractacus." Lewis spent only four years with the BBC, resigning in 1926 because his artistic nature baulked at the growing bureaucracy within the organization. He wrote one of the first books on the subject of radio, *Broadcasting from Within*, which was published in 1924.

After working as a flight instructor in World War II, Lewis came under the influence of the ideas of the Russian mystic, George Gurdjieff, and set up a farming community in South Africa to preserve the philosopher's ideas. Thereafter, he worked as a radio producer for the United Nations and then briefly for Associated Rediffusion at the time of the launch of commercial television in the UK. Beginning in from 1956, he became involved as the organizer of the *Daily Mail*'s Ideal Home Exhibition.

Lewis spent the last years of an extraordinary life on the island of Corfu and continued to write books and plays. He married three times and died in London in January 1997, two months short of his 99th birthday.

LICENSE FEE. From its foundation, the license fee has been the mainstay of **British Broadcasting Company/Corporation (BBC)** finance. The system was introduced on 1 November 1922, set at a price of 10 shillings. The fee remained unchanged until 1946 when it was doubled to one pound. With the advent of television, the license was combined for both media, rising in 1965 again to 25 shillings. In 1971, a television-only license was introduced, and from that time onward radio in the UK has been license free for consumers. Apart from its value as revenue, the compulsory license fee offered a very useful measurement of the potential total audience for radio, particularly prior to the introduction of a systematic listener research unit in 1936.

LIDDELL, ALVAR (1908–1981). Coming from a Swedish background, nevertheless this **British Broadcasting Corporation (BBC)** announcer was the on-air epitome of "received" pronunciation. Beginning his career as a singer, he joined the corporation in 1932. It was Liddell who was present at the microphone to announce or introduce some of the most significant moments of UK—and world—history, such as the abdication of King Edward VIII and Neville

Chamberlain's broadcast of 3 September 1939 informing the nation that war had been declared. He retired in 1969.

LIFE WITH THE LYONS. First broadcast on the **Light Programme** in November 1950, this highly successful family situation comedy show starred American husband and wife Ben Lyon and Bebe Daniels (billed as "Hollywood's happiest married couple") and their real-life offspring, Richard and Barbara. Owing something to the quick-fire style of George Burns and Gracie Allen, the show was written by Bebe and revolved around fictional situations in the bringing up of their children. The show ran through 10 series, produced the spin-offs of two films (1953 and 1954) and a book of recipes by Molly Weir, who played the family's housekeeper, Aggie MacDonald, finally ending its last run in May 1961. Also between 1955 and 1961 were three television versions.

LIGHT PROGRAMME. With the coming of World War II, and the creation of the **Forces Programme**, the **British Broadcasting Corporation (BBC)** had taken a major step toward streaming of radio output, with the transfer of "light" entertainment into predominantly one network, with other material carried by the **Home Service**. After the war, the latter service continued, and the Forces Programme, which, with its successor, the **Allied Expeditionary Force (AEF) Programme**, had proved hugely popular with domestic listeners, was transformed into the new Light Programme. The change came on 29 July 1945, with a broadcast of music from the BBC Theatre Organ, played by **Sandy Macpherson**. On 30 September 1967, the Light Programme became **Radio 2**.

THE LISTENER. The second weekly journal established by the **British Broadcasting Corporation (BBC)** after *The Radio Times* was launched in January 1929, it had the aim of "capturing the fugitive word in print." Initially a medium for transcriptions of broadcast talks, it expanded to become a respected journal containing reviews and general **features**. One of its original acknowledged aims was to "promote the BBC's work in adult education, by linking up the interests of the occasional listener with those of the serious, regular student." In its lifetime, it had some distinguished editors, including

Richard Lambert (1929–1939), Anthony Howard (1979–1981), and Alan Coren (1987–1989). From a circulation peak of 150,000 in the early 1950s, it gradually declined until 1990 when it was selling a mere 17,000 copies a week. With losses amounting to £1 million a year by this time, the BBC decided to close it down, and the last issue was in January 1991.

Reporting its 10th anniversary celebration in January 1939, the **BBC Handbook** for 1940 quoted one critic as saying that it would be "invaluable to the historian as a guide to the multiple and changing interests and tastes of the age." This view remains today an accurate assessment of the magazine's legacy. *See also* JOURNALS.

LISTENING IN (1). Although not broadcast itself, this stage show is noteworthy in that it was the first of its kind based on the new medium of radio. Billed as a "Musical Burlesque in Fifteen Radio Calls," *Listening In* opened in London in July 1922, with Will Hay as "Professor Broadcaster."

"LISTENING IN" (2). As will be seen from the above, "Listening In" was the common phrase used to denote the act of experiencing radio programs in the first years of the new medium. **John Reith** disliked the phrase, as implying some form of eavesdropping, and in his early book *Broadcast Over Britain* (1924), went out of his way to denounce this "objectionable habit," writing:

> This is a relic of the days when he actually did listen in to messages not primarily intended for him; now he is the one addressed, and he accordingly listens. Only the unlicenced listen-in.

LISTEN WITH MOTHER. This much-loved program for the under-fives began in January 1950. A 15-minute mix of stories, songs, and nursery rhymes set to music by Ann Driver, it was broadcast originally—and for many years—at 1:45 p.m., prior to **Woman's Hour**. Its presenters were Daphne Oxenford and Julia Lang, although for the last seven years of its life they were replaced by Nerys Hughes and Tony Aitken. For several generations of small children, its theme tune—the Berceuse from Gabriel Fauré's *Dolly Suite* and its traditional opening words, "Are you sitting comfortably? then I'll begin . . ." became iconic, and there was a national outcry when, in

September 1982, the program was taken off air, having already been transferred to a less-effective morning place in the schedule, resulting in reduced listening figures.

LOCAL RADIO. Historically, UK radio has always been firmly rooted in localness and regionality. The first **British Broadcasting Company (BBC)** stations created between 1922 and 1924 were essentially local, born out the limitations of transmitter power at the time.

The concept of a network of **British Broadcasting Corporation (BBC)** local radio stations, which began in 1967 with the establishment of **Radio Leicester** began as an experiment initiated by the then director of BBC Radio, **Frank Gillard**. Gillard had conceived the idea after a visit in the 1950s to the United States but determined that the BBC model would be strongly speech and community-based. Initially, stations were closely involved with local authorities who even partly funded the experiment in its early days.

Over the years, BBC local radio has been at the forefront of a number of funding crises, and threats of closure have occasionally arisen. By 2005, however, the network of 40 stations, grouped in 11 regions, was in a strong position, and audiences were loyal, largely from a 55+ demographic. Added to this, a number of ethnic inner city stations reflected the growing multicultural nature of the UK. BBC local radio increasingly sought to play proactive roles in their communities, in many cases working to a policy of developed interactivity with audiences, working in and with those communities rather than limiting their involvement to that of the traditional broadcaster/listener relationship.

In October 1973, **Independent Local Radio (ILR)** began with the establishment of the **London Broadcasting Company (LBC)** and **Capital Radio**, and for nearly 20 years **commercial radio** in Britain developed on a purely local basis, initially with a strong community base founded on a public service ethic (hence the early insistence on the use of the term "independent" rather than "commercial" radio). As the digital revolution of the late 1990s and early 21st century gained momentum, local multiplexes developed alongside their national equivalents, providing opportunities for new digital-only local stations.

Concurrent with this came the movement toward another tier of local broadcasting in the form of **community radio,** which developed out of a limited experiment, with the first full **licenses** being granted in the spring and early summer of 2005.

THE LOCAL RADIO COMPANY. In May 2004, the Local Radio Company was formed to purchase the complete share capital of Radio Investments, a long-time investor in UK **commercial radio.** Radio Investments had been a share holder in **Capital Radio** in 1973. Since that time, the company specialized in the development of local stations, and the new company, based in High Wycombe, came into control of 26 radio stations, with a wide geographical spread of Britain, from Falkirk in Scotland to the Isle of Wight. In 2005, a 27th station was added to the roster of the Local Radio Company in the form of Durham FM. The company also runs First Radio Sales, selling advertising to local stations across the country.

LODGE, OLIVER (1851–1940). The eminent English physicist, born in Penkull, Staffordshire, studied at the Royal College of Science and University College, London, becoming in 1881 professor of physics at Liverpool University. In 1900, he was appointed first principal of Birmingham University and was knighted in 1902. Especially distinguished for his work with electricity, he was a pioneer of wireless telegraphy. In 1894, he demonstrated wireless telegraphy across more than 50 yards to the British Association. He established the importance of tuning to wireless communications and patented a circuit for this purpose in 1897. Unfortunately, he dismissed the possibilities and did not pursue his research in the area. Nevertheless, he received the Albert Medal for his work from the Royal Society of Arts in 1919. Lodge was a frequent and popular broadcaster of talks, and became interested in psychical research and communication with the spirit world, seeking to bring science and religion together. Among his writings on the subject of wireless are *Signalling across Space without Wires* (1897) and *Talks about Wireless* (1925).

LONDON BROADCASTING COMPANY (LBC). First heard on 8 October 1973, LBC was the UK's first legal land-based **commercial radio** station. Initially, the station weathered troubled times both in terms of finance and listenership, and has, over its subsequent existence, been the subject of a number of takeovers, reinventions, and franchise renewals. Closely connected in its initial incarnation with **Independent Radio News**, in the early 21st century, it was bought by the **Chrysalis** Group, which invested heavily in high profile presenters in its relaunch of the station. Apart from the continuity of its name, LBC remains what it was when commercial radio began in Britain, committed to—and licensed to provide—an all-speech program format.

LONG, NORMAN (1893–1951). Long was a musical comedian, whose act revolved around semisung monologues to his own piano accompaniment. His significance was that, having been first heard on the opening evening of transmissions from both **Marconi House** and **Savoy Hill**, he could claim to be the first comic whose reputation was created principally by the medium of radio. He also took part in the first Royal Command Performance to be broadcast (1927).

Long later appeared on commercial stations, including **Radio Luxembourg**, and many of his routines used radio as their subject, including "London and Daventry Calling" (1926), "Luxembourg Calling" (1935), and his satire on **British Broadcasting Corporation (BBC)** censorship, "We Can't Let You Broadcast That" (1933). He retired after World War II, and ran a hotel in Salcombe, Devon, until his death.

LONGWAVE. The term is an archaic one, still used to describe the section of the radio spectrum used in broadcasting around the 1500 meters wavelength. Like **mediumwave (MW)**, its transmitters utilize **amplitude modulation (AM)**. Longwave (LW)'s advantage over mediumwave is that its ground wave is capable of greater distance than the higher frequencies employed in MW transmissions. It has also been of value in the past due to its capacity for being receivable on the most rudimentary of radio sets.

LONG MARCH OF EVERYMAN. Broadcast from November 1971 on **Radio 4**, over six months, this epic series of 26 programs, each lasting 45 minutes, was the most ambitious social history project ever mounted by **British Broadcasting Company/Corporation (BBC)** radio. Produced by Michael Mason, a vast cast of historians contributed, and there was a major sonic contribution by the **BBC Radiophonic Workshop**. The then managing-director of BBC Radio, **Ian Trethowan**, was a great advocate of the series, describing it as "a demonstration of faith that radio continues to be as effective in imaginative broadcasting as it is on all sides acknowledged to be in the fields of music and of news."

LORD HAW HAW. *See* JOYCE, WILLIAM.

LORD OF THE RINGS. First broadcast in 1981 on **Radio 4**, this ambitious and highly successful adaptation of the J. R. R. Tolkien epic was created by Brian Sibley and Michael Bakewell. In its original form, it was broadcast in 26 episodes, later repeated twice—in 1982 and 2002, in 13 hour-long episodes. The **British Broadcasting Corporation (BBC)** also issued the broadcast commercially. The production contained many major personalities from the theater, including Ian Holm, Michael Hordern, and Robert Stephens.

LUX RADIO THEATRE. First heard by UK audiences from **Radio Luxembourg** in 1938, the program was broadcast on Sundays to large audiences. The great London theater producer C. B. Cochran took over the show and it became a vehicle for some of the major stars of the time, among them Flanagan and Allen, Beatrice Lillie, Jessie Matthews, and Elsie Randolph.

LYNN, VERA (1917–). Vera Lynn made her first broadcast in 1935 with the Joe Loss Orchestra, but her career was made by her role in radio during World War II. Working with producer Howard Thomas, she hosted the radio series *Sincerely Yours* in November 1941, in which she read dedications and messages for those in the armed forces from loved ones at home. This, together with songs such as "We'll Meet Again" and "The White Cliffs of Dover," established her as a major star, and earned her the popular title of "The Forces' Sweetheart." After the war, she continued in radio and television, including a 1951 series for **Radio Luxembourg**, *Vera Lynn Sings*.

She was the first British artist to reach the top of the U.S. charts with her song, "Auf Wiedersehn Sweetheart." She remained a much-loved symbol for a whole generation, and played a major part in the broadcast celebrations marking the 60th anniversary of the end of World War II, in 2005. She received an OBE in 1969, and a Damehood in 1975.

LYTTELTON, HUMPHREY (1921–). Educated at Eton College and Camberwell School of Art, Lyttelton saw war service from 1941–1946 in the Grenadier Guards. During this time he became proficient on the trumpet and in 1947 joined George Webb's Dixielanders. The following year, he formed his own band and signed to Parlophone Records in 1949. In that same year, partnered by clarinetist Wally Fawkes ("Trog"), he founded the *Daily Mail* cartoon strip, *Flook*, a project he continued to work on until 1953. In 1956, his band supported Louis Armstrong in London, and produced the first British jazz record to become a hit, *Bad Penny Blues*. At the same time, Lyttelton developed other career strands, including radio. From 1967, he hosted **Radio 2**'s *Best of Jazz* and in 1972, commenced hosting the comedy radio series, *I'm Sorry I Haven't a Clue*.

– M –

MACCOLL, EWAN (1915–1989). This songwriter, singer, and writer was born in Lancashire as Jimmy Miller. As a young man, he joined the Communist Party, a member of which he remained until 1960, and through the 1930s he worked on experimental theater projects with Joan Littlewood, whom he later married. He appeared—as Jimmy Miller—in some of the Manchester radio features under the aegis of **E. A. Harding** during the 1930s. He was married three times in his life, ultimately to Peggy Seeger; in the late 1950s, they collaborated with **Charles Parker** on the creation of the **Radio Ballads**, fusing song, location actuality, and the spoken word to create a new form of radio **feature**.

MACGREGOR, SUE (1941–). Raised in South Africa, Sue MacGregor trained as a reporter on *The World at One* before presenting *Woman's Hour* from 1972–1987, when she joined the *Today* program, where she stayed for more than 17 years, becoming the program's longest-serving presenter when she left in 2002. She was awarded the CBE in 2002 for services to broadcasting. *See also* WOMEN.

MACKENZIE, KELVIN (1946–). From 1998–2005, Kelvin Mackenzie was chairman and chief executive of the **Wireless Group** and the owner of **TalkSport** and 13 regional and local radio stations in Britain. A former editor of the *Sun* newspaper, Mackenzie has always been a controversial media figure, and in 2003, launched an unsuccessful attempt at suing the **Radio Joint Audience Research (RAJAR)** organization jointly owned by the **British Broadcasting Corporation (BBC)** and the **Commercial Radio Companies' Association (CRCA)** for allegedly operating an audience measurement system that was corrupt, which, he claimed underestimated TalkSport's reach. He also sought to change the method of measurement from that of diaries to electronic monitoring. The sale of the Wireless Group to Ulster Television in May 2005 was said to have profited Mackenzie personally by approximately £6 million.

MACNEICE, LOUIS (1907–1963). Distinguished as a poet, MacNeice worked for the **British Broadcasting Corporation (BBC)** from 1940, producing many remarkable radio **features**, initially created out of his own writing in support of the war effort. Of these, the most important were *Alexander Nevsky* (1941) based on the film by Serge Eisenstein, and *Christopher Columbus* (1942), which marked the 450th anniversary of the crossing to America. This featured Laurence Olivier in the title role and an original score by William Walton.

Postwar, MacNeice's most famous work was the poetic drama, *The Dark Tower*, which was first heard on the **Home Service** in January 1946, with a second production in 1956, starring Richard Burton. The work was an allegory concerning fate and free will, and the title was taken from the poem by Robert Browning, *Childe Roland to the Dark Tower Came*.

MACPHERSON, SANDY (1897–1975). Real name, Roderick Hallowell Macpherson. Originally the organist of the Empire Cinema, Leicester Square, and succeeding **Reginald Foort** as **British Broadcasting Corporation (BBC)** staff organist in 1938, the quiet Canadian tones of his presentation endeared him to millions. He was born in Paris, Ontario, he served in the Canadian Forces in World War I, and thereafter he worked as a cinema pianist before working as an organist on the Loew circuit. In 1928, he came to London and began his 10-year tenure at Leicester Square.

He was a prolific radio entertainer, and at the outset of World War II, he virtually sustained radio broadcasting for the first few days, broadcasting no less than 45 programs in two weeks. It was MacPherson who may be said to have created the radio request program, linking millions of servicemen and women with their families with his melodic organ playing and his gentle, cozy style of presentation. By July 1952, he had made 6,000 programs. Subsequently, he had long-running shows on the **Light Programme**, among them *From My Post-Bag* and *The Chapel in the Valley*. He died on his 78th birthday.

MACPHERSON, STEWART (1908–1995). Curiously, this Canadian broadcaster came to Britain a year after his namesake (above) began broadcasting for the **British Broadcasting Corporation (BBC)**. Originally an ice hockey commentator, he worked as a BBC war correspondent, commentating on the Arnhem campaign from the air, and later gained a popular following as the host of a number of successful radio programs, among them *Down Your Way* of which he was the first presenter, *Ignorance Is Bliss*, and *Twenty Questions*. His style was fast moving and his sporting commentaries conveyed a unique sense of excitement. In 1949, he received the vote for "Voice of the Year" in the National Radio Awards.

Despite his success in UK radio, MacPherson was unsettled in Britain, and decided to accept an offer by **Edward R. Murrow** of a job as news and sports commentator at a Columbia Broadcasting System (CBS) radio station in Minneapolis. It is a mark of the affection with which he was held in Britain, that, at his departure from the BBC, King George VI and Queen Elizabeth invited MacPherson to record his last *Twenty Questions* program at Buckingham Palace.

His time in Minneapolis was not a success, and when CBS sold the station in 1960, he accepted a post with a sports organization in his native Winnipeg, moving back into broadcasting shortly afterward when a new television station opened in the city. One of his first actions was to revive the *Twenty Questions* format on the station. He retired in 1974 and died in April 1995.

MADDEN, CECIL (1902–1987). After a period working in theater management in Paris, Madden joined the **British Broadcasting Corporation (BBC)** Talks Department in 1933, and became responsible for the outside broadcasting elements of the new magazine program, *In Town Tonight*. He became a senior producer with the new **Empire Service**, and in 1936, moved into television, preparing for the first high-definition TV service.

With the outbreak of World War II and the close-down of BBC Television, Madden returned to radio, and in 1940 he was made head of overseas entertainment. It was Madden who conceived the idea of the **Allied Expeditionary Force (AEF)** service. During the war years, he was responsible for discovering many artists who were to become well-known stars in the UK, including Petula Clark and the Beverley Sisters.

When UK television resumed transmissions in June 1946, Madden returned to his former post of programs organizer. In this, he may be seen as one of the founding fathers of British TV. He was awarded an MBE in 1952, and retired from the BBC in 1964, although he continued to lead an active and creative life until his death in May 1987.

MAIN WILSON, DENNIS (1925–1997). This distinguished producer of light entertainment programs for both radio and television is associated mostly with his successes in sound on *The Goon Show* and *Hancock's Half Hour*. Main Wilson joined the **British Broadcasting Corporation (BBC)** in 1941 and during the war attended the Royal Military Academy, becoming an army captain and landing at Juno Beach on D-Day. Returning to radio in 1951, he at once began work on *The Goon Show*, and in 1954 produced the first of no less than 68 episodes of *Hancock's Half Hour*. Three years later, he moved to television production work, where, among many other programs, he was responsible for Johnny Speight's *'Til Death Us Do Part*. Despite continuing success in the medium, it was his radio years he remembered with most pride.

THE MAN BORN TO BE KING. Between December 1941 and October 1942, a 12-part **serial** was broadcast on Sunday evening during *Children's Hour*, which caused considerable controversy both within the **British Broadcasting Corporation (BBC)** and in the wider context of morality. *The Man Born to Be King* was written by the novelist Dorothy L. Sayers and told the dramatized story of the life of Christ. When BBC executives wanted to alter her script, she tore up her contract but was mollified when **Val Gielgud**—with whom she had worked successfully in the past—was appointed as producer.

Later, at a press conference, Sayers read extracts from the work; she included passages that angered many, due to her use of slang language. Many complaints were received, and the issue was even debated in the House of Commons. Scripts were adjusted in the light of this, and the transmission demonstrated a work of great power and importance. Indeed, the sequence was repeated many times in its original broadcast form, in 1949, 1951, and 1965, and broadcast again in a new production, freshly adapted by Raymond Raikes, as the **Radio 4** *Classic Serial* in 1975.

MANSELL, GERARD (1921–). Mansell was in charge of the **Home Service** from 1965, and remained until 1969, bridging the network's time of rebirth in 1967 into **Radio 4**. It was Mansell who saw the creation of the news program, the *World at One*. He was also involved in the creation of the document, *Broadcasting in the Seventies*, which caused considerable controversy. From 1972–1981, he was director, External Services and wrote a history of the **World Service**, entitled *Let Truth Be Told*.

MANSFIELD, DAVID (1954–). David Mansfield was appointed chief executive, **GCap Media** group in May 2005, when the **Capital Radio** and **GWR** groups merged. He resigned from the post in September of the same year. Prior to this, he was chief executive, Capital Radio from July 1997, having joined the Company in 1993 as commercial director. He had begun his career as a marketing executive at Scottish Television and Grampian Sales in 1977. Following a number of management roles, he joined Thames Television in 1985 as marketing controller. He served as deputy director of sales and marketing, where he was responsible for the day-to-day sales operation of the company until leaving to join Capital Radio in 1993.

MARCONI, GUGLIELMO (1874–1937). Hailed by many as the father of wireless, Marconi's principal experiments were conducted in the UK, including the famous transmission in 1901, when it was claimed that a transmission of the Morse code for the letter "S," sent from a station in **Poldhu**, Cornwall, was received at St John's, Newfoundland, making this the first transatlantic electronic communication and winning for Marconi worldwide fame. (Some scholars have questioned if indeed the signal was received as history states.)

Marconi was born in Bologna, Italy, and from an early age had followed the experiments of James Maxwell, Heinrich Hertz, and Oliver Lodge in electrical science and the existence of radio waves. In 1895, he succeeded in sending a wireless signal over a distance of more than a mile on his father's estate at Pontecchio in Italy. Frustrated by the lack of interest shown in his native land, he came to England the following year and was granted the world's first patent for a system of wireless telegraphy. In July 1897, he formed the Wireless Telegraph and Signal Company, renamed in 1900, Marconi's Wireless Telegraphy Company. See also MARCONI COMPANY.

In 1900, his most famous patent, for "tuned or syntonic telegraphy," was taken out, and then came the Poldhu experiment, which was crucial because it demonstrated that wireless waves were not affected by the curvature of the earth.

While serving as a commissioned officer for the Italian Army during World War I, Marconi investigated the development of **shortwaves**, which he continued into the 1930s. In his lifetime, he received many honors, including, in 1909, the Nobel Prize for Physics; in 1914, he was appointed Honorary Knight Grand Cross of the Royal Victorian Order in the UK.

MARCONI COMPANY. Established initially in 1897 by **Guglielmo Marconi** as the Wireless Telegraph and Signal Company, and carrying Marconi's name from 1900, it was at the Marconi Company's Chelmsford headquarters that the great experiments of 1920 were carried out, culminating in the historic transmission of a recital by the singer Dame Nellie Melba in June of that year.

In 1921, the company received a license from the postmaster general to transmit publicly from a small station at **Writtle** near Chelmsford, with the call sign, **2MT**, and these commenced in February 1922, led by **P. P. Eckersley**. Shortly after this, the **Marconi Company** began broadcasting from Marconi House in London's Strand, using the callsign,

2LO. In November of that year, the station became the starting point for the newly formed **British Broadcasting Company (BBC)**.

MARCONI-STILLE SYSTEM. In 1924, the German inventor Curt Stille created a machine capable of recording sound on steel wire, and a version of this was bought in 1931 by Louis Blattner, who brought it to England and developed it under the title of the Blattnerphone. Blattner sold his machine to the **British Broadcasting Corporation (BBC)** that year, but at the same time the **Marconi Company** was in the process of purchasing the UK rights to Stille's original patents. As a result, Marconi and the BBC jointly produced a number of steel tape recorders under the name of "The Marconi-Stille System," with the strong motivation of a requirement to broadcast to various different time zones, at the creation of the **Empire Service** in 1932. *See also* BLATTNERPHONE.

MARSHALL, HOWARD (1900–1973). Marshall was one of the most distinguished commentators at **British Broadcasting Corporation (BBC)** outside broadcasts, including sporting and events of national importance and significance. Coming from a print journalism background, in 1928, he was the BBC's assistant **news** editor and during the 1930s and 1940s, he was well known for his cricket commentaries. He also described the coronations of 1937 and 1953 for radio listeners, and between those two events, served as the director of public relations for the Ministry of Food from 1940–1943, and as a war correspondent from 1943–1945. As such, he was among the broadcasters who described the Normandy D-Day landings in 1944.

MASCHWITZ, ERIC (1901–1969). Maschwitz joined the **British Broadcasting Company (BBC)** at **Savoy Hill** in 1926 and was editor, *The Radio Times* from 1927–1933, when he became director of variety. He was thus responsible for light entertainment during what many have called "The Golden Age." Programs included *In Town Tonight* and *Scrapbook*. Maschwitz was a multitalented man, successful as a songwriter (among many others he wrote the lyrics for "These Foolish Things") and as a novelist (using the pseudonym of "Holt Marvell" he cowrote the detective novel *Death at Broadcasting House* with **Val Gielgud**).

MATHESON, HILDA (1888–1940). Matheson was one of the true founders of radio journalism at the **British Broadcasting Company/ Corporation (BBC)**. During World War I, she had worked for MI5, prior to which she had been political secretary to Nancy Astor. She was recruited by **John Reith** in 1926 as the BBC's first director of talks, and she transformed the output, bringing some of the greatest cultural and intellectual voices of the time to the air, including H. G. Wells, George Bernard Shaw, and Vita Sackville-West, who became her lover.

It was Matheson who understood for the first time that there is a specific skill and art to direct presentation on radio. In 1931, she resigned from the BBC, after she clashed with Reith over the issue of the censorship of a talk on James Joyce. She then went on to oversee the African Survey, continuing her work with MI5/MI6 at the outbreak of war, and running the Joint Broadcasting Committee. In 1940, debilitated by overwork, her health failed and she died during surgery.

MAXWELL, CHARLES (1910–1998). Maxwell began his radio career in prewar **commercial radio**, one of the first announcers on **Radio Luxembourg** and was associated also with **Radio Normandy**. Here, together with **Bob Danvers-Walker** and **Roy Plomley**, he helped develop the station's brief persona of **Radio International**, broadcasting to British troops in France during the first months of the war. He later joined the **British Broadcasting Corporation (BBC)** as a producer, and worked as such on a number of highly successful radio programs, among them, the hit comedy show, *Take it from Here*.

MCCULLOCH, DEREK (1897–1967). McCulloch—"Uncle Mac" to generations of children —had suffered severe injuries in World War I and had subsequently lost a leg in a road accident. Notwithstanding, his career in children's radio entertainment was long and distinguished. He joined the **British Broadcasting Company (BBC)** in 1926 as an announcer and became organizer of *Children's Hour* in 1933, and the program's director in 1938. He became known for his closing farewell at the end of programs—"Goodnight children—everywhere," which he introduced during World War II. He was also the voice of "Larry the Lamb" in the *Children's Hour* series, ***Toytown***. Although he left the staff of the BBC in 1950, he returned to broadcast ***Children's Favourites*** on Saturday mornings from 1954–1964. He chaired ***Nature Parliament***, a program that had been his own idea.

MCINTYRE, IAN (1931–). McIntyre joined the **British Broadcasting Corporation (BBC)** as a **talks** producer in 1957 and was involved with the **current affairs** program, *At Home and Abroad*. During the 1960s, he worked at Conservative Central Office in Edinburgh and stood unsuccessfully for Parliament in 1966. During the late 1960s, he was an occasional presenter of Third Programme/Radio 3 **documentaries** and became the main presenter of the flagship current affairs series, ***Analysis***, between 1970–1975, presenting 91 editions. McIntyre worked closely with the producer, **George Fischer**, on this and other talks programs during this period. He was appointed controller, **Radio 4** in 1976, moving to **Radio 3** as controller in 1978. He retired from the BBC in 1987. McIntyre was a champion of Reithian values within the BBC, and wrote an important biography of **John Reith**.

MCWHINNIE, DONALD (1920–1987). Donald McWhinnie was a major figure in the development of adventurous drama while assistant head of the **British Broadcasting Corporation's (BBC)** Radio Drama Department in the 1950s. As such, he worked on the production of works by key European dramatists, among them **Samuel Beckett**.

MEDIUMWAVE. *See* AMPLITUDE MODULATION.

MEET THE HUGGETTS. This comedy series, which ran from 1953–1961, was based on characters that had first appeared in a film entitled *Holiday Camp* in 1947. On radio as on film, "Mr. and Mrs. Huggett—Joe and Ethel" were played by **Jack Warner** and Kathleen Harrison. A succession of six young actresses played their voluptuous daughter, Jane.

"MELBA" BROADCAST, THE. One of the most important events in the early history of British radio was the broadcast—on 15 June

1920—of a song recital by the Australian Prima Donna, Dame Nellie Melba (1861–1931). The 30-minute transmission from the **Marconi Company** works in New Street, Chelmsford, was commissioned by Lord Northcliffe, the proprietor of the *Daily Mail* newspaper. The paper promoted the concert enthusiastically in the days preceding it, and at 7:10 p.m., after a studio announcement, Melba ran up and down the scale as a sound check, what she referred to as her "Hallo to the world." The concert itself was scheduled to begin at 7:15 p.m., and punctually at that time, Melba sang "Home Sweet Home," followed by "Nymphes et Sylvains" (in French) and "Addio" from *La Boheme* (in Italian). This was to have been the official end of the recital. There had been, however, some technical problems during the third song, and Melba was persuaded by the engineer in charge of the broadcast, **H. J. Round**, to sing an encore. In fact, she sang several more songs, including "Chant Venitien," a repeat performance of "Nymphes et Sylvains," and ending with the first stanza of "God Save the King."

Although by the time of the Chelmsford broadcast, Melba's greatest years were behind her, she was still a household name and was extremely popular with a wide audience. "Home Sweet Home" was one of her most famous songs, and its inclusion at the start of this recital would have had enormous impact. In fact, the concert was a great success, and the Marconi Company received more than 400 immediate reception reports from all over the world, including Northern Persia, Madrid, The Hague, Sweden, Norway, and Berlin, as well as from a large number of ships equipped with radio receivers, en route to various ports. The day after the event, the *Daily Mail* reported: "Art and science joined hands and the world listening in must have counted every minute of it precious."

MEN TALKING. In prewar broadcasting, one of the problems facing producers within the **British Broadcasting Company/Corporation (BBC)** was the dilemma of ridding their **talks** programs of scripted speech, while preserving control over the content, particularly in areas of contentious or controversial ideas. In 1937, the producer Roger Wilson created a talks series entitled *Men Talking*, based on a series from the United States, *The Chicago Round Table.* The talks were unrehearsed and unscripted, and speakers were chosen not only for their expertise or knowledge on particular subjects but for their ability to be at ease and to voice opinion. The nature of the program style, "controlled" by a chairman, was popular and was instrumental in breaking down barriers between the elitism the BBC was sometimes accused of and the working-class parts of its audience.

MERRY-GO-ROUND. Two programs have carried this title. One was a children's show on **Radio Luxembourg** in 1954. Far more important, however, was the wartime program of this name, a comedy series that featured material gathered from the three armed forces. Having initially been targeted at forces in the Mediterranean and the Middle East, in January 1945, it expanded its remit more globally.

Postwar, it divided into three force-specific shows, *Stand Easy* (army), **Much-Binding-in-the-Marsh** (air force), and *Waterlogged Spa* (navy). Many future stars of radio appeared in these shows, notably **Charlie Chester** in *Stand Easy* and **Eric Barker** in *Waterlogged Spa*.

MESSITER, IAN (1920–). Messiter was a radio producer who joined the **British Broadcasting Corporation (BBC)** in 1942. He was instrumental in developing the career of **Bernard Braden** and **Barbara Kelly** and devised the program that was a major initial vehicle for their talents, *Leave Your Name and Number*. He also worked on *It's That Man Again (ITMA)*, *The Piddingtons*, and *Twenty Questions*, on which program it was his task to sack a drunken **Gilbert Harding**. He was said to be the most prolific inventor of radio and television game shows in the world, but by far his most famous creation was *Just a Minute*, based on experiences as a boy at Sherborne School in Dorset.

METCALFE, JEAN (1923–2000). Originally joining the **British Broadcasting Corporation (BBC)** as a typist, her warm voice was noticed by a radio producer on the telephone and she successfully auditioned as an announcer. During World War II, she became the most popular presenter on the request program, *Forces Favourites*, and stayed with the show after the war, when it became *Two Way Family Favouites*. It was here that she met her future husband, **Cliff Michelmore**, "on air"; she was presenting from London while he hosted the other link of the program from Hamburg. It was 18 months before they actually met, in 1949, and they married the following year. In 1955, she was voted Daily Mail Broadcasting Personality of the Year. Metcalfe also presented *Woman's Hour* and, after some years away from broadcasting, returned to host national radio's first counseling program, *If You Think You've Got Problems*, from 1971–1976. See *also* WOMEN.

MIDGET RECORDER. Two recording devices using this name were employed by sound broadcasters in Great Britain during the 1940s and 1950s, and both machines in their own way revolutionized outside broadcasting.

(1) "Midget" or "Riverside Portable." As D-Day approached, the **British Broadcasting Corporation (BBC)** realized that this was to be a period of the war unprecedented in its mobility, and for its correspondent to be in a position technically to report accurately on current events, they would need to be equipped with personal recording devices that were fully portable. The answer to this need came in the form of the "Midget" or "Riverside" portable, developed by BBC engineers in conjunction with the **Marguerite Sound Studios**. The machines weighed 35 pounds and recorded sound onto a double-sided 10-inch disk. The freedom this machine gave BBC reporters made possible the nightly program, *War Report*. It also facilitated some of the most remarkable eye-witness accounts of the war, from such broadcasters as **Richard Dimbleby**, **Frank Gillard**, **Stanley Maxted**, and **Godfrey Talbot**. Their use of the device brought the actual sounds of warfare into British homes for the first time. Between 1944 and 1945, 72 machines were manufactured. This technology changed the way news was reported forever.

(2) EMI "Midget" Tape Recorder. This first really truly portable tape recorder was first produced by Electrical and Musical Industries (EMI) in about 1950. It was a product of the miniaturization brought about by the development of integrated circuits, and used early transistors, rather than the more bulky and unreliable valves (tubes). The compact portability of the machine was also enabled by the small electric motor. Used initially for news gathering, it was famously the tool that unlocked location and actuality for radio **feature** makers, including the legendary *Radio Ballads* made by **Charles Parker** and **Ewan MacColl**. It was the precursor of the **Uher**.

MIDDLETON, CECIL HENRY (1887–1945). In 1931, the **British Broadcasting Corporation (BBC)** contacted the Royal Horticultural Society, seeking an expert in gardening matters who would also be able to broadcast regularly for them. The result was C. H. Middleton, whose regular program, *The Week in the Garden*, became immensely popular; "Mr. Middleton" as he was known quickly attained the status of national personality. In 1934, he created the Sunday series, *In Your Garden*, which continued through the war, and which he was still presenting at his death in 1945. He was also a regular guest on *The Brains Trust*.

MILLIGAN, SPIKE (1918–2002). Milligan was a comic genius whose best-known radio creation was *The Goon Show*, a program of surreal, anarchic humor that changed attitudes to radio comedy from the time of its first appearance on the **Light Programme** in the 1950s. Born in India as Terence Milligan, the son of an army officer, he served in Italy and Tunisia in World War II, during which time he met **Harry Secombe**, later another key member of the Goons. In 1951, the two joined forces with two other ex-servicemen, Michael Bentine and **Peter Sellers**, and *The Goon Show* team was complete. The show ran for six years.

Milligan was a sensitive man, given to bouts of deep depression. He had been shell-shocked in the war and suffered a number of nervous breakdowns caused, among other things, by the sheer stress of having to write scripts for *The Goon Show* under the considerable pressure of a weekly deadline. He had a huge influence on British comedy, combining music hall ideas with surreal absurdity, blended with a fascination for language. He was awarded a CBE, and in 2000, an honorary knighthood, although he had refused to swear allegiance to the Queen.

MILNE, ALASTAIR (1930–). Having worked as a producer of influential television programs for the **British Broadcasting Corporation (BBC)**, Milne succeeded **Ian Trethowan** as **director-general** in 1982, at a time of considerable government interference in BBC policy, an interference that was often supported by members of the BBC **Board of Governors**, including the **chairman**, **Marmaduke Hussey**. Thus Milne frequently found himself in conflict with both the government and his own Board, regarding the BBC's independence, on one occasion calling the governors "a bunch of amateurs." In the end, he was forced to resign in 1987. His autobiography was published in 1988.

MITCHELL, DENIS (1911–1990). Although born in the UK, Denis Mitchell's family moved to South Africa when he was six years old. There, he gained his first radio experience, writing scripts for the South African Broadcasting Corporation. Initially interested in drama, during World War II, he was attached to an entertainment unit. At the end of hostilities, he joined the staff of the South African Broadcasting Corporation.

It was at this time that Mitchell became fascinated by the concept of the documentary approach, and in particular the witness of "real" people. He met **D. G. Bridson** on a visit to South Africa, and on his advice returned to the UK in 1949, where, a year later, he became features producer for the **British Broadcasting Corporation (BBC)** in Manchester. His work was characterized by the voices of people seldom heard in radio at the time—the homeless, the unemployed, and criminals. He would often work alone, meeting people on the streets by chance, and recording them in their own surroundings, rather than in the studio.

From 1955, Mitchell took his techniques and interests to television, and in 1962, left the BBC to form Denis Mitchell Films, making documentaries on social issues for most of the major television companies.

MOIR, JAMES (1941–). As controller, **Radio 2** from 1996–2003, James Moir successfully implemented a strategy to attract a new audience to the network, while continuing to provide programs that would appeal to its existing—maturer—listenership. This resulted in creating a radio brand that consistently and increasingly increased its position as the most listened-to radio station in the UK. Perceiving that the necessary realignment of **Radio 1** with a younger target audience disenfranchised some of its older audience, Moir redeveloped Radio 2, taking on many of the former Radio 1 presenters, creating a station that proved unassailable in terms of listenership in the early years of the 21st century.

Ironically, Moir's background, prior to his 1996 appointment, was exclusively in television. Joining BBC TV's Light Entertainment Department in 1963 as a production trainee, he became a production manager six months later, subsequently rising through the roles of producer (1970) and executive producer (1980) to the post of head of variety, Light Entertainment Group (January 1982). He became head of the Group in 1987, and was appointed deputy director of Corporate Affairs for the BBC in 1993. In recognition of his work in radio, he was awarded a fellowship of the **Radio Academy** in 1998.

MONDAY NIGHT AT SEVEN/EIGHT. In April 1937, the **British Broadcasting Corporation (BBC)** began a series of shows that were a blend of variety and magazine content entitled *Monday at Seven.* The program was an hour in duration, and later became *Monday Night at Seven* (from October 1938). A schedule change in November 1939 turned the program into *Monday Night at Eight,* and with basically an unchanged format, the show ran through eight series until March 1948. The tradition of this very popular program was revived from 1959–1962 in *Monday Night at Home,* initially presented by **Rene Cutforth**.

MOORE, RAY (1942–1989). One of **Radio 2**'s most popular presenters, in the early morning schedule for many years, Moore had a wry Liverpool humor. He began his career as a presenter of the 1966 **Light Programme** show, *Pop North.* A very heavy smoker, he developed throat cancer, which forced his retirement in 1988, a year before his death from the disease.

MP3. At the turn of the 20th century, the potential for the creation of MPEG, Audio Layer 3 made the download and transfer of sound files from the Internet a major issue for the global music industry. Controversy arose when copyrighted songs were distributed illegally from websites.

In 2004, the technology began to impact directly on radio, through the development of possibilities perceived through the popularity of Apple's MP3 player, the **iPod**. Downloadable radio became a growing phenomenon, and numerous sites appeared, offering the service in various degrees of professionalism. In Britain, the **British Broad-**

casting Corporation (**BBC**) began experimenting with downloadable programs in the early spring of 2005, the first program being so offered on its websites being **Radio 4**'s cultural discussion program, *In Our Time*.

MRS. DALE'S DIARY. A daily drama serial of immense following at the peak of its reputation, *Mrs. Dale's Diary* began on the **Light Programme** in January 1948. It revolved around the daily diary of a fictional doctor's wife, who recounted happenings in her family, living in "Parkwood Hill," South London. Mrs. Dale herself was played first by Ellis Powell. A familiar part of the program was its improvised harp theme, performed by Sidonie Goossens.

In attempts to keep the **serial** relevant a number of changes were introduced over the years of its run. In February 1962, the title changed to *The Dales*, and the family moved out to the Home Counties. At the same time, the famous harp theme was replaced by a more contemporary and less reflective signature tune, written by Ron Grainer. Just over a year later, Ellis Powell was replaced as Mrs. Dale by the ex-film actress, singer, and dancer Jessie Matthews. The program continued after the birth of **Radio 2**, and finally ended in April 1969 after just over 21 years on air.

MUCH-BINDING-IN-THE-MARSH. Growing out of the tripartite Forces program, *Merry-Go-Round*, *Much-Binding-in-the-Marsh* was based on a fictional Royal Air Force (RAF) station, changed in its postwar incarnation into a country club. It began in January 1947 and starred **Richard Murdoch** and **Kenneth Horne**, who also cowrote the show.

Sam Costa, Maurice Denham, and Dora Bryan also appeared in a number of the series, which ran until 1953 (although by this time the title had been abbreviated to simply *Much-Binding*). Murdoch wrote a monthly spin-off chronicle accompanying the program in the *Strand Magazine* in 1948. Famous also was the theme song, written and sung by Murdoch and Horne.

It was repeated as late as the 1980s. The show was said to be a great favorite among members of the Royal Family, and among certain politicians, including Conservative prime minister John Major.

MUIR, FRANK (1920–1998). Brought up in London's East End, Muir began writing for radio during World War II. Having served as an airman, at the end of hostilities he joined the **British Broadcasting Corporation (BBC)** as a comedy writer, working with the comedian **Jimmy Edwards**. It was **Ted Kavanagh** who first teamed his talents with those of **Denis Norden** in 1947, beginning a long partnership that produced, among other hits, *Take It from Here*. Moving into television, the pair never abandoned their radio roots, and Muir latterly developed a new **series** as a writer/presenter in the successful radio series *Frank Muir Goes into . . .* , produced by another long-term collaborator, Simon Brett. Muir and Norden both regularly appeared on radio panel games, notably *My Word* and *My Music*. The Frank Muir and Denis Norden Archive at the University of Sussex contains more than 600 of their scripts, and was deposited there in 2000 by Norden himself and Muir's son, Jamie.

MURDOCH, RICHARD (1907–1990). Murdoch worked in *Band Waggon* with **Arthur Askey**, and later in *Merry-Go-Round*, where he began his partnership with **Kenneth Horne**, which continued in *Much-Binding-in-the-Marsh*. In 1962, he began the **Light Programme** series, *The Men from the Ministry*, initially with Wilfrid Hyde-White and subsequently with Deryck Guyler. Murdoch continued working up to the end of his life, and was appearing on *Just a Minute* just a year before his death.

MURPHY, FRANK (1889–1955). Murphy, who was to give his name to one of the great British radio manufacturing companies, was, from an early age, a gifted student of mathematics, and after Oxford, worked for the Post Office and Western Electric as an engineer, prior to serving in communications during World War I. In 1919, he met (Charles) Rupert Casson, a young copywriter. Together, they formed the Engineering Publicity Service (EPS), an advertising company serving clients in the field of engineering. Murphy Casson, as the company became known, was successful, but for Frank Murphy, unfulfilling; in 1928, he withdrew to begin his own radio manufacturing company.

By 1936, Murphy Radio, based in Welwyn Garden City, was acknowledged as one of the leaders in the field, based on Murphy's own personal insistence on two cardinal virtues of reliability and value for money. Murphy sets were not always the most stylish, but they were durable and consistently high-performing.

Murphy was a man of high principles, and in 1937 resigned from the board of his now highly successful radio business to develop a new venture of good-quality furniture aimed at a mass market. The venture failed, and despite various subsequent attempts at developing new ideas, including immigration to Canada in 1947, Murphy ended his life in a round of occasional jobs, including taxi driving and teaching mathematics in a Toronto high school.

MURRAY, JENNI (1950–). Jenni Murray has been the regular presenter of **Radio 4**'s *Woman's Hour* since 1987. Born in Barnsley, Yorkshire, she gained a degree in French and drama from Hull University, and joined BBC Radio Bristol in 1973. After a number of subsequent posts in television, she joined **Radio 4** as a presenter on the *Today* program in 1985. She has also presented the Radio 4 media magazine program *The Message* and has worked as a print journalist for a number of major UK national newspapers. She holds an OBE for services to broadcasting.

MURRAY, PETER (1928–). One of Britain's most popular and experienced **disc jockey**s of the postwar era, and a successful television personality, Pete Murray came from a theater background. He joined **Radio Luxembourg** in 1950, and remained with the station until 1955, during which time he hosted numerous programs, including *Top Twenty*. He also worked for the **British Broadcasting Corporation (BBC)**, presenting *Pete's Party* for the **Light Programme**, and sharing a good-natured on-air rivalry with fellow Light Programme presenter, **David Jacobs**.

When **Radio 1** launched in 1967, Murray was one of the original team, moving in 1969 to **Radio 2**, where, for more than 10 years, he presented *Open House*. In 1983, he was dropped from the schedule, but immediately joined the **London Broadcasting Company (LBC)**, where he continued his career successfully for a number of years more. Occasionally he returned to the stage for acting roles. On TV, he hosted *Six-Five Special*, and later, *Top of the Pops*.

MURROW, EDWARD R. (1908–1965). One of the world's great broadcasters, more than any other, it was Murrow through his graphic descriptions of London air raids and their effects in World War II who gave millions of Americans a true sense of the impact of the conflict at a time when Great Britain stood very much alone against the forces of Nazi Germany. His nightly introduction, "This . . . is London," became a familiar trademark in the same way that Stuart Hibberd's voice intoning the same words, was instantly identifiable.

Murrow later flew on Royal Air Force (RAF) bombing raids, and he was—exceptionally for a non-British citizen—awarded an OBE for his war reporting. He had been a participant in the founding of the Columbia Broadcasting System (CBS), as its director of talks from 1935–1937, its European director from 1937–1946, and postwar, its director of public affairs from 1946–1947. In 1961, he was appointed by President John F. Kennedy as director of the United States Information Agency, where part of his responsibility was the output of **Voice of America**.

MUSIC. There is a long tradition of patronage of "live" music in British radio, dating back to the earliest broadcasts. This has been partly due to the role played by the **British Broadcasting Corporation (BBC)** as a public service organization, and partly because of regulatory issues that restricted the amount of music played from commercial recordings. The BBC has fostered—and continues to maintain—a large number of orchestras; during the 1920s, '30s, and '40s, the Corporation augmented these with dance bands and smaller ensembles. Up until World War II, the use of records in BBC programs was often seen as merely a substitute for live music, with a few notable exceptions. Contrary to BBC policy, the **commercial radio** stations broadcasting from the Continent during the 1930s existed very much on a diet of commercial records. These stations and their musical output exposed the BBC to criticism for its somewhat staid musical policy, particular on Sundays, when the Reithian (*See* REITH, JOHN) idea of "The Lord's Day" informed an output in which popular music had no place.

Examination of program schedules from prewar radio stations in Great Britain show the strong influence of light orchestral music rather than jazz, although dance orchestras increasingly established "swing" in the repertoire, and the coming of American bands in wartime created a strong appetite for such music. At the same time, the necessity of linking members of the military forces with loved ones at home saw the growth of record request programs, such as *Two Way Family Favourites*, creating personalities out of presenters, including Cliff Mitchelmore and **Jean Metcalfe**.

After the war, the BBC was slow to respond to the growth of the new popular music, and in particular during the 1950s and '60s became increasingly out of touch with trends in youth culture. At this time, the main source of popular music on radio aimed at the young was **Radio Luxembourg**, which established its *Top Twenty* program in 1948. Even this was based on sheet music sales rather than records, and it was not until 1952, with the establishment of the first pop chart in the *New Musical Express* magazine, that it became overtly a program of the best-selling records in the United Kingdom. During the 1960s, the crisis in UK music radio came to a head with the establishment of **pirate radio** stations, such as **Radio Caroline** and **Radio London**, transmitting from ships moored outside UK territorial waters, and broadcasting American-style music radio of a kind previously unheard by British audiences. Given that this coincided with the explosion of 1960s youth popular music culture, the effect was dramatic, and drove the BBC into creating generic radio stations in 1967, including, for the first time, a network aimed specifically at the youth audience, **Radio 1**.

In September 1946, the BBC created a consciously elitist cultural network in the **Third Programme**, broadcasting not only classical orchestral music, but challenging drama and discussions. In 1967, this became **Radio 3**, which continues to be the largest purveyor of live concert music in the world. Additionally, more recently, it has widened its musical brief to include world music and jazz. Classical music has continued to play a large part in radio in Great Britain on other stations; notably, in 1992, **Classic FM** became the first national commercial station in the UK, and has continued successfully with a policy of light classical music scheduled in the style of popular music radio. Establishing jazz as a popular format has been somewhat more problematic, and commercial stations seeking an all-jazz format have often been forced to modify their playlists to embrace a less niche form of content.

From the establishment of land-based commercial radio in 1973, until changes in regulation in 1990, **Independent Local Radio (ILR)** was legally committed to the support of live music through agreements with the Musicians Union. After 1990, this commitment ceased, and at the same time, output on such stations became increasingly playlist bound, and "appointment to listen" specialist shows gave way to an overall station "sound," formats aimed at a specific demographic identified in station policy. The development of digital playout systems with playlists created by computers further divorced presenters from their audiences, to a certain extent reversing one of music radio's major contributions to the medium, the personality **disc jockey (DJ)**.

The creation of personalities in popular music radio within Great Britain—disc jockeys—began somewhat spasmodically in the late 1920s and '30s, with the work of broadcasters, such as **Christopher Stone** and his colleague **Doris Arnold**, one of the first female disc jockeys. In this era, records were usually played on BBC programs by way of reviewing new material, and announcements frequently included details, such as record label and number. The prewar band leader **Jack Jackson** developed innovative ways of interacting with commercial recordings in his shows, using comedy material from radio programs to form a dialogue with the music. These techniques were highly influential, and were subsequently developed by a number of other presenters. It was, however, with the arrival of the offshore stations in the 1960s that DJs were truly established as a major part of UK radio. From this time, presenters, such as **Kenny Everett**, **John Peel**, **Johnnie Walker**, and "**Emperor Rosko**," became major personalities in the youth culture of the time and brought U.S.-style music radio to British audiences for the first time, creating, in the process, a refreshing, inventive, and often creative style of broadcasting. Many of these presenters were signed by the BBC with the creation of Radio 1, the first voice on the network being the former Radio Caroline and Radio London presenter, **Tony Blackburn**. There have also been strong followings for women DJs, such as **Annie Nightingale** and **Jo Whiley**.

Alternatives to the niche programming of music radio have also existed: *Sing Something Simple*, a gentle program of light vocal music, was broadcast on the **Light Programme/Radio 2** for many years as a 30-minute medley, late afternoon, Sundays by Cliff Adams and his singers, while Radio Luxembourg's *Smash Hits* program from the 1950s used the conceit of inviting listeners to request their most hated records for destruction. During the first years of the 21st century, popular music radio in Great Britain faced new challenges with the growth of technology permitting the download of music from the Internet and a decline in radio listening among younger audiences. At the same time, the range and quality of music radio across all genres remained impressive.

– N –

NATIONAL PROGRAMME. On 9 March 1930, the **British Broadcasting Corporation (BBC)** streamlined its radio services by creating the National Programme, which as its name suggests, carried a full service uniformly nationwide. In the same year, to complement this the **Regional Service** was born, creating the opportunity for geographical variation. This system of networking continued until September 1939 when both programs were absorbed into the newly named **Home Service**.

NATIONAL RADIO AWARDS. Established in 1950, and running for five years, the National Radio Awards were sponsored by the *Daily Mail*, and were the first awards for broadcasters in Britain. The first radio awards, presented by Lady Rothermere, went to:

Outstanding Actor:	James McKechnie
Outstanding Actress:	Gladys Young
Voice of the Year:	**Richard Dimbleby**
Outstanding Variety Series:	*Educating Archie*

In the second ceremony, by now opened up to television in addition to radio, in 1952, the radio awards went to:

Personality of the Year:	**Wilfred Pickles**
Outstanding Radio Program:	*Take It from Here*

In 1953, radio gained the following awards:

Personality of the Year:	**Gilbert Harding**
Outstanding Actor:	Howard Marion Crawford
Outstanding Actress:	Gladys Young
Most Popular Musical Entertainer:	Tom Jenkins
Most Entertaining Program:	*Educating Archie*
Most Promising New Program:	The *Al Read* Show

The fourth series of awards, issued in January 1954, produced the following results for UK radio:

Personality of the Year:	Gilbert Harding
Outstanding Actor:	James Mckechnie
Outstanding Actress:	Marjorie Westbury
Most Popular Musical Entertainer:	Tom Jenkins
Most Entertaining Program:	***The Archers/Take It from Here***
Most Promising New Program:	*The Name's the Same*

The fifth and final year of the awards took place in January 1955. The radio prizes went to the following:

Personality of the Year:	**Jean Metcalfe**
Outstanding Actor:	Richard Williams
Outstanding Actress:	Marjorie Westbury
Most Popular Musical Entertainer:	Cyril Stapleton
Most Entertaining Program:	*The Archers*
Most Promising New Program:	*Hello Playmates*

NAUGHTON, BILL (1910–1992). Born in County Mayo, Ireland, but brought up in Bolton, Lancashire, Naughton is an important example of a writer whose work has transferred successfully from radio to film and television. He is noted for his graphic and realistic stories describing working-class life in postwar Britain. His first piece of radio was *Timothy*, broadcast on the **Home Service** in 1956. He was a member of an elite group of new writers who were given opportunities by the development of the **Third Programme** in the 1950s and early 1960s. (Others included **Samuel Beckett**, Harold Pinter, and

John Osborne.) Notable among more than 15 radio plays has been *Alfie Elkins and His Little Life*, produced by **Douglas Cleverdon**, which was ultimately to become the film *Alfie*, starring Michael Caine, in a role originally created by Bill Owen on the Third Programme in 1962. Other "cross-overs" have been *All In Good Time* (**Radio 3**, 1973), which became the film, *The Family Way*, and *My Flesh, My Blood*, later to become a successful stage play and film as *Spring and Port Wine*.

NAVY LARK, THE. This spoof of life in the Royal Navy was one of the most popular UK radio comedy series of all time, as well as being the longest running (prior to **Weak Ending** gaining the distinction) from 1959–1977. Set aboard *"HMS Troutbridge,"* the series was successful less because of its innovative writing and production than for the brilliance of its ensemble of actors and the quality of the characterization. The three leading characters were "The No. 1," initially played by Dennis Price and after the first series, by Stephen Murray, "Sub-Lieutenant Phillips," played with suave idiocy by Leslie Phillips, and Chief Petty Officer Pertwee, played by Jon Pertwee. Other parts were in the hands of Richard Caldicott, Heather Chasen, Michael Bates, Ronnie Barker, and Tenniel Evans. The program was conceived by Laurie Wyman.

NAVY MIXTURE. This wartime series began in February 1943 on the **General Forces Programme**. In its time, it provided early exposure for many variety artists who were to become household names in postwar Britain, among them **Peter Brough**, **David Jacobs**, and **Jimmy Edwards**. The last series started in July 1947 and ended in November of the same year. Elements of the program were incorporated and revived into a new format, which became the successful comedy series, *Take It from Here*.

NETWORK CHART SHOW. This program, created by the **Unique Broadcasting Company**, was a rundown of the UK's top-selling records, and was notable in that it was the first syndicated show on Independent Local Radio (ILR). It began in 1984, hosted by **Capital Radio**'s David Jensen, and, from the following year, sponsored by the coffee company, Nescafé. Broadcast from 5:00 p.m.–7:00 p.m. on Sunday evenings, it was taken by almost the entire ILR network, at a period when consolidation of ownership had not been approached as an issue, thus creating effectively the first real national commercial competition to the **British Broadcasting Corporation (BBC)**. At its peak, it claimed to reach 20% of the nation's 10- to 24-year-olds. It was also broadcast by a number of other countries.

NETWORK THREE. This **British Broadcasting Corporation (BBC)** service was introduced in 1957 on the **Third Programme** frequency. The idea behind it was to provide a daytime service that would draw an audience that might consider the high cultural evening schedule of the Third to be intimidating.

NEWS. The first news to be broadcast by the **British Broadcasting Company (BBC)** was also the first program; **Arthur Burrows** read a bulletin on 14 November 1922 from Marconi House. It was, however, to be some years before the BBC had complete freedom to develop a news policy unrestricted by agreements with newspaper proprietors and press agencies. During the **General Strike** of 1926 it had, of necessity, to develop independent sources of news, but this was short-lived.

It was with the coming of World War II that major breakthroughs occurred that were to define the future of newsgathering and the use of location-based reporters as a key factor within the process. (*See* WARTIME BROADCASTING). The program, *War Report*, was particularly significant in this respect. It was the necessities of the situation and the requirement for portability and durability of reporters' equipment during the Allied advances after D-Day that shaped news programs thereafter. In more recent military conflicts the use of bi-media reporters, "embedded" with troops in situations directly linked to action, have provided material of an immediate nature to both radio and television, using satellite technology to provide coverage virtually instantaneously.

Subsequently technology has continued to play a major part in the way news is gathered, both within the BBC and beyond. With the coming of **commercial radio**—and in particular the first station, the

London Broadcasting Company (LBC), and **Independent Radio News (LBC)** in October 1973—news styles of radio journalism developed, with the growing use of reporters from ethnic backgrounds, etc.

Forms of news presentation have varied over the history of UK radio; during World War II, the major BBC bulletin was at 9:00 p.m., and it was at this time that news readers began to identify themselves by name, guarding against the possibility of their material becoming confused with propaganda broadcasts. In recent years, the concept of rolling news services, such as the service provided by **Radio 5 Live**, have provided an alternative to the set-piece bulletins and news programs to be heard on **Radio 4**, or the on-the-hour short summaries to be heard on many music stations. The continuing technological advances in web usage have provided radio broadcasters with further mechanisms for the dissemination and complementary development of news stories.

NEWSBEAT. This 15-minute program of hard and soft news was created by **Radio 1** in 1974, with the aim of engaging its youth audience in current affairs. Always fast moving, the format was highly successful and enduring.

NEWS QUIZ. This long-running topical game show began in 1977. Panelists comment on current affairs in an amusing format devised by John Lloyd. It was subsequently adapted for television as *Have I Got News for You?*

NIGHTINGALE, ANNIE (1943–). Formerly a newspaper journalist, Brighton-born Nightingale joined **Radio 1** in 1970, becoming the network's first female **disc jockey**. Her *Sunday Request Show* ran from 1982–1994 and gained something of a cult following. In 1996, she was seriously injured in a mugging incident in Cuba. She has continued her association with Radio 1 into the 21st century, as well as working on other **British Broadcasting Corporation (BBC)** networks, including work on *Woman's Hour*, *Pick of the Week*, and *Front Row*. In the 2001 New Year Honours list, she received an MBE for services to radio broadcasting and in 2004 was inducted into the **Radio Academy Hall of Fame**.

NIGHT THOUGHTS. This **radio poem**, a "radiophonic poem" as its author called it, was written by David Gascoyne (1916–2001) and was first broadcast on the **Third Programme** on 7 December 1955, with music especially composed by Humphrey Searle. Produced by **Douglas Cleverdon**, the cast included Robert Harris, Hugh David, David William, Frank Duncan, Alan Reid, Peter Claughton, Norman Shelley, Robert Marsden, Gladys Young, Jill Balcon, and Leonard Sachs. Gascoyne later spoke of the pain of writers' block the commission produced in him, and the compassionate tolerance of Cleverdon, enabling him to complete the work at his own pace. The result was one of British radio's great masterpieces.

NORDEN, DENIS (1922–). With his writing partner, **Frank Muir**, Norden created many of the most famous British radio comedies, including *Take It from Here* and *Breakfast with Braden*. He also became increasingly known as a broadcaster in his own right and regularly appeared in radio game shows such as *My Word* and *My Music*. In television, he was host of a successful occasional series of programs that exposed TV fluffs and errors, entitled *It'll Be Alright on the Night*.

NORMAN, R. C. (1873–1963). Ronald Collet Norman was **chairman** of the **British Broadcasting Corporation (BBC)** from 1935 to 1939. He had a good relationship with **John Reith** and proved to be an intelligent and knowledgeable chairman. He had worked in local politics, notably with London County Council from 1907 to 1922. After leaving the BBC, he served with a number of cultural institutions in Britain, including the National Trust.

NORMAN AND HENRY BONES. This long-running series of stories about two boy-detectives, sons of the Reverend Henry Bones, was the creation of a schoolmaster, Anthony C. Wilson. The first in the series, *Mystery at Ditchmoor*, was broadcast on **Children's Hour** in July 1943, produced by **Josephine Plummer**. The two boys were played by Charles Hawtrey as Norman and Peter Mullins as Henry. Mullins was later replaced in the part by Patricia Hayes.

– O –

OFFFICE OF COMMUNICATION (OFCOM). OFCOM was created in December 2003 when previous regulators, the **Radio Authority (RA)** and the Independent Television Commission (ITC), were abolished. The aim was to establish an overarching regulatory body in response to the perceived convergence of media in the digital age. Thus, by its own definition, Ofcom is "the regulator for the UK communications industries, with responsibilities across television, radio, telecommunications, and wireless communications services." Its remit is to balance choice and competition in the media industries with the duty to "foster plurality, informed citizenship, to protect viewers, listeners and customers, and promote cultural diversity." It also takes an active role in the encouragement of the development of new electronic media and communications.

OGILVIE, F. W. (1893–1949). Sir Frederick Wolff Ogilvie was **director-general** of the **British Broadcasting Corporation (BBC)** from 1938–1942, succeeding **John Reith**. Ogilvie's background was that of an economics academic, having been vice-chancellor of Queen's University, Belfast, prior to his appointment. It fell to Ogilvie to defend the BBC's independence in the early war years, when there was questioning from elements in both the press and the government as to the very future of the BBC. Overseas programs increased during his time, but there were issues relating to delays in implementation, and overspending, and he was replaced in 1942 jointly by **R. W. Foot** and **Cecil Graves**. A criticism of Ogilvie was that he lacked leadership qualities; Reith wrote of him in his autobiography, "I was quite sure he was not the man for the BBC." After his time with the corporation, Ogilvie became principal of Jesus College, Oxford, and became a vocal critic of the postwar BBC.

OLIVER, VIC (1897–1965). Oliver was of Austrian aristocratic stock, the son of Baron Victor von Samek. In 1922, he relinquished his hereditary title. He was an extremely accomplished musician, playing the violin and piano and even touring the United States as a concert pianist in 1927. Later, he began to develop comedy routines involving his music and in so doing became an influence on later acts, such as Victor Borge. He became part of the wartime team of *Hi Gang* with **Ben Lyon** and **Bebe Daniels**. After the war, he continued to blend comedy and music, forming the **British Concert Orchestra** and acting as Master of Ceremonies for *Variety Playhouse*. He was married to Sir Winston Churchill's daughter, Sarah, but the couple divorced in 1945.

ONE MINUTE, PLEASE. This popular panel game was the forerunner of *Just a Minute* and devised by Ian Messiter, and had its first broadcast in August 1951. The initial broadcast had **Roy Plomley** as chair, with panelists including **Gilbert Harding** and **Kenneth Horne**. One of the favorite team members was the cartoonist **Gerard Hoffnung**, who first became known to British audiences on the program.

ONEWORD RADIO. This national **digital radio** station dedicated to books and literature-based talk was launched in 2000. It suffered when **BBC 7** subsequently began broadcasting, using a similar format, and the station went through a period of stagnation. In 2005, it was jointly acquired by **UBC Media** and Channel 4, after which it began an attempt at regeneration, moving to new studios and launching fresh programming in its schedule. Mostly the station's output from the start has been in the genre of "talking books."

OPPORTUNITY KNOCKS. The well-known talent show began on the **Light Programme** in February 1949, before moving to **Radio Luxembourg** in 1950. It was hosted by **Hughie Green**, who devised the program, produced by **Dennis Main Wilson** for the **British Broadcasting Corporation (BBC)** and by Gordon Crier on Radio Luxembourg, where it was sponsored by Horlicks. With the coming of Independent Television (ITV), the program transferred to television, where it continued to enjoy great success for many years.

ORIGINAL 106. In September 2005, a new **commercial radio license** was awarded for the Solent region of the UK, to serve the area bounded by Bournemouth and Southampton. The franchise was hotly contended but was given to Original 106. Original 106 was 95% owned by CanWest Mediaworks, a wholly owned subsidiary of the CanWest Global Communications Corporation and Seven Broadcast of Canada. The station offered "adult alternative radio aimed at 40- to 59-year-olds" and was scheduled to begin broadcasting in 2006.

OTHER PEOPLE'S HOUSES. *See SOS.*

OUTSIDE BROADCAST (OB). Both the **British Broadcasting Corporation (BBC)** and **commercial radio** operators were involved with the development of outside broadcasts. From the earliest days, the desire of broadcasters to move beyond the bounds of the studio led to some adventurous experiments. In fact, the precursor of outside broadcasts could be said to be the prewireless relays of the **Electrophone** Company, based in Gerrard Street, London, from as early as 1894. The principle here was of a live performance from a theater, concert hall or church, which was relayed via telephone line to subscribers. There was, however, no real radio production in the sense it was to become known. The first BBC OB was in January 1923, from Covent Garden. Beatrice Harrison made her famous broadcast of her duet between a **Cello and the Nightingale** in 1924, and the BBC's Outside Broadcasts Department was formally constituted in 1925.

Sports commentary began in January 1927, when the England/Wales rugby match was broadcast "live" from Twickenham. A week later, the first soccer match commentary to be broadcast came from Highbury, and featured Arsenal against Sheffield United. There was some doubt in these early days that a listener would be able to follow the action without some form of aid, and for a time a representation of the playing area would be included in *The Radio Times*, divided into numbered squares. As commentary proceeded, a second voice would call out the number of the square corresponding to the point of action on the pitch.

Difficulties in sports commentaries have, for the most part, been less significant than had been initially feared, due largely to the skill of a new breed of broadcaster that emerged with the new form. Even snooker has been attempted, and notably resulted in the first woman commentator, Thelma Carpenter, herself an amateur champion at the sport, who was engaged by the BBC to provide commentary on a match in 1936.

Also during the 1930s, commercial stations such as **Radio Normandy** and agencies including the **J. Walter Thompson Organization** mounted variety shows that were recorded for transmission from continental locations. Among the most successful of these was *Radio Normandy Calling*.

Portability of recording developed up to and through World War II and enabled the BBC's **war correspondents** to provide graphic descriptions of events and places that hitherto had been impossible to relay to audiences at home. In addition, many "live" transmissions of events of State, such as the coronation of King George V, led to a considerable enrichment of the texture of British radio.

OVALTINEY'S CONCERT PARTY. One of the most significant children's programs ever broadcast on UK radio, the *Ovaltiney's Concert Party*, was first broadcast from **Radio Luxembourg** in December 1934, featuring **Jack Payne** and his Band, and the child impersonator, **Harry Hemsley**. Young listeners could join the League of Ovaltineys, and weekly messages were sent to members in code. The program ran on Sunday early evening until Radio Luxembourg closed down at the outbreak of war, but returned when the station reopened in very much the same format, and using its famous theme song, "We are the Ovaltineys," possibly the best known and most successful British advertising jingle ever created:

> "We are the Ovaltineys, little girls and boys,
> Make your request, we'll not refuse you,
> We are here just to amuse you.
> Would you like a song or story,
> Will you share our joys?
> At games or sports we're more than keen,
> No merrier children could be seen,
> Because we all drink Ovaltine,
> We're happy girls and boys."

– P –

PAIN, NESTA (1905–1995). After a brilliant academic career, gaining a first in classics at Liverpool University and then going on to

Somerville College, Oxford, to undertake a Ph.D. in comparative philology, Nesta Pain married at the age of 21 and had her only child. From this time, she became closely involved with Liverpool Playhouse and wrote two plays. In 1942, having separated from her husband, she moved to London with her 15-year-old daughter and joined the **British Broadcasting Corporation (BBC)**, where she began writing and producing programs for both the **External Services** and domestic audiences.

In 1947, Pain became part of the **Features** Department, working under **Laurence Gilliam**, and stayed for 12 years, writing, producing, and directing a wide range of material and becoming a passionate advocate of the radio feature. In 1957, she was responsible for persuading John Mortimer to write his first radio play, *The Dock Brief*, which won a Prix Italia in the same year.

Pain was seconded to television in 1956 but continued to work in radio features until 1964, when she resigned. A year later, the department was closed. She took a part-time post as a scriptwriter/producer and continued to produce a range of acclaimed programs, including a serialized life of Queen Victoria. After her retirement, she was impeded by poor eyesight, although she remained mentally active and creative until her death. She remained a champion of the radio feature, claiming that it was "the one unique form that radio has achieved in its short history."

PARFITT, ANDY (1958–). Parfitt's appointment to the post of controller, **Radio 1** in March 1998, occurred as a result of his predecessor, **Matthew Bannister**'s appointment as director, **BBC Radio** the previous year. Parfitt had begun his career in the **British Broadcasting Corporation (BBC)** in 1980 as a studio manager before a secondment to the **British Forces Broadcasting Service (BFBS)** in the Falkland Islands. He returned to the BBC in 1984 and became a producer for **Radio 4**, working on arts and magazine programs. In 1989, he was a part of the launch team of the original **Radio 5**, becoming the network's assistant editor.

In 1993, Parfitt moved to Radio 1 as chief assistant to the controller, being promoted successively to the posts of editor, commissioning and planning, and then managing editor, before succeeding Bannister. In 2002, he oversaw the conception and launch of **1Xtra**, a new **digital radio** service for fans of new black music.

PARKER, CHARLES (1919–1980). This highly influential producer is best remembered for his eight *Radio Ballads*, which he made between 1958 and 1964 with Ewan MacColl and Peggy Seeger. After war service as a submarine commander, Parker gained his degree from Queen's College, Cambridge, in 1948. In the same year, he joined the North American Service of the **British Broadcasting Corporation (BBC)**, and then became a producer in the BBC External Service.

In 1954, Parker became senior **features** producer for the BBC Midland Region in Birmingham, and began experimenting with the new portable EMI **Midget** tape recorder. The first result of this experimentation was *The Ballad of John Axon*, broadcast in 1958. Seven other ballads followed, but his funding was withdrawn in 1964. He continued to work with Ewan MacColl, and with him produced the 14-part series, *The Song Carriers*.

In 1972, Parker was forced into early retirement, although he continued to produce radio in a "guest" capacity until 1976. Thereafter, he fostered his already considerable interest in social-action theater, producing some of the first multimedia work for Arnold Wesker's Centre 42, and becoming a founder member of Banner Theatre of Actuality in 1974. Here, he attempted to extend the concept of the radio ballad form to the stage and other media.

Parker became a sought-after lecturer on the university circuit, expounding vigorously his views on oral history and mass communication. He had also assembled a vast archive, which, on his death, was deposited at the Central Library in Birmingham.

PASTERNAK, MICHAEL. *See* "EMPEROR ROSKO."

PAUL TEMPLE. Created in April 1938 by Francis Durbridge as an eight-part adventure **serial** in the **British Broadcasting Corporation (BBC)** Midland Region, the show was originally called *Send for Paul Temple* and was such a success with its sophisticated format— that of an intellectual and attractive married couple working as amateur sleuths to defeat crime—that it ran for a full 30 years, finally ending in spring 1968. For 25 of those years, it was produced by the same man, Martyn C. Webster. During its lifetime, six actors played Paul Temple, and two actresses played his wife, "Steve."

PAYNE, JACK (1899–1969). Payne was a successful band leader who made his first broadcast as conductor of the Hotel Cecil dance band in 1924, and became so popular that the **British Broadcasting Company (BBC)** invited him to form its first dance orchestra, which he led from 1928–1932, during which time he became a household name through his radio broadcasts. In 1932, he resigned his BBC post to take his own band on tour, but he continued to be a major radio personality, fostering many vocalists with his band in the prewar years.

In the later 1930s, when dance bands both in Great Britain and the United States were swamping the popular music market, he formed his own theatrical agency, although with the outbreak of war, Payne formed a new band, and became popular as a troop entertainer. After the war, he became a successful radio presenter, including on *Say It with Music*, the title taken from his own theme tune, which ran for three years on the **Light Programme** from 1954–1957.

PC 49. The subtitle of this extremely popular postwar **British Broadcasting Corporation (BBC)** series was "Incidents in the career of Police Constable Archibald Berkeley-Willoughby." The concept—original for its time—was that the central character was an upper-class police constable, an ex-public schoolboy, playing against the stereotype of members of the UK police force coming from more working-class stock. The eponymous hero was played by Brian Reece and the program was created from an idea by the Australian crime journalist, Alan Stranks. Each episode was a self-contained adventure in its own right, and proved so popular in its six years of air-time, 1947–1953, that it spawned spin-offs of a number of books, two films, and cartoon representations, notably in the boys' *Eagle* comic, which continued to publish the exploits of PC 49 until March 1957, exactly four years after the last radio series.

PEACH, LAWRENCE Du GARDE (1890–1974). After an academic career in his native Sheffield, which included a Ph.D. in 1921, Peach became increasingly interested in drama for specific target markets, and from 1923, he began to explore the possibilities afforded by the new medium of radio. Particularly fascinated by the opportunities within the area of children's drama, he contributed many dramatized historical and biographical programs for *Children's Hour*. Moving through various fields of endeavor—including politics—Peach continued involvement with drama both on the provincial stage and on radio. In addition, during the 1950s, he wrote more than 20 children's titles for the educational publishers, Wills and Hepworth, for their Ladybird imprint. With a total of more than 400 radio plays broadcast on the **British Broadcasting Company/Corporation (BBC)** through the 1920s and beyond, du Garde Peach may hold the claim for the most prolific ever radio playwright.

PEASE, JOSEPH (1860–1943). Joseph Albert Pease, Lord Gainford of Headlam, was the first **chairman** of the **British Broadcasting Company (BBC)**. He had worked in the family coal and iron business prior to entering Parliament, where he served in Lloyd George's Liberal government as postmaster general. He was chairman until 1927, and after his time with the BBC worked for the Federation of British Industries.

PEEL, JOHN (1939–2004). Born John Robert Parker Ravenscroft in Heswall near Liverpool, Peel first worked in radio as a disc jockey for WRR in Dallas in the early 1960s. Returning to Britain at the height of the North Sea "**pirate radio**" boom, he joined **Radio London** before coming to **Radio 1** at its creation in August 1967. He remained on the station for the rest of his life, the only survivor of its original DJ lineup. He was famous and much-loved for his championing new bands throughout his career, including Joy Division, The White Stripes, and the Undertones, whose song "Teenage Kicks" remained his all-time favorite record. Earlier, he had given studio time in his *Peel Sessions* to emerging stars of a previous generation, such as David Bowie, Captain Beefheart, and Marc Bolan. Uniquely, Peel remained an icon to youth culture—even at the age of 65—while becoming a favorite of middle-class England with his **Radio 4** weekly program, *Home Truths*. In 1998, he received an OBE and, in 2003, was given a place in the **Radio Academy Hall of Fame**. He died while on a working holiday in Peru in October 2004.

PEOPLE ARE FUNNY. Ross Radio Productions for Pye Radio produced this **series** for **Radio Luxembourg**, beginning in November

1953. It ran for 72 weeks in two series, the second beginning in August 1955. Performed in front of a live audience, it was a fast-moving audience-participation comedy show, directed by one of the UK's most energetic pioneers and champions of **commercial radio**, **John Whitney**.

PERKINS, JOHN (1945–). Managing Director, **Independent Radio News (IRN)** since 1989, John Perkins began his radio journalism career in 1974 at Radio City in Liverpool as the new station's political reporter after working as a reporter on various daily newspapers. He moved to the London all-news station, **London Broadcasting Company (LBC)**, the following year, and was one of the presenters chosen for LBC's experiment in U.S.-style rolling news format. In 1978, he joined IRN, where he worked as home affairs editor and industrial editor. In 1982, Perkins was appointed managing editor of LBC and IRN and in 1986 became editor, IRN. His appointment as managing director of IRN came three years later.

John Perkins's time at IRN has coincided with a number of major developments in distribution and funding; he oversaw the introduction of satellite distribution of the service, and of funding by commercials rather than cash payments. This proved the turning point for the organization, which had been dogged by financial problems from its inception. IRN went on to become arguably one of the world's most successful radio news broadcasters, producing substantial profits and returning millions of pounds each year to client stations in the form of "loyalty bonuses." *See also* INDEPENDENT RADIO NEWS (IRN).

PETTICOAT LINE. Conceived by **Anona Winn** and **Ian Messiter** in January 1965, the program was a feminist panel discussion, in a sense a version of the ***Any Questions*** format. It ran until 1979, and featured panelists, such as Renee Houston, Katharine Whitehorn, Marjorie Proops, and Jane Asher.

PHILIPS-MILLER RECORDING SYSTEM. After a number of experiments into sound on film, in 1931 a Dr. J. A. Miller developed a system that became the basis of the Philips-Miller recording process, with tape and equipment manufactured by Philips in Eindhoven, The

Netherlands. This was a sound-only system and its use was as a radio recording medium. The requirements of quality and instant play-back were answered at a stroke in this superior technical advance, which was picked up in the prewar years by both **British Broadcasting Corporation (BBC)** and commercial companies alike, with the most widespread use initially among the latter.

The idea of film that required processing before broadcast clearly prevented the instant use of recorded work in play-back form. This was circumvented in the Philips-Miller system by having a groove or pattern cut in a cellulose base of film, coated with gelatin, on which was placed a skin of black mercuric oxide three microns thick. A v-shaped cutter recorded sound signals by tracing a pattern in the oxide, leaving a transparent track down the center of the film. This optical pattern could be "read" by a photoelectric cell. The result, manufactured and sold under the trade name, Philimil, was the highest quality of recorded sound known before World War II.

With advances in magnetic tape developments after the war, particularly as a result of German quality improvements, the Philips-Miller System was no longer relevant and fell into disuse.

PHONE-IN. The term was coined in the United States in 1968 and was first heard as a phrase in the United Kingdom in 1971. **BBC** Radio Nottingham has been claimed to be the first UK station to hold a phone-in, in 1968. During the 1970s, with the growth of local radio, the genre became a staple of output, being cheap and frequently controversial. This also fueled the development of the "shock-jock" style of presenter, who would debate—often violently and abusively—with his callers. The trend, which began in the U.S., was explored on the **London Broadcasting Company (LBC)** and **TalkSport** by such presenters as **Brian Hayes** and **James Whale**. On national radio, the first **Radio 4** phone-in was *It's Your Line* in the 1970s, and in 1989, *Any Answers*, which had previously been a letters-only response to *Any Questions* became a phone-in.

PICK OF THE POPS. This record program, originally two hours long, began on the **Light Programme** in October 1955, introduced by **Franklin Engelmann**, billed as a choice of "current popular gramophone records." Before long, Engelmann was replaced by **Alan Dell**

and then **David Jacobs** in a late-night Saturday slot. In 1961, Alan Freeman became the host, and a new formula emerged of new releases in the first hour, and the top ten in the second, broadcast in reverse order. At this time, the show moved to Sunday afternoons and was to be absorbed into **Radio 1** when the station was created in 1967. In later incarnations, broadcast by **Radio 2** on Saturday afternoons, the program moved toward a retrospective format, and when Freeman finally retired, the show, now made by the independent production company, **Unique Broadcasting**, was hosted by Dale Winton, featuring two top tens from past years.

PICKLES, WILFRED (1904–1978). Pickles, a Halifax-born man who moved into regional radio in 1931, made radio history in two principal ways. First, during World War II, he read the news despite having a strong northcountry accent, thus breaking the mold of the somewhat formal **British Broadcasting Corporation (BBC)** newsreading style. Second and more significantly, his highly popular series, *Have a Go*, gave the microphone on location to the people who came to the show, creating an ad-lib program of considerable oral history significance through local storytelling within the format of a quiz show. With his wife Mabel as prize-giver—"What's on the table, Mabel?" was a catchphrase—the program became a national institution. As a broadcaster, he was extremely versatile, from singing and story-telling to stand-up comedy, pantomime, straight acting, and newsreading.

Pickles was also a much beloved broadcaster to young people, and for more than 20 years, from 1942–1963, he captivated Northern children with his *Pleasant Journey* talks on *Children's Hour*. His work, and that of others in the North Region of the BBC, went a long way toward the democratizing of British radio. Significantly, in a 1949 volume of his autobiography, *Between You and Me,* he wrote: "I wish the men who make the restrictive decisions at the BBC could get out and meet the people." With his slogan, "presenting the people to the people," Pickles broke through some of the social barriers that British public service broadcasting had created around itself and in so doing became one of its best-loved personalities.

PIDDINGTONS, THE. In 1949 and 1950, the Australian Sidney Piddington and his wife, the former actress Lesley Pope, brought this program to British radio, indulging in what they referred to as "their own kind of mystery." The series involved a wide range of mind-reading stunts, many incredibly complex and skillful. Part of the mystery was the very way it was achieved; every show ended with the words, "Telepathy or not telepathy? You are the judge." Publicity for the show was considerable, and public debate on the Piddingtons's methods was rife. Producer **Ian Messiter** kept his peace about the trick of it. Prior to their BBC series, the couple had presented their act on Australian radio from 1947.

PIRATE RADIO. The term is used to denote a form of sound broadcasting contravening **licensing** regulations either within the country of origin, or reception or both. In the United States, pirate radio stations are sometimes called "bootleg" stations. Although there seems to be no specific historical point from which the use of the term, "pirate" may be traced, it would appear to have been utilized from the earliest days of broadcasting. Long before the term was used in this context, it had been used in the field of publishing to describe illegal reprints of already published works.

In Great Britain, the term was used in the 1930s, to describe the activities of **Radio Luxembourg**. This station was considered a "pirate" internationally, rather than some of the other Continent-based stations broadcasting to the UK and therefore contravening the monopoly of the **British Broadcasting Corporation (BBC)**; while stations such as **Radio Normandy**, **Radio Toulouse**, and others were broadcasting in English and aimed at UK audiences, they were doing so with the agreement and support of continental radio stations with legitimate wavelengths. Radio Luxembourg, however, was illegally using a wavelength that had been assigned to another potential broadcaster, namely Warsaw Radio, which had been allocated the frequency by international agreement but had at the time (November 1933) not yet begun broadcasting on it.

Thus, a UK precedent for the term was established, equating it with "theft." This definition was applied again by the Wilson Labour Party government of the 1960s in its decision to close down the offshore radio stations, such as **Radio Caroline**, **Radio London**, and others (*See* MARINE BROADCASTING [OFFENCES] ACT). In Britain, licenses were required both to transmit and to receive; thus, these stations were pirates and, it being illegal to listen to unlicensed stations, listeners as well as broadcasters, were breaking the law.

Advocates of such stations referred to them, not as "pirate" but as "free" radio, and a number of such stations, beginning illegally, have subsequently become licensed, government-approved organizations. One such has been the London-originating music station, **Kiss FM**. Pirate radio in Britain has frequently been seen as a catalyst for change, providing a revivifying force that has often generated a reevaluation of traditional radio services, and, in most cases, an absorption of techniques, styles, technology, and personnel into the mainstream. A number of UK-based ethnic "pirates" have demonstrated a consumer need that has resulted in legitimizing their activities and the granting of a government license, particularly in the field of **community radio**. Notwithstanding this fact, in the late fall of 2005, the government media industry regulator, the **Office of Communication (Ofcom)**, confirmed its intention of prohibiting any such stations from broadcasting.

Pirate radio can also be seen as touching on other areas, such as national and international propaganda. For example, the traditional voice of Hanoi, the Voice of Vietnam, had a U.S.-sponsored anticommunist counterpoint in the Voice of Free Vietnam. The use of the Internet, and the ease with which Internet radio stations are able to function, has increasingly overtaken the idea of terrestrial "pirate" radio stations, although the element of danger and innovation that the term implies in its most positive form continues to have a powerful impact on radio generally.

PITTAS, CHRISTOS (1945–). Born in Alexandria, Egypt, of Greek parents, the composer Christos Pittas grew up in Cyprus, where he began his musical studies. In 1970, he came to England as a student and since then has lived mostly in London. His works often explore forms that combine sound, movement, and speech. Since 1971, he has worked extensively for the **BBC Radio Drama** Department, composing original musical scores for many productions, and working with a large number of directors, including Ian Cotterel, Martin Jenkins, and **John Theocharis**, and specializing in radio interpretations of the classical repertoire, including *The Theban Trilogy* by

Sophocles (director, David Spencer, 1983) and *The Birds* by Aristophanes (John Theocharis, 1990).

PLOMLEY, ROY (1914–1985). Initially working as a small-parts actor, Plomley joined **Radio Normandy** in 1936 as an announcer, and subsequently went on to produce and present much of the **International Broadcasting Company (IBC)**'s outside broadcast output, notably the touring stage variety show, *Radio Normandy Calling*. He was involved with the establishment of the short-lived **Radio International** during the first months of World War II and narrowly escaped capture, returning to England, where he established his most enduring creation, *Desert Island Discs* for the **British Broadcasting Corporation (BBC)** in 1942. As a radio panel show host, he chaired *We Beg to Differ* and *One Minute, Please* on the **Light Programme** and from 1946–1949 was MC of the same network's *Accordion Club*.

PLOWDEN, BRIDGET (1910–2000). A public servant who had a considerable influence on the development of education, in particular at primary level, Bridget, Lady Plowden, became involved in broadcasting administration and regulation in 1970, initially as a deputy chairman of the **British Broadcasting Corporation (BBC)** governors. The then **chairman Lord Hill** had hoped and intended that she would succeed him, but instead, in 1975, she became chairman of the Independent Broadcasting Authority (IBA), where she became deeply interested in the program output of both Independent Television (ITV) and the fledgling **Independent Local Radio (ILR)**. In this role, she was well liked and made it a policy to visit new stations as they came on air.

PLOWRIGHT, PIERS (1937–). One of the most distinguished features producers of his generation, Piers Plowright was educated at Christ Church, Oxford. He joined the British Council in 1963 and worked as radio and TV officer in Khartoum, Sudan, from 1964–1967. In 1968, he joined the **British Broadcasting Corporation (BBC)** English Radio Department, working from **Bush House** in London. An attachment to BBC Radio Drama in 1973 led to a permanent post for Plowright the following year as executive producer for the **Radio 2 serial**, *Waggoners' Walk*. He remained with the program until 1978 when he became a producer of plays and features, with responsibility, from 1980, for short stories and features on **Radio 3** while maintaining production work on **Radio 4**.

Between 1982 and 1990, Plowright was one of two features producers working in the Drama Department, winning Italia Prizes for his radio documentaries, *Nobody Stays in This House Long* (1983), *Setting Sail* (1986), and *One Big Kitchen Table* (1988). From 1990, he was a senior features producer in Features, Education and Arts Radio (a department that changed its name several times before his retirement from the BBC in 1997). In 1998, he was made a fellow of the Royal Society of Literature, and after he retired from program making, he continued to present occasional features and **talks** on Radios 3 and 4, while maintaining an active role as a freelance lecturer and writer. *See also* FEATURES.

PLUGGE, LEONARD (1889–1981). Captain Leonard Plugge, for many, was the founding father of commercial radio in Britain. His father was a Belgian citizen of Dutch descent. Plugge was educated in London and Brussels and gained a degree in civil engineering at University College, London. In World War I, he joined the Royal Naval Volunteer Reserve, transferring in 1918 to the air force, where he became a captain, a title he used in civilian life for the rest of his career. He remained with the air force until 1921, working on the technical side and representing the air force at aeronautical control commissions in Berlin and Paris, for which he was elected a fellow of the Royal Aeronautical Society in 1921.

From 1923–1930, Plugge worked in London for the Underground Railways group of companies, and during this time he became fascinated with the possibilities of the new medium of radio. In 1924, he traveled through France and Italy by train, exploring the concept of portable radio reception. In 1926, he was the first person to have a radio installed in a private car, and the following year he announced plans to tour through Europe with a colleague, each in their own car, with the intention of examining the possibility of keeping in touch with one another by wireless; thus he predicted the creation of the car telephone, which came 40 years later.

In 1925, he set up an experimental transmission from the Eiffel Tower in Paris, broadcasting a 15-minute fashion talk, sponsored by the London store, Selfridges. Since the broadcast received no publicity, it went virtually unnoticed. Plugge, however, was a born entrepreneur, and during the early 1930s, while experimenting with the concept of the car radio, he was traveling through Normandy in France and arranged a meeting with Fernand Legrand—who was at that time himself exploring the possibilities of wireless transmissions from the town of Fécamp. Thus was born the successful partnership that created **Radio Normandy** and ultimately the network that was the **International Broadcasting Company (IBC)**.

Leonard Plugge had been helped in his initial research into continental stations by his early work, paid for by the **British Broadcasting Company/Corporation (BBC)**, which was to research and publish program details from international radio stations for the BBC journal, *World Radio*.

Plugge pronounced his name, "Plooje"—although when he fought a 1935 General Election campaign under a "Free Radio" ticket, his slogan became "Plug(ge) in for Chatham." He won the seat, although he lost it in the General Election of 1945. This marked the end of his period of influence, with the closure, prewar, of his commercial interests in France, and the loss of his French holdings.

It has been claimed that his name is the origin of the term "record plugger," being a promoter of commercial recorded material for radio. This has, however, not been proven.

He married in 1934 and had two sons and a daughter. In 1972, Plugge moved Hollywood, California, and died there of a heart attack in February 1981. *See also* COMMERCIAL RADIO.

PODCASTING. *See* MP3.

POLDHU. In 1900, **Guglielmo Marconi** came to Cornwall, and set up an experimental wireless station on cliffs above Poldhu cove, on the Lizard Peninsula. The design of the station was predominantly by Sir **Ambrose Fleming**. The exposed location of the station resulted in considerable storm damage, and the first experimental signals traveled only a short distance. On 12 December 1901, however, the first transatlantic wireless signal was sent from here, and picked up 1,800 miles away on Signal Hill, St. John's, Newfoundland, where Marconi had established an aerial, which was held airborne by kites, and a receiving station. The prearranged signal sent was the Morse code for the letter "S."

In 1903, the site was visited by the Prince and Princess of Wales, and the nearby Poldhu Hotel (now a retirement rest home) continues to be a place of pilgrimage for radio enthusiasts. The original wireless station buildings were demolished in 1937, when the **Marconi Company** erected a commemorative granite obelisk that stands on the edge of the cliff close to the site.

POSTE PARISIEN. The first European radio station ever to be owned entirely by a newspaper (*Le Petit Parisien*), Poste Parisien was housed in state-of-the-art studios off the Champs Elysees in Paris in its 1930s prime, having started broadcasting as La Poste Petit Parisien in July 1923. Its transformation into an ultra-modern studio complex, together with the development of a 60-kW transmitter capable of UK reception, resulted from the flotation of the station in October 1929, which raised 5,500,000 French francs.

In partnership with the **International Broadcasting Company (IBC)**, Poste Parisien gradually expanded its UK transmissions up to 18 hours per week by the outbreak of World War II. Recordings of the station's French output from the period include a station call signal of a gong—identical to the sound later utilized by **Radio Luxembourg**.

POST OFFICE. The role of the Post Office, originally the General Post Office (GPO) in British radio has been considerable. From the earliest days, the power of the postmaster general (PMG) as arbiter of content and licenser of broadcasters, listeners, and, initially, of receivers ensured that government policies relating to broadcasting were firmly administered and controlled. After the **"Melba" broadcast** of 15 June 1920 from **Chelmsford**, the postmaster general of the time, the Rt. Hon. Albert Illingworth, announced to the House of Commons that further experimental broadcasts would be suspended because of "interference with legitimate services," the phrase being used to refer to complaints from the newly established air-traffic control system installed at London's Croydon airport. Thus was the Post Office the controller and guardian of frequency use, even prior to the creation of the **British Broadcasting Company (BBC)**.

The GPO issued **licenses** for listeners and introduced a stipulation in 1922 that holders of such licenses could only listen to BBC programs on British-made equipment manufactured by a member company of the BBC and approved by the Post Office. Such receivers carried a circular stamp of approval, with the logo "BBC/PMG" and a registration number. With the growth of homemade sets, rules were laid down by the Post Office that each of the constituent parts of the receiver should bear the stamp of approval. When the company became the **British Broadcasting Corporation (BBC)** in 1927, this regulation was no longer necessary, although the Post Office continued to control licensing.

The direct involvement of the postmaster general continued until 1969, when a Supplemental Royal Charter (Cmnd 4194) was granted, following a Post Office Act of the same year, which transferred the powers of the postmaster general with regard to broadcasting to the newly created government post of the minister of posts and telecommunications. *See also* BBC CHARTER.

POTTER, GILLIE (1888–1975). This comedian's real name was Hugh Peel. Potter was an educated and sophisticated humorist who specialized in an English "upper-class" persona, (utilizing the epithet of "Lord Marshmallow of Hogsnorton"). Although he was a highly successful stage artist, his style was particularly suited to radio, and he frequently broadcast 15-minute studio talks, without a "live" audience. He made his radio debut in 1931, and his style, with its love of language and word-play, quickly endeared itself both to prewar audiences and to the **British Broadcasting Corporation (BBC)**, who found in his witty style a counterpoint to the broader music hall acts. He made his last radio series, *Mr. Gillie Potter*, in 1952. In the early 1960s, he retired to Bournemouth, and his last broadcast appearance was as part of the panel game show *Sounds Familiar* in 1970.

POTTER, STEPHEN (1900–1969). Stephen Potter worked as a writer and critic, producing a series of studies of literary figures, including D. H. Lawrence and Samuel Taylor Coleridge, before joining the **British Broadcasting Corporation (BBC)** as a writer/producer in the **Features** Department in 1938, later rising to become head of features and poetry. During the war, he produced a number of features and **documentaries**, on literary themes and also relating to the current conflict, before developing a series of satirical programs with Joyce Grenfell under the collective title of *How*. These dealt in a humorous way with everyday issues, with titles such as *How to Give a Party* and *How to Talk to Children*. In all, there were 29 *How* programs, starting in 1943. In 1946, *How to Listen to Radio* was the first program heard on the newly created **Third Programme**.

Potter's lightness of touch as a producer helped the genre of the radio feature develop toward a new impressionistic style, utilizing natural dialog and little in terms of sound effects. Among notable successes were his *Professional Portraits*, *New Judgements*, and his production of Nevill Coghill's version of Chaucer's *The Canterbury Tales*. In 1947, Potter began working on a new book, which became *The Theory and Practice of Gamesmanship*. Such was the success of the book, that he left the BBC to concentrate once more on his writing, and a series of sequels followed.

POWELL, ALLAN (1876–1948). Sir Allan Powell, **chairman** of the **British Broadcasting Corporation (BBC)** from 1939 to 1946, was responsible for maintaining the BBC's independence during the difficult war years. It was Powell who dismissed **F. W. Ogilvie** as **director-general**, replacing him with **Cecil Graves** and **R. W. Foot**, and subsequently, **William Haley**.

PM. This news magazine program, running from 5:00 p.m.–6:00 p.m. on weekday evenings, effectively bridging the **Radio 4** schedule from afternoon to evening, first went on air in 1970. Over the years, its format has barely changed, with its dual presenter style, and its blend of heavy and light news items.

THE POWER BEHIND THE MICROPHONE. This remarkably prophetic book, written by **Peter Eckersley** in 1942, extended the concept of "wired" radio as developed during the 1930s through **relay exchanges**, to a vision of a system that only at the start of the 21st century came to fruition in Britain through the establishment of cable transmission systems. It is worth quoting from Eckersley's work, predicting as it does, effectively the digital revolution in the context of living standards in the UK that would not manifest themselves for half a century:

I have a dream about the future. I see the interior of a living-room. The wide windows are formed from double panes of glass, fixed and immovable. The conditioned air is fresh and warm . . . Flush against the wall there is a translucent screen with numbered strips of lettering running across it . . . these are the titles describing the many different "broadcasting" programmes which can be heard by just pressing the corresponding button . . . Not a hint of background noise spoils the sound even though some of the performances take place half across Europe, the quality is so lovely that reproduction criticizes every detail of the playing and speaking.

Of course it is only a dream, but not so completely fantastic as some might imagine. It could all be done by using wires rather than wireless to distribute programmes. Let a cable, no thicker than a man's finger, be laid along the streets, outside the houses, and the main part of the installation is completed. The cable would only contain two or three conductors and tappings would be made on to these for branch feeders to bring the service into the houses. The branch ends in the houses would be connected to house receivers. The street cables would be taken to transmitters which would inject programmes into them. [Eckersley, P. P. The Power Behind the Microphone. London: The Scientific Book Club, 1942.]

PRIESTLAND, GERALD (1927–1991). Joining the **British Broadcasting Corporation (BBC)** as a graduate trainee to the **news** division in 1948, Gerald Priestland received numerous overseas postings as a reporter, including Asia, Europe, the Middle East, and the United States, where he interviewed Martin Luther King shortly before the Civil Rights leader's assassination. He moved into television thereafter, returning to the UK, but taking on the host role for *Newsdesk* on **Radio 4** in 1970, a post he retained for four years.

A breakdown in the mid-1970s, brought on by his experiences in covering the Vietnam War, led Priestland to a profound religious faith, and in 1976, he became a Quaker. In 1977, he became the BBC's religious affairs correspondent and created an unprecedented response from the public through his series, *Priestland's Progress*, in which he brought religious faith to a mass audience and prompted a postbag of more than 20,000 letters. He became a popular voice on the *Today* program, and even after his retirement, he was heard weekly in the *Pause for Thought* spot on **Terry Wogan**'s morning **Radio 2** program.

PRIESTLEY, J. B. (1894–1984). Priestley was a prolific writer and his plays—both on stage and on radio—were successful from the mid-1930s. Prior to World War II, however, he had held no great regard for radio. This was to change with a series of **talks**, begun in June 1940, as an attempt by the **British Broadcasting Corporation (BBC)** to counter the propaganda broadcasts of **William Joyce**. Priestley wrote and presented the series, entitled *Postscript*, which went out after the 9:00 p.m. news on Sunday evenings. What characterized these broadcasts were both the content—a straightforward honesty and communicable determination that touched the national mood in a similar way to that of Winston Churchill's broadcasts—and Priestley's style, a bluff, north-country voice, talking directly to his listener.

His Socialist politics at one point offended Conservative sensibilities in October 1940, and he was removed from the air, to be briefly reinstated in January 1941. Much later, the talks from these months were collected and published in the book, *All England Listened*, (1967).

PRIX ITALIA. The Prix Italia is the oldest and most prestigious international competition for radio, television, and related media in the world. It awards prizes for productions in the fields of **drama, documentaries** (including both cultural and **current affairs**), the performing arts, and music. The competition was founded in Capri in 1948, and annually it is hosted by a major Italian city. Only members of the Prix Italia are permitted to enter its competition; membership is made up of 80 public and private radio and television companies, representing 42 countries from five continents. Its general assembly meets annually to select a president from one of its members.

PROGRAM SHARING. This was a concept of exchanging program material between independent radio stations, which operated from 1976 to 1990. It was first administered by the **Independent Broadcasting Authority (IBA)** and subsequently by the **Association of Independent Radio Contractors (AIRC)**. Programs from local stations around Great Britain were centrally copied and offered to other companies, free of charge. The scheme helped to overturn prejudice against the fledgling commercial industry by disseminating programs.

The funding for the enterprise—the advertising, copying, and distribution costs—came from a controversial tax raised by the IBA called **secondary rental**. The range of work was considerable and demonstrated a notable difference in programming to that permitted after the 1990 **Broadcasting Act**, when regulations were relaxed and effectively ended much creative speech and arts coverage on commercial radio in Britain.

PURVES, LIBBY (1950–). Libby Purves presented **Radio 4**'s conversation program, *Midweek* from 1983. After joining the **British Broadcasting Corporation (BBC)** in 1971 as a studio manager, at the age of 28, she joined **Brian Redhead** as copresenter on the *Today* program, becoming the show's first woman presenter. She was also the first person to broadcast "live" from Beijing, hosting *Today* from there in 1978. Other programs have included *The Learning Curve* and a number of **documentaries**. She has also been a print journalist, and has written travel books, works on childcare, several novels, and a book in praise of radio, *Radio: A True Love Story* (2002).

PYE, WILLIAM GEORGE (1869–1949) and PYE, HAROLD JOHN (1901–1986). William and Harold Pye, father and son, together created one of the most prestigious of British radio manufacturing firms, which was to become known ultimately as "Pye of Cambridge." William Pye had started his own business in 1896, as a scientific instrument manufacturer. During World War I, the Pye company made optical and electrical instruments for the armed services. After the war, with the coming of the **British Broadcasting Company (BBC)** and radio broadcasting, it began manufacturing receivers.

In 1923, William's son, Harold, joined the company, and the following year was made a partner. Pye junior was an excellent engineer and salesman, and he was able to design sets that proved attractive to consumer needs, paying particular attention to the receiver cabinets as furniture. During this period, the famous Pye "Fretwork Sunrise" began to appear on the cabinets of Pye sets. Harold had noticed the motif on a colleague's cigarette case, and utilized it with effect from 1927. It was used for 10 years, and briefly reappeared on a 1948 model. It remains an iconic image of UK radio manufacture in the 1930s.

Meantime, William Pye was maintaining his instrument business, and in 1929, sold the radio branch to Charles Orr Stanley. The company continued to trade as Pye Radio, and, after 1937, as Pye Ltd., while William's original company, W. G. Pye and Co., continued under William's leadership until 1936, when William retired in 1936, selling his interest to Harold. Pye Junior ran the company until 1947, developing, as in the previous war, a working relationship with the government in the manufacture of military equipment. He then sold this company to Pye Ltd., and thereafter, although the Pye name continued for many years, the family no longer controlled it. Harold retired at the early age of 46.

– Q –

QUEEN'S HALL. Almost adjacent to **Broadcasting House** in London, standing where a modern hotel and the **British Broadcasting Corporation (BBC)** office block, Henry Wood House, now resides, Queen's Hall was used for the Promenade Concerts until it was destroyed by bombs in May 1941. It was here that the **BBC Symphony Orchestra** gave its first ever concert, in October 1930, under the leadership of Arthur Catterall.

QUERY PROGRAMME. Said to be the first radio **Quiz Show**, *Query Programme* ran for a series of eight editions beginning in May 1926. The concept behind the program was that listeners should place a series of named radio performers in their correct *Radio Times* billings. Weekly winners were invited to spend an evening at the London station, **2LO**.

QUIGLEY, JANET (1902–1987). Janet Quigley was involved as a producer with many important war and postwar **British Broadcasting Corporation (BBC)** radio initiatives. Prior to her BBC career, she had worked in publishing and with the Empire Marketing Board. Her first job in the Corporation, which she joined in 1936, was in the **Talks** Department, where she was assigned the task of researching topics for talks which that appeal to **women**. One of her major initiatives from this time was the 12-part series, *Towards National Health*, broadcast in 1937, which covered fitness and nutrition.

She worked on *Women at War*, which began in October 1941, designed initially for women serving in the armed forces. Quigley also produced the lighter series, *Kitchen Front*. In 1944, she was awarded the MBE for her work on wartime talks. She left the BBC a year later to marry, but returned in 1950 as editor of **Woman's Hour**. In 1956, she was promoted to Talks Department management, where, in 1957, with Isa Benzie, she was instrumental in the creation of the flagship news program, **Today**. She also helped to create the program for the blind, **In Touch**.

Quigley referred to what she called radio's capacity for "indirect propaganda" as a means of conveying valuable social messages, and her ability to impose this quality on the programs with which she was associated over 30 years could be seen as one of her greatest contributions to the medium. She retired in 1962, but thereafter continued to write for radio, serializing more than 20 books for *Woman's Hour.*

QUIZ SHOWS. In Britain, the birth of the radio quiz could be said to be in 1926, with **Query Programme**, although it was not to be until 1937 that the concept was explored further. **Monday Night at Seven** contained an element entitled *Puzzle Corner*, and in 1938, **Children's Hour** carried a series of spelling contests between teams from different parts of the country chaired by **Freddy Grisewood** and entitled *Spelling Bee*. Subsequently, the genre has developed to the extent that it is not possible to chronicle all programs. It is notable, however, that during the immediate prewar years, and onward from 1939, there was a proliferation of quiz programs feeding a growing appetite in the British radio audience. Among these, contained within the 1944 program, *Merry-Go-Round* was the first quiz to offer a cash prize, *Double or Quits Cash Quiz*. **Alastair Cooke** chaired *Transatlantic Quiz* in 1945, and this was followed by **Round Britain Quiz** in 1947. The trend continued with the popular schools quiz, *Top of the Form*, which ran on the **Light Programme** from 1948–1986. *What Do You Know?* which began in 1953 under the chairmanship of **Franklin Engelmann** evolved into *Brain of Britain* with Robert Robinson in 1967. The most popular of all radio quizzes, however, remains *Have a Go*, which began in 1946 with Wilfred Pickles.

QUOTE . . . UNQUOTE. A long-running panel game broadcast on **Radio 4**, at one time on **Radio 2** and also the **World Service**. It was devised by Nigel Rees, who also presented the program, and had its first broadcast in 1976.

– R –

RADIO 1. Britain's first national pop music station first broadcast on 30 September 1967 as part of the streamlining of **British Broadcasting Corporation (BBC)** radio into generic strands. The network was a necessary response to the challenge thrown down by **pirate radio**, and employed many of the personalities who had been heard on such stations as **Radio Caroline** and **Radio London**, including **Tony Blackburn**, who, as breakfast show presenter, was the first voice to be heard on the new network.

Initially, because of needle time restrictions, under its first controller, Robin Scott, the new station was something of a compromise; output was shared for a time with **Radio 2**, and the networks separated only for specific programs at certain times of the day. At first only heard on **mediumwave (amplitude modulation, AM)**, Radio 1 opened its first **frequency modulation (FM)** frequency, broadcasting alongside its AM transmissions, in 1988. By the end of the decade, it could be heard in stereo by three quarters of the UK population.

By the early 1990s, the network was passing through a period of crisis caused partly by an upsurge in **commercial radio** success, but also by the fact that personnel on Radio 1 had changed little since its creation, and were becoming increasingly out of touch with the youth audience. **Matthew Bannister**, then controller of the network, set about redefining its brand image. Many of the old order left, the audience continued to decline, and the last years of the 20th century were difficult.

By 2005, Controller **Andy Parfitt** had consolidated station policy, acutely aware that one of Radio 1's key issues is, and always has been, the balance between being relevant to its core youth audience in terms of music policy, and its role as a **public service** broadcaster. In the first five years of the 21st century, this has resulted in some award-winning **documentary** features, frequently made by independent production companies, highlighting problems of drugs, AIDS, and youth violence.

RADIO 2. Created at the same time as **Radio 1**, the network replaced the old **Light Programme**, and brought with it many of the **features** and programs from that network. Since September 1967, the station has frequently been in the vanguard of UK radio broadcasting; in January 1979, it was the first **British Broadcasting Corporation (BBC)** network to broadcast a 24-hour schedule. In August 1990, it was the first to broadcast on **frequency modulation (FM)** only.

For some years, Radio 2 had a somewhat staid reputation, as being designed for an older generation. It was in January 1996, with the appointment of Controller **James Moir**, that this began to change. Moir began cleverly rebuilding the network into the most listened-to radio station in the country, combining music interest for an audience disenfranchised by the reduced age of the target audience on **Radio 1**, while retaining the loyalty of older listeners.

In May 2002, Radio 2 won the Sony Gold Award for Station of the Year for the second year running, an achievement it was to repeat at the 2005 event. Its hold over the UK radio market seemed virtually unassailable under Moir's successor, **Lesley Douglas**, and a continuing problem for **commercial radio**, lacking its resources but frequently seeking to draw on the same audience.

RADIO 3. In many ways, Radio 3 has come to represent the **British Broadcasting Corporation (BBC)** public service ethic in its most uncompromising form. Created in this name on 30 September 1967, it grew out of former networks; the **Third Programme** had become **Network Three**, and the cultural high tone was retained for this new incarnation.

Radio 3 is the greatest patron of the arts—particularly music—within the BBC, with a high proportion of its output given over to live relays of concerts, frequently by one of the corporation's five orchestras. It also broadcasts drama and features, and its discussion programs, such as *Night Waves*, engage at a high level with arts, culture, and contemporary issues.

Successive controllers have explored the network's identity in various ways. During the **Promenade Concerts**, it is the audio source of accessing every concert, and lately, particularly under Controller **Roger Wright**, it has explored ethnic music and jazz increasingly as part of its output, sometimes to the chagrin of certain elements of its listenership.

RADIO 4. Evolving out of the old **Home Service** in September 1967, this was the fourth and last station of **Frank Gillard**'s generic streaming policy at the time. The UK's primary speech network, broadcasting a mix of **news**, debate, **features**, comedy, and drama, it is unique in the UK, and globally. It has created innovative work, such as the *Hitchhiker's Guide to the Galaxy*, alongside programs that have become much-loved institutions, including *The Archers*. Its commitment to drama is extensive, with at least one play broadcast every day of the week.

Successive controllers have become aware of the network's particular relationship with its audience; Radio 4 listeners have always been vocal regarding change to the station's output. Recent Controllers **Helen Boaden** and **Mark Damazer** have been aware of this issue, when developing the schedule, seeking to combine adjustments and refinements with a sensitivity of approach to listeners' perceptions and requirements of the network.

Radio 4 remains capable of innovation; it has explored the concept of interactive radio in its drama, *The Dark House*, and in 2005 created the opportunity for listeners to download certain of its programs from its website, "**podcasting**" Melvin Bragg's intellectual discussion/debate, *In Our Time*. Radio 4's success has been called by its critics, its largest problematic issue; broadcasting to a certain demographic of the UK, sometimes nicknamed "Middle England," it has historically found it difficult to attract an audience from the younger elements of the UK population.

RADIO 5. On the day **Radio 2** relinquished its old **mediumwave (AM)** frequency, (27 August 1990), the **British Broadcasting Corporation (BBC)** used that frequency to create a new radio station, Radio 5. This was a hybrid of **news**, **sports**, and youth speech programming, including some innovative and interesting plays aimed at the teenage market. From the start, the lack of brand identity made the network problematic, and audiences remained small. In March 1994, it was relaunched as **Radio 5 Live**.

RADIO 5 LIVE. This **British Broadcasting Corporation (BBC)** network was born out of controversy in a number of ways. At the same time that **Radio 5** was perceived to be failing, BBC radio was moving toward the idea of a rolling news service and had originally earmarked the **Radio 4 longwave** frequency for this purpose. There was, however, considerable opposition to this from listeners in parts of the UK—and Europe—where there was not adequate **frequency modulation (FM)** reception. Thus, the failure of Radio 5 provided an opportunity to escape this impasse.

Launched on 26 March 1994, Radio 5 Live created a blend of tabloid-like **news** coverage, magazine programs, and high-quality **sports** coverage. It also developed a strong web-based identity and for a time led the way in terms of the relationship between a radio station and its web presence.

The coming of **digital radio** gave listeners the opportunity of hearing the station in other than its **amplitude modulation (AM)** quality, and station chiefs used this new technology to launch an alternative service, Radio 5 Live Sports Extra, an occasional service, enabling the network to cover two major sporting events simultaneously.

RADIO ARANJUEZ. *See* EAQ MADRID.

RADIO ATHLONE. This Irish radio station presents a unique case in the history of prewar commercial radio broadcasting into the United Kingdom: a state-run broadcaster, initially part-funded by **license** fees and part by customs duties. It opened in 1933, and from the start operated a UK concession, initially granted to Radio Athlone Publicity, and subsequently—briefly—to the **International Broadcasting Company (IBC)**, before, in May 1935, the Irish government made a decision that no non-Irish advertisers would be permitted to sponsor programs.

Thereafter, the only sponsored programs on the station became those supported by the Hospitals Trust, which were advertised by 1937 in *Radio Pictorial* as being one hour per night, seven nights a week. At the same time, transmitter power had been increased from an already powerful 60 kW to 100 kW, the most that was permitted to Ireland under international agreement. By the end of that year, the station was billed as Radio Eireann, although the program output remained unchanged until the outbreak of war.

RADIO AUTHORITY (RA). Created out of the 1990 Broadcasting Act to replace the **Independent Broadcasting Authority (IBA)**, the Radio Authority was designed to be the regulator of all radio broadcasting in Great Britain outside the **British Broadcasting Corporation (BBC)**. This included local and national **commercial radio**, as well as the regulation and **licensing** of student and hospital broadcasting and **Restricted Service License (RSL)** stations. Its first chair was Lord Chalfont, and its first chief executive was Peter Baldwin. The Radio Authority was intended to be a "light touch" regulator, but as the decade proceeded, commercial broadcasters sought for a further easing of regulation and greater opportunities for consolidation. In the **2003 Broadcasting Act**, the Radio Authority was deemed to be no longer appropriate to the converging digital world of modern media, and in December 2003 it was replaced by the wider-reaching regulatory powers of the **Office of Communications (Ofcom)**.

RADIO BALLADS. This ground-breaking concept of **feature** making grew out of the partnership between the husband and wife folk team of **Ewan MacColl** and Peggy Seeger and the BBC producer, **Charles Parker**. In all, there were eight "Ballads." These were (with transmission dates):

The Ballad of John Axon	2 July 1958
Song of a Road	5 November 1959
Singing the Fishing	16 August 1960
The Big Hewer	18 August 1961
The Body Blow	27 March 1962
On the Edge	13 February 1963
The Fight Game	3 July 1963
The Travelling People	17 April 1964

The programs not only developed a new narratorless technique of documentary storytelling, utilizing new mobile recording technology, but gave a direct voice to working-class communities, elevating their stories to a kind of radio "art." The best known of the eight programs is *Singing the Fishing*, which won the **Prix Italia** in October 1960.

RADIO CAROLINE. The brainchild of **Ronan O'Rahilly**, the first of the UK **pirate radio** stations of the 1960s, and extremely important in the development of UK postwar radio. Radio Caroline shaped the music radio revolution that led to the creation of **Radio 1** by the **British Broadcasting Corporation (BBC)**, and ultimately, the launch of **commercial radio** in the UK in October 1973.

Radio Caroline began broadcasting on 29 March 1964, from a ship moored off the Thames Estuary. Its first voice was that of **Simon Dee**. After merging with **Radio Atlanta** shortly thereafter, the original ship sailed around the coast to the Isle of Man, where it became Radio Caroline North, while Atlanta became Radio Caroline South.

When the offshore stations were outlawed in August 1967 by the Marine Broadcasting Offences Act, Caroline alone defied the ban, with **Johnnie Walker** and Robbie Dale continuing to broadcast, moving the station into legend. Administration was established in Holland, and thereafter the Caroline brand has continued in various guises through sinkings, changes of ships, raids by the UK Department of Trade and Industry, and hurricanes. In 2004, it was heard again, through the new medium of satellite radio, a continuing icon in UK radio, even when reduced to little more than a famous name.

RADIO CITY. There have been two stations by this name.
1. In the early summer of 1964, during the period of **pirate radio** expansion, a World War II fort, nine miles off the east coast of England, on the Shivering Sands sandbank, was occupied by a company run by David Sutch ("Screaming Lord Sutch") and launched later that year as Radio City. The station was involved with various controversies, including a murder, during its short existence.
2. When land-based **Independent Local Radio (ILR)** was approved in 1972, a number of station **licenses** were granted after the initial franchises of the **London Broadcasting Company (LBC)**, **Capital Radio**, and **Radio Clyde**. One of these was Radio City in Liverpool, on air since 1974 and broadcasting to Merseyside, Cheshire, and parts of Wales and Lancashire. The station's first

controller was **Gillian Reynolds**, who in taking on the post, became the first female controller in UK **commercial radio**.

RADIO CLYDE. This Glasgow Independent Local Radio (ILR) station was the first **commercial radio** operation to be established outside London when it began broadcasting in December 1973. Run by James Gordon, later Lord Gordon of Strathclyde, it became, with Radio Forth, the foundation of **Scottish Radio Holdings**. Particularly in its early days, the station was noted for its drama and **talks** production, under the hand of—successively—Hamish Wilson and Finlay Welsh.

RADIO CÔTE D'AZUR. This French radio station, originally based in the Municipal Casino at Juan-les-Pins, was one of those utilized by the **International Broadcasting Company (IBC)** to carry programs to the UK in English. Although the station itself changed its name to Radio Méditerranée for domestic transmissions, the IBC, broadcasting to the UK from 1934, kept the title "Radio Côte d'Azur (Juan-les-Pins)" as a more evocative brand, advertising output in *Radio Pictorial* and inviting listeners to "tune in on Sundays to the Sunny South." Shortly before the outbreak of World War II, however, the station's domestic name was also being used for its international output, with an increasing amount of English-language programming.

RADIO DATA SYSTEM (RDS). This transitional technology for **frequency modulation (FM)** usage grew out of developments made by Swedish engineers in 1976. The principal benefits of the RDS (RBDS in the U.S.) were that radios using the system would automatically retune to locate the strongest FM signal, while carrying the Enhanced Other Networks (EON) feature, thus enabling travel broadcasts to be detected and permitted to interrupt received programs. This was particularly useful for car radios. The system also permitted display of station information.

Designed for use with FM analog, much of the RDS technology was incorporated into UK **digital radio**, as this new platform gradually began to supercede FM transmissions.

RADIO EIREANN. *See* RADIO ATHLONE.

RADIO INTERNATIONAL. After the closure of **Radio Normandy** in 1939, the **International Broadcasting Company (IBC)** used its resources and transmitter to create programs for the British Expeditionary Forces in France until it was closed down by a joint British and French Government ruling on 3 January 1940. In its short life, it predated the **British Broadcasting Corporation (BBC)**'s **Forces Programme**, which opened within days of its demise.

RADIO JOINT AUDIENCE RESEARCH (RAJAR). RAJAR was established in 1992 to operate a single audience measurement system for the UK radio industry. The company is wholly owned by the **British Broadcasting Corporation (BBC)** and the **Commercial Radio Companies Association (CRCA)**. The structure is that of a "deadlocked" company, board decisions requiring the agreement of both parties.

In addition to BBC and CRCA representation, membership of the board recognizes the interests of the advertising community, which is represented by the Institute of Practitioners in Advertising (IPA). In recent years there has been much discussion within the British industry relating to the adjustment of RAJAR's methods of monitoring an increasingly complex market. The traditional method of audience measurement has been through the issue to listeners of personalized diaries, to be completed according to the individual's listening habits. Increasingly, pressure from some areas was brought to bear for the introduction of a system of electronic metering.

RADIO LEICESTER. Radio Leicester was the first local radio station in Britain run by the **British Broadcasting Corporation (BBC)**, commencing transmissions on 8 November 1967, under the managership of **Maurice Ennals**.

RADIO LONDON. Not to be confused with **British Broadcasting Corporation (BBC)**, Radio London, launched in 1970, prior to being rebranded as Greater London Radio (GLR) in 1988, was one of the seminal **pirate radio** stations, operating from the North Sea, which went on air in December 1960. A former U.S. minesweeper was moored off Frinton-on-Sea, Essex, the station was the major competitor to **Radio Caroline**, and it became the platform for many

UK **disc jockeys** who went on to become household names in radio, including **John Peel**, **Tony Blackburn**, and **Kenny Everett**. The station was relaunched in May 2005, with programs created in Frinton, and transmitted from Holland back to the UK.

RADIO LUXEMBOURG. This famous station went on the air from the Villa Louvigny in Luxembourg city in late 1933, after a series of test transmissions that had begun in March that year. It originally broadcast on a wavelength of 1190 meters, and its policy—together with **Radio Normandy** and other stations operated by the **International Broadcasting Company (IBC)**—was to beam sponsored programs at Britain, attacking the public service monopoly of the **British Broadcasting Corporation (BBC)**. In particular, the station targeted Sunday listeners, denied entertainment by the BBC's Sabbatarian principles, and at its peak in the mid-1930s achieved huge audiences with such programs as *The Ovaltineys* and *The Palmolive Program*.

Radio Luxembourg closed down on 21 September, 1939, shortly after the outbreak of hostilities. Because of its strategic significance, the station, with its giant transmitter, situated on the Junglinster Plateau, was used by both German and Allied forces at various times during World War II. It was used as a relay for the transmission of the propaganda broadcasts of **William Joyce ("Lord Haw-Haw")**, and following the station's liberation by American forces on 10 September 1944, it started programming aimed at the retreating German army under the station name "Radio Twelve-Twelve," after the U.S. 12th Army, who were operating the programs.

Radio Luxembourg reopened its commercial English-language transmissions on 1 July 1946, and on 2 July 1951 switched to its well-known wavelength of 208 meters, mediumwave. The 1950s proved to be a second golden age of sponsorship for the station; it once again offered populist listening to an audience to which the BBC did not cater. With the coming of **pirate radio** in the 1960s and the BBC's creation of **Radio 1** in 1967, Radio Luxembourg's audience began to decline. In August 1990, it launched a new satellite channel, but it finally closed down on 30 December 1992.

RADIOLYMPIA. See *RADIO SHOW*.

RADIO LYON. Radio Lyon began broadcasting to its French community in 1924, but licensed English-language transmissions that began under the title "Radio Lyons" in the autumn of 1936. The UK agency was Broadcast Advertising of London, with a program department at the commercial recording studios of **Vox**. Thus, it was one of the few independent commercial operations of the time outside of the activities of the **International Broadcasting Company (IBC)**, **Wireless Publicity**, or the **J. Walter Thompson Organization**.

The station's output had many original features, including the marketing of its chief announcer, Tony Melrose, as "the golden voice of Radio Lyons." Adopting a visual pun on its name in the symbol of two lions on its program publicity material, it also created an early version of a music chart in 1937, when it broadcast a list of the 12 most popular tunes requested by listeners. It continued its transmissions in English up to the start of World War II.

RADIO NEWSREEL. Initially started in July 1940 as a daily program for North America, the **British Broadcasting Corporation (BBC)** initiated a Pacific edition in October that year and an African version in October 1941. It was first broadcast to British audiences in November 1947, and continued to be broadcast to domestic audiences until April 1970, thereafter continuing on the **World Service**. Its theme tune, "Imperial Echoes," became famous.

RADIO NORMANDY. The fruit of a speculative partnership between the entrepreneur **Leonard Plugge** and a businessman from Fécamp on the Normandy coast, Fernand leGrand, this was the first station to beam regular sponsored programs from the Continent to Britain. In so doing, it formed the foundation of Plugge's **International Broadcasting Company (IBC)**, which flourished throughout the 1930s. First transmissions were under its nonanglicized name, "Radio-Normandie," on 11 October 1931, on 246 meters, mediumwave.

In 1935, a wavelength change to 1304 meters improved British reception greatly, although the station never achieved the nationwide coverage of **Radio Luxembourg**'s giant transmitter. Indeed, the marketing branch of the IBC made a virtue of this, claiming to potential advertisers that they deliberately targeted "The prosperous south" of the country. The station gave early opportunities to a number of young broadcasters who were to achieve success elsewhere, among them **Bob Danvers-Walker** and **Roy Plomley**. It developed a sophisticated policy of outside broadcast recording, notably the touring variety show *Radio Normandy Calling*. For some months after the outbreak of World War II, the IBC sought to reinvent the station as a service for British troops under the title **Radio International**. On 3 January 1940 however, this closed down, and after the war, changes in French media regulation made it impossible for the station to resume its transmissions.

RADIO NORMANDY CALLING. In 1938, at the height of the prewar **commercial radio** boom in Britain, the **International Broadcasting Company (IBC)** created a traveling show, recorded on location at various venues around the UK. The aim, particularly in the north of the country, was to raise awareness of **Radio Normandy**, which was less well known in the region than **Radio Luxembourg**, because of relative transmitter power. It was presented by **Roy Plomley**, and had a theme sung by "The Belles of Normandy":

Radio Normandy calling you,
Bringing you music from out the blue,
Laughter and rhythm, so when you hear . . . (Bell rings)
You know it stands for
Radio Normandy coming through,
With lots of enjoyment for all,
So be sure to listen to
Radio Normandy Calling.

The program existed in both an on-air and off-air version, the latter being used solely as a promotional vehicle, from which specific acts were selected for the broadcast version, once a week.

RADIO PARADE. In 1933, British International Pictures, based at Elstree, made a feature film that included many of the top radio variety stars of the time. Entitled *Radio Parade of 1933*, it clearly borrowed from U.S. films of the time, including some of those made by Busby Berkeley, as well as Hollywood's *Big Broadcast* series. Unfortunately, the film no longer exists.

A restored version of the sequel, *Radio Parade of 1935*, remains, and contains an innovative color sequence, and a host of major radio personalities. The film is noteworthy in that its main plot revolves around a staid **British Broadcasting Corporation (BBC)**, run by an autocrat (Will Hay impersonating **John Reith** under the name of "Garland").

RADIO PARIS. Beginning broadcasting in 1921 to a French domestic audience, Radio Paris was carrying some programs made by the **International Broadcasting Company (IBC)** early in 1933, but shortly afterward, the stake with the UK company seems to have ended. Thereafter, the station became involved with the early radio aspirations of a group of entrepreneurs led by the newsaper the *Sunday Referee* and Radio Publicity (Universal).

Broadcasting on **longwave (LW)**, it became a popular broadcaster of English-language programming until December 1933. This output, however, had been threatened by a French government decision to take the station out of private hands and turn it into a state-run enterprise. At this time, a new station was being developed in Luxembourg, and negotiations led to a shift of UK programming, transmitted on Sundays, from Paris to Luxembourg. In early December 1933, output was broadcast on both stations simultaneously, with the chief announcer, **Stephen Williams**, encouraging listeners to retune to the new wavelength, guided by the sound of his voice. Thus was created **Radio Luxembourg**'s first UK output. Radio Paris opened under state control on 17 December. From this time, UK transmissions from the station ceased.

RADIO PICTORIAL. This populist magazine began as a journal of general broadcasting "gossip" in January 1934. By August of that year, it was carrying full details of **commercial** broadcasts from the Continent, in the face of a British ban on newspaper publicity for the services. At first there were articles relating to **British Broadcasting Corporation (BBC)** programs and personalities, but these diminished as the decade proceeded. With the coming of war, and the ending of the programs it publicized, the magazine also ended its life, the final edition appearing on 8 September 1939. *See also* JOURNALS.

RADIO POEMS. Radio and poetry have long been linked and there has been a large number of commissions for radio poems—works specifically designed to be interpreted by and through the medium. In many cases, these have been linked to **drama**, in others, the genre has been used to illuminate **features**. The **British Broadcasting Corporation (BBC)** producer **Douglas Cleverdon** was particularly active in this field, fostering and developing relationships with leading poets during the 1940s and 1950s, such as David Jones, David Gascoyne, and Dylan Thomas. Perhaps the most famous radio poetic drama was Thomas's *Under Milk Wood*, produced by Cleverdon in 1954. Other poets who have been attracted to the medium have included **Louis MacNeice**, Michael Symmons Roberts, George Macbeth, and Julian May.

RADIO SHOW. The first UK radio exhibition took place in the Horticultural Hall, London, from 30 September to 7 October 1922. In March 1923, the *Daily Mail* Ideal Home exhibition included a display and demonstration of equipment, and by 1925, with the new technology now established as a major business, an exhibition at the Royal Albert Hall featured 122 stands mounted by 63 suppliers. This led to the establishment of an annual radio show, that—from September 1926—was staged in the Empire Hall, Olympia, London, by the Radio Manufacturers Association, and subsequently in partnership with the **British Broadcasting Company (BBC)**.

"Radiolympia," as it was originally known, and, after its transfer to the Earls Court complex, "The Radio Show," was for 40 years (aside from the war years) the showcase for the British industry, covering television from 1936 in addition to sound broadcasting. Programs were broadcast live from the exhibition throughout its history, including in 1934 *Variety from Olympia* with **Henry Hall** and the **BBC Dance Orchestra** and a special edition of *In Town Tonight*. The annual event even had a theme tune composed in its honor in 1937, "Listen to Your Radio."

The first postwar Radiolympia was in 1947. As the Radio Show, it continued to be a major annual week of celebration of the medium, until in 1966, the BBC decided it was no longer appropriate, and it was ended. There was one revival, in 1988, when more than 93,000 people visited the "BBC Radio Show" at Earls Court.

RADIO TIMES. It was in response to a boycott by the British Newspaper Proprietors' Association in 1923 that **John Reith** launched *The*

Radio Times, subtitled "the Official Organ of the **British Broadcasting Company (BBC)**." The first edition of this weekly listings magazine was published on 28 September 1923. From the start, it contained a range of features, letter pages, competitions, and advertisements. It also developed a tradition of commissioned art covers, marking special occasions, the seasons of the year, anniversaries, etc.

When first published, the schedules were printed from Sunday to Saturday, following **John Reith**'s view of Sunday—the first day of the week—as "The Lord's Day." This continued until October 1960, when the broadcasting week became reflected in the journal's pages as running from Saturday to Friday. Up until the end of 1936, the magazine was *The Radio Times*; with its edition of 8 January 1937, however, it received a major style overhaul, at which point the word "The" was dropped from its title and the journal was thereafter known simply as *Radio Times*.

With the advent of television, the journal began to accommodate TV schedules, and there have been a number of attempts over the years, to integrate radio and television programs. Since 1989, radio programs have been grouped at the back of the magazine, and increasingly the brief has widened to include non-BBC programming and digital stations. In spite of the predominance of television within its pages in latter years, the magazine retains its original title. *See also* JOURNALS, *THE LISTENER*, WORLD RADIO.

RADIO TOULOUSE. Radio Toulouse played a key part in the story of English-language commercial broadcasts from the Continent, in that it was the first station to broadcast sponsored programs regularly to Great Britain from France, in 1928, shortly after the illegal boosting of its transmitter strength. These were record programs, sponsored by **Vox** and presented by **Christopher Stone**. Thereafter, irregular English-language programming came from the station, although in early 1933 the **International Broadcasting Company (IBC)** was broadcasting *The IBC Half Hour* from the station on a regular basis.

In 1933, the station was destroyed by fire and did not reopen until 1937, when it recommenced transmissions from a greatly improved site. At this time, the UK concession moved to the W. E. D. Allen Agency. The company gained from the expertise of **Peter Eckersley**, who had become a business associate. Somewhat surprisingly, the opening of the new English service in 1937 began with an inaugural address by Winston Churchill, followed by a talk by Eckersley. Program listings continued in *Radio Pictorial* until May 1938. Thereafter, traces of UK transmissions disappeared.

RAY, TED (1906–1977). Born Charles Olden in Wigan, Ted Ray grew up in Liverpool and learned his comedy trade on the Music Hall stage, where his act, wisecracking interspersed with violin playing carried the sobriquet, "Fiddling and Fooling." He began his radio career in 1939 and in 1949 gained his own half-hour radio show, *Ray's a Laugh*, which the **British Broadcasting Corporation (BBC)** used as a replacement for *It's That Man Again (ITMA)*. The program ran for more than 10 years. He was also a long-term regular member of the off-the-cuff comedy quiz, *Does the Team Think*. His theme tune was "You are my Sunshine."

RAY'S A LAUGH. The comedy series based around **Ted Ray** and a cast that included Kitty Bluett, Patricia Hayes, and Kenneth Connor ran from 1949 to 1961 on the **Light Programme.** The first series contained no less than 64 episodes and featured a young **Peter Sellers**. Indeed, later, Sellers was to cite Ray as one of his great comedic influences.

READ, AL (1909–1987). Read, a comedian who came from a Lancashire background, was, until he broke into radio comedy, the latest generation in his family's business of meat pie manufacturing. After becoming resident comedian in *Variety Fanfare* in 1951, he quickly became a popular favorite with audiences for his comedy of social observation, drawn largely from Lancashire working-class life. *The Al Read Show* ran through the late 1950s and into the 1960s on the **Light Programme.**

REDHEAD, BRIAN (1929–1994). With a background in print journalism, Redhead came to **Radio 4**'s flagship morning program, *Today*, in 1975. Although known for his confident and often combative style of interviewing—particularly politicians—he was keenly interested in comparative religion and, in particular, Christianity, and often presented programs reflecting this interest. He was chair of the *Radio 4 Debates* from 1989, and—nine years before his debut on the *Today* program, was host of *A Word in Edgeways* from 1966. Born on Tyneside, he retained a passionate commitment to the North of England, an engagement reflected in his election, shortly before his death, as chancellor of Manchester University.

REGIONAL PROGRAMME. The concept of a regional service for the **British Broadcasting Company (BBC)** came from Chief Engineer **Peter Eckersley** in 1924, but the Regional Service did not begin until 21 October 1929; at that time, the 2LO transmitter moved to Brookman's Park and London Regional was born. Other regional services were created in the Midlands (1931), Scotland (1932), West and Wales (1933), and Northern Ireland (1934), all providing a localized alternative to the **National Programme**, which had begun under that name in 1930. The Regional and National Programmes merged on 1 September 1939 to become the **Home Service**. After the war, regional programs returned but as op-outs from the main Home Service.

REITH, JOHN CHARLES WALSHAM (1889–1971). Sir John, later Lord Reith of Stonehaven, was born in Stonehaven, the son of a Scottish Presbyterian minister. Following his education at Glasgow Academy and Gresham's School in Norfolk, he served an engineering apprenticeship with the North British Locomotive Company. Reith was a major in the Royal Engineers in World War I from 1914–1915, when he was badly wounded. In 1919, he became general manager of William Beardmore & Co., an engineering firm in Glasgow, and shortly afterward, at the age of 33, he was appointed general manager of the newly formed **British Broadcasting Company (BBC)**.

From the start, Reith held a high-minded vision that the BBC's role was to inform, educate, and entertain; this concept was to shape the development of public service broadcasting in Britain ever after. Within seven months, he launched *The Radio Times* as the journal of the new organization, circumventing boycotts from the Newspaper Proprietors' Association. One of his great achievements of the early years was to enable the BBC to negotiate the events of 1926 when Britain was hit by the General Strike, and newspapers ceased publication. In this, he saw a great opportunity to demonstrate the immediacy and news power of radio.

When the company changed to corporation under Royal **Charter** on 1 January 1927, Reith became its first **director-general**, a post he retained until 1938. He was knighted in 1927. Reith was a complex man whose concepts created the term *Reithian*, a word still used to describe the ideology that inspired his attitude to public service broadcasting. Aspects of his paternalistic attitude and an autocratic style of management brought him considerable criticism. In particular, the Sabbatarian policy upon which he insisted in the prewar years of the BBC, forbidding light entertainment on Sundays, created opportunities for **commercial radio** entrepreneurs using Continental station bases to directly attack the BBC's monopoly.

It was at the bidding of Prime Minister Neville Chamberlain that Reith left the BBC in 1938, to become chairman of Imperial Airways. Although his post-BBC years were filled with achievement and recognition—he was created baron in 1940 and was chairman of the Commonwealth Telecommunications Board from 1946 to 1950, during which time (1948) the BBC inaugurated the **Reith Lectures** in his honor—there remained a sense that he felt betrayed by the direction that British broadcasting took after his departure from a position of direct influence. He wrote two volumes of autobiography: *Broadcast Over Britain* (1924) and *Into the Wind* (1949). He also kept a diary, which was subsequently published.

REITH LECTURES. The **British Broadcasting Corporation (BBC)** inaugurated the Reith Lectures in 1947, naming them after the first **director-general**, **John Reith**. The Corporation each year invites a leading figure to deliver a series of lectures, with the aim to advance public understanding and debate about significant issues of public interest. The lecture series is broadcast on **Radio 4**, and the first series was given in 1948 by Bertrand Russell. Chronologically, speakers and topics have been:

1948	Bertrand Russell	Authority and the Individual
1949	Robert Birley	Britain and Europe
1950	John Zachary Young	Doubt and Certainty in Science
1951	Lord Radcliffe	Power and the State

1952	Arnold Toynbee	The World and the West
1953	Robert Oppenheimer	Science and the Common Understanding
1954	Sir Oliver Franks	Britain and the Tide of World Affairs
1955	Nikolaus Pevsner	The Englishness of English Art
1956	Sir Edward Appleton	Science and the Nation
1957	George Kennan	Russia, the Atom, and the West
1958	Bernard Lovell	The Individual and the Universe
1959	Peter Medawar	The Future of Man
1960	Edgar Wind	Art and Anarchy
1961	Margery Perham	The Colonial Reckoning
1962	Prof. George Carstairs	This Island Now
1963	Dr. Albert Sloman	A Universe in the Making
1964	Sir Leon Bagrit	The Age of Automation
1965	Robert Gardiner	A World of Peoples
1966	J. K. Galbraith	The New Industrial State
1967	Edmund Leach	A Runaway World
1968	Lester Pearson	Peace in the Family of Man
1969	Dr. Frank Frazer Darling	Wilderness and Plenty
1970	Dr. Donald Schon	Change and Industrial Society
1971	Richard Hoggart	Only Connect
1972	Andrew Schonfield	Europe: Journey to an Unknown Destination
1973	Prof. Alastair Buchan	Change without War
1974	Prof. Ralf Dahrendorf	The New Liberty
1975	Dr. Daniel Boorstin	America and the World Experience
1976	Dr. Colin Blakemore	Mechanics of the Mind
1977	Prof. AH Halsey	Change in British Society
1978	Rev. Dr E Norman	Christinity and the World
1979	Prof. Ali Mazrul	The African Connection
1980	Ian Kennedy	Unmasking Medicine
1981	Prof. Laurence Martin	The Two Edged Sword
1982	Prof. Denis Donoghue	The Arts without Mystery
1983	Sir Douglas Wass	Government and the Governed
1984	Prof. John Searle	Minds, Brains and Science
1985	David Henderson	Innocence and Design
1986	Lord McCluskey	Law, Justice and Democracy

1987	Prof. Alexander Goehr	The Survival of the Symphony
1988	Prof. Geoffrey Hosking	The Rediscovery of Politics
1989	Jacques Darras	Beyond the Tunnel of History
1990	Rabbi Dr Jonathan Sacks	The Persistence of Faith
1991	Dr. Steve Jones	The Language of the Genes
1992	No Lecture Series	
1993	Edward Said	Representation and the Intellectual
1994	Marina Warner	Managing Monsters
1995	Sir Richard Rogers	Sustainable City
1996	Jean Aitchison	The Language Web
1997	Patricia Williams	The Genealogy of Race
1999	Anthony Giddens	Runaway World
2000	Chris Patten	Respect for the Earth
	Sir John Brown	
	Thomas Lovejoy	
	Gro Harlem Brundtland	
	Vandana Shiva	
	HRH The Prince of Wales	
2001	Tom Kirkwood	The End of Age
2002	Prof. Onora O'Neill	A Question of Trust
2003	V. S. Ramachandrian	The Emerging Mind
2004	Wole Soyinka	Climate of Fear
2005	Lord Broers	The Triumph of Technology
2006	Daniel Barenboim	In the Beginning Was Sound

RELAY EXCHANGES. The development of relay exchanges—organizations specializing in the dissemination of radio programs down telephone wires opposed to wirelessly from transmitters—was a crucial factor in the advance of **commercial radio** in Britain before World War II. Their existence is also significant in that they predated by many years the development of cable broadcasting in the UK.

The idea of sending material down a telephone wire for public—as opposed to private—consumption, had been present from the 1890s (*See* ELECTROPHONE). With the development of radio on a mass audience scale in the late 1920s and early 1930s, the idea of wired relays, under license to the Post Office as controller of the lines, became a key issue in British radio. One of the most enthusiastic supporters of "wired broadcasting" was the first Chief Engineer

Peter Eckersley for the **British Broadcasting Company (BBC)**. After his departure from the Corporation in 1929, Eckersley worked strenuously at developing the medium, one of the benefits of which was that the vagaries of signal fade and strength could be eliminated; this was particularly useful in blocks of flats and other poor reception areas.

Eckersley's experiments gave prospective listeners a choice of four programs, on a subscription basis. With the BBC offering two—the **National** and **Regional** services—the way was therefore open for competition on an equal technical quality basis. This—and the fact that a subscription to a relay service was cheap, and therefore attractive to the poorer parts of society—was of major significance to the issue of commercial competition from the Continent. The BBC sought to reach agreement with two of the relay companies—Standard Radio Relay Services and Radio Central Exchanges—that they would relay only BBC programs. The scheme was thwarted by the Post Office, however, with the argument that "it would be unfair to impose restrictions on relay subscribers which were not imposed on the private owners of wireless sets."

Major relay subscription areas were established in Leicester, Derby, Nottingham, Sheffield, Middlesborough, Newcastle, and Carlisle. For obvious reasons of reception, Wales—North and South—was "wired," and the city of Hull boasted the most extensive wired network in Europe. The growth of relay services in Britain during the first half of the 1930s was remarkable:

	Exchanges	Subscribers
1931	132	43,889
1932	194	82,690

From this almost doubling of subscribers, the growth over subsequent years was startling:

	Exchanges	Subscribers
1935	343	233,554

By 1939, the number of relay exchanges had fallen, partly because of a vigorous campaign against the services by radio receiver manufacturers. In December of that year, there were 284 exchanges, with 270,596 subscribers. Nonetheless, taking into account the number of listeners per household, relay services were, by this time, reaching a total audience of 1,033,677. The war saw an end to relay exchanges, and in spite of pressure from enthusiasts such as Eckersley (*see THE POWER BEHIND THE MICROPHONE*) it was to be more than 60 years before the concept of wired—or cable—transmission would be readopted in Britain.

RELAY STATIONS. When the **British Broadcasting Company (BBC)** established its first eight stations in 1922–1924, it achieved a geographical spread of the United Kingdom, which it quickly sought to enhance by the establishment of a series of relay stations, responsible only for transmitting program material, rather than originating it. These stations were, in chronological order of opening:

Sheffield (6FL), 16 November 1923
Plymouth (5PY), 28 March 1924
Edinburgh (2EH), 1 May 1924
Liverpool (6LV), 11 June 1924
Leeds/Bradford (2LS), 8 July 1924
Hull (6KH), 15 August 1924
Nottingham (5NG), 16 September 1924
Stoke-on-Trent (6ST), 21 October 1924
Dundee (2DE), 12 November 1924
Swansea (5SX), 12 December 1924

By 1939, the number of relay exchanges had fallen, partly due to a vigorous campaign against the services by radio receiver manufacturers. In December of that year, there were 284 exchanges, with 270,596 subscribers. Nonetheless, taking into account the number of listeners per household, relay services were by this time reaching a total audience of 1,033,677. The war saw an end to the exchanges, and in spite of pressure from enthusiasts, such as Eckersley (*See THE POWER BEHIND THE MICROPHONE*), it was to be more than 60 years before the concept of wired—or cable—transmission would be readopted in Great Britain.

RESTRICTED SERVICE LICENSE (RSL). The concept of the restricted service license radio station was created by the then regulator of UK **commercial radio**, the **Radio Authority**. It has subsequently been developed by the regulatory successor, the **Office of Communication (Ofcom)**. It was part of the widening of public access to radio broadcasting, and successful **licensees** are permitted to run a radio station, usually for up to 28 days, either on **frequency modulation (FM)** or **amplitude modulation (AM)** on low power. The scheme is particularly attractive to charities, festivals, and other specific events. More extended versions can be available for such institutions as hospitals and student organizations. It also permits those planning to apply for a full-time license, for example, potential **community radio** stations, to test audiences within their target area. RSLs are issued at Ofcom's discretion, subject to frequency availability and adherence to various specified basic rules and technical criteria.

REYNOLDS, GILLIAN (1935–). A well-known radio critic, Gillian Reynolds began her career in this field in 1967 as the radio critic of the *Guardian*. In 1974, she was the founding program controller of the Liverpool **Independent Local Radio (ILR)** station, **Radio City**. This made her the first woman controller of a commercial radio station in the UK. Thereafter, she became the radio critic of the *Daily Telegraph* and one of the most respected voices in British radio criticism.

Reynolds is chairman of the **Charles Parker Archive** at Birmingham Central Library, and served for five years on the Consultative Committee of the National Sound Archive. She became the first fellow of the **Radio Academy** in 1990 and in 1999 was made an MBE for services to journalism.

RIDERS OF THE RANGE. Created by **Charles Chilton**, this was the first UK-made radio series in the genre of the Western. Broadcast on the **Light Programme** from 1949–1953, the series was based as far as possible on known information relating to the history of the American West. Chilton also scripted a "spin-off" cartoon series in the children's comic book *The Eagle*. The music for the program was created by The Four Ramblers, one of whom, Val Doonican, went on to achieve fame in a solo singing career.

THE ROBINSON FAMILY. Initially billed as "A day-to-day history of an ordinary family" (changing by its end to "an everyday story of everyday people," and thus predating *The Archers'* subtitle of "An everyday story of country folk"), *The Robinson Family* was the first exploration of the genre of the daily **serial** by the **British Broadcasting Corporation (BBC)**, starting in July 1945. In order to create a sense of authenticity, the production team, writers, and actors were not billed. It was broadcast at 2:45 p.m. each afternoon on the **Home Service**, and ended its run on Christmas Eve 1947.

"ROMANY." The Reverend George Bramwell Evens (1883–1943) was a Methodist minister whose roots lay in gypsy stock, and in October 1932, he began a popular series of "walks" in the studios of the **British Broadcasting Corporation (BBC)** North Region, in Manchester. Initially, the *Out with Romany* programs were heard only in the North of England, but from 1938 they were broadcast on the **National Programme**. In these simulated nature walks, Evens was joined by two children, Murel Levy and Doris Gambell, and a spaniel, named "Raq." The programs became extremely popular, and spawned a series of books by Evens.

ROSS, JONATHAN (1960–). One of the most popular entertainers in the UK media, Ross's hosting of his highly successful Saturday morning program on **Radio 2** has complemented his television work, and in 2005 an independent panel commissioned by *Radio Times* voted him the most successful radio broadcaster in Britain. Born in the East End of London, Ross's first radio work was in 1987, when he stood in for two weeks on **Radio 1**. The following year, he joined Richard Branson's **Virgin** Radio station, where he was produced by **Chris Evans**. Meanwhile, he continued to make freelance appearances on the **Radio 4** program *Loose Ends* from 1987–1989.

In 1998, Ross returned to Virgin Radio with *The Jonathan Ross Show*, working with his producer, Andy Davies, for the first time. The format, of producer and presenter sharing on-air banter, proved popular, and when Radio 2 controller **Jame Moir** brought him to the network, the format transferred with Ross, and achieved new heights of critical and audience success. In 2000, he won a **Sony Radio Academy Award** for music presentation; other awards have included Radio Program of the Year and Radio Personality of the Year at the annual **Television and Radio Industries Club (TRIC)** in 2000 and 2001, respectively.

ROUND, HENRY JOSEPH (1881–1966). H. J. Round was a highly gifted radio engineer and inventor, who joined the **Marconi Company** in 1902. After working in the United States for the company, where he devised the elements of direction finding, he returned to Britain to work personally with **Guglielmo Marconi**, before further travel to Ireland and South America in 1912, where he operated two wireless stations on the upper reaches of the Amazon, redesigning them to operate on two separate wavelengths by day and by night, the first time that deliberate use had been made of wavelength differences to solve problems of transmission.

World War I saw Round in distinguished service, working in communications, notably when through his wireless operations, the movements of the German fleet prior to the Battle of Jutland were detected. He also designed the first telephony transmitters and receivers for airborne use. For his services, he received the Military Cross in 1918. After the war, he helped set up the experimental station at **Chelmsford**, and engineered the first public broadcast entertainment on 15 June 1920, a recital by the Australian prima donna, Dame Nellie Melba (*See* "MELBA" BROADCAST). When, two years later, the **Writtle** experiments led to the establishment of **2LO** in **Marconi House**, London, the transmitter was designed by Round.

Other contributions were the creation of the artificial echo system and the Sykes-Round microphone. In 1931, he set up in private practice as a research consultant, and continued to work, largely on the defense applications of wireless, both for the Admiralty and the Marconi Company for many years. Round filed 117 patent applications throughout his life, the last of which was recorded in 1962 when he was 81.

ROUND BRITAIN QUIZ. The concept behind this long-running **quiz** program was that a team from the British regions challenges a team from London on varied and often complex areas of general knowledge. The program began in November 1947, and among its various quiz masters has been **Gilbert Harding**.

ROUND THE HORNE. Written by a team of writers led by **Barry Took** and Marty Feldman, and including Brian Cooke, Johnnie Mortimer, and Donald Webster, this famous comedy series was the successor to *Beyond Our Ken*. Both programs revolved around **Kenneth**

Horne, and *Round the Horne*, which ran on the **Light Programme** from March 1965 to June 1968. At its peak, 15 million listeners a week tuned in regularly to hear a blend of innuendo, camp, familiar catchphrases, and wordplay from a regular team including **Kenneth Williams**, Betty Marsden, Hugh Paddick, and Bill Pertwee. In 2002, a stage version, *Round the Horne Revisited*, devised by Brian Cooke, recreated the program with actors impersonating the original players with considerable success.

RUSSELL, AUDREY (1906–1989). Born in Dublin and trained as an actress, she joined the London Fire Brigade shortly before World War II broke out, and worked actively in this capacity through the London blitz. Based near **Broadcasting House**, she came to the notice of the **British Broadcasting Corporation (BBC)** after being interviewed on the effects of air raids. As a result, she was invited to make a series of broadcasts on the work of the Auxiliary Fire Service. This resulted in a secondment to the Air Ministry, from where she broadcast a series of talks on the work of the Women's Auxiliary Air Force.

In 1942, the BBC appointed her as traveling reporter for the magazine program ***Radio Newsreel*** with the specific task of touring Britain, reporting on the effects of war from various parts of the country. Russell became an accredited war correspondent, and sent dispatches from Belgium, Holland, Norway, and Germany. After the war, she became a reporter for the **Home Service**, although her great skill—and love—was for commentary rather than reportage.

In 1947, Russell was part of the outside broadcast team covering the wedding of Princess Elizabeth, and this led to her becoming one of the key members of commentary teams covering state occasions for the BBC; she worked on relays from the Festival of Britain in 1951, and went on the first of many royal tours in 1952. She was in Westminster Abbey, commentating on the coronation of Queen Elizabeth II in 1953, and went on to cover numerous other events of national significance, including the funeral of Winston Churchill in 1965, and the Silver Jubilee of 1977.

Russell was the only **woman** to become an accredited war correspondent in World War II and the first woman news reporter on the Home Service. She became a freeman of the City of London in 1967 and was appointed MVO in 1976.

– S –

SAGA RADIO. Saga Radio grew out of the Saga brand created in the 1950s by Sidney De Haan, who identified a growth market for providing products and services to older members of the community—initially the retired population. Beginning with the holiday market, Saga diversified into magazine publication (1984) and insurance and investment from 1987.

It was the success of *Saga Magazine* that encouraged the company to explore the possibilities of radio at a time when the UK **commercial radio** sector was about to enter a period of change and growth. Undertaking preliminary work on an application for the first national commercial **license** (*See* CLASSIC FM), the company then went on to undertake its own research, leading to the establishment of Saga Radio in 1994. Market research showed that radio services for listeners aged 50 and over were lacking, and, given that this age group was identified clearly as Saga's brand target, the group moved forward in the application process for a number of licenses. These included the West Midlands, Yorkshire, and East Midlands licenses. In 1999, Saga appointed Ron Coles as its director of radio, and since that time the group has invested heavily in **digital radio**, with both its Saga Radio regional stations, and its digital-only Primetime Radio national station.

SARONY, LESLIE (1897–1985). This well-known songwriter and entertainer enjoyed considerable success during the 1920s and 1930s as a stage and recording artist, and in 1935 formed, with pianist Leslie Holmes, the variety double act they called "The Two Leslies." In November 1936, they created an occasional comedy series entitled *Radio Pie*, which Sarony himself devised, which featured a cast of well-known variety performers including **Tommy Handley** and Anne Ziegler. It proved to be so popular that in 1939 a stage version toured Britain, to considerable acclaim.

Holmes retired in 1946, and Sarony continued the act for three more years with Michael Cole before returning to solo variety work in the late 1940s. He continued to work until near the end of his life, in demand as a "straight" character actor in stage productions ranging from the work of **Samuel Beckett** and Shakespeare to a film role in *Chitty Chitty Bang Bang*. In 1983, he appeared in his second royal variety performance, less than two years before his death from cancer in February 1985.

SATURDAY CLUB. Hosted by Brian Matthew, this live program of popular music began on the **Light Programme** in 1957 as *Saturday Skiffle Club*, and continued until 1969. Initially, it was one of the very few shows catering to a youth market on **British Broadcasting Corporation (BBC)** radio. It featured a blend of interviews, records, and "live" sessions with leading artists and bands. The program was responsible for introducing many U.S. artists to UK radio audiences; in 1960 the show featured sets with Gene Vincent and Eddie Cochran, and in June 1966, to celebrate its 400th edition, guests included Cliff Richard and the Shadows, Billy Fury, Marianne Faithfull, **Humphrey Lyttelton**, and the Beatles.

SATURDAY SKIFFLE CLUB. This precursor of the broader-ranging *Saturday Club* grew out of the UK trend for young people to make their own music. Brian Matthew, who continued to host the program after its name change, introduced many professional artists in the field, including Chas McDevitt and Nancy Whiskey, who had a major hit with their version of *Freight Train* and other groups of the era, among them the Vipers and Johnny Duncan and the Blue Grass Boys. The program was produced by Jimmy Grant. In April 1958, **Radio Luxembourg** capitalized on the trend by introducing *Amateur Skiffle Club*.

SAVEEN, ALBERT (1915–1994). Working under his surname, Saveen was a highly successful ventriloquist and the first to have his own series on radio—a **Light Programme** show called *Midday with Daisy May*. Saveen was originally a printer; a cockney who developed a sophisticated presentation style with his doll, "Daisy May," he had suffered lung damage during the war and later said it was the effect of this that inadvertently led him to create the voice he used in his ventriloquist act.

SAVILLE, JIMMY (1926–). A former Yorkshire miner, Saville's extrovert style was first heard on **Radio Luxembourg**, before he moved in 1968 to **Radio 1**, where he presented *Saville's Travels*, a highly popular program that in 1989 transferred to **commercial radio**.

SAVOY HILL. This was the first permanent home of the **British Broadcasting Company (BBC)**. Two Savoy Hill was part of a building owned by the **Institution of Electrical Engineers (IEE)** on the Thames Embankment, adjacent to the Savoy Hotel. The IEE leased the building to BBC, and the building was the scene of some of the most important early radio experiments, notably in **drama**. The BBC in the form of **2LO** moved into Savoy Hill on 2 February 1923, and broadcasting began from the premises on 1 May of that year. Photographic images of the studios show broadcasting in a more elegant time; one of the studios was modeled on the Lounge of Eastbourne's **Grand Hotel**, itself the origin of a famous series of light orchestral music programs that ran into the 1970s. Because of the building's proximity to the Savoy Hotel, a number of the dance bands employed by the hotel became regular broadcasters, most notably the **Savoy Orpheans**. The last program, *The End of Savoy Hill*, produced by **Lance Sieveking**, took place on 14 May 1932, ending with a final announcement by **Stuart Hibberd**, after which an unidentified voice from the new headquarters was heard, ensuring complete continuity: "This is **Broadcasting House** calling . . ."

SAVOY ORPHEANS. The Orpheans became the most famous of the Savoy Hotel dance bands to perform from Savoy Hill during the 1920s, becoming major radio and recording stars. The band recorded prolifically from its formation in 1923 until 1927, initially under Debroy Summers, who led the first direct relay from the hotel on 11 October 1923, then with Cyril Ramon Newton and finally with the pianist Carroll Gibbons.

SCOTT, ROGER (1943–1989). After a stint as a merchant seaman, Roger Scott began his broadcasting career on U.S. and Canadian radio stations during the 1960s, before joining the renowned biscuit factory radio station, **United Biscuits Network (UBN)**. In 1973, he was a member of the original on air team at **Capital Radio**, where his afternoon shows gained significant audiences with particular emphasis on features, such as *Three o'Clock Thrill* and *Hitline*. After 15 years, he moved from Capital to **Radio 1** in 1988 (although he had appeared on **British Broadcasting Corporation (BBC)** Radio in the early 1970s under the pseudonym, "Bob Baker"). His devotion to the **music** he played and his eschewing of the cult of personality gained him a loyal fan base, and he broadcast his *Saturday Sequence* and *Late Night Sunday* programs until shortly before his early death from throat cancer.

SCOTTISH RADIO HOLDINGS (SRH). Scottish Radio Holdings grew out of the third **commercial radio license** to be granted in the UK, when **Radio Clyde** went on air in January 1974, serving Glasgow. The first two London stations—**London Broadcasting Company (LBC)** and **Capital Radio** had had troubled starts a few months earlier, and endured some initial financial problems. Clyde on the other hand was an immediate success.

In 1990, UK radio ownership rules were relaxed, and this enabled the two main Scottish stations, Radio Clyde and **Radio Forth**, to merge in 1991, thus creating Scottish Radio Holdings. In 1995, the company expanded into print, buying newspaper and magazine interests in Ireland, Northern Ireland, and Scotland. Meantime its radio division continued to expand, acquiring Today FM, Ireland's independent national station and the Dublin-based FM104. SRH's radio division comprised 22 **analog** services, one digital service, and six digital licenses. In June 2005, the group was acquired by **Emap** Radio.

SCRAPBOOK. This highly popular and valuable series of historical **documentaries** was the first of its kind, starting in December 1933 with *Scrapbook for 1913*. The premise behind the series was that each program would base itself upon one year, which would then be examined historically through archives, music, and reconstruction. The programs were researched by the journalist, Leslie Baily, who devised the idea, and who also created two books based on the series, which ran until 1974. The 40th anniversary of the founding of the **British Broadcasting Company (BBC)** was marked in 1962 by *Scrapbook for 1922*. The programs were presented by **Freddy Grisewood**.

SECOMBE, HARRY (1921–2001). Harry Secombe was famed for his work on the ground-breaking radio comedy series, *The Goon Show*, in which his stock character was "Neddy Seagoon." The program, on which he worked with **Spike Milligan**, **Peter Sellers**, and **Michael Bentine**, was first broadcast in 1949 and ran for nine years. Secombe moved into television and film and was an accomplished singer. He was knighted in 1981.

SELLERS, PETER (1925–1980). Born in Southsea on the south coast of England, Peter Sellers is known as one of the UK's most gifted comic actors, in later years enjoying considerable success in film. However, it was as a member of the revolutionary *The Goon Show* that he is best remembered in radio terms.

Drafted into the Royal Air Force (RAF) at the age of 18, Sellers's ambition to become a pilot was thwarted by his poor eyesight. Thus, he became an official RAF concert entertainer. Seeking to develop a career in this field after the war, he contacted the producer, Roy Speer, who engaged him for the 1948 program, *Showtime*. This, in turn, led to *The Goon Show*. A number of comic recordings followed, and subsequently he participated less in radio as his film career burgeoned.

SERIALS. The serial genre may be divided into two forms: dramatized and nondramatized. The former of these was the first to be broadcast by the **British Broadcasting Company (BBC)**. From September 1923 to February 1924, the BBC transmitted a serialized reading of an adventure novel for boys by Herbert Strang, entitled *Jack Hardy*. In December 1925, the BBC ran a three-part serial entitled *The Mayfair Mystery*, which was in the form of a competition, inviting listeners to find the correct solution to a detective story for a prize of £100. The first adult serialized reading was *At the Villa Rose*, read in five episodes by Campbell Gullan in July 1926.

The first drama serial was Hilda Chamberlain's *Ghostly Fingers*, broadcast in three parts on the evenings of 23 and 28 August 1926, with parts one and two being transmitted on the first of those evenings. However, it was not until June 1935 that the first true dramatized radio serial in the modern sense was broadcast by the **British Broadcasting Corporation (BBC)**. This was *The Mystery of the*

Seven Cafes, produced by A. W. Hanson and featuring **Norman Shelley** in the central role. By the time the war broke out, **commercial radio** was developing the genre of the popular radio serial, inspired by the experiences of U.S. agencies such as the **J. Walter Thompson Organization**.

After the war, a number of children's serials gained large audiences, including *Norman and Henry Bones* and *Toytown*. Crossover programming between generations was achieved with the 1950s science fiction serial, *Journey into Space*, while *Mrs. Dale's Diary*, later renamed *The Dales*, and starting in 1948, appealed to a largely female daytime audience. This was replaced by *Waggoners' Walk* in 1969, running until 1980. The most successful serial on UK radio is *The Archers*, a daily serial with an omnibus edition broadcast on Sundays. This began in 1950 and continues to the present. The **World Service** created a serial for an international audience, entitled *Westway*, in 1997, which, despite considerable success with listeners globally, was axed in a round of cost cutting in 2005. *See also* SOAP OPERAS.

SERIES. The genre of the radio series was first successfully developed in the United States. The concept was—and remains—a program that operates on a regular basis—usually weekly—using the same formula of personnel, style, and content, broadcast at the same time on the same day. Comedy series and **quiz shows** have historically fallen conveniently into this category. For comedy the most durable format—one that was to form the blueprint for many that followed—was created first by **Band Waggon** in 1938. This, however, was not the first comedy series; that honor goes to *Radio Radiance* (1925), featuring **Tommy Handley**. In the same year, the BBC broadcast the first series of popular **music** programs, entitled *Winners*. Through the 1930s, **commercial radio** capitalized on the concept of familiarity and habit in the radio audience, and virtually all programs on these stations were made as series. At the same time, social issues were addressed in BBC series such as *Time to Spare*, which focused on the plight of the unemployed.

There have been—and continue to be—series in every genre on UK radio; in the field of **news** and **current affairs**, **Radio 4** has long provided in-depth coverage through programs such as *Analysis* and

From Our Own Correspondent, weekly series of informed comment and reportage. Comedy series have included many classic programs, among them, the **Goon Show**, **Round the Horne** and *Take It from Here*. The long-running *I'm Sorry I Haven't a Clue* owes much of its success to the personalities of its participants, while series of readings, such as the daily **Book at Bedtime**, have become institutions. Daily programs include the news programs, *Today,* and *World at One*, as well as **Woman's Hour** and *You and Yours*, all on Radio 4.

SHAPLEY, OLIVE (1910–1999). Olive Shapley was a highly imaginative and creative **documentary** program maker and broadcaster, who spent 40 years in the **British Broadcasting Corporation (BBC)**, working in both radio and television. Joining the Corporation in 1934 after an education at Oxford, she worked with some of the most significant names in broadcasting. Starting in **Children's Hour**, in Manchester, she became North Region controller of the program.

She became part of the thriving left-wing Features Department developed by **A. E. Harding**, and between 1937–1939 made a number of social-action documentaries, such as *Miners' Wives*, *They Speak for Themselves*, and *The Classic Soil*. This last program, written by Joan Littlewood, compared the living conditions of the Manchester working class with those described by Frederick Engels 100 years previously. In 1939, she married John Scarlett Alexander Salt, director of programs in Manchester, and resigned her staff position because of the ruling that married couples were not both permitted to work for the BBC.

As soon as World War II was declared, however, Shapley returned as a freelancer and made memorable programs about the effect of war on ordinary people's lives. Among her documentaries after the outbreak of war were *Women in Europe* and *Women in Wartime*. From 1942–1945, Shapley and her husband lived and worked in New York, where she continued to contribute material for *Children's Hour* and created **Letter from America**, which was subsequently taken over by **Alistair Cooke**.

After the war and her return to the UK, and the death of her husband in 1947, she became involved in the creation of **Woman's Hour**, a program with which she was associated for more than 20 years, both as producer and presenter. She was also a part of early postwar

British television, and in 1952, she married again, to Christopher Gorton, a textiles executive in Manchester. He died in 1959.

She continued to work in radio and television until her retirement in 1973. Thereafter, she worked and campaigned on a range of social-action issues and traveled widely. In 1996, she published her autobiography, *Broadcasting a Life*.

SHELLEY, NORMAN (1903–1980). Having made his early radio reputation in Australia and New Zealand, Norman Shelley first broadcast for the **British Broadcasting Corporation (BBC)** in 1926, and by the end of the 1930s he had become known as one of UK radio's most versatile and respected actors, becoming an original member of the BBC's wartime repertory company. He was a regular reader on *Book at Bedtime*, and later in life he appeared for a time in *The Archers*, playing "Colonel Danby" up until the time of his death.

Shelley's most famous part, however, was that of Winston Churchill. On 4 June 1940, Churchill had made his famous speech, "We will fight them on the beaches . . ." to the House of Commons. The British Council had wanted Churchill to record the speech for broadcast as propaganda to the United States, but Churchill refused to read it again, suggesting that someone else should read it in his stead. Shelley was approached and recorded it, later claiming that Churchill was pleased with the impersonation. Apparently many listeners in the United States believed they were listening to Churchill himself. Later, stories began to circulate that Shelley was responsible for more broadcasts purporting to be Churchill. This has been largely disproved.

SHENNAN, BOB (1962–). Bob Shennan began his radio career at Hereward Radio in 1985 as a journalist, having graduated with a degree in English from Cambridge. He joined the **British Broadcasting Corporation (BBC)** as a trainee producer in Radio Sport in 1987, going on to become a senior producer in 1989 and editor of Radio Sport in 1992. After elevation to the post of head of Radio Sport in 1994, he assumed responsibility for BBC TV and radio **sports** coverage in 1997. In 2000, he was appointed controller of **Radio 5 Live** with responsibility for all aspects of the network's output.

SHORTWAVE. Prior to the development of the global possibilities for radio programming afforded by the Internet, shortwave broadcasting remained for many years the main means of long-distance sound transmission. **Guglielmo Marconi** had experimented with the medium, although the first engineer to use it for broadcast was Frank Conrad of Westinghouse in the United States.

The long-distance capability of shortwave relates to a section of the ionosphere containing reflective properties, causing signals in the range one to three megahertz to "bounce." This layer was named the "Kennelly-Heaviside Layer," after the American Arthur Kennelly (1861–1939) and the British Sir Oliver Heaviside (1850–1925), who had independently discovered the existence of the layer, 55 to 95 miles above the surface of the earth. It subsequently became known as the "E-Layer."

Shortwave broadcasting played a significant part in the technical development of international broadcasting by the **British Broadcasting Corporation (BBC)**, and during the postwar period was widely used for propaganda purposes. It was for this reason that many large-scale shortwave stations were state controlled or were national broadcasters rather than privately run companies, although some of these continue to use the medium in a limited way. Since the end of the Cold War and the diminishing amount of jamming of signals by hostile powers, shortwave transmission and reception have improved, although since the year 2000, there has been a steady decline in general usage.

SIEPMANN, CHARLES (1899–1985). Born in England, where the first half of his life was spent, Charles Siepmann later moved to the United States, where his influence on media affairs matched that of his prewar years with the **British Broadcasting Corporation (BBC)**. He joined the newly established corporation within a year of its creation under **charter**. Beginning in 1927 as the deputy director of adult education, he became director of the department in 1929. In 1932, when the department was merged with **talks**, he took on the role of director of the combined units, creating a period of considerable creativity in the genre.

Internal departmental tensions led to his move to a newly created post of director of regional relations. The importance of this was twofold; although the **Regional Programme** had been established in technical terms, this was the first time the social and cultural implications of broadcasting regionally had been explored, and Siepmann came to understand the significance of local and regional planning, which would profoundly affect the long-term future of broadcasting in the United Kingdom.

From 1936–1939, Siepmann was director of program planning. Thereafter, after gaining American citizenship, he worked for the U.S. government, where he worked as a consultant to the Federal Communications Commission (FCC), and authored an important report, entitled *Public Service Responsibilities of Broadcast Licensees*, a critique of program and advertising practices on a number of U.S. stations. The work remained highly controversial. From 1946 until the end of his career, Siepmann was involved in academia in the U.S., remaining all his life a staunch believer in the public service ideals he had upheld during his time with the BBC.

SIEVEKING, LANCE (1896–1972). Prior to his radio career, Sieveking served as a pilot in the World War I and was shot down in 1917. Joining the **British Broadcasting Company (BBC)** in 1924, he worked first as the assistant to the director of education before progressing to become the first head of **Outside Broadcasts** for BBC Radio. His approach to the problems of presenting **sport** on radio was innovative and imaginative; the first such event was the 1927 Twickenham encounter between England and Wales. Having personally hired the commentator, H. B. T. Wakelam, he placed a blind rugby enthusiast next to him, to enable him to focus his commentary on an audience without the benefit of vision.

Later moving into the field of radio drama, Sieveking was prolific both in production and adaptation. Here he found a genre that fascinated him philosophically. In his 1934 book, *The Stuff of Radio*, he wrote: "It is interesting to reflect that practically all the things which go to make up the daily broadcast programmes existed before broadcasting was invented, and are now being transmitted just as they stand, very much as the water which existed before water companies is now being transmitted to the water companies' subscribers . . . No, there is only one true stuff of radio. One kind of thing, one genre of arranged sounds, that is peculiarly, particularly, and integrally *the* stuff of radio. The radio-play, and the 'feature-program,' are of this genre." The well-known broadcaster and cricket commentator, **John Arlott**, later called Sieveking "probably the most creative pioneer of British broadcasting."

SILVEY, ROBERT (1905–1981). One of the pioneers of UK radio audience research, Silvey originally worked for the London Press Exchange from 1929–1936, and was involved in researching listenership for early **commercial radio** interests in Great Britain. In October 1936, he joined the **British Broadcasting Corporation (BBC)** to set up Listener (later Audience) Research, of which he remained head until his retirement in 1968.

Silvey devised two research strategies: a continuous survey of listening, which provided estimates of audience size for individual programs, and "panels" of listeners (and later viewers), who were sent questionnaires on a weekly basis to obtain their opinions of selected programs. The survey, involving interviewing a representative sample of the audience regarding their listening—and viewing—for the previous day, ran from December 1939 and continued long after Silvey's retirement.

Silvey, and **Stephen Tallents**, with whom he worked, encountered considerable suspicion from some BBC staff about audience measurement, many believing it would lead to a tyranny of chasing audience figures and result in less quality programming.

After he left the BBC, Robert Silvey lectured widely in the United States, Canada, and Europe on audience research and involved himself with the work of Amnesty International. He was awarded an OBE in 1960, and in 1974, he published *Who's Listening? The Story of BBC Audience Research*.

SIMON, ERNEST (1884–1968). Sir Ernest Emil Darwin Simon, Lord Simon of Wythenshawe, was **chairman** of the **British Broadcasting Corporation (BBC)** from 1947–1952. Having begun political life as a Liberal MP in 1923, he joined the Labour Party in 1946 and was granted a peerage in 1947. He supported the view that BBC chairmen and governors should be granted greater executive responsibility. Unlike previous chairmen, he adopted a highly proactive policy of spending a substantial part of his work week in his office at **Broad-**

casting House. He was a founder of the *New Statesman* magazine and was an important figure in the rebuilding of postwar Britain. His home city was Manchester with which he maintained close connections, chairing the City Council there until 1957.

SIMS, MONICA (1925–). A distinguished producer for many years and editor of *Woman's Hour* from 1964–1967, Monica Sims was controller of **Radio 4** from 1978–1983. In her long career, she was also head of children's television programs, and a member of the British Board of Film Classification. She received an OBE.

SINGING THE FISHING. This August 1960 **feature** by **Charles Parker**, **Ewan MacColl**, and Peggy Seeger was the most famous of the **Radio Ballads** produced by this team from 1958–1964, and established fully, the radio ballad as a new form. The third in the series, it took as its subject Britain's herring fishing communities and featured the singing of Norfolk fisherman, Sam Larner. The program took nearly four months to make and utilized 250 reels of taped actuality and interviews. On transmission, it was critically lauded and won the **Prix Italia** award for radio in October 1960. It was subsequently broadcast in 86 countries and issued as a commercial recording.

SING SOMETHING SIMPLE. This program began on the **Light Programme** in July 1959. The format was simple and unchanging; created by musical arranger Cliff Adam (1923–2001), it revolved around his choir—Cliff Adam's Singers—who presented a half-hour of continuous song, characterized by a gentle, sentimental nostalgia. The singers were accompanied by accordionist Jack Emblow, and the formula proved enduringly popular for an older generation of listener. Starting on Fridays, it soon moved to a Sunday afternoon slot, where it continued on **Radio 2** until Adam's death in 2001. *See also* MUSIC.

6 MUSIC. The first **British Broadcasting Corporation (BBC)** digital music station launched at 7:00 a.m. on 11 March 2002, with Phill Jupitus's *Breakfast Show*. The service was widely publicized as "the first new BBC music station for 32 years." The station controllership is shared with **Radio 2**. Thus at the time of its launch, the controller was **James Moir**.

SMASH HITS. This **Radio Luxembourg** program from the 1950s revolved around the premise of listeners' least-liked records. Members of the audience would write requests for a record to be destroyed on-air, stating their reasons. After the record was played for one time, it would be "smashed." The series proved to be highly popular, first broadcast in December 1952 and running in various forms until 1956. *See also* MUSIC.

SNAGGE, JOHN (1904–1996). Snagge joined the **British Broadcasting Company (BBC)** after coming down from Oxford in 1924. His first role was that of the station director of the Stoke-on-Trent station, but in 1928, he became an announcer at **Savoy Hill**. Among many other BBC posts, he was strongly associated with Outside Broadcasts during the 1930s, and was best remembered for his radio commentary on the Varsity Boat Race, which he performed from 1931–1980. His remark during a moment of confusion in the 1949 race, "I don't know who's ahead—it's either Oxford or Cambridge," remains a favorite. Beyond this, he was the voice of the BBC at many key historical moments, announcing for example the D-Day landings, VE Day, VJ Day, and the deaths of King George VI and Queen Mary. In the years before his final retirement from broadcasting in 1981, he made in excess of 100 programs for BBC Radio London under the title *John Snagge's London*.

SOMERVILLE, MARY (1897–1963). Born in New Zealand, Mary Somerville was educated in Scotland and Oxford, and while at college, met **John Reith**, who was then running the **British Broadcasting Company (BBC)**. Somerville, a passionate believer in education and a mature student at Oxford, wrote to Reith in February 1925 offering her services to the BBC on a voluntary basis to help develop the use of radio in schools to supplement what she saw as the over-rigid scholasticism of the education system. As a result, she was appointed schools assistant in July 1925, working under J. C. Stobart, the company's director of education.

Thereafter, Somerville devoted her whole career, despite poor health, to the development of radio as an educational tool, fusing the ideals of scholarship with the techniques of the new medium. In 1929, she became responsible for the broadcasting of all programs to schools, and by 1950 had risen to the post of controller, **talks** (home sound), becoming the first woman to reach the post of controller in the BBC.

SONY RADIO ACADEMY AWARDS. These awards are seen by the UK radio business as the industry's equivalent of the British Academy of Film and Television Arts (BAFTA) awards for film and television in the UK, or Oscars, for film in the United States. First presented as the Sony Radio Awards in 1983, the aim from the start was to recognize excellence in British radio. In a later agreement between Sony UK and the **Radio Academy**, the country's main industry organization, the names of the two institutions were combined in the title. The awards take the form of a nominations event in which shortlisted entries are announced, followed about a month later by a banquet-event, usually in the Grosvenor House Hotel on London's Park Lane, at which the actual winners are announced.

SOS. In 1933, the **British Broadcasting Company (BBC)** ran a series of programs, presented by the writer S. P. B. Mais, which were eye-witness accounts of unemployment. The series came from the **Talks** Department, ran in tandem with a complementary series, *Other People's Houses*, and was followed a year later by another 12-part **series** of programs on unemployment, *Time to Spare*. The programs were controversial and drew strong responses from all sides. At the same time, they remain as landmarks in the development of public service broadcasting in the United Kingdom. These were the first attempts by the BBC to examine and analyze social issues in human terms.

SOS MESSAGES. These messages, requesting relatives to establish contact with a sick or dying relative, have been broadcast by **British Broadcasting Company/Corporation (BBC)** radio services since 1923, as part of its public service remit. The format is unchanging, and follows a strict pattern of words. Once a very familiar part of **Home Service** and **Radio 4** continuity, increasingly sophisticated communication technology has rendered the service less necessary, although broadcast announcements of this type continue to be heard.

SPORT. The development of radio as a medium for sports commentary was initially seen as problematic. In early soccer commentaries, it was felt that listeners would require a visual aid to assist them in picturing the action of the game; a numbered grid, representing the playing area, was placed in *The Radio Times*, and alongside the commentator describing the play, another voice would call out the number of the square in which the action was taking place. In addition, full radio sports coverage required the development of technical resources, and critically, agreement with the Press Association. It was with the creation under **charter** of the **British Broadcasting Corporation (BBC)** in 1927, that this agreement was achieved, and organized coverage of sporting events was launched on radio, with a flurry of events.

In January of that year came both the first commentary of a rugby international (England v. Wales) and a soccer match (Arsenal v. Sheffield United.) In March 1927, the first horse racing commentary was broadcast, of the Grand National Steeplechase. In April, the first commentary of the Oxford v. Cambridge boat race on the River Thames in London began a long tradition that continued well into the era of television coverage of the event, and in the same month came the first coverage of the major soccer event in the UK sports calendar, the FA Cup Final (Cardiff City v. Arsenal). This was followed in May by the first commentary on a cricket match (Essex v. the New Zealand touring team) and in June, the first Wimbledon tennis tournament.

The establishment of radio as a medium for sports coverage saw the creation of a new kind of broadcaster with both specialist knowledge and the ability to describe—often at high speed—the action as it developed before them. Such broadcasters included **George Allison**, (soccer) **Eamonn Andrews** (boxing), **John Snagge** (the Boat Race), and **Raymond Glendenning** (horse racing). In addition to outside broadcasts, a number of magazine programs fed the appetite for sport, including *Sports Report*, which began in 1948. The necessity to cover extended sporting events, such as cricket, with matches lasting between three and five days, led to all-day commentaries, such as *Test Match Special* (**TMS**), which has covered every international test match since 1957. For some, the service is controversial, as it adopts **Radio 4**'s **longwave** service, displacing regular programs, in addition to being carried by a digital service.

A number of sports-specific stations have developed in recent years, including **Radio Five Live**, which carries sport in addition to a general rolling news format, and its digital companion station **Radio Five Live Sports Extra**, activated at times when two or more major sporting events occur concurrently. Additionally, the **commercial radio** station, **TalkSport**, carries a strongly male-biased schedule of commentary, comment, and **phone-in** content nationally.

STOLLER, TONY (1947–). Tony Stoller was a key figure in **commercial radio** regulation for many years, following an early career in regional newspapers. He held senior posts in the radio division of the **Independent Broadcasting Authority (IBA)** for five years, after moving in 1974 from the position of marketing services manager of the *Liverpool Daily Post and Echo*. After a time as the first director of the **Association of Independent Radio Contractors (AIRC)**, the trade organization for commercial radio companies, he was for four years managing director of Thames Valley Broadcasting (Radio 210) in Reading.

Stoller was chief executive of the **Radio Authority (RA)**, which, prior to the creation of the **Office of Communication (Ofcom)**, licensed and regulated all commercial radio services in the UK. In April 2003, Stoller became Ofcom's external relations director, responsible for building the organization's structure and presence in the Home Nations, and for creating a climate among stakeholders and opinion leaders in order to enable Ofcom to carry out its regulatory duties, both nationally and internationally. In 2003, he was awarded a CBE for his services to broadcasting, and retired in 2005.

STONE, CHRISTOPHER (1882–1965). Stone has been claimed to be the first British broadcaster to make a profession of playing records full-time on radio. He began doing so for the **British Broadcasting Corporation (BBC)** in 1927, and later moved to **commercial radio** in the 1930s, where he became increasingly popular on **Radio Luxembourg**.

Stone was educated at Eton College and Christ Church, Oxford. In 1914, he enlisted in the Middlesex Regiment and the following year was commissioned in the Royal Fusiliers. He was rewarded for his service in World War I with the Distinguished Service Order (DSO) and the Military Cross (MC). It was in July 1927, while acting as joint editor—with his brother-in-law, Compton Mackenzie—of the magazine the *Gramophone* that he became associated with radio record programs. The key to his success was his casual approach and spontaneity; at a time when virtually all speakers and presenters on radio worked from scripts, Stone insisted on a conversational ad-lib approach. In his own words, "I never had any words written down. I insisted on being free to meander along in my own fashion and tell a few personal stories prompted by the records I played." This style quickly endeared him to British radio audiences, tired of more formal presentation, and he gained an extremely large following.

Stone was lucratively involved in many sponsorship deals, and recorded promotional material for many commercial services. As a result of this, and his continuing association with Radio Luxembourg, he was blacklisted by the BBC, although after the war, with the climate of commercial radio from Europe changed, he returned to the corporation for a time, working on a number of charity appeals that raised £100,000 in four years.

Stone was also a successful writer, the author of eight novels, and *Christopher Stone Speaking*, a nonfiction work written in 1933, in which he expressed his own views relating to the current state of radio, including the debate relating to BBC and commercial interests.

STREET, ARTHUR GEORGE (1892–1966). Street was a Wiltshire-born farmer who turned to writing articles on farming affairs in the late 1920s and subsequently wrote a number of books, including more than 30 novels and cameos of country life. His autobiography of his early years farming in Britain and Canada, *Farmer's Glory*, was published in 1932. In the same year, he made his first broadcast, quickly becoming a popular commentator on current affairs in general and rural life in particular.

Street was particularly liked for his gruff, down-to-earth turn of phrase and opinions. After the war, he became a regular member of the panel for the new **current affairs** opinion program, *Any Questions*, which originated in the **British Broadcasting Corporation (BBC)** West Region center of Bristol.

SUNDAY BROADCASTING POLICY. During the 1930s, a significant aspect of **British Broadcasting Corporation (BBC)** broadcasting strategy was its Sunday policy. In this, perhaps as much as anywhere else in corporation affairs of the time, thinking inspired by the upbringing and attitudes of **John Reith** influenced public service broadcasting. The issues raised by the corporation's Sunday broadcasting policy were of profound importance to the development of UK broadcasting between 1930–1939.

John Reith, the son of a man who became moderator of the General Assembly of the Free Church of Scotland, believed fervently all his life that Sunday was an institution "which belonged to the maintenance of a Christian presence." He stated his position on Sunday broadcasting within two years of the creation of the British Broadcasting Company, in his book, *Broadcast Over Britain* (1924):

> The surrender of the principles of Sunday observance is fraught with danger, even if the Sabbath were made for man. The secularising of the day is one of the most significant and unfortunate trends of modern life of which there is evidence . . . it is a sad reflection on human intelligence if recreation is only to be found in the distractions of excitement.

To understand how this attitude related to Sunday programs on BBC radio, it is only necessary to examine a Sunday listings page from an edition of *The Radio Times* of the era. For example, the **National Programme** page for Sunday 5 April 1935 shows that transmissions began at 10.30 a.m. with a weather bulletin for farmers, followed by a 15-minute interlude. There then followed part one of the St. Matthew Passion, then a program of classical orchestral music, and a chamber recital by a string quintet. Most of the afternoon was devoted to the second half of the St. Matthew Passion, followed by a talk for children entitled *Joan and Betty's Bible Story*. After this came program 10 in the series, *Heroes of the Free Church*. This took the time to 5:10 p.m., when came *How to Read an Epistle*, prior to a performance of Richard Brinsley Sheridan's play, *The Rivals*. Thereafter, the diet of religious talks and chamber music resumed until close down with a *Religious Epilogue* at 10:45 p.m.

This paternalistically inspired Sabbatarianism on the part of the legal monopoly broadcaster laid the BBC open to challenge, and this came first from the entrepreneur, **Leonard Plugge**. Plugge's actions in the development of **commercial radio** broadcasting from continental stations directly attacked the "BBC Sunday," and the creation of **International Broadcasting Company (IBC)** programs from **Radio Normandy** and other stations inspired others, such as **Wireless Publicity**, who developed **Radio Luxembourg** from 1933. All competition centered around breaching the BBC's monopoly at its most vulnerable—that is to say, on Sundays.

For many working-class people of the time, Sunday was the only day of rest in an otherwise grueling week. Wages were poor, unemployment was high, and the international situation was threatening and depressing. Capitalizing on all this, the commercial enterprises provided a diet of populist entertainment that drew huge audiences away from the BBC. Indeed, only the outbreak of World War II ended this threat to the Corporation's monopoly, which could otherwise have changed the face of British broadcasting permanently.

SWANN, MICHAEL (1920–1990). Sir Michael Meredith Swann, Lord Swann of Coln St. Denys, was one of the most popular **chairmen** of the **British Broadcasting Corporation (BBC)**. Unlike his predecessor, **Lord Hill**, he did not involve himself in program decisions and thus maintained a good working relationship with **directors-general Ian Trethowan** and **Charles Curran**. Under his chairmanship, the BBC came through some potentially difficult times, including the aftermath of the report of the **Annan Committee** and **license fee** negotiations.

SYKES COMMITTEE. A government committee set up in 1923 under the chairmanship of Sir Frederick Sykes, it was to examine issues of finance, organization, and control relating to the future of British broadcasting. The committee's discussions were strongly influenced by the initial development of wireless in the United States, which had been free and chaotic. The British Post Office pressed for a disciplined structuring of wavelengths and usage.

The Sykes Committee considered whether advertising should be permitted within the British system, deciding that, although it should not in general terms, certain forms of "sponsorship" should be allowed, whereby commercial concerns could support concerts and should be acknowledged on air for doing so. In effect, this was hardly used by the early **British Broadcasting Company (BBC)**.

Other issues considered by the committee related to concerns voiced by the **Newspaper Proprietors' Association**, which was concerned on behalf of its members about the development of **news** on the BBC, which it saw as infringing on its interests. A further recommendation of the committee was that the BBC should receive an increased share of revenue derived from the **license** fee and collected by the Post Office from the public. *See also* CRAWFORD COMMITTEE.

– T –

TAKE IT FROM HERE. This show, which ran on the **Light Programme** from 1948–1960, was the first completely new comedy **series** to emerge after World War II. It was written by **Frank Muir** and **Denis Norden** and starred **Jimmy Edwards**, Joy Nichols, and Dick Bentley. The first producer was Charles Maxwell, who, before the war, had worked for **Radio Luxembourg**. Joy Nichols left the program in 1952 and was ultimately replaced by June Whitfield and the singer Alma Cogan. One of the new elements that entered the program with the coming of Whitfield was the long-running saga of "The Glums," with Bentley playing "Ron" and Whitfield as "Eth." For the 13th and last series, the writing was taken over by Eric Merriman and Barry Took.

TAKE YOUR PICK. This comedy **quiz** program was produced by Star Sound Studios for **Radio Luxembourg** from 1953–1960, by which time it had transferred to television. Originally sponsored by Beecham's Pills, its host was Michael Miles.

TALBOT, GODFREY (1908–2000). After an early career in newspaper in Manchester, Godfrey Talbot joined the **British Broadcasting Corporation (BBC)** in 1937 as press officer for the North Region. With the coming of war in 1939, he transferred to London, where he worked initially as a copy editor. With the need for BBC war reporters established, Talbot delivered his first reports during the London Blitz and, proving his value as a broadcaster, was sent in 1942 to follow General Bernard Montgomery and the Eighth Army and report on its advance from El Alamein to Tripoli. For this work, he was mentioned in dispatches and received a military OBE.

After the war, Talbot was responsible for organizing the BBC's news gathering operation; one of his suggestions was for a series of specialist correspondents, among them one attached to Buckingham Palace, a post to which he was himself appointed, becoming the first BBC court reporter. He became the "voice" on radio for many state occasions and reported on then Princess Elizabeth's 1951 Canadian tour. He retired in 1969, although he continued to be heard in occasional broadcasts and commentaries.

TALKS. The idea of scripted talks, usually by key intellectual figures in their respective fields, was a genre championed by **John Reith** within the **British Broadcasting Company (BBC)** from its earliest days. The traditional prescribed length was 15 to 20 minutes, and the earliest of these was by E. B. Towse, in December 1922. Frequently, as with **Oliver Lodge** and **J. B. Priestley**, talks were given in **series** and became regular "appointment to listen" programs. Specialist themes developed in literature, film, and music, and transcripts often appeared in the *Listener*. H. G. Wells and C. S. Lewis were frequently employed to give talks. Many talks were aimed at children, among them *Zoo Man* and *Out with Romany*. (*See* "ROMANY").

Illustrated talks, such as the series *Talking about Music* have sometimes crossed from one network to another, while personalities such as **Charles Hill** as the *Radio Doctor* and **Cecil Middleton** with his gardening talks gained major audiences prewar and postwar respectively. The traditional length of a radio talk evolved to 15 or 20 minutes. However, postwar, the literary critic Lionel Trilling once gave a talk on the **Third Programme**, which lasted for 65 minutes—thought to have been the longest broadcast by one voice, uninterrupted. One of the greatest—and longest-running—series of talks has been *Letter from America*, by **Alastair Cooke**.

TALLENTS, STEPHEN (1884–1958). A distinguished civil servant for much of his career, Tallents was a public relations expert who played an important part in the development of publicity and the early development of audience measurement in the **British Broadcasting Corporation (BBC)**. Joining the corporation from the General **Post Office**

(GPO) in 1935 as controller of public relations, he had aspirations to succeed **John Reith**, although when Reith left the BBC in July 1938, the appointment went elsewhere. In May 1940, he was made responsible for the overseas services of the BBC, but because of internal conflicts, was forced to resign in September 1941.

TAPE RECORDING. The possibility of recording programs had been explored relatively early by radio engineers; during the 1920s, visits were made to view German experiments in the use of tape, but the quality was not deemed of a sufficient standard to warrant further development. Producers within the **British Broadcasting Company/Corporation (BBC)** held two points of view: some believed that "live" broadcasting was better, that it produced stronger and sharper performances from artists and speakers. Others, such as **Lance Sieveking** and **Val Gielgud**, saw creative and practical possibilities in what was known as "bottled" programs. The introduction of the **Empire Service** in 1932, broadcasting to differing time zones, made recording essential, and the means of answering the requirement came with the use of steel tape and the **Blattnerphone/Marconi-Stille** system.

This was later superceded by **disc recording**, using technology devised in Britain by **Cecil Watts** and also, for a time, by the **Philips-Miller** film system. It was not until World War II that staff at the BBC's **monitoring service** came to understand the great advances made by German sound engineers in the use of magnetic tape. In 1945, the BBC acquired a German army Magnetophon Tonnschreiber B magnetic tape recorder, and this, together with other acquisitions, led to experimentation that moved the Corporation toward the gradual adoption of tape as the preeminent recording medium, a system that would last into the digital age.

The creation of the **EMI Midget** tape recorder in the 1950s—and subsequently other portable machines, such as the **Uher**—gave journalists and producers a combination of quality and flexibility that had previously been largely lacking. Quarter-inch tape recording—principally at speeds of 7.5 inches per second (IPS) or 15 IPS, using flexible oxide-covered plastic tape, easily edited with a chinagraph pencil and razor blade—became the stock-in-trade for a generation of broadcasters. Tape machines of this type could still be found in some BBC studios into the 21st century.

TARRANT, CHRIS (1946–). Although principally a television presenter and game show host, Tarrant's tenure as Breakfast Show **disc jockey** on London's **Capital Radio** (1987–2003) earned him induction into the **Radio Academy**'s Hall of Fame in December 2003. In addition, his work on the program has been honored by a Gold Award in the **Sony Radio Academy Awards**, as well as another Gold in 2001 for career achievement in 2001. Additionally, he was named Radio Personality of the Year in 1990.

TELEGRAPHY ACTS. The early evolution of British broadcasting was established out of regulations that predated it in its transmitted form. A series of government acts in the late 19th and early 20th centuries set down rules that contained the foundations of a regulated broadcasting system.

The first telegraph companies in Great Britain were privately owned; during the 1860s, it was becoming increasingly clear that commercial and government business would rely more and more on telegraphic communications. In the 1863 Electric Telegraph Act, clauses 21 and 49 established the origins of state control. Initially, the role of the postmaster general was seen to be dominant.

The 1868 Electric Telegraphy Act empowered the **Post Office** to create, acquire, and operate telegraph business in addition to existing privately operated ones, wherever required by the public interest. A year later, the 1869 Telegraph Act gave the Post Office further power, stating: "The Postmaster General, by himself or by his deputies, and his and their respective servants and agents, shall, from and after the passing of this Act, have the exclusive privilege of transmitting telegrams within the United Kingdom of Great Britain and Ireland."

Guglielmo Marconi's systems of wireless transmission were becoming widely adopted by 1903, when the Berlin Convention set out an agreement, signed by the major powers, establishing a plan for universal compulsory intercommunication, by which no wireless station was permitted to refuse the reception of a signal from another station using another system of transmission. This was seen as being of particular importance at times of war or national or international emergency. Great Britain was not in a position to sign the agreement, because no existing legislation existed in the country at the time, which would enable it to enforce the articles of the Convention.

Accordingly, the Wireless Telegraphy Act of 1904 contained an Explanatory Memorandum enabling British delegates to sign relevant documents at a second Berlin Convention in 1906. This important Act took into account the already-dominant view that the new medium would develop quickly and widely. It gained for the state wide powers for the regulation of wireless telegraphy, while enabling the individual enthusiast to develop interests in wireless for private use. From this time, however, it was compulsory for every operator of wireless telegraphy to possess an official **license**.

TELEVISION AND RADIO INDUSTRIES CLUB (TRIC). Formed in 1931, the Television and Radio Industries Club was founded "to promote mutual understanding and goodwill amongst those engaged in the audio, visual, communication and allied industries." Membership embraces the communication, entertainment, manufacturing, and service sectors, from program makers and broadcasters to radio producers and makers. The organization hosts the annual TRIC awards.

TEST MATCH SPECIAL (TMS). Radio's international cricket commentary service, which proudly boasts "ball-by-ball" commentary of every Test Match series that has taken place in England since 1957, in addition to coverage of many games played overseas (since 1990). The preservation of its continuous service during matches has frequently provided the **British Broadcasting Corporation (BBC)** with scheduling problems, as wavelengths have changed over the years. Currently "TMS" is broadcast on **Radio 4**'s **longwave** frequency, and **Radio 5 Live**'s Sports Extra **digital** service. The program has been characterized over the years by the personalities of its presenters; **John Arlott**, **Brian Johnston**, Fred Truman, Christopher Martin-Jenkins, and others. The mix of styles has produced a unique blend of professionalism and school-boy humor that is somehow peculiarly English and eccentric.

THEOCHARIS, JOHN (1932–). John Theocharis was born and educated in cosmopolitan Alexandria. In his early twenties, he worked at the local radio station, broadcasting in Greek, English, and French. He taught in Ethiopia and published his early poetry in Athens. His love of English literature and theater brought him to London, where he won a scholarship to the Royal Academy of Dramatic Art (RADA). Subsequently, he joined the **BBC World Service**. His production for the Greek Service of a long-lost play by Menander (the first in any medium) drew the attention of **Martin Esslin**. He was appointed senior producer and features editor, capacities in which he served **Radio 3** and **Radio 4** for more than 20 years.

Dividing his time between **drama** and **features**, he found the cross-fertilization of the two disciplines a great source of inspiration. He directed many modern British and continental plays (among the latter *Outside the Jeweller's* by Pope John Paul II); as well as classical drama and many Greek tragedies. As editor, he ran the BBC Radio Drama Features unit for many years, and made a large number of major features, including drama-documentaries, such as *The Lady Chatterley Trial* and his coproduction of *The Chicago Conspiracy Trial* (New York Festivals International Radio Award).

Favoring original sounds and treating radio as a visual medium as much as possible, he has recorded features in many parts of Europe, and as a freelance director since 1992, has made documentaries and dramas for numerous broadcasters worldwide. He has also served for many years as Radio Jury Member/Chairman for Prix Futura, Prix Europa, and the International Prix Marulic, and as a regular BBC representative at the International Features Conference.

THESE YOU HAVE LOVED. The title of this long-running **music** program, devised and presented for many years by **Doris Arnold**, was taken from Rupert Brooke's poem *The Great Lover.* It began in November 1938 and established Arnold as the first female **disc jockey** in the UK. The content was that of extracts of classical and light classical music, requested by listeners, and became extremely popular during World War II as a link between the armed forces personnel and their loved ones at home. The program went through many series, and Arnold herself broadcast her 300th edition in March 1951. She continued to host the program, which ran intermittently through the 1960s. For the last five years of its existence however, from 1972–1978, it was presented by Richard Baker. The last edition of all was broadcast—appropriately—on 11 November (Armistice Day) that year.

THIRD PROGRAMME. As part of the **British Broadcasting Corporation's (BBC)** postwar reorganization, the Third Programme was established on 29 September 1946 as a cultural channel specializing in classical **music**, **drama**, experimental works, and "highbrow" **talks** and **features**. It was thus the first totally new radio network to be created after the war. Its tone and ambition were summed up by the poet Henry Reed who stated that "[It acknowledges] that some listeners are fools and some are not, and that we cannot wait for the fools to catch up with their betters." That said, among its lighter items was a much-loved series by **Stephen Potter** and **Joyce Grenfell** called *How To.* . . . The first episode of this program was transmitted on the network's opening night with *How to Listen*. Shortly after its inception, the station was taken off the air for 16 days in February 1947 as the result of a fuel crisis that hit Britain. Initially beginning by broadcasting only in the evenings, it gradually increased its output, although its focus was frequently blurred by the "bolting on" of other services—**Network Three**, **The Music Programme** and **Third Network**. In 1967, it became **Radio 3**, and in recent years, successive controllers have sought to widen its appeal through the introduction of jazz and world music.

THOMAS, HOWARD (1909–1986). Howard Thomas was, in the latter part of his career, one of the key founding figures in UK commercial television, which began in 1955. Prior to this, however, he had had a long and successful career in radio, including working both for the **British Broadcasting Corporation (BBC)** and for the prewar commercial sector. Working for the London Press Exchange (LPE) from 1937, he began writing scripts for the BBC, and in 1938, set up the **Commercial Radio** Department of the LPE, writing and producing many of the programs himself, for **Radio Luxembourg** and **Radio Normandy**.

In 1940, having been rejected for military service due to poor eyesight, he took a staff post with the BBC; through the years of World War II, he produced over 500 programs, including *Sincerely Yours*, featuring **Vera Lynn**. He also created *The Brains Trust* and was personally responsible for the selection of panel members. In 1944, disillusioned with the BBC, he resigned and subsequently developed his second highly successful career as a film and television producer, initially with Pathé Pictures, the subsidiary of the Associated British Picture Corporation. When the company was invited by the Independent Television Authority to apply in 1955 for a weekend contract to service the North and Midlands, Thomas formed ABC Television and continued to work in commercial television until his retirement at the age of 70 in 1979. He received a CBE in 1967.

THOMPSON, JOHN (?–). Coming from a publishing background, John Thompson was the first director of radio at the **Independent Broadcasting Authority (IBA)** from 1972–1987, when he was succeeded by his deputy, **Peter Baldwin**.

THOMPSON, MARK (1957–). Mark Thompson came through the ranks of the **British Broadcasting Corporation (BBC)** to senior management beginning in 1979 as a production trainee. After a range of television jobs, he became director of Nations and Regions in 1996, and director of television in 2000. After two years as chief executive of Channel Four Television from 2002 to 2004, he returned to the BBC as **director-general** after the resignation of **Greg Dyke**.

TIME TO SPARE. See SOS.

TIMPSON, JOHN (1928–2005). A popular radio broadcaster of the 1970s and 1980s, who developed as an author of the English countryside after his retirement from the **British Broadcasting Corporation (BBC)**. He presented the *Today* program from 1970–1976 and from 1978–1986. He was well known while on the program for his on-air relationship with **Brian Redhead**. He was chairman of the **Radio 4** series *Any Questions* from 1984–1987, and subsequently made a number of series as a freelance for the network, including *Timpson's England*.

TODAY. This has remained **Radio 4**'s flagship morning **news** and **current affairs** magazine program for 50 years. Its form and character have, however, changed in that time. Beginning on the **Home Service**, in 1957, conceived by a team including **Janet Quigley** and **Isa Benzie**, its original format was that of a light magazine program. Since that time, it has become much more of a hard news program with a strongly political agenda. This has been reflected in the range of its presenters, from the avuncular **Jack De Manio** to the aggressive style of **John Humphrys**. The program's uncompromising agenda has led on occasion to tensions with politicians and political parties, none more so than in 2003, when **Andrew Gilligan**'s report on information gained from the government weapon's inspector, Dr. David Kelly, over government claims of Iraqi military capability led to the **Hutton Enquiry** and the ultimate resignation of senior **British Broadcasting Corporation (BBC)** figures.

TOOK, BARRY (1928–2002). Took was a comedian and scriptwriter and a successful presenter both on radio and television. In 1951, he won a radio talent show as a comedian, and his skill as a scriptwriter of comedy radio soon showed itself in such programs as *Beyond Our Ken*. His greatest achievement, however, was that show's successor, *Round the Horne*, which he cowrote with Marty Feldman. He was for some years the host of the **Radio 4** program *The News Quiz*.

TOPICAL TAPES. The Topical Tapes project grew out of the **British Broadcasting Corporation's (BBC)** Overseas Regional Service at **Bush House**, which directed material to specific areas of the world, by direct transmission and through tape and cassette distribution. The service began in November 1962 and provided subscribers with a regular weekly service of English-language topicality to supplement the services available by **shortwave** transmission. Approximately 12 weekly magazine programs were produced on subjects, such as development, international business, books, or science, and were distributed to—and broadcast by—more than 35 countries; and in the United States alone by more than 100 stations. The subject matter was always topical, in that the material was designed to remain relevant for approximately two weeks, the time being governed by the longest estimated time taken for tapes posted in London to reach the furthest recipients, in the South Pacific. The service was closed down in March 1996 due to a funding crisis, after almost 34 years.

TOP OF THE FORM. Commencing in 1948 on the **Light Programme**, *Top of the Form* was a schools' **quiz** program in which teams of four from UK secondary schools competed in a knock out competition featuring general knowledge questions. It was a highly successful format, and ran until 1986.

TOP TWENTY. This program, broadcast on **Radio Luxembourg**, began in 1948, and was thus the earliest chart show broadcast on radio for British audiences. It was also significant in that it was transmitted on Sundays, which had frequently been seen as a day inappropriate for such broadcasting. It continued in various forms until the closure of Radio Luxembourg in 1992, but it's most radical change came in 1952. Prior to this point, the program—although using records as illustration—was a representation of the top-20 sheet music sales in UK popular music. As purchasing moved away from sheet music toward the growing consumption of gramophone records, fueled by the developing popular music industry of the 1950s and 1960s, record sales became the significant unit of interest. In 1952, with the creation, in the *New Musical Express* magazine, of the first weekly printed chart of record sales, the program switched its emphasis to reflect this. *See also* MUSIC.

TORCH, SIDNEY (1908–1990). Starting his musical career as an organist, Sidney Torch became conductor of the Royal Air Force (RAF) Concert Orchestra during World War II and thereafter became widely known as a composer of light orchestral music. In 1953, he worked with the **British Broadcasting Corporation (BBC)** to devise *Friday Night Is Music Night*, and conducted the **BBC Concert Orchestra** for nearly 20 years on the **Light Programme**, later **Radio 2**, until his retirement in 1972. He broadcast on countless occasions, including frequent celebrity concerts and relays from the Royal Festival Hall, London, as part of the BBC's regular light **music** festivals. He was awarded the MBE in 1985.

TOYTOWN. This extremely popular and long-running children's program was first broadcast as part of *Children's Hour* in July 1929, with **series** running intermittently until February 1963, by which time its parent program had already been axed by **Frank Gillard**. Originally taken from the book *Tales from Toytown* by S. Hulme Beaman, the stories were adapted for radio by **Derek McCulloch**, who also narrated the programs and played the part of the central character, "Larry the Lamb." There were 36 stories in all, and the program's much-loved signature tune was "Parade of the Tin Soldiers."

TRAIN, JACK (1902–1966). Jack Train was a genuine radio personality, created by radio and a versatile and popular user of the medium. Prior to his first work in the medium, he had appeared in a West End Review, *Many Happy Returns*, in 1928, the same year as his radio debut, and worked with Nervo and Knox of the "Crazy Gang" vaudeville act for five years. He first came to major public attention in 1939 as one of the stars of ***It's That Man Again (ITMA)*** in which he played a variety of rich comic characters. Train had a considerable gift for mimicry and was a multivoiced entertainer perfectly suited to the fast-moving, character-based format of the show.

After the war, he hosted record programs for the **Light Programme**, and was a long-term panel member of *Twenty Questions*, where his ability to improvise without a script made him a popular favorite with radio audiences again. He also appeared in many films, including one that developed the success of his radio **quiz** show, *The Twenty Questions Murder Mystery*.

TRANSISTOR. The development of the transistor as a replacement for the **Valve** within radio receivers had a major effect on the portability of the medium. Originally created by research scientists at the Bell Laboratories in the United States in 1947, the device consisted of the addition of a second contact point to a crystal diode with a pointed "**cat's whisker**" touching its surface. Initially, the application of this miniaturized form of amplification was slowed down by the difficulty of manufacturing the invention. After early experimentation, the Japanese company Totsuko (later to become Sony) began work on the use of transistors during the 1950s, and in March 1957 produced the first true "pocket" radio, the TR-63. During the 1960s, social changes in Great Britain and the growing youth market for popular music created a large demand for mobile radio technology, and what became known as the "Transistor Age" was born. By 1963, 36% of all radios sold in Britain were imported from Japan, and the tiny sets of the time enabled teenagers to tune in to their music anywhere, thus escaping the dominance of television.

TRAVIS, DAVE LEE (1945–). Born David Griffin, he trained as a designer and took a part-time job as a club **disc jockey** in his native Manchester, where he changed his name to Dave Lee Travis. Becoming known simply as "D. L. T.," he joined **Radio Caroline** South in September 1965, transferring to the North station in 1967, where he remained until the **Marine Offences Bill** of August, that year. He joined **Radio 1**, and remained with the station until 1994, when he resigned on air in protest against the changes to the network at that time being instigated by the controller, **Matthew Bannister**. In the meantime, in 1990, his **World Service** record program, *A Jolly Good Show*, was revealed to receive the largest postbag of any English-language program on the network. After leaving Radio 1, he joined the **Classic Gold** network, presenting a long-running morning program, as well as working on a number of syndicated shows for other stations.

TRETHOWAN, IAN (1922–1990). Sir Ian Trethowan was managing director of **British Broadcasting Corporation (BBC)** Radio from 1970–1976 and was thus the incumbent at the time of the significant *Broadcasting in the Seventies* paper. During his time, Radio 4 gained its first **woman** newsreader (Sheila Tracy). In 1977, Trethowan succeeded Sir **Charles Curran** as **director-general** of the BBC. His background was print journalism, and his first job was as an office boy for the *Daily Sketch* at the age of 16. He joined the BBC from Independent Television News as a parliamentary commentator in 1963. His time as director-general coincided with a period of considerable difficulty for the BBC, with shrinking income from **license** fees and government criticism via the **Annan Report**. He was remembered as being a warm and genial person of considerable intelligence. He survived a heart attack in 1979 and stayed in the post until he was 60 in 1982, subsequently serving as a board member for numerous other organizations, including Thames Television and the British Council. His death in 1990 was from motor neurone disease.

"TUNE IN." The song, recorded by **Jack Payne** and his Band, was the theme tune of **Radio Luxembourg** from its inception in 1934, and it was also commercially issued, with some success. In common with a number of the station's other elements, it was revived when the station returned to civilian output after World War II. Its refrain was:

Tune in, Tune in,
Just sit in your easy chair
And through the air to anywhere
Tune in, keep tuning in.

TWENTY QUESTIONS. A variation of a well-known parlor game, *Animal, Vegetable, Mineral, Twenty Questions* started in 1947 and ran until 1976 on the **Light Programme**, also going out for a time on **Radio Luxembourg**. The show was produced in front of a live audience, and the first chairman was **Stewart MacPherson**, later replaced by **Gilbert Harding**, who was himself dismissed from the program for being drunk on air. Long-term panelists included **Anona Winn**, **Richard Dimbleby**, and **Jack Train**.

TYDEMAN, JOHN (1936–). After actively developing his interest in theater while at Cambridge, John Tydeman joined the **British Broadcasting Corporation (BBC)** in 1959, spending 25 years in the Radio **Drama** Department, and rising to become its head in 1986. As a radio director, his chief interest was in fostering contemporary dramatists and new talent. In this capacity, he was responsible for discovering Joe Orton and producing his first play, *Ruffian on the Stair*. Tydeman won the **Prix Italia** in 1970, and the Prix Futura in 1979 and 1983. In 1994, he received the **Sony Radio Academy Award** for services to radio.

Since his retirement from the BBC in 1994, Tydeman has remained actively involved with radio drama, working all over the world, including the United States, where he directed for National Public Radio, working closely with the poet Archibald MacLeish and playwright Edward Albee. He also directed plays for audiobooks on CD and cassette, and has served twice as the chairman of the Prix Italia radio drama jury.

– U –

UHER. For more than 30 years—until the advent of high-quality cassette recording and subsequently of **digital** recording—the German Uher portable tape machine was the mainstay of professional radio interviewing and news reporting. Strong, robust, and simple to use, the *Report* series had a number of tape speeds, although for professionals 7.5 inches per second was the preferred speed for broadcast quality. Set to this speed, the 5-inch tape reels produced 15 minutes of recording. The machine was standard issue when **British Broadcasting Corporation (BBC) local radio** began and developed, from 1967.

ULLSWATER REPORT. The purpose of this committee, under the chairmanship of Lord Ullswater, appointed in 1935, was "to consider the constitution, control and finance of the broadcasting service in this country and advise generally on the conditions under which the service, including broadcasting to the Empire, television broadcasting and the system of wireless exchanges, should be conducted after the 31st December 1936." The significance of the date was the expiry of the **British Broadcasting Corporation**'s **(BBC) charter**, and it came at a crucial time, given the competition from **commercial** interests in the form of populist programming from such organizations as **Radio Luxembourg** and the **International Broadcasting Company (IBC)**. Ullswater mostly ratified and confirmed the previous status of issues relating to the BBC's structure and character, renewing the charter for a further 10 years. It did however criticize the Corporation for its program content in certain areas, notably its heavy **Sunday program policy**, and concerns were voiced that the BBC did not consult the political parties on major issues as much as it should and that there were signs that the Corporation was beginning to usurp certain areas of political patronage.

"UNCLE CARACTACUS." *See* LEWIS, CECIL.

"UNCLE MAC." *See* MCCULLOCH, DEREK.

UNDER MILK WOOD. This "play for voices" by **Dylan Thomas** was produced first by **Douglas Cleverdon** for the **BBC Third Programme** in January 1954. Thomas himself had died two months earlier. Had he lived, he would have played the part of First Voice himself. Instead, the part was given to Richard Burton, whose performance in the role has become legendary. The play—which runs for 90 minutes—grew out of a 1945 radio talk Thomas had given on the Welsh Regional **Home Service** entitled *Quite Early One Morning*, which begins: "Quite early one morning in the winter in Wales, by the sea that was lying down still and green as grass after a night of tar-black howling and rolling . . . ." Many of the characters in his talk find their way ultimately into the finished work. In his play, which evolved tortuously over a period of years and which owed its existence almost entirely to Cleverdon's persuadings, Thomas created a work that is at once a poem and a definition of the radio listening experience. Taking place over one day in a fictional Welsh village, the piece was commissioned not by the Radio **Drama** Department of the **British Broadcasting Corporation (BBC)** but by the **Features** Department. The music was created by Thomas' boyhood friend, the composer Daniel Jones.

UNIQUE BROADCASTING COMPANY/UBC MEDIA GROUP. Formed in 1989, Unique was a pioneer of sponsored programs for Independent Local Radio. Founded by **Noel Edmonds**, Simon Cole, and **Tim Blackmore**, the company was to grow and expand over subsequent years, eventually—as UBC Media—becoming the leading independent production company in the UK. In 1992, the **British Broadcasting Corporation (BBC)** began experimenting with independent production for radio, and Unique soon won contracts with all five networks. In 1999, the company floated on the UK stock market as UBC Media Group plc, and used the investment to expand into digital broadcasting through **Oneword** and Classic Gold Digital. In August 2005, Edmonds cashed in his stake in the company for £1.35 million.

UNIVERSAL PROGRAMMES COMPANY (UPC). This was the production wing of the **International Broadcasting Company (IBC)**, and its role was to package sponsored programs in Britain, for transmission from the IBC's continental stations. UPC was based at 37 Portland Place—just 200 yards from **Broadcasting House**—during the 1930s.

UNIVERSAL RADIO PUBLICITY. Formerly known as Radio Publicity, Ltd., this pioneering independent producer of sponsored programs is known to have been active as early as 1929, when it produced a program of dance music on **Radio Paris**, sponsored by Revelation Suitcases. After the company's name change, in October 1930, it also broadcast nightly sponsored shows on Irish radio.

– V –

VALVE. Invented by Sir **John Ambrose Fleming** in 1904 and patented the following year, the two-electrode radio rectifier, also known as the thermionic valve, vacuum diode, kenetron, Fleming valve, and, in the United States, the vacuum tube, was to be of crucial significance in the development of radio and the amplification of received signals within sets. The term "valve" was used by Fleming because the device allows electrical current to pass in one direction only. This piece of technology enabled electrons to flow from the negatively charged cathode to the positively charged anode; as the current within the tube is moving from negative to positive, incoming signals' oscillations are rectified into a detectable direct current. Although Fleming's invention predated the creation of wireless networks by almost two decades, the valve was initially neglected due to its cost and the development of the cruder but cheaper **cat's whisker**. By the 1950s, the large, fragile valve was giving way to the new technology of the **transistor**, although while it ceased to be a part of radio receivers, it continued to be used in transmitters.

VARIETY BANDBOX. This weekly Sunday evening show, devised by **Cecil Madden**, was originally designed for the armed forces, beginning in December 1942 on the **Overseas Programme** and transferring in February 1944 to the **Forces Programme**, where demand soared for its star-studded entertainment. Sunday variety on **British Broadcasting Corporation (BBC)** Radio was, until World War II, a rare thing, and British audiences had had to turn to the **commercial** stations, such as **Radio Luxembourg** and **Radio Normandy** for such fare. Once established in the public consciousness, *Variety Bandbox* achieved numerous seasons over several years. The final edition was broadcast on 28 September 1952, by which time it had moved to a Monday evening slot on the **Light Programme**. Among stars who took part over the 10 years of its existence were Issy Bonn,

Reg Dixon, Arthur English, FRANKIE HOWERD, Margaret Lockwood, **Al Read**, Max Wall, and Bernard Miles. In its final series, the resident orchestra was that of Cyril Stapleton.

VARIETY DEPARTMENT. Originally, Variety provision within the **British Broadcasting Corporation (BBC)** came under the same heading as **drama**. This was, however, changed in 1933, when a specific Variety Department was created under the directorship of **Eric Maschwitz**, then editor of *Radio Times*. The role of the department was to fill BBC airtime with just under 18 hours of vaudeville, operetta, light music, dance music, and comedy. The first series to come out of the new department was *In Town Tonight*. The department grew quickly, and during its existence it was housed in a number of BBC premises, including **Broadcasting House**, St. George's Hall, and Aeolian Hall. Many major popular shows originated in this department, including legends such as *It's That Man Again (ITMA)*, *Variety Bandbox*, *Band Waggon*, *Ack-Ack, Beer-Beer*, and *Garrison Theatre*.

VARIETY FANFARE. Billed as "heralding variety in the North," the series ran for a time as *Fanfare*, changing its name in July 1949, after which it ran for several more months, featuring comedians such as **Cyril Fletcher** and **Frankie Howerd**, and musical acts, including the harmonica player Tommy Reilly and the singer Betty Driver.

VARIETY PLAYHOUSE. This major Saturday evening series began May 1953, hosted initially by **Vic Oliver** on the **Home Service**. It ran until 1963, and during its life many of the top names in British light entertainment appeared on the program. The mix was varied; the first show featured—among others—Jean Sablon and Benny Hill, and subsequent programs saw appearances by such artists as the violinist Campoli, the singer Billy Eckstine, and the actor Sir Donald Wolfit. Its content over 10 years reflected changes in entertainment trends during the era.

VAUGHAN-THOMAS, WYNFORD (1908–1987). A friend of Dylan Thomas, he shared the poet's delight in words and applied it to the art of the radio commentator, giving his work a Celtic lyrical quality in which his Welshness was always a factor. Among many famous broadcasts, his commentary from a Lancaster bomber over Berlin in 1943 became famous, as did his other war-reports such as describing General Bernard Montgomery crossing the Rhine and a transmission from the Hamburg studio used by **William Joyce** shortly after Joyce had made his final broadcast. Later, he was a familiar voice at state and royal occasions and was one of the radio commentary team at the 1981 wedding of Prince Charles and Lady Diana Spencer. A man who loved the landscape of Britain, he presented the monthly program *The Countryside in*... until his death at the age of 79.

VIC SAMSON, SPECIAL INVESTIGATOR. Broadcast in a short-lived series on **Radio Luxembourg** from mid-August 1939, this was the first daily adventure serial aimed at children, and preempted the BBC's **Dick Barton, Special Agent** by seven years. The eponymous hero worked for Scotland Yard and was assisted by his schoolboy brother, Bob. The series disappeared at the closure of Luxembourg when war broke out and was never revived subsequently.

VERY HIGH FREQUENCY (VHF). *See* FREQUENCY MODULATION (FM).

VIKING RADIO. This commercial station based in Hull commenced broadcasting in 1984, and was notable for being the first to divide its **frequency modulation (FM)** and **mediumwave (MW)** services, providing alternative services for its listeners, a trend that was later to become common practice on **Independent Local Radio (ILR)** stations. This was, however, at this time only on weekends, to provide an alternative service for sports fans. The station split its frequencies completely in 1989, with the launch of its Classic Gold service. *See also* COUNTY SOUND.

VIRGIN RADIO. Originally owned by entrepreneur Richard Branson, Virgin Radio became the UK's first national pop **music** station when it began broadcasting on 30 April 1993 as Virgin 1215. Its policy was that of playing quality rock, featuring a high proportion of album tracks, and this has remained the backbone of its output.

   In 1997, **Capital Radio**, exploiting the climate of radio deregulation that permitted groups to consolidate into multistation ownership, attempted to buy Virgin Radio from Richard Branson. In the event, the issue was referred to the UK Monopolies and Mergers Commission. Before a ruling on the purchase could be reached, the Ginger Media Group, owned by **Chris Evans**, stepped in and bought the station. Subsequently purchased by **Scottish Media Holdings** in 2005, the station became the subject of considerable renewed speculation regarding its ownership.

Broadcasting to most of Great Britain was via **mediumwave (MW)**, and the development of **digital radio** was clearly significant for a station such as Virgin; accordingly, it was a part of the multiplex launched by **Digital One** in the spring of 1999. Technical innovation—an issue of considerable interest to the station's core audience—has always been part of Virgin Radio's policy; its web presence is extremely sophisticated, and it was one of the early sites to experiment with online broadcasting. It has also used satellite platforms to reach an increasingly global audience. In March, 2005, it was the first UK commercial radio station to offer a "**podcasting**" of a daily show.

VOCALION CONCERT. This half-hour record program was significant in that it was the first commercial radio series to be advertised (*Sunday Referee*). Featuring records on the *Broadcast* label, it ran from October 1931–January 1932, initially on **Radio Toulouse**, and subsequently on **Radio Paris**. There is, however, evidence that versions of the program were broadcast earlier than that, with **British Broadcasting Corporation (BBC)** reception reports dating from 1929.

VOICE OF AMERICA (VOA). Funded by the United States government, this service began in 1942, initially broadcasting only in German. It was, however, later to grow to 44 languages, including English, and had a not inconsiderable listenership in Britain immediately after the war and during the 1950s. One reason for its popularity in the United Kingdom—apart from its commentary in the postwar age of uncertainty brought about by the Cold War—was the fact that British audiences had developed a taste for the more relaxed style and accents of U.S. presenters during the war. The service itself grew out of a perceived need, in that in 1939, the United States was the only world power without a government-sponsored international radio service. Today, VOA is a multimedia service claiming to reach 100 million listeners globally.

VOICE OF THE LISTENER AND VIEWER. This pressure group was founded as Voice of the Listener in 1983 by Jocelyn Hay to campaign for the preservation of Reithian (*see* REITH, JOHN) standards in radio broadcasting. It was initially created in opposition to a proposal to transform **Radio 4** into a rolling news format network. Once established, it became clear that other issues in broadcasting required a consumer organization to act and speak on behalf of listeners. Formed as it was in a period when radio was moving into a period of deregulation, it was a strong lobbyist of Parliament during the passage of the 1990 Broadcasting Act. The following year, broadening the brief to television, the word "Viewer" was added to the title.

VOIGT, PAUL (1901–1981). One of the leading inventors of sound equipment, Paul Voigt was born on 9 December 1901, just three days before the first transatlantic signal by **Guglielmo Marconi**. Born in London of German parents, Voigt was educated at Dulwich College, and even as a child he was fascinated by the mechanics of wireless. He joined the southeast London electronics firm of J. E. Hough, manufacturing gramophone records and machines, later moving into radio set manufacture.

Voigt became a specialist in microphones, amplifiers, and above all, loudspeakers. After his employers went out of business in 1933, Voigt formed Voigt Patents, and concentrated on manufacturing loudspeakers for public arenas such as cinemas and dance halls. He was among the pioneers who predicted the later growth of music radio and recordings in the home. Near the end of World War II, he suffered a breakdown and decided to move to Canada to continue his work on loudspeakers. Emigrating in April 1950, he found work with the Canadian Radio Authority. In his last years he almost completely neglected audio, becoming involved in the theory of electromagnetic induction, some of Albert Einstein's work, and whether the speed of light was an invariable constant or slowed toward the extremes of the universe. However, it is for his technical work in the areas of sound production and reception that he is best remembered.

– W –

WAGGONERS' WALK. After the demise of ***Mrs. Dale's Diary/ The Dales***, **Radio 2** sought to introduce a more socially relevant daily **serial** that would reflect modern life. The result was *Waggoners' Walk*, which was broadcast Monday–Friday from 1969–1980 (2,824 episodes). **Piers Plowright** was one of its first producers.

WALKER, JOHNNIE (1945–). Johnnie Walker has been one of the major figures in the development of **music** radio in the UK since his time on the **pirate radio** station **Radio Caroline**. When the **Marine Offences Bill** took effect on 14 August 1967, Walker, and his fellow Caroline **disc jockey**, Robbie Dale, defied the legislation and continued broadcasting past the midnight deadline, when all other offshore stations had fallen silent. It was reputed that, on this occasion, the audience was more than 20 million listeners Europe-wide.

From 1969–1976, Walker worked for **Radio 1**, where he gained a reputation for his knowledge of and respect for the music he played on his programs, pioneering then new names, such as Steve Harley, Lou Reed, Fleetwood Mac, and Steely Dan. Often outspoken and controversial, Walker left Radio 1 in 1976 after a disagreement with the station controller, **Johnny Beerling**, and moved to San Francisco, where he recorded a weekly program broadcast on **Radio Luxembourg**.

In the first years of the 1980s, he returned to the UK, and after periods on local radio in the west of England, he worked on **Radio 5** before joining **Radio 2** to take over the early evening drive-time program upon the retirement of **John Dunn** in 1998. He moved to a Sunday evening slot in 2006.

WALTERS, JOHN (1939–2001). This award-winning **British Broadcasting Corporation (BBC)** producer and broadcaster began as an artist and teacher, later becoming a musician, working with the Alan Price Set, and even playing on the same bill as the Beatles in their last ever British stage appearance. He joined **Radio 1** at its creation in 1967. Two years later, he began his long association with **John Peel**, a partnership that lasted more than 20 years. His wry and witty sense of humor and turn of phrase made him a popular broadcaster in his own right. For a time, he hosted his own programs, *Walters Weekly* (which became *Walters Week*) on Radio 1, and *Largely Walters* on **Radio 4**, in addition to creating a series of comic monologues featured in programs by other broadcasters. He left the BBC staff in 1991.

WARTIME BROADCASTING. The role of the **British Broadcasting Corporation (BBC)** during World War II is important and must be considered from two perspectives: home front and overseas broadcasting. By the time of commencement of hostilities, the Corporation had had time to establish its policy clearly, including, where appropriate, evacuating and/or resiting of certain services. Within days of the announcement, a "Supplementary Edition" of *Radio Times* was published, carrying the banner, "Broadcasting Carries On."

Because a depleted workforce on the domestic scene was augmented by many who found themselves in an unfamiliar situation, morale was a crucial issue, and the BBC created a number of new programs to cater to this requirement, such as *Workers' Playtime* and *Music while You Work*. Other programs supported the government's "Dig for Victory" campaign, including *The Kitchen Front*, *Back to the Land*, and *The Radio Allotment*. In the early days, **J. B. Priestley**'s *Postscript* program, broadcast after the Sunday evening news, countered the lowering of morale caused by the broadcasts of **William Joyce**, and in the last year of the war, Allied progress across Europe was monitored by the nightly *War Report* program.

The **Variety Department** created a range of light entertainment programs, many of which were to move into radio legend, such as *Band Waggon* and *It's That Man Again (ITMA)*. A new, relaxed style began to emerge in programming, partly caused as the war continued by the influx of U.S. and Canadian broadcasters, who, together with the BBC, created a tripartite Forces broadcasting service that gave UK domestic audiences—who could also listen—a taste for a new style of radio.

At the same time there were some who felt that BBC programs were becoming more vulgar and were catering to a lower common denominator than previously. The Forces Programme was requested to use material that was aimed at raising of standards and providing more informative content; this led to the creation of *The Brain's Trust*, which, with a weekly postbag of up to 4,000 letters, became the first "serious" program to attract a mass audience.

As with domestic programming, the BBC's overseas output had been primed for the event of war for several years. Countering German propaganda broadcasts became an increasing concern of the British government from 1933, when the Nazis came to power, and the BBC was asked to respond; this it did in 1938 with the creation of the **Arabic Service** as well as services in Spanish and Portuguese. Between 1940–1941, the BBC increased its overseas output threefold. Crucially, a special service to North America was created that demonstrated to the United States the true situation in a beleaguered Great Britain, with dramatized documentary programs, such as *The Stones Cry Out*.

At this time, services also began in every major European language. In 1941, as the expanding provision dictated the need for more space, the BBC took over the **Bush House** studios, formerly used by the **J. Walter Thompson Organization**'s **commercial radio** division. This became the headquarters of the European Service, and went on to be—for many overseas listeners even after the war—the true home of BBC radio. It was from Bush House, on the BBC's French Service, that Charles de Gaulle made his first broadcast—on 18 June 1940—four days after the fall of Paris. From this, the French Resistance was created with a force estimated to be 56,000 strong.

It is hard to overestimate the importance of the role of the BBC during World War II. The Corporation had entered the war somewhat demoralized, with areas of its output under siege from commercial interests, such as the **International Broadcasting Company (IBC)** and **Radio Luxembourg**. By 1945, the BBC was an organization commanding global respect. This may be measured by the fact that in September 1939 it was transmitting in seven languages. By 1945, there were more than 40 services, and the staff of the BBC had more than doubled.

WAR REPORT. *War Report* was first broadcast by **British Broadcasting Corporation (BBC)** radio after the nine o'clock news on D-Day, 6 June 1944, and continued nightly until 5 May 1945. From the initial landings until the final defeat of Nazi Germany, it gave millions of listeners a nightly picture of the progress of the war through the eyes of the men on the spot.

Using the new recording technology of the **Midget** disc recorder, relatively lightweight and portable, BBC correspondents such as

Richard Dimbleby, Frank Gillard, Wynford Vaughan-Thomas, and **Godfrey Talbot** relayed vivid word pictures to the waiting audience in Great Britain. Reports usually reached the listener within 24 hours of having been recorded. Among the most famous reports was Richard Dimbleby's moving account of the liberation of the Belsen concentration camp. Fundamentally, the necessities created by the policy decision to cover the last stages of the war in this way changed radio as a news-gathering medium forever.

WARNER, JACK (1895–1981). Jack Warner (real name Horace John Waters) was the brother of **Elsie and Doris Waters**. Having initially trained as an engineer, just prior to the outbreak of World War I, he worked as a mechanic in Paris and gained a good working knowledge of French. From 1914–1918, he worked as a driver with the Royal Flying Corps, based in France, after which he returned to his work as a mechanic, this time in England. His war years had seen his beginnings as an entertainer in concert parties, but he was over 30 before he became a professional entertainer.

In 1935, he made his West End debut, at which point he changed his name to Warner. It was, however, with his role in the radio show, *Garrison Theatre* in 1939, that his fame was assured. After the war, he played Joe Huggett in the successful radio comedy show, *Meet the Huggetts*. Thereafter, an increasingly successful career in television and film beckoned, and as PC George Dixon in the popular TV series, *Dixon of Dock Green*, which ran from 1955–1976, he reached a major new audience.

With no formal training, Warner's great gift was sincerity, a quality heard and understood by the radio microphone, which established him as a major British star with an affectionate following.

WATERS, ELSIE AND DORIS. Elsie (1893–1990) and Doris (1899–1978) were together one of the most famous and popular comedy double acts in British variety, and, as their on-stage personas, "Gert and Daisy," two cockney women, appeared in every medium. Two sisters, they never married and lived together all their lives. Their first radio broadcast was in 1929, and this led to a record contract. For one of their commercial recordings, they created the characters for which they were ever known; this was played on air by **Christo-**

pher Stone, and a highly successful career resulted. It was said that the East London working-class sound of the act appealed to an audience alienated by the Reithian **British Broadcasting Corporation's (BBC)** policy of standard English presentation.

In March 1934, the Waters sisters appeared on *Henry Hall's Guest Night*, and two months later they appeared in their first Royal Variety Performance. The act was a particular favorite of Queen Elizabeth, later the Queen Mother. During World War II, they regularly appeared on such programs as *Workers' Playtime*. After the war, they both received OBEs. "Gert and Daisy" continued to perform until the 1970s.

WATTS, CECIL (1896–1967). Watts was a musician who had worked in the early days of **2LO** as a musician. His major contribution, however, was the invention of **direct disc recording**, a technology he devised in order to replay rehearsals to his band, but which was adopted as a revolutionary instant recording device by program makers. In order to manufacture the number of discs required, which he and his wife Agnes called the Marguerite Sound System [later Studios] (MSS) based on a name that occurred on both sides of their family, he established a factory, initially in London's Shaftesbury Avenue, then in Charing Cross Road, and subsequently at Kew.

The demand came first from **commercial radio**, although the **British Broadcasting Corporation (BBC)** began to buy the Watts discs in quantity in April 1934. The importance of the invention was that for the first time broadcasters had access to an instant, cheap, and durable playback system, and the development of the recording of program material was immeasurably enhanced. Watts later developed a means of cleaning discs during playback, a device he called the "Dust Bug."

WEAK ENDING. The longest-running British radio comedy program ever, which went out from **Radio 4** on Friday evenings from 1970, produced by Simon Brett and **David Hatch**. It was originally written by Pete Spence. Since then, the program has had 27 producers and more than 65 writers, among them Jimmy Mulville, Griff Rhys Jones, and **Douglas Adams**. Growing out of the tradition of Oxbridge satire, the show frequently found itself on dangerous ground, as in 1980, when the journalist and broadcaster Derek Jameson attempted—and failed—to sue over a biting sketch that attacked him for his alleged lack of intellect.

WESTERN BROTHERS. Kenneth (?–1963) and George (?–1969) Western, were a double act that satirized the British upper classes. Known as "The Wireless Cads," they were actually cousins and had solo careers until they first met in 1925, when they formed one of the most successful acts on stage and radio. They broadcast from the 1930s onward, including during and after World War II, although the peak of their fame and success was undoubtedly during the 1930s, when they were featured in cabaret, variety, and radio. Frequently, their monologues and routines used the paternalistic BBC as a target, with such items as "O Dear, What Can the Matter Be, No One to Read Out the News," "The Old School Tie," and "We're Frightfully BBC." The style was that of a languid, unison drawl, and on stage, they wore evening dress and monocles.

WHALE, JAMES (1951–). This controversial and aggressive talk-show host developed a style similar to some of the U.S.-based "shock-jocks," engaging in belligerent debate with **phone-in** callers, and frequently verbally attacking their views on air. First heard on Metro Radio in the 1970s, he moved to Radio Aire in 1981, where his program was also televised by Yorkshire TV. After leaving radio to concentrate on television, he returned to work on the national talk station, **TalkSport**, where in 2005, he was broadcasting a late-night phone in.

WHAT DO YOU KNOW? This **quiz** show created by John P. Wynn for the **Light Programme** was chaired by **Franklin Engelmann** and contestants competed for the title "Brain of Britain." The program was first broadcast in 1953 and transferred to television in 1958 under the title *Ask Me Another*. In 1967, the radio version was renamed *Brain of Britain*.

WHILEY, JO (1965–). Jo Whiley joined **Radio 1** in 1993 and became known for her extensive and in-depth knowledge of popular **music**;

her programs frequently feature interviews and live sessions with major contemporary musicians. She has been associated with the Glastonbury Festival, and copresented for Radio 1 from the Festival with **John Peel**. In 1998, she received the **Sony Radio Academy Award** for **disc jockey** of the year. *See also* WOMEN.

WHITBY, TONY (1929–1975). Tony Whitby was controller of **Radio 4**, in the early 1970s, and was involved with the development of many highly significant programs during his time on the network, including *Kaleidoscope* and *I'm Sorry I Haven't a Clue*.

WHITE, PETER (1947–). Peter White, blind since birth, has been the main presenter for the **Radio 4** program for the visually impaired, *In Touch*, which he joined in 1974. He began his radio career in 1971 with Radio Solent in Southampton. Since 1995, he has been the **BBC**'s disability affairs correspondent. Between 1995 and 2005, he wrote four series of autobiographical talks for Radio 4. He also presented many programs for television, and in 1999, he published his autobiography, *See It My Way*.

WHITLEY, JOHN HENRY (1866–1935). Whitley became **chairman** of the **British Broadcasting Corporation (BBC)** in 1930, succeeding **George Clarendon**. Coming from a family cotton business, Whitley became an MP and subsequently Speaker of the House of Commons. Following the dispute between **John Reith** and Clarendon a document was drawn up that laid out the rights and duties of the chairman and the members of the Board of Governors. This became known as the Whitley Document and established a status quo whereby the BBC presented a unified face to the outside world. Reith and Whitley maintained a good relationship and Whitley died in office. *See also* OLIVER WHITLEY.

WHITLEY, OLIVER (1912–2005). Oliver Whitley, the son of **J. H. Whitley** joined the **British Broadcasting Corporation (BBC)** in 1935, and in 1939, was attached to the **Monitoring Service**, which was at that time expanding into a 24-hour operation monitoring 150 foreign news bulletins every day. Whitley resigned in 1941 and spent wartime service in the navy. He rejoined the BBC after the war in 1946, and was immediately seconded to the Colonial

Office to advise on the development of broadcasting in British overseas territories. He returned in 1949 as head of the **General Overseas Service**; in 1955 he was appointed assistant controller, Overseas Service.

In 1958, Whitley left **Bush House** and took up the post of appointments officer and then controller of staff training and appointments. He became chief assistant to **Hugh Greene** during the latter's tenure as **director-general** of the BBC and served on the Board of Management. He ended his career in the Corporation as the first managing director of the **External Services**, a post he held from 1969 until his retirement in 1972.

WHITNEY, JOHN (1930–). John Whitney became involved in radio in 1951 when he founded Ross Radio Productions, producing programs for **Radio Luxembourg**. A particular success from this time was *People Are Funny*. Always a passionate advocate of **commercial radio**, he cofounded the Local Radio Association, an organization created to encourage the introduction of self-funding radio in the UK, in 1964. He was founding managing director of **Capital Radio** from 1973–1982, at which time he was appointed director-general of the **Independent Broadcasting Authority (IBA)**, a post he held until 1989.

Whitney was chairman of the **Association of Independent Radio Contractors (AIRC)** from 1973–1975 and again in 1980. Among his numerous executive posts, he has been chairman of the **Sony Radio Academy Awards** and chairman of **Radio Joint Audience Research (RAJAR)**.

WILLIAMS, KENNETH (1926–1988). This highly talented actor is remembered for his camp portrayal of an array of bizarre comedy characters—in particular in *Beyond Our Ken* and *Round the Horne*. A great and much-loved raconteur, he was a regular and brilliant member of the *Just a Minute* team for nearly 20 years. He had earlier worked with **Tony Hancock** in *Hancock's Half Hour*. Williams was a complex person with a serious side that embraced a great love of poetry and art.

WILLIAMS, STEPHEN (1908–1994). Williams was an important figure in **commercial radio** history before and after World War II.

After spending time at **Radio Normandy**, he worked for **Radio Paris** at the time of the transfer of output to the fledgling **Radio Luxembourg** in December 1933. It was Williams who was responsible for the launch and early development of the station.

During World War II, he became the broadcasting officer for the Entertainments National Service Association (ENSA). Among programs he worked on from this time were *Variety Bandbox* and *It's All Yours*. Returning to Luxembourg in January 1945, he became the first postwar director of the station when it relaunched. In 1948, he joined the **British Broadcasting Corporation (BBC)**, where for 14 years he produced *Have a Go*. He was also involved in the establishment of BBC Radio Enterprises in the mid-1960s.

WILTON, ROBB (1881–1957). Referring to himself as a "comedy character actor," Robb Wilton was already a star of music hall and repertory theater by the time he made his first radio appearance—on **2LO**—in 1922. Born in Liverpool, he developed a rich strain of northern English humor that centered around a bumbling bureaucratic inefficiency. He became a major radio star in the late 1930s, and through the war years the British public found solace in his sketches and routines revolving around "muddling through"; by creating this loveable persona, he caught the mood of the nation. His last radio appearance was on *Blackpool Night* in August 1956. He died in May of the following year.

WINN, ANONA (1907–1994). Born in Australia, Anona Winn first trained as a pianist and then as an opera singer (under Dame Nellie Melba) prior to coming to Great Britain. She first broadcast on radio in 1928 in *Fancy Meeting You*. Widely known as a singer, composer, impressionist, and actress, she had made more than 300 broadcasts by the mid 1930s and had fronted her own dance band, "Anona Winn and Her Winners." Postwar, her considerable fame rested mostly on her role as a panelist in *Twenty Questions* from 1947 and her presentation of *Petticoat Line* from 1965 (a program she also devised).

WIRELESS GROUP. The company, which owned the national commercial speech station **TalkSport** as well as 13 regional and local radio stations, was run by **Kelvin MacKenzie**, a former editor of the

Sun newspaper, from 1998–2005, when the group was purchased by Ulster Television for £98.2 million.

WIRELESS PUBLICITY. Founded as a production house in 1936 by **Radio Luxembourg**, in premises on London's Thames Embankment, Wireless Publicity was created, like its rival companies, the **Universal Programmes Company** and **Universal Radio Publicity**, to package sponsored programs for the station. As with its parent company, it was revived after the war, and in 1954, its name was changed to Radio Luxembourg, London.

WOGAN, TERRY (1938–). Born in Limerick, Ireland, Terry Wogan's first role in radio was with Radio Telefis Eireann (RTE) as a newsreader/announcer. After two years working in documentary features, he moved into light entertainment as a **disc jockey** and presenter of **quiz** and variety programs. His first job with **British Broadcasting Corporation (BBC)** radio was presenting the **Light Programme** music show, *Midday Spin*, and when **Radio 1** started, he presented *Late Night Extra* on weekday evenings. Later, he presented the afternoon program on **Radio 2**, in April 1972 taking over the breakfast show.

Wogan left radio for a period to concentrate on television, including *Wogan*, a chat show that ran for seven years on BBC 1 TV, three nights a week. It was, however, as a radio presenter that Wogan has been most celebrated. In 1993, he returned to Radio 2 to present the breakfast show again, this time retitled *Wake Up to Wogan*. A series of honors followed; in 1994, he won the **Sony Radio Academy Award** for the Best Breakfast Show in 1997, he received an OBE in the New Year's Honors List, and in 2005, he was awarded an honorary knighthood, in addition to receiving the award for Radio Broadcaster of the Year at the Broadcasting Press Guild awards.

WOMAN'S HOUR. Founded by **Norman Collins**, creator of the **Light Programme**, in October 1946, it originally occupied an afternoon slot, 2:00 p.m.–3:00 p.m., a time conceived as being the one hour in the day when **women** at home would have time to themselves. The program's format—a series of magazine items and studio interviews on matters relating to women, and a read serialized book (later dramatized)—has changed little, although the content has altered to reflect the altering role of women in society.

In 1990, **Radio 4** moved the program—amidst considerable controversy—to a morning place in its schedule, where it has remained. Although its first presenter was a male, subsequently the program has been presented by a series of women, including **Jean Metcalfe**, **Marjorie Anderson**, **Sue MacGregor**, and **Jenni Murray**.

WOMEN. From the first days of UK broadcasting and the creation of the **British Broadcasting Company (BBC)**, the role and perception of women both as broadcasters and listeners has been at once crucial and frequently contradictory. In the latter case, there was a long-held view informing policy among broadcasters that a man's place was in the workplace while a woman's was in the home, making her therefore an available audience for programs of a particular type and style. Early examples of men's attitudes toward women within the medium show that they were frequently patronized and marginalized both as staff members and as consumers of radio, attitudes that reflected the Victorian roots from which the first broadcasters emerged. The first programs specifically aimed at women listeners had content that was suggested by a Women's Advisory Committee, and the coming in 1946 of the long-running *Woman's Hour* has seen an evolution of styles and attitudes, hosted by a succession of highly distinguished broadcasters, including **Jean Metcalfe**, **Marjorie Anderson**, **Sue MacGregor**, and **Jenni Murray**. At the same time, the existence of such a program has at times been criticized as a form of compartmentalizing women's issues and ideas. The perception of a stereotypical image of the woman listener at various times was carried over into a number of broadcasting **journals**, including *Radio Pictorial* during the 1930s.

A number of **serials** and **soap operas**, such as *Young Widow Jones*, *Mrs. Dale's Diary,* and *Waggoners' Walk* demonstrated media perceptions of women in society at various stages of British broadcasting history. In the field of light entertainment, **Mabel Constanduros** was significant during the 1930s in creating a unique voice for British radio comedy. Likewise, **Elsie and Doris Waters**, in the personas of their cockney characters, "Gert and Daisy" established themselves as a radio institution that survived for over 40 years.

The first woman announcer to introduce a program was Sheila Borrett, in July, 1933. A month later in the same year, the news was read by a woman for the first time, although this was discontinued soon afterward. It was not until 1974 that the news on **Radio 4** was read by a woman (Sheila Tracy), and shortly afterward Sandra Chalmers and **Gillian Reynolds** became managers of BBC and commercial radio stations, respectively. Other distinguished broadcasters included **Audrey Russell** in the field of live commentary and **Doris Arnold** in **music** presentation.

Early and highly influential women producers included **Olive Shapley**, **Nesta Pain**, and **Hilda Matheson**, who were innovators and developers of radio techniques that were subsequently widely adopted. Nevertheless, the official prejudices within the BBC meant that there was little equality; for instance, if a woman staff member married a male who also worked for the BBC, the woman was required to resign from her post. The history of women in UK radio provides many examples of inequalities while demonstrating the major part played in all areas, including production, presentation, technical work, and management. In the modern BBC, **Helen Boaden** and **Lesley Douglas**—as controllers of Radio 4 and **Radio 2**, respectively—have significantly contributed to the development of radio in the UK, and **Jenny Abramsky**'s role as director of radio and music has been instrumental in steering BBC policy through major changes in the way radio is both made and consumed. Beyond the BBC, the diversity of women's roles in modern society has been reflected in many ways, including feminist community radio stations, lesbian radio, and local Asian radio.

In general presentation, **Annie Nightingale** and **Jo Whiley** have achieved real status and authority in popular music presentation, while Jenni Murray has presented both news and specialist media programs, as has **Libby Purves**. **Mary Somerville** helped develop the BBC's policies relating to educational broadcasting from 1925, and **Bridget Plowden**, in her role as chairman of the **Independent Broadcasting Authority (IBA)**, was a key figure in the evolution of **commercial radio** within the UK.

WOOD NORTON. This medieval mansion in Worcestershire was purchased by the **British Broadcasting Corporation (BBC)** in 1939 in order to relocate its broadcasting operations away from urban sites during wartime. A dozen studios were built, and within a year Wood Norton had become one of the largest broadcasting centers in Europe, averaging 1,300 radio programs a week. It was also, for a time, a monitoring station, with linguists tuning in to overseas broadcasts. After the war, Wood Norton became the BBC's engineering training center. Purpose-built facilities in the grounds are still used for this.

WORKERS' PLAYTIME. In 1940, the minister for labour, Ernest Bevin, requested that the **British Broadcasting Corporation (BBC)** devise a program that would support and cheer workers in factories supporting the war effort. The result was *Workers' Playtime*, beginning as a weekend show in May 1941, and moving into a thrice-weekly slot from October that year, when Bevin himself introduced the program. Hosted by Bill Gates, the program comprised variety "turns"—notably **Elsie and Doris Waters**, who were regulars throughout the show's career in their characters of "Gert and Daisy" and two pianos, and was always transmitted as an **outside broadcast** from a factory canteen, the location of which was kept secret for security reasons during the war years, the announcement telling the listener only that it came from a "works somewhere in England." It long outlived its original intention, the final edition under the original name coming from a factory in Hatfield Heath in October 1964, when guests introduced by Gates included Anne Shelton, **Cyril Fletcher**, and Val Doonican.

THE WORLD AT ONE. Created by Andrew Boyle, launched in October 1965, and hosted in its early years by **William Hardcastle**, *The World at One*, a daily half-hour **news** magazine program on the **Home Service** that was to continue on **Radio 4**, is an example of a policy, encouraged by **Frank Gillard** during his time as director of sound broadcasting at the **British Broadcasting Corporation (BBC)**, and **Gerard Mansell**, of moving speech output away from scripted contributions and into the field of live debate.

WORLD RADIO. Almost as soon as radio began in an organized form in the United Kingdom, early adopters of receiver technology sought to experiment by exploring the airwaves in attempts to locate more and more distant radio stations. Within the context of this climate, the **British Broadcasting Company (BBC)** founded *World Radio*, initially the *Radio Supplement*, in 1925, two years after its domestic *The Radio Times*. Subtitled, the *Official Foreign and Technical Journal of the BBC*, its purpose was to foster awareness of international radio, and the journal contained articles and listings, together with wavelengths and broadcasting times. As the BBC moved toward its new **Empire Service**, the journal was expanded in 1932, in spite of objections from the trade press.

The interest in international listening during the 1920s and early 1930s gave *World Radio* its purpose; compared to *The Radio Times*, its circulation was extremely modest, as the following comparison demonstrates:

	The Radio Times	*World Radio*
1930	1,334,063	153,595
1931	1,575,151	181,513
1932	1,825,951	157,545

The year 1931 proved to be the highpoint in sales for *World Radio*, and thereafter sales diminished. The journal ceased publication in 1939.

It was a curious and ironic fact that in the first years of the 1930s, *World Radio* was carrying listing for stations, which themselves were supported by sponsorship, broadcasting from the Continent into the UK. As a BBC journal, this was inappropriate, while at the same time, the Corporation had commercial factors to consider in the sale of its magazines. Although most of the listings were terse and factual, occasionally a study of the pages of *World Radio* reveals a sponsor's message, and toward the end of the journal's life, it was carrying full details of **Radio Normandy** programs. It is no coincidence that **Leonard Plugge**, while developing his **commercial radio** interests, had gained a contract from the BBC itself "to supply, translate and sub-edit foreign wireless programs" for *World Radio*. See also JOURNALS.

WORLD RADIO NETWORK (WRN). World Radio Network was created in 1992 by three former **British Broadcasting Corporation**

(BBC) staff members who aimed to take advantage of emerging technologies to improve the distribution of international **shortwave** radio. The company's first contract was to deliver programs from Vatican Radio to listeners via the Astra satellite. WRN then began to create its own branded radio channels carrying daily scheduled programs, many from international shortwave broadcasters. These channels were distributed to listeners via **analog** and later **digital** satellite, cable, the internet, and local **AM/FM** relays, enabling listeners to hear international radio in greatly improved audio quality, particularly in comparison to shortwave.

Channels were themed according to language, and WRN developed services in English, German, French, Russian, and Arabic. International broadcasters find in WRN a conduit for the daily or weekly dissemination of their programs in high-quality audio; these include Radio Netherlands, China Radio International, Radio Canada International, Deutsche Welle, and Radio Australia. Distribution has continued to develop as new technologies have offered themselves, among them **podcasting**, **Digital Audio Broadcasting (DAB)**, and mobile telephony.

In recent years, the company has taken advantage of its aggregation and distribution infrastructure to offer a wide range of transmission services to other broadcasters. It also developed an extensive brokerage service, buying time on shortwave, AM and FM transmitters on behalf of clients.

WORLD SERVICE. From the early days of the **British Broadcasting Company (BBC)**, there was interest in creating a broadcasting service that could link the British Empire. The development of **shortwave** was a key element in this technically, and although the main advances in this were during the 1920s, the BBC was not financially in a position to undertake this. Given that the **license** fee provided UK listeners with a service, **John Reith** initially argued that the British public should not be required to fund a service beyond the domestic confines of broadcasting. This view was reversed in 1931, as in the throes of a financial crisis, the creation of such a service was deemed to be in the national interest. On 19 December 1932, the Empire Service was opened, and on Christmas Day, King George V spoke to the Empire for the first time.

The service operated through five separate two-hour transmissions at different times of the day, aimed at specific areas of the world. Gradually, transmission increased until by September 1939 the service was operating 18 hours a day. Programs were frequently re-broadcasts, or relays of domestic shows, although from 1934, there was a specific **News** Department. The first programs broadcast other than in English were those of the **Arabic Service**, which began January 1938; later the same year, broadcasts in French, German, and Italian were added, countering the increasing number of propaganda broadcasts coming from Europe at the time. **Wartime broadcasting** saw a very considerable development of overseas broadcasting from the UK, and it was to accommodate this that the BBC took over the **J. Walter Thompson** radio studios in **Bush House**, London.

It was during the years 1939–1945 that the title "Empire Service" was abolished, and was replaced by the General Overseas Service. With the election of a postwar Labour government, the decision was made to continue the multilanguage services that had been established, funded by the government, but with content decided by the BBC. This was the basis upon which the newly titled "External Services" were built and the key element that has established the global uniqueness of the service itself.

The postwar years were, however, difficult: with spending cuts brought about by economic depression, and a serious confrontation between the Anthony Eden government and the BBC over the 1956 Suez Crisis, during which the BBC's determination to broadcast both sides of the argument raised for a short time the possibility of the BBC coming under direct government control. Other issues emerged with the development of the Cold War with the Soviet Union, and the reputation of the BBC for impartial reporting of world events at a time when propaganda continued to be rife, was a major factor—together with the application of the **transistor** to receiver technology—in growth in listenership. In 1965, the General Overseas Service was renamed "The World Service," and in 1988, the title was extended to include all External Services of the BBC.

In 1991, the World Service moved into television and today broadcasts as BBC World. In radio, the development of satellite technology has enabled **frequency modulation (FM)** relays in many areas of the world. Added to this, in 1995, the BBC's Polish service was the first to go online, and this subsequently increased to cover all 43 languages covered by the service in addition to English. The World Service now broadcasts 24 hours a day in English and for varying durations in its other languages.

WRIGHT, STEVE (1954–). Joining **Radio 2** in April 1996 as part of the redesign of the station instigated by controller, **James Moir**, Steve Wright initially presented two weekend shows, on Saturday and Sunday mornings, but later moved to weekday afternoons, while continuing with his *Sunday Lovesongs* program. Born in Greenwich, London, he first joined the **British Broadcasting Corporation (BBC)** as a researcher and record librarian, leaving in 1975 to work briefly in European radio. Thereafter, he made programs for the **London Broadcasting Company (LBC)** and then Thames Valley Radio (Radio 210) in 1976. Three years later, he was at **Radio Luxembourg** and then joined **Radio 1** in January 1980, where he presented various shows.

In January 1994, after a highly successful period as the afternoon program host, he took over the breakfast show, where he remained until 21 April 1995 when he resigned in dramatic fashion in protest against the reforms on the network then being undertaken by Controller **Matthew Bannister**. Wright has won a wide range of awards for his work in UK **music** radio.

WRITTLE. Situated near **Chelmsford** in Essex, home of the **Marconi Company**, the village of Writtle was the location of the first regular public broadcast program in the UK, which commenced in February 1922. The circuit was almost identical to that of a standard Marconi telephone, and the transmitter fed a four-wire aerial 250 feet long and 100 feet high, originally radiating on a wavelength of 700 meters.

The equipment was housed in a former army hut, and the station took the call sign 2MT, Two Emma Toc, broadcasting a weekly half-hour program of technical information, testing, occasional music, and entertaining banter, principally from its main presenter, Captain **P. P. Eckersley**. The station closed on 17 January 1923. Writtle remained a company site for many years thereafter. The historic hut was later removed for use by a local school but was subsequently retrieved and is now housed at the Chelmsford Science and Industry Museum,

Sandford Mill. The site of the hut is today commemorated by a nearby information board at Melba Court, named after Dame Nellie Melba, who made Britain's first entertainment broadcast from the company's New Street works in Chelmsford (*See* "MELBA" BROADCAST). The board was unveiled in 1997 by Marconi's daughter, Princess Elletra Marconi. The site itself was sold, and the land was used for housing development in the 1990s.

In the village of Writtle, the Church of All Saints contains a window commemorating the work of Marconi. It was dedicated by his grandson, Prince Guglielmo Marconi Giovanelli, in 1992. The Writtle station may be seen as the true birthplace of UK radio as a public entertainment form.

– Y –

YOU AND YOURS. This daily consumer and social affairs magazine began its life on **Radio 4** in 1970. Initially a half-hour slot, its duration was extended during the 1990s by Controller James Boyle to just under an hour.

YOUNG, JIMMY (1925–). Young was a popular singer for many years, with two chart-topping hits in the mid-1950s. It was, however, as a radio presenter that he made his greatest mark. Working as a **disc jockey** for the **Light Programme** he presented *Flat Spin* in 1949 and later *Housewives' Choice* intermittently from 1955 to 1960. Thereafter, he worked at **Radio Luxembourg** for a number of years. When **Radio 1** launched in 1967, he was a member of the original team, and his mid-morning program was broadcast on both Radio 1 and **Radio 2** for some time. In 1973, he moved to Radio 2 exclusively, and remained in the morning slot until replaced by **Jeremy Vine** in 2003. Young was known for his interviews with high-ranking world figures, including every British prime minister from 1964. Said to be Margaret Thatcher's favorite interviewer, he was knighted for his services to radio.

YOUNG, STUART (1934–1986). Stuart Young came from an accounting background and a number of directorships to become a governor of the **British Broadcasting Corporation (BBC)** in 1981. He had originally felt that the Corporation should be funded by advertising, but changed his thoughts on this to the extent that, as **chairman** (a role to which he was appointed in 1983), he was to lead the BBC's successful argument to the **Peacock Committee** for a continuation of **license** funding. It was a time of tension between the BBC and the government over editorial matters, particularly in television. When Young died in office in 1986, his place was taken by Vice-Chairman Lord Barnett until the appointment of **Marmaduke Hussey**.

YOUNG WIDOW JONES. Toward the end of the Continent-based commercial revolution of the 1930s, agencies such as the **J. Walter Thompson Organization** began developing variations of the soap operas then popular on U.S. radio. Among these was *Young Widow Jones*, broadcast on **Radio Luxembourg** from October 1938 and sponsored by Milk of Magnesia. It was billed in ***Radio Pictorial*** as "The moving story of a woman's heart and woman's love. Living in the small town of Appleton, Peggy Jones, in her twenties, with two children to support, ponders long on the question of what she owes to her children and what she owes to herself. A story of joy and despair, life and love as we all know it." The series was based on the U.S. original, *Young Widder Jones*, and this, and other such programs, introduced British audiences to a genre that, postwar, was to become highly significant.

YOUR HUNDRED BEST TUNES. Devised by **Alan Keith**, and presented by him on Sunday evenings since 1959 until his death in 2003, when the mantle was assumed by Richard Baker, the title was originally *The Hundred Best Tunes in the World*. Beginning on the **Light Programme**, it moved to the **Home Service** during the 1960s and subsequently transferred to **Radio 2**. The **musical** choice has always been undemanding, relaxing, and comforting.

YOUR OLD FRIEND DAN. This popular prewar series on **Radio Normandy** began in September 1936, and featured the Canadian broadcaster, Lyle Evans. The format was that of songs, instrumental music, and homespun philosophy that made Evans (as "Dan") a well-known personality in the last years of peace. The program was sponsored by Johnson's Wax Polish.

– Z –

ZOO MAN, THE. This regular feature on *Children's Hour* began in 1924, presented by the *Daily Mail* journalist, Leslie Mainland. Later, it was recreated by David Seth-Smith the curator of birds and mammals at London's Regent's Park Zoo in January 1934, who maintained regular **talks** in the slot until 1945. **British Broadcasting Corporation (BBC)** Regions sometimes gave the idea a more local slant by appointing their own "Zoo Man."

Bibliography

A. Direct Sources   305
   1. Official Sources   305
   2. Public Journals   305
   3. Commentaries, Biography and Autobiography   305
B. Historical, Analytical and Interpretative   307
   1. Historical Reference Works   307
   2. Cultural and Theoretical   309
   3. Journals   311
   4. Articles and Papers   312
   5. Pamphlets   312
   6. Websites   312
C. Making Radio   313
   1. Technical   313
   2. Production   313
   3. Radio Advertising   314
   4. Commercial Radio   314
   5. Music Radio   314
   6. Radio Drama   315
   7. Radio Journalism   315
   8. International Radio   315
   9. Radio Texts   316

INTRODUCTION

Because radio as a public entertainment is less than 100 years old, the library of works relating to it is both concise and potent. This collection of works divides broadly into three kinds; (1) the writings of its creators; (2) the histories; and (3) growing in size and importance, reflective works of theory and cultural studies. In the United Kingdom, as elsewhere in the world, radio is increasingly seen as an important subject, worthy of academic study, and because of the medium's continuing ability to reinvent itself according to new technologies, also an important and continuing source of cultural reference.

In the early days of UK radio, the wonder—almost strangeness—of the new medium caused many of the pioneers to reflect in print on their first experiences. Thus John Reith's *Broadcast over Britain*, Arthur Burrows' *The Story of Broadcasting*, and Cecil Lewis's *Broadcasting from Within*—works from three of the most important founding fathers of British radio, written within three years of the creation of the British Broadcasting Company in 1922, provide very direct and impassioned witness to those first heady years. These works are invaluable, particularly when read alongside some of the primary material cited in this bibliography, including the official government reports, created as radio in the UK sought to define itself within the model of a public service ethic. For this reason, these commentaries, autobiographies, and personal reflections have been included within section A, Direct Sources. For the same reason, journals such as *Radio Times*, *Radio Pictorial*, and the *BBC Handbooks* are included here under "Public Journals," listing magazines and other regular publications that are intended by broadcasters for their audiences and offer direct information for those seeking to understand the *zeitgeist* of the time.

For the serious student of UK radio—indeed, broadcasting—history, an indispensable source is Asa Briggs' five-volume *History of Broadcasting in the United Kingdom*. Told principally from a BBC perspective, it is nonetheless a work to which all other scholars of British media history owe a great debt. Likewise, the same author's *The BBC: The First Fifty Years* provides extremely useful insights. Section B of the bibliography contains details of historical works such as this, together with analytical and interpretative writings, coming from the developing academic discipline of Radio Studies in Great Britain. Here, the reader will find books grouped with journals, papers, pamphlets, and websites.

Section C is entitled "Making Radio." Here are sections dealing with the practicalities of creating the medium in its diverse forms; because radio platforms—transmission and receiver technology—are rapidly changing and evolving, it is important to understand the nature and essence of the form itself through a perception of its various facets. Even today's instruction manuals will become tomorrow's historical primary source texts, as have those of radio's short past already. The section begins with the technical, and includes Edward Pawley's seminal *BBC Engineering 1922–1972*. Next, production itself, offering an understanding of some of the multifarious skills required in the medium. Radio advertising and commercial radio are clearly linked, and the genres of music radio, radio drama, and radio journalism offer texts both historical and contemporary as source and textbooks for the radio scholar at every level.

Texts on international radio have been included; because of the very nature of the medium, radio is always potentially international; however, most of the works cited here relate to the work of the BBC World Service, and the nature of wartime propaganda broadcasting. Finally, the semidirect source of the radio-based text; a number of UK radio programs have spawned either spin-off books or specific studies. Both types are included here, maintaining the theme of this bibliography's aim, which is to be both reflective and directly engaged with primary sources relating to radio in the United Kingdom.

A: DIRECT SOURCES

1. Official Sources

Report of the Imperial Wireless Committee 1919–20. Cmnd. 777. (Norman Committee). London: HMSO, 1920.
Broadcasting Committee Report, Cmnd. 1951. (Sykes Committee) London: HMSO, 1923.
Report of the Broadcasting Committee, Cmnd. 2599. (Crawford Committee). London: HMSO, 1925.
Report of the Television Committee 1934–5. Cmnd. 4793. (Selsdon Committee). London: HMSO, 1935.
Report of the Broadcasting Committee, Cmnd. 5091. (Ullswater Committee). London: HMSO, 1936.
Broadcasting Policy White Paper. Cmnd. 6852. London: HMSO, 1946.
Report of the Broadcasting Committee 1949. Cmnd. 8116. (Beveridge Committee). London: HMSO, 1951.
Broadcasting Policy. White Paper. Cmnd. 9005. London: HMSO, 1953.
Report of the Committee on Broadcasting, Cmnd. 1753. (Pilkington Committee). London: HMSO, 1962.
Report of the Committee on the Future of Broadcasting, Cmnd. 6753. (Annan Committee). London: HMSO, 1977.
The Development of Cable Systems and Services. White Paper. Cmnd. 8866. London: HMSO, 1983.
Report of the Committee on the Financing of the BBC, Cmnd. 9284. (Peacock Committee). London: HMSO, 1986.
Broadcasting in the 1990s: Competition, Choice and Quality. White Paper. Cmnd. 517. London: HMSO, 1988.

2. Public Journals

BBC Handbook. [Sometimes called *BBC Year Book* and *BBC Annual*]. Annually. London: BBC, 1928–87.
Radio Pictorial. Weekly. London: Bernard Jones Publications, 1934–1939.
Radio Times. Weekly. London: various publishers, 1923–present.
The Listener. Weekly. London: BBC, 1929–1991.

3. Commentaries, Biography and Autobiography

Adie, Kate. *The Kindness of Strangers.* London: Headline, 2002.
Barker, Eric. *Steady, Barker.* London: Secker and Warburg, 1956.
Boyle, Andrew. *Only the Wind Will Listen: Reith of the BBC.* London: Hutchinson, 1972.

Bridson, D. G. *Prospero and Ariel: The Rise and Fall of Radio, A Personal Recollection*. London: Gollancz, 1971.
Burrows, Arthur. *The Story of Broadcasting*. London: Cassell, 1924.
Carney, Michael. *Stoker: The Life of Hilda Matheson OBE 1888–1940*. Llangynog: Michael Carney, 1999.
Cleghorn Thomson, David. *Radio Is Changing Us*. London: Watts, 1937.
Coulton, B. *Louis MacNeice in the BBC*. London: Faber and Faber, 1980.
Dimbleby, Jonathan. *Richard Dimbleby*. London: Hodder and Stoughton, 1975.
Eckersley, Myles. *Prospero's Wireless*. Romsey: Myles Books, 1998.
Eckersley, Peter. *The Power behind the Microphone*. London: The Scientific Book Club, 1942.
Eckersley, Roger. *The BBC and All That*. London: Sampson Low, Marston, 1946.
Evens, E. *Through the Years with Romany*. London: University of London Press, 1946.
Fielden, Lionel. *The Natural Bent*. London: Andre Deutsch, 1960.
Fletcher, Cyril. *Nice One Cyril*. London: Corgi Books, 1980.
Gielgud, Val. *Years in a Mirror*. London: Bodley Head, 1964.
Glover, Fi. *Travels with My Radio*. London: Ebury Press, 2002.
Gorham, Maurice. *Sound and Fury: Twenty-one Years in the BBC*. London: Percival Marshall, 1948.
Green, Hugh. *The Third Floor Front*. London: Bodley Head, 1969.
Grisewood, Freddy. *The World Goes By*. London: Secker and Warburg, 1952.
Grisewood, Harman. *One Thing at a Time: An Autobiography*. London: Hutchinson, 1968.
Guthrie, Tyrone. *Squirrel's Cage*. London: Cobden–Sanderson, 1931.
Hall, Henry. *Here's to the Next Time*. London: Odhams, 1956.
Harding, Gilbert. *Along My Line*. London: Putnam, 1953.
———. *Master of None*. London: Putnam, 1958.
Hawkins, Desmond. *When I Was: A Memoir of the Years between the Wars*. London: Macmillan, 1989.
Heatley, Michael. *John Peel: A Life in Music*. London: Michael O'Mara Books, 2005.
Heppenstall, Rayner. *Portrait of the Artist as a Professional Man*. London: Owen, 1969.
Hibberd, Stuart. *This—Is London*. London: MacDonald and Evans, 1950.
Hill, Trevor. *Over The Airwaves, My Life in Broadcasting*. Lewes: The Book Guild, 2005.
Hunter, Fred. "Hilda Matheson and the BBC, 1926– 1940." In *Women and Radio*, edited by Caroline Mitchell. London: Routledge, 2000.
Kavanagh, Ted. *Tommy Handley*. London: Hodder and Stoughton, 1949.
Lewis, Cecil. *Broadcasting from Within*. London: Newnes, 1924.
MacPherson, Stewart. *The Mike and I*. London: Home and Van Thal, 1948.
Marconi, Degna. *My Father, Marconi*. London: Frederick Muller, 1962.
Marconi, Maria Cristina. *Marconi, My Beloved*. Boston: Dante University of America Press, 2001.

Martland, Peter. *Lord Haw Haw: The English Voice of Nazi Germany.* London: The National Archives, 2003.
Maschwitz, Eric. *No Chip on My Shoulder.* London: Jenkins, 1957.
McIntyre, Ian. *The Expense of Glory: A Life of John Reith.* London: HarperCollins, 1993.
Messiter, Ian. *My Life and Other Games.* London: Fourth Estate, 1990.
Miall, Leonard. *Inside the BBC: British Broadcasting Characters.* London: Weidenfeld and Nicolson, 1994.
——. (ed.) *Richard Dimbleby, Broadcaster.* London: BBC, 1966.
Moseley, Sydney. *Broadcasting in My Time.* London: Rich and Cowan, 1935.
Moseley, Sydney. *The Private Diaries of Sydney Moseley.* London/Bournemouth: Max Parrish/The Outspoken Press, 1960.
Nicolson, Harold. *Diaries and Letters.* London: Collins, 1967.
Payne, Jack. *Signature Tune.* London: Paul, 1947.
Pickles, Wilfred. *Between You and Me.* London: Werner Laurie, 1949.
Plomley, Roy. *Days Seemed Longer: Early Years of a Broadcaster.* London: Eyre Methuen, 1980.
Priestland, Gerald. *Something Understood.* London: Andre Deutsch, 1986.
Purves, Libby. *Radio: A True Love Story.* London: Hodder and Stoughton, 2002.
Reith, John. *Broadcast Over Britain.* London: Hodder and Stoughton, 1924.
——. *Personality and Career.* London: George Newnes, 1925.
Reith, John. *Into the Wind.* London: Hodder and Stoughton, 1949.
Rowntree, Seebohm. *Poverty and Progress.* London: Longman's, 1941.
Shapley, Olive. *Broadcasting a Life.* London: Scarlet Press, 1996.
Sieveking, Lance. *The Stuff of Radio.* London: Cassell, 1934.
Stone, Christopher. *Christopher Stone Speaking.* London: Elkin Matthews and Marrot, 1933.
Stuart, Charles (ed.). *The Reith Diaries.* London: Collins, 1975.
Thomas, Howard. *With an Independent Air: Encounters during a Lifetime of Broadcasting.* London: Weidenfeld and Nicolson, 1977.
Train, Jack. *Up and Down the Line.* London: Odhams, 1956.
Trethowan, Ian. *Split Screen.* London: Hamish Hamilton, 1984.
Watt, John (ed.). *Radio Variety.* London: Dent and Sons, 1939.
Watts, Agnes. *Cecil E. Watts, Pioneer of Direct Disc Recording.* London: Agnes Watts, (privately published), 1972.
White, Peter. *See It My Way.* London: Little, Brown and Company, 1999.

B: HISTORICAL, ANALYTICAL, AND INTERPRETATIVE

1. Historical Reference Works

Baker, A. J. *A History of the Marconi Company.* London: Methuen, 1970.
BBC. [No author credited]. *Broadcasting House.* London: BBC, 1932.

Beachcroft, T. O. *British Broadcasting*. London: Longman, Green and Co., 1946.
Black, Peter. *The Biggest Aspidistra in the World*. London: BBC, 1972.
Briggs, Asa. *Governing the BBC*. London: BBC, 1979.
———. *The History of Broadcasting in the United Kingdom, Vol. 1: The Birth of Broadcasting, 1896–1927*. Oxford: Oxford University Press, 1995.
———. *The History of Broadcasting in the United Kingdom, Vol. II: The Golden Age of Wireless, 1927–1939*. Oxford: Oxford University Press, 1995.
———. *The History of Broadcasting in the United Kingdom, Vol. III: The War of Words, 1939–1945*. Oxford: Oxford University Press, 1995.
———. *The History of Broadcasting in the United Kingdom, Vol. IV: Sound and Vision, 1945–55*. Oxford: Oxford University Press, 1995.
———. *The History of Broadcasting in the United Kingdom, Vol. V: Competition, 1955–1974*. Oxford: Oxford University Press, 1995.
———. *The BBC, The First Fifty Years*. Oxford: Oxford University Press, 1985.
Brochand, Christian. *Histoire Générale de la Radio et de la Télévision en France, Tome 1, 1921–1944*. Paris: La Documentation Française, 1994.
Carpenter, Humphrey. *The Envy of the World, Fifty Years of the BBC Third Programme and Radio 3*. London: Weidenfeld and Nicolson, 1996.
Chignell, Hugh. *BBC Handbooks, Accounts and Annual Reports (1927–2002)*. Wakefield: Microform Academic Publishers, 2003.
Cox, Jim. *The Great Radio Soap Operas*. New York: McFarland, 1999.
Crissell, Andrew. *Understanding Radio*. London: Methuen, 1994.
———. *An Introductory History of British Broadcasting*. London: Routledge, 2002.
———. (ed.). *More Than a Music Box: Radio Cultures and Communities in a Multi-Media World*. Oxford: Berghahn Books, 2004.
Currie, Tony. *The Radio Times Story*. Tiverton: Kelly Publications, 2001.
Donovan, Paul. *The Radio Companion*. London: Grafton, 1992.
Douglas, George H. *The Early Days of Radio Broadcasting*. Jefferson, N. C.: McFarland, 1987.
Duval, René. *Histoire de la Radio en France*. Paris: Éditions Alain Moreau, 1979.
Fernandez, Francisco José Montes Fernández. *Los Orígenes de la radiodifusión exterior en España*. Madrid: RTVE, 1988.
Foster, Andy, and Steve Furst. *Radio Comedy 1938–1968*. London: Virgin, 1996.
Gifford, Denis. *The Golden Age of Radio*. London: Batsford, 1985.
Gilliam, Laurence (ed.). *BBC Features*. London: Evans Brothers, 1950.
Gorham, Maurice. *Forty Years of Irish Broadcasting*. Dublin: The Talbot Press, 1967.
Hartley, Ian. *2ZY to NBH: An Informal History of the BBC in Manchester and the North West*. Altrincham: Willow Publishing, 1987.
Hawkins, Desmond. *War Report: D-Day to VE-Day*. London: Ariel Books, BBC, 1985.
Hennessey, Brian. *Savoy Hill: The Early Years of British Broadcasting*. Romford: Ian Henry Publications, 1996.
Kenyon, Nicholas. *The BBC Symphony Orchestra: The first fifty years, 1930–1980*. London: BBC, 1981.

Lambert, R. S. *Ariel and All His Quality*. London: Victor Gollancz, 1940.
Méadel, Cécile. *Histoire de la Radio des Années Trente*. Paris: Anthropos/INA, 1994.
Morris, John. *From the Third Programme: A Ten Years' Anthology*. London: Nonesuch Press, 1956.
Nicholas, Sian. *The Echo of War: Home Front Propaganda and the Wartime BBC, 1939–45*. Manchester: Manchester University Press, 1996.
Reid, Colin. *Action Stations: A History of Broadcasting House*. London: Robson Books, 1987.
Smith, Anthony. *British Broadcasting*. Newton Abbot: David and Charles. 1974.
Snagge, John, and Michael Barsley. *Those Vintage Years of Radio*. London: Pitman, 1972.
Scannell, Paddy, and David Cardiff. *A Social History of British Broadcasting, 1922–1939, Serving the Nation*. Oxford: Blackwell, 1991.
Shingler, Martin, and Cindy Wieringa. *On Air: Methods and Meanings of Radio*. London: Arnold, 1998.
Sterling, Christopher H. (ed.). *The Museum of Broadcast Communications Encyclopedia of Radio*. New York: Fitzroy Dearborn, 2004.
Street, Seán. *Crossing the Ether: British Public Service Radio and Commercial Competition 1922–1945*. London: John Libbey Media, 2006.
———. *A Concise History of British Radio, 1922–2002*. Tiverton: Kelly Publications, 2005.
———. "Radio For Sale: Sponsored Programming in British Radio during the 1930s." In *Sound Journal*. www.kent.ac.uk/sdfva/sound-journal/street19991.html, ed. Alan Beck. Canterbury: 1999. [accessed 20 July 2005]
———. "Recording Technologies and Strategies for British Radio Transmission before the 2nd World War." In *Sound Journal*. www.kent.ac.uk/sdfva/soundjournal/street002.html, ed. Alan Beck, Canterbury: 2000. [accessed 20 July 2005]
Tomalin, Norman. *Daventry Calling the World*. Whitby: Caedmon of Whitby, 1998.
Took, Barry. *Laughter in the Air*. London: Robson Books, 1976.
Wander, Tim. *2MT Writtle: The Birth of Broadcasting*. Stowmarket: Capella Publications, 1988.
Whitehead, Kate. *The Third Programme: A literary history*. Oxford, Clarendon Press, 1989.
Wood, R. *A World in Your Ear*. London: Macmillan, 1979.

2. Cultural and Theoretical

Baily, Leslie. *Leslie Baily's BBC Scrapbooks, Volume 2: 1918–1939*. London: George Allen and Unwin, 1968.
Baldwin, Stanley. *On England, and Other Addresses*. London: Philip Allan, 1936.
Briggs, Susan. *Those Radio Times*. London: Weidenfeld and Nicolson, 1981.
Black, Peter. *The Biggest Aspidistra in the World: A Personal Celebration of 50 Years of the BBC*. London: BBC, 1972.

Burns, T. *BBC: Public Institution, Private World.* London: Macmillan, 1977.
Cardiff, David. "The Serious and the Popular: Aspects of the Evolution of Style in the Radio Talk 1928–1939." In *Media, Culture and Society: A Critical Reader,* edited by Richard Collins et. al. London: Sage, 1986.
Carey, John. *The Intellectuals and the Masses: Pride and Prejudice among the Literary Intelligensia, 1880–1939.* London: Faber and Faber, 1992.
Clark, J. *Culture and Crisis in Britain in the 1930s.* London: Lawrence and Wishart, 1979.
Coase, R. H. *British Broadcasting—A Study in Monopoly.* London: The London School of Economics/Longmans, 1950.
Cooke, Alistair. *The Patient Has the Floor.* London: The Bodley Head, 1986.
Crisell, Andrew. "Look with Thine Ears: BBC Radio 4 and Its Significance in a Multi-Media Age." In *More Than a Music Box,* ed. Andrew Crisell. Oxford/New York: Berghahn Books, 2004.
Crisell, Andrew (ed.). *More Than a Music Box—Radio Cultures and Communities in a Multi-Media World.* Oxford/New York: Berghahn Books, 2004.
Curran, Charles. *A Seamless Robe: Broadcasting—Philosophy and Practice.* London: Collins, 1979.
Curran, James, and Jean Seaton. *Power without Responsibility: The Press and Broadcasting in Britain.* London: Routledge, 1997.
Douglas, Susan J. *Listening In: Radio and the American Imagination.* New York: Times Books, 1999.
Emery, Walter B. *National and International Systems of Broadcasting: Their History, Operation and Control.* East Lansing, Mich., 1969.
Engelman, Ralph. *Public Radio and Television in America: A Political History.* Thousand Oaks, Calif.: Sage, 1996.
Giddings, Robert. "John Reith and the Rise of Radio." In *Literature and Culture in Modern Britain, Vol. 1, 1900–1929,* ed. Clive Bloom. London: Longman, 1993.
Gilder, Eric. *Mass Media Moments in the United Kingdom, the USSR and the USA.* Sibiu, Romania: Lucian Blaga University of Sibiu Press, 2003.
Goldie, Grace Wyndham. *Facing the Nation: Television and Politics 1936–1976.* London: The Bodley Head, 1977.
Hendy, David. *Radio in the Global Age.* Cambridge: Polity Press, 2000.
———. "Reality Radio: The Documentary." In *More Than a Music Box,* ed. Andrew Crisell. Oxford/New York: Berghahn Books, 2004.
Hilmes, Michele, and Jason Loviglio (eds.). *A Radio Reader: Essays in the Cultural History of Radio.* New York: Routledge, 2002.
Hutchby, Ian. "The Organisation of Talk on Talk Radio." In *Broadcast Talk,* edited by Paddy Scannell. London: Sage, 1991.
Jennings, Hilda, and Winifred Gill. *Broadcasting in Everyday Life, A Survey of the Social Effects of the Coming of Broadcasting.* London: BBC, 1939.
Kerwin, Jerome. *The Control of Radio.* Chicago: University of Chicago Press, 1934.
Koshar, Rudy (ed.). *Splintered Classes, Politics and the Lower Middle Classes in Interwar Europe.* New York: Holmes and Meier, 1990.

Lacey, Kate. "Continuities and Change in Women's Radio." In *More Than a Music Box*, ed. Andrew Crisell. Oxford/New York: Berghahn Books, 2004.

Leavis, F. R. *Mass Civilisation and Minority Culture*. London: The Minority Press, 1930.

Lewis, P. M. and J. Booth. *The Invisible Medium: Public, Commercial and Community Radio*. London: Macmillan, 1989.

Linehan, Andy (ed.). *Aural History: Essays on Recorded Sound*. London: British Library, 2001.

MacDonald, Barrie. *Broadcasting in the United Kingdom: A Guide to Information Sources*. London: Mansell, 1993.

Marwick, Arthur. *Class: Image and Reality*. London: Collins, 1980.

McDonnell, James (ed.). *Public Service Broadcasting, A Reader*. London: Routledge, 1991.

Mitchell, Caroline (ed.). *Women and Radio: Airing Differences*. London: Routledge, 2000.

Paulu, Burton. *British Broadcasting: Radio and Television in the United Kingdom*. Minneapolis: University of Minnesota Press, 1956.

Pegg, Mark. *Broadcasting and Society 1918–1939*. Beckenham: Croom Helm, 1983.

Scannell, Paddy (ed.). *Broadcast Talk*. London: Sage, 1991.

———. "The Relevance of Talk." In *Broadcast Talk,* edited by Paddy Scannell. London: Sage, 1991.

———. *Radio, Television and Modern Life*. Oxford: Blackwell, 1996.

Siepmann, Charles. *Radio, Television and Society*. New York: Oxford University Press, 1950.

Silvey, Robert. *Who's Listening? The Story of BBC Audience Research*. London: George Allen and Unwin, 1974.

Starkey, Guy. "BBC Radio 5 Live: Extending Choice through 'Radio Bloke'?" In *More Than a Music Box,* ed. Andrew Crisell. Oxford/New York: Berghahn Books, 2004.

Street, Seán. *Radio Waves: Poems Celebrating the Wireless*. London: Enitharmon Press, 2004.

Williams, Raymond. *Culture and Society*. Harmondsworth: Pelican Books, 1963.

Williams, Raymond. *Television: Technology and Cultural Form*. London: Fontana, 1974.

Wolfe, Kenneth M. *The Churches and the British Broadcasting Corporation 1922–1956: The Politics of Broadcast Religion*. London: SCM Press, 1984.

3. Journals

The Circular Note: Journals of the Vintage Radio Programmes Collectors' Circle. Harrogate.

Historic Record and AV Collector. London.

Journal of Advertising History. Norwich: MCB University Press.
Journal of Media Practice. Bristol: Intellect.
Journal of Radio Studies. Washington: Broadcast Education Association.
Media Culture and Society. London: Sage.
The Radio Journal: International Studies in Broadcast and Audio Media. Bristol: Intellect/Radio Studies Network.

4. Articles and Papers

Lewis, Peter. "Opening and Closing Doors: Radio Drama in the BBC." *The Radio Journal* 1, no 3 (February 2004): 161–176.
Long, Paul. "British Radio and the Politics of Culture in Post-War Britain: The Work of Charles Parker." *The Radio Journal* 2, no. 3 (July 2005): 131–152.
Moores, Shaun. "'The Box on the Dresser': Memories of Early Radio in Everyday Life." *Media Culture and Society* 10, no. 1. 1988.
Street, Sean. "BBC Sunday Policy and Audience Response 1930–45," *Journal of Radio Studies* 7, no. 1. (Spring 2000) 161–179.
———. "Programme-Makers on Parker: Occupational Reflections on the Radio Production Legacy of Charles Parker." *The Radio Journal* 2, no. 3. (July 2005): 187–194.
Wall, Tim. "Policy, Pop & the Public: The Discourse of Regulation in British Commercial Radio." *Journal of Radio Studies* 7, no. 1. (Spring 2000): 180–195.
Williams, Stephen. "Pioneering Commercial Radio the 'D–I–Y' Way." *Journal of Advertising History* 10, no. 2 (1987): 7–14.

5. Pamphlets

Calling All Nations: BBC Overseas Broadcasting. London: BBC, 1943.
Twenty-five Years of British Broadcasting. London: BBC, 1947.
Capital, Local Radio and Private Profit. London: Comedia Publishing Group/Local Radio Workshop, 1983.

6. Websites [All accessed 20 July 2005]

Chronomedia: www.terramedia.co.uk/Chronomedia/index.htm
Commercial Radio Companies Association (CRCA): www.crca.co.uk
Media UK: www.mediauk.com
Ofcom: www.ofcom.org.uk
Old Radio Broadcasting Equipment and Memories: www.roger.beckwith.btinternet.co.uk/bh/menu.htm
Radio Academy: www.radioacademy.org
Radio Days: www.otr.com/index.shtml

Radio Rewind: www.radiorcwind.co.uk
The Wireless Works: www.wirelessworks.co.uk/info/info.htm

C: MAKING RADIO

1. Technical

Alkin, G. *Sound Recording and Reproduction.* London: Focal Press, 1991.
Batten, Joe. *Joe Batten's Book: The Story of Sound Recording.* London: Rockliff, 1956.
Berry, Richard. "Speech Radio in the Digital Age." In *More Than a Music Box,* ed. Andrew Crisell. Oxford/New York: Berghahn Books, 2004.
Biel, Michael J. *The Making and Use of Recordings in Broadcasting before 1936.* Evanston Illinois: UMI Dissertation Service, 1996.
Bussey, Gordon. *Marconi's Atlantic Leap.* Coventry: Marconi Communications, 2000.
Hill, Jonathan. *The Cat's Whisker: Fifty Years of Wireless Design.* London: Oresko Books, 1978.
———. *Radio! Radio!* Bampton: Sunrise Press, 1986.
Pawley, Edward. *BBC Engineering 1922–1972.* London: BBC, 1972.
Reade, Leslie. *Marconi and the Discovery of Wireless.* London: Faber and Faber, 1962.
Reddin, Harry. *Wires, Wheels and Wings: A Wireless Mechanic's Diary.* Durham: The Pentland Press, 1994.
Tarrant, D. R. *Marconi's Miracle: The Wireless Bridging of the Atlantic.* St. John's, Newfoundland: Flanker Press, 2001.

2. Production

Barnard, Stephen. *Studying Radio.* London: Arnold, 2000.
Crook, Tim. *Radio Presentation: Theory and Practice.* London: Focal Press, 2002.
Gordon, Janey. *The RSL: Ultra Local Radio.* Luton: The University of Luton Press, 2000.
Holsopple, C. *Skills for Radio Broadcasters.* London: TAB Books, 1988.
Horstmann, Rosemary. *Writing for Radio.* London: A and C Black, 1997.
Kaye, Michael, and Andrew Popperwell. *Making Radio: A Guide to Basic Radio Techniques.* London: Broadside Books, 1992.
Macloughlin, Shaun. *Writing for Radio.* Oxford: How to Books, 2001.
McInerney, Vincent. *Writing for Radio.* Manchester: Manchester University Press, 2001.
McLeish, Robert. *Radio Production.* London: Focal Press, 1994.
McWhinnie, Donald. *The Art of Radio.* London: Faber and Faber, 1959.

Mills, Jenni. *The Broadcast Voice*. Oxford: Focal Press, 2004.
Nisbett, Alec. *The Technique of the Sound Studio*. London: Focal Press, 1994.
Priestman, Chris. *Web Radio*. London: Focal Press, 2001.
Starkey, Guy. *Radio in Context*. Basingstoke: Palgrave Macmillan, 2004.

3. Radio Advertising

Arnold, Frank A. *Broadcast Advertising—The Fourth Dimension*. New York: John Wiley, 1931.
Butler, George, Ed. Jill Firth. *Berlin, Bush House and Berkeley Square*. London: privately printed memoir, 1985.
Crawford, Sir William, and H. Broadley. *The People's Food*. London: William Heinemann, 1938.
Dyer, Gillian. *Advertising as Communication*. London: Routledge, 1982.
Dygert, Warren B. *Radio as an Advertising Medium*. New York: McGraw-Hill, 1939.
International Broadcasting Company (IBC). *This Is the I.B.C.* London: IBC, 1939.
Kaldor, Nicholas, and Rodney Silverman. *A Statistical Analysis of Advertising Expenditure and the Revenue of the Press*. Cambridge: Cambridge University Press, 1948.
Montague, Ron. *When the Ovaltineys Sang*. Southend-on-Sea: privately printed pamphlet, 1993.
Nevett, T. R. *Advertising in Britain, a History*. London: Heinnemann/The History of Advertising Trust, 1982.
Radio Advertising Bureau (RAB). *Commercial Radio Revenues*. London: Radio Advertising Bureau, 2002.
Sturmey, S. G. *The Economic Development of Radio*. London: Duckworth, 1958.
Turner, E. S. *The Shocking History of Advertising*. London: Michael Joseph, 1952.

4. Commercial Radio

Baron, Mike. *Independent Radio*. Lavenham: Terence Dalton, 1975.
Carter, Meg. *Independent Radio: The First 25 Years*. London: Radio Authority, 1998.
Henry, Stuart, and Mike von Joel. *Pirate Radio Then and Now*. Poole: Blandford Press, 1984.
Nichol, Richard. *Radio Luxembourg, the Station of the Stars: An Affectionate History of 50 years of Broadcasting*. London: Comet, 1983.
Skues, Keith. *Pop Went the Pirates*. Sheffield: Lambs Meadow Publications, 1994.

5. Music Radio

Barnard, Stephen. *On the Radio: Music Radio in Britain*. Milton Keynes: Open University Press, 1989.

Chapman, Robert. *Selling the Sixties: The Pirates and Pop Music Radio*. London: Routledge, 1992.
Garfield, Simon. *The Nation's Favourite: The True Adventures of Radio 1*. London: Faber and Faber, 1998.
Wall, Tim. *Studying Popular Music Culture*. London: Hodder Arnold, 2003.

6. Radio Drama

Beck, Alan. *The Invisible Play, BBC Radio Drama 1922–1928*. Canterbury: Sound Journal Publications, 2000.
Crook, Tim. *Radio Drama, Theory and Practice*. London: Routledge, 1999.
Drakakis, J. (ed.) *British Radio Drama*. Cambridge: Cambridge University Press, 1981.
Felton, F. *The Radio Play: Its Techniques and Possibilities*. London: Sylvan Press, 1949.
Gielgud, Val. *British Radio Drama, 1922–1956*. London: Harrap, 1957.
Hughes, Richard. *Plays*. London: Chatto and Windus, 1924.
Lea, Gordon. *Radio Drama and How to Write It*. London: George Allen and Unwin, 1926.
Rodger, Ian. *Radio Drama*. London: Macmillan, 1982.

7. Radio Journalism

Beaman, Jim. *Interviewing for Radio*. London: Routledge, 2000.
Crook, Tim. *International Radio Journalism*. London: Routledge, 1998.
Gage, Linda. *A Guide to Commercial Radio Journalism*. London: Focal Press, 1999.

8. International Radio

Browne, Donald. *International Radio Broadcasting*. New York: Praeger, 1982.
Camporesi, Valeria. *Mass Culture and National Traditions: The BBC and American Broadcasting, 1922–1954*. Fucecchio: European Press Academic Publishing, 2000.
Kuhn, Raymond. *The Media in France*. London: Routledge, 1995.
Lean, E. Tangye. *Voices in the Darkness*. London: Secker and Warburg, 1943.
Lemaitre, Jean. *Allo! Allo! Ici Radio Normandie*. Fécamp: L. Durand et Fils, 1984.
Mansell, Gerard. *Let the Truth Be Told, 50 Years of BBC External Broadcasting*. London: Weidenfeld and Nicolson, 1982.
Pedrick, Gale (ed.) *The World Radio and Television Annual: Jubilee Edition*. London: Sampson Low, Marston & Co., 1947.
Rolo, C. J. *Radio Goes to War*. London: Faber ad Faber, 1943.
Tangye Lean, E. *Voices in the Darkness: The Story of the European Radio War*. London: Secker and Warburg, 1943.

Tomlinson, J. D. *The International Control of Radiocommunications.* Ann Arbor, Mich.: University of Michigan, 1945.
Walker, Andrew. *A Skyful of Freedom: 60 Years of the BBC World Service.* London: Broadside Books, 1992.
Wood, James. *The History of International Broadcasting.* London: Peregrinus/ Science Museum, 1994.
Smulyan, Susan. *Selling Radio, The Commercialization of American Broadcasting 1920–1934.* Washington, D.C.: Smithsonian Institution Press, 1994.

9. Radio Texts

Baseley, Godfrey. *The Archers: A Slice of My Life.* London: Sidgewick and Jackson, 1971.
Brough, Peter. *Educating Archie.* London: Paul, 1955.
Cannell, J. C. *In Town Tonight.* London: George G. Harrap, 1935.
Chilton, Charles. *Journey into Space.* London: Herbert Jenkins, 1954.
Cooke, Alistair. *Letter from America, 1946–2004.* London: Penguin/Allen Lane, 2004.
Donovan, Paul. *All Our Todays.* London: Cape, 1997.
Duncan, Peter. *In Town Tonight.* London: Werner Laurie, 1951.
Edwards, Rex. *The Dales.* London: BBC, 1969.
Garner, Ken. *In Session Tonight: The Complete Radio 1 Sessions.* London: BBC Books, 1993.
Grevatt, Wallace. *BBC Children's Hour: A Celebration of Those Magical Years.* Lewes: The Book Guild, 1988.
Hulme Beaman, S. G. *Tales of Toytown.* Oxford: Oxford University Press, 1928.
May, Derwent. *Good Talk: An Anthology from BBC Radio.* London: Victor Gollancz, 1968.
———. *Good Talk 2: An Anthology from BBC Radio.* London: Victor Gollancz, 1969.
Murrow, Edward R. *In Search of Light: The Broadcasts of Ed Murrow, 1938-61.* London: Macmillan, 1968.
Priestley, J B. *Postscripts.* London: Heinnemann, 1962.
Thomas, Howard. *Britain's Brains Trust.* London: Chapman and Hall, 1944.
Webb, Geoffrey. *The Inside Story of Dick Barton.* London: Convoy Publications, 1950.
Worsley, Francis. *Anatomy of ITMA.* London: Pilot Press, 1946.

About the Author

Seán Street (L.R.A.M. Drama, Royal Academy of Music; Ph.D., Bournemouth University) is a writer, an academic, a poet, and a broadcaster. He has worked as a radio practitioner since 1970 and is frequently to be heard as producer/presenter in his own features on BBC Radios 3 and 4. He is an elected member of the Trustees of the Radio Academy, a fellow of the Royal Society of Arts, and has written widely on radio history; his *Concise History of British Radio* (2005) is on many media department reading lists, and *Radio Waves—an Anthology of Poems Celebrating the Wireless* (2004), drew widespread critical praise. His study of pre-World War II radio in the UK, *Crossing the Ether* (2006), examined the little-explored subject of attacks on the BBC monopoly by commercial radio in Britain during the 1930s. He is a board member of two UK radio stations, 2CR FM and Hope FM, and is professor of radio at Bournemouth Media School, Bournemouth University, where he directs the MA in Radio Production; as part of the course, in 2000, he founded the Bournemouth Internet Radio Station (BIRSt). His doctorate was on the subject of commercial radio history, and he is director of the Centre for Broadcasting History Research in the Bournemouth Media School.

Dr. Street is also the author of a number of books of literary critical history, including *The Dymock Poets* (1994), *The Wreck of the Deutschland* (1992), and editor of *A Remembered Land* (1994). His plays have been widely performed, including *Honest John* (1993), commissioned by the Royal Theatre, Northampton, which won the Central Television Award for new drama. *Beyond Paradise* (1998), his one-man play about

Charles Darwin, is currently touring, with the ex-RSC actor, Christopher Robbie as Darwin. He has published six collections of his own poems, including *A Walk in Winter* (1989), *This True Making* (1992), and *Radio and Other Poems* (1999). Other stage and multimedia work includes the Royal National Theatre-commissioned "Urban Sonnets" for *Metropolis Kabarett* (2001), directed by Henry Goodman.